Changes in Argument Structure

Linguistic Insights

Studies in Language and Communication

Edited by Maurizio Gotti,
University of Bergamo

Volume 277

PETER LANG
Bern · Berlin · Bruxelles · New York · Oxford

Tamara Bouso

Changes in Argument Structure
The Transitivizing Reaction Object Construction

PETER LANG
Bern · Berlin · Bruxelles · New York · Oxford

Bibliographic information published by die Deutsche Nationalbibliothek
Die Deutsche Nationalbibliothek lists this publication in the Deutsche Nationalbibliografie; detailed bibliographic data is available on the Internet at ‹http://dnb.d-nb.de›.

For generous financial support thanks are due to the following institutions: the Spanish Ministry of Education (grant FPU2012/01669), the European Regional Development Fund, the Spanish Ministry of Science and Innovation (grant FFI2017-86884-P) and the Regional Government of Galicia (Directorate General for Scientific and Technological Promotion, grants ED431D 2017/09 and ED431B 2017/12).

ISSN 1424-8689
ISBN 978-3-0343-4095-3 (Print)
E-ISBN 978-3-0343-4265-0 (E-PDF)
E-ISBN 978-3-0343-4266-7 (EPUB)
E-ISBN 978-3-0343-4267-4 (MOBI)
DOI 10.3726/b17960

Wabernstrasse 40, CH-3007 Bern, Switzerland
bern@peterlang.com, www.peterlang.com

Acknowledgements

This book is a revised and improved version of my dissertation, defended at the University of Santiago de Compostela in 2018. I am greatly indebted to my supervisors, Professors Teresa Fanego and Belén Méndez Naya, for their unconditional support, and their helpful suggestions during the planning and development of this project. I also owe a great debt of gratitude to Professors Graeme Trousdale and Martin Hilpert, for their extreme kindness, and the priceless feedback I received from them during my research stays at the University of Edinburgh (2014), and the Université de Neuchâtel (2016, 2019).

I am also grateful for the encouragement and counsel of a number of colleagues I met along the way: Montserrat Martínez-Vázquez, Nikolaos Lavidas, Jóhanna Barðdal, Elly van Gelderen, Damián Blasi, Daniel Ross, and most especially, of those of the research teams headed by Professors Alexander Bergs (Osnabrück University), and Britta Mondorf (Johannes Gutenberg-Universität Mainz). In addition, I thank the research team *Variation, Linguistic Change and Grammaticalizaton* (VLCG), of which I am a member, and the research network *English Linguistics Circle* (ELC). For generous financial support I acknowledge the following institutions: the Spanish Ministry of Education (grant FPU2012/01669), the European Regional Development Fund, the Spanish Ministry of Science and Innovation (grant FFI2017-86884-P) and the Regional Government of Galicia (Directorate General for Scientific and Technological Promotion, grants ED431D 2017/09 and ED431B 2017/12). Finally, a special word of gratitude goes to my mother for being my greatest support and for always reminding me what matters most. To her, I dedicate this monograph.

Contents

PART I Transitivization, Reaction Objects and Construction Grammar

PART II Hands-On with Data: A Usage-Based Approach to the History of the ROC

List of Abbreviations

agt	Agent
B&T	Bosworth & Toller's *An Anglo-Saxon Dictionary*
BNC	*British National Corpus*
CLMET	*Corpus of Late Modern English Texts*
CLMET3.0	*Corpus of Late Modern English Texts, version 3.0*
CLMET-EV	*Corpus of Late Modern English Texts (extended version)*
COC(s)	Cognate object construction(s)
COCA	*Corpus of Contemporary American English*
COHA	*Corpus of Historical American English*
DAT	Dative
DIR	Directional
DNC	Definite null complement
DOE Web Corpus	*Dictionary of Old English Web Corpus*
EEBO	*Early English Books Online*
EModE	Early Modern English
EOC	Expressive Object Construction
Exp	Experiencer
Gmc	Germanic
HC	*Helsinki Corpus of English Texts*
HTOED	*Historical Thesaurus of the Oxford English Dictionary*
$_i$	Coreferentiality
INC	Indefinite null complement
LME	Late Middle English

LModE	Late Modern English
ME	Middle English
MED	*Middle English Dictionary*
ModE	Modern English
N	Noun
NOM	Nominative
NP	Noun phrase
N_V	Deverbal noun
OBJ	Object
OBJ_1	Object 1 (indirect object)
OBJ_2	Object 2
OBL	Oblique
OE	Old English
OED	*Oxford English Dictionary*
P N construction	Preposition noun construction
pat	Patient
PDE	Present Day English
PC	Predicative complement
POSS	Possessive
PP	Prepositional phrase
PPCEME	*Penn-Helsinki Parsed Corpus of Early Modern English*
PPCMBE	*Penn-Helsinki Parsed Corpus of Modern British English*
PPCME2	*Penn-Helsinki Parsed Corpus of Middle English*
PRED	Predicator
R	Relation
REC	Recipient
RO(s)	Reaction object(s)
ROC(s)	Reaction object construction(s)
SEM/Sem	Semantics

sent. agt.	Sentient agent
SUBJ	Subject
Subsch.	Subschema
Syn	Syntax
(In)tr.	(In)transitive
V_{INTR}	Intransitive verb
X, Y, Z	Variables
YCOE	*York-Toronto-Helsinki Parsed Corpus of Old English Prose*

1. Introduction

1.1 Aims and scope

This monograph is concerned with the characterization and diachronic development of the so-called English reaction object construction (ROC; Levin 1993, 97–98), as in *She* ***mumbled*** *her adoration* and *The door* ***jingled*** *a welcome*. The ROC consists of an intransitive verb (*mumble*, *jingle*) followed by a nonsubcategorized object that expresses a reaction or an attitude of some kind (*adoration*, *welcome*), such that the whole syntactic unit acquires the overall extended meaning "express, communicate, signal X by V-ing", that is, 'She expressed, communicated her adoration by mumbling' and 'The door expressed, signalled a welcome by jingling' in the examples above. In the terminology of Construction Grammar (Goldberg 1995, 2006, 2019), the theoretical framework adopted here, the ROC is defined as a *valency-increasing argument structure construction*, that is, an argument structure construction that contributes an extra argument (*her adoration* and *a welcome* in the examples above) to the event structure of the intransitive verb it blends with. In this respect, the ROC can be aligned with other constructions which also show a similar process of argument augmentation such as the causative property resultative construction (*He* ***wiped*** *the table clean*; Broccias 2008, 27), the cognate object construction (*The hart* ***lept*** *a great leap*; Visser 1963–1973: I, § 424 (b): 416) and the *way*-construction (*She* ***giggled*** *her way up the stairs*; Israel 1996, 218).

The three constructions just mentioned have been extensively studied over the last decades, mostly from a synchronic perspective (Jones 1988, Jackendoff 1990, Massam 1990, Goldberg 1995, Boas 2003, Goldberg and Jackendoff 2004, Höche 2009, Horrocks and Stavrou 2010, to mention just a few), but also from a diachronic viewpoint (Israel 1996, Broccias 2008, Mondorf 2011, Traugott and Trousdale 2013, Lavidas 2018, Perek 2018), an interest which is partly due to the emergence of Construction Grammar and to its application to language change (Lakoff 1987, Fillmore, Kay, and O'Connor 1988, Goldberg 1995, 2006, Hilpert 2013, Traugott and Trousdale 2013). By contrast, ROCs have so far eluded systematic investigation. The few linguists who have dealt with them have mainly focused on (i) the *nonprototypical features* of reaction objects in relation to other nonsubcategorized objects such as cognate objects and *way*-objects (Martínez-Vázquez 1998, Felser and Wanner 2001, Mateu 2001, 2014, Mirto 2007, 2012, 2017, Kogusuri 2009b, 2011, Bouso 2014a), and (ii) the *characterization*, the *frequency* and *context* of occurrence of the ROC in PDE and Spanish (Martínez-Vázquez 2010, 2014a, 2014b, 2015, 2016, 2017, Bouso 2012). If synchronic studies on the ROC are scarce, historical studies devoted to its diachronic development are non-existent. This monograph aims to fill this gap by offering a detailed characterization of the modern ROC from a Construction Grammar perspective and by addressing key historical issues such as *when* the ROC emerges, *how* it develops over time, and *what* mechanisms of change and factors may have propelled its development. These are considered to be the main contributions of this book, which hopes to raise questions and avenues for future research on the ROC from either a synchronic or a diachronic perspective.

My study on the ROC is in line with other diachronic studies on English verbs' argument structure, a field of research which has attracted much scholarly attention of late. The areas which have been explored include (a) processes of *argument remapping* where there is a reorganizacion of the argument structure of a verb, (b) processes of *argument reduction* that imply the demotion or suppresion of one of its arguments, and (c) processes of *argument augmentation* where an extra argument is added, as in the case of the valency-increasing argument structure constructions mentioned above.

For the purposes of explanation, I will briefly discuss each of these processes in turn. I will first show a clear case of argument remapping based on van Gelderen (2014), then some examples of argument reduction, these based on Möhlig and Klages (2002), and finally, before heading into the research questions and hypotheses (§ 1.2), I will touch upon some general synchronic and diachronic features of the three types of valency-increasing constructions previously mentioned: the causative property resultative construction (e.g. *He wiped the table clean*), the cognate object construction (e.g. *The hart lept a great leap*) and the *way*-construction (e.g. *She giggled her way up the stairs*).

In processes of *argument structure remapping* there is a reorganization of the original argument structure of the verb. A clear example of one such process can be observed in the history of some *psych*-verbs such as *fear* (< OE *fǣran* 'to terrify, frighten') and *like* (< OE *(ge-)lícian* 'please'), which possessed a different argument structure in earlier stages of English. *Psych*-verbs, or experiencer verbs, are those that "express mental states and involve the inclusion of an experiencer argument" which may act like the subject or the object of the sentence (van Gelderen 2014, 100).[1] For instance, the *psych*-verb *fear* occurs with a subject experiencer (example (1)), whereas the *psych*-verb *frighten* takes an object experiencer, as shown in example (2).

(1) He **fears** that alien.

(2) That alien **frightens** him.

As explained by van Gelderen (2014, 104), many of the verbs that are now *psych*-verbs have become so recently (e.g. *worry* and *thrill*), a few subject experiencer verbs have remained stable over time – *dread*, *hate* and *love* were already in use in Old English (OE) with basically the same semantic structure – , while some originally object experiencer verbs such as *fear* and *like* have been reanalysed as subject experiencers over the course of history. This is illustrated in Fig. 1.1.

One possible cause of argument structure remapping is the loss of the morphologically overt causative affix *-j/-i*. This explanation fits well with the history of *fear* summarized here in Tab. 1.1. According to the *Oxford English Dictionary* (OED), the origins of *fear* (< OE *fǣran*) lie in the causative verb **fǣrjan* ('to terrify, frighten') which had the Germanic causative affix *-j/-i*. During ME, OE *fǣran* phonologically developed into *fēren*, and acquired the meaning 'to fear (something), to be afraid' where the object experiencer argument becomes the subject of the sentence (example (4) in Tab. 1.1). This remapped argument structure is the one that *fear* shows in Present Day English (PDE), whereas

1 Common labels used in the literature to refer to verbs that subcategorize for an experiencer argument are 'impersonal verbs' (Fischer and van Der Leek 1983, 346), and 'experiencer verbs' (Allen 1995, 20 ff; see also Allen 1986).

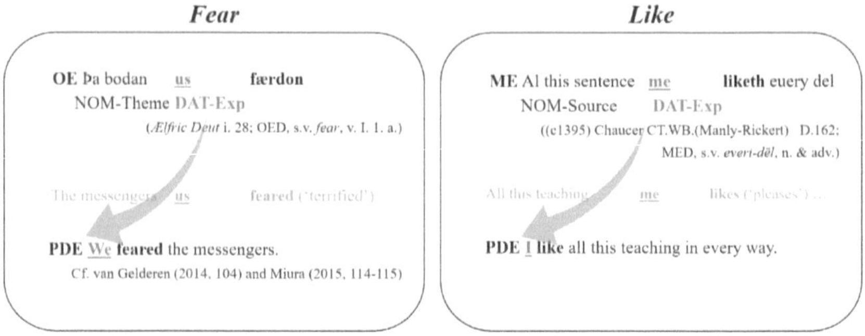

Fig. 1.1: *Fear* and *like* as examples of argument remapping

the object experiencer pattern is now expressed by the verb *frighten*, formed by means of the noun *fright* ('fear') and the causative affix *-en* (e.g. *The alien frightens* <u>*me*</u>).

Moving now onto processes of *argument structure reduction*, commonly referred to outside Construction Grammar as *detransitivization* processes, these imply the suppression of one of the arguments of the event structure of the verb. Clear examples of this type of process have been described in Möhlig and Klages (2002), who deal with

Tab. 1.1: History of the *psych*-verb *fear*: From 'terrify' to 'fear'. Adapted from van Gelderen (2014)

Form and meaning		**Example**	**Changes**
OE *fǽran* (<**fǽrjan*) 'to terrify, frighten' (B&T, s.v. *fǽran*)	(3)	OE Þa bodan <u>us</u> **færdon** **NOM-Theme DAT-Exp** (Ælfric *Deut* i. 28; OED, s.v. *fear*, v. I. 1. a.) The messengers <u>us</u> **feared** ('terrified') PDE <u>We</u> **feared** the messengers	Loss of the affix *-j/-i*
ME *fēren* 'to fear (something), to be afraid' (MED, s.v. *fēren* (v.(1)))	(4)	ME And that schold <u>every wys man</u> **fere** (a1393 Gower CA Frf 3 2.578; cited in van Gelderen 2014, 107) And that should <u>every wise man</u> **fear**	Phonological changes Adoption of a new meaning Subject experiencer

coreferential intransitive uses, generic uses, ergative uses and middle uses of a number of originally transitive verbs.

Coreferential intransitive uses developed through a stage where they showed coreferential reflexive pronouns (e.g. *John washed the clothes > John washed himself > John washed Ø).* This example of detransitivization is mainly restricted to verbs belonging to the lexical domain of body-care or directed body-movement such as *wash*, *shave*, *dress* and *move*, which require an animate agent. Although the loss of –*self* reflexives does not seem to be tied to any specific historical period, Görlach (1999, 78) pointed out that "[m]any grammarians have noted an increase" in coreferential intransitive uses in the nineteenth century alongside other processes of transitivization (i.e. argument augmentation) and detransitivization (i.e. argument reduction). Interestingly, Jespersen (1909–1949: III, § 16.2: 325–331) also noted that the omission of the "cumbersome *self*-pronoun whenever no ambiguity is to be feared" is characteristic of Modern English (ModE) and more recently, Rohdenburg (2009) has taken Jespersen's argument one step further and demonstrated that the suppression of overtly reflexive uses continues to the present day, with American English clearly leading the way.[2] Interestingly, the reverse process, that of argument augmentation (i.e. transitivization), has been identified with 'non-argument reflexives', that is, with structures where reflexives do not express the *referential* identity of two participants (Siemund 2014, 52). Examples of these uses are shown in (5), where these 'obligatory reflexive verbs' cannot occur without the reflexive pronoun (see (6)), the pronoun itself cannot be coordinated with a full noun phrase (NP) (see example in (7)), nor can it be replaced by another NP (see (8)). As demonstrated by Siemund (2014, 70), the use of these non-argument reflexives has increased since ME times and they are probably still on the rise.

(5) **absent** oneself, **content** oneself, **ingratiate** oneself, **perjure** oneself, **pride** oneself, etc.

(6) John absented *(himself) from the meeting.

2 Apart from Jespersen (1909–1949) and Rohdenburg (2009), the decline of the reflexive has been documented by Kirchner (1951), König and Siemund (2000), Peitsara (1997) and Mondorf (2010, 2011).

(7) John absented *himself and his colleague.

(8) John absented *his colleague from the meeting.

(Siemund 2014, 52)

Like coreferential intransitive uses, *generic uses* of transitive verbs also represent a case of argument reduction. These refer to intransitive verbal uses where the object is implied by the cultural context (e.g. world knowledge), as shown in the Old and Modern English examples (9)-(12) for the transitive verbs *read*, *drink*, *wash* and *drive*.

(9) OE (Northumbrian) *Lindisf. Gospels: Mark* xiii. 14 *Qui legit intellegat* : seðe **redes** oncnauað (OED, s.v. *read*, v. 6. a.) (PDE '[This] understands he who reads')

(10) 1640 J. Fletcher & J. Shirley *Night-walker* iv. sig. H2v, Give me the bottle, I can **drink** like a Fish now, like an Elephant. (OED, s.v. *drink*, v.[1] 11. II. a.)

(11) 1697 T. Tryon *Way to Health* (ed. 3) vi. 101 It [*sc.* rain-water] Brews and **Washes** to greater advantage than others. (OED, s.v. *wash*, v. I. 2. h.)

(12) 1717 M. Prior *Alma* iii. 140 The man within the coach that sits..Is safer much..than he that **drives**. (OED, s.v. *drive*, v. I. 5. c.)

The force that drives the generic use with these transitive verbs is the collocational binding they exhibit with their objects (some kind of writing, some liquids, clothes and vehicles). Givón (1984, 108–109) refers to these suppressed objects as "highly stereotypical/predictable/habitual" and observes that "[t]he referential identity of such objects is thus seldom an issue in the discourse, and they are thus often suppressed, leaving the verb a surface-*intransitive*" (109). This explains why generic uses are not possible with transitive verbs like *dress*, *open*, *break* or *fill*, which contrary to the verbs in (9)-(12), occur with a larger number of object types. Interestingly, generic uses are reminiscent of the use of cognate objects with intransitive verbs (e.g. *She smiled an enigmatic smile* and *The hart lept a great leap*) in which the encoding of the object is important for pragmatic purposes (see Klages 1996). This leads us to the third example of detransitivization provided by Möhlig and Klages (2002), that concerning *ergative uses* which apply to those verbs that show transitive-causative and intransitive-inchoative alternations such as the verb *open* in *Mary opened the door* vs. *The door opened*. These uses pose problems regarding the directionality of the development, which seems to be "more or less impossible to establish on the grounds of diachronic data" (Möhlig and Klages 2002, 241).

Finally, the last case of detransitivization identified by Möhlig and Klages concerns *middle uses* such as the intransitive use of the verb *read* in *This book reads well.* Middle uses are "characteristically marked by the occurrence of an adverb of manner which is almost always obligatory in the predicate frame" (Möhlig and Klages 2002, 244). Contrary to other examples of detransitivization, middle uses emerged later in time, as they were non-existent in Old and Middle English (Visser 1963–1973: I, § 168: 158), scarce in Early Modern English (EModE), but prolific from the eighteenth century onwards, especially in the nineteenth and twentieth centuries (Denison 1993, 392–393).

Worth of note here is that to these four cases of detransitivization described by Möhlig and Klages (2002), one more detransitivization use has been recently identified by Mondorf and Schneider (2016) for the causative *bring* in *bring X to infinitive* as in the LModE example *She brought miss Hariot to confess* (2016, 439). As shown in their diachronic corpus data from the fifteenth to the twentieth century, causative *bring* goes from taking fully fledged objects (*miss Hariot* in the example above), to being basically restricted to reflexives in the present day (PDE *?I brought him to laugh* vs PDE *I just can't bring myself to do it*). The process of detransitivization is mainly justified by the fact that causative *bring* involving reflexives such as *I just can't bring myself to do it* scores lower than prototypical transitive structures on the set of Hopper and Thompson's parameters of transitivity (1980), among other reasons, because reflexive objects are not as affected by the action denoted by the verb as prototypical objects such as *B* in the prototypical transitive structure *A murdered B*.

Finally, the argument structure of verbs may also undergo a process of *argument augmentation*. This type of process involves strategies in which the verbal territory of a verb is systematically extended, either by the addition of an extra argument to the verb, as in the causative property resultative construction (*He wiped the table clean*) or by the transitivization of a previously intransitive structure as in the case of the cognate object construction (*The hart lept a great leap*), the *way*-construction (*She giggled her way up the stairs*) and the construction under examination in this monograph, the reaction object construction (*She mumbled her adoration*).

In causative property resultative constructions as in (13) and (14), an adjectival phrase (i.e. *full of water* and *clean*) is attached to a transitive verb (e.g. *drink* and *wipe*) (Levin 1993, 99–101; Goldberg and Jackendoff 2004, Broccias 2008). Interestingly, this process of argument augmentation attested in causative property resultatives is not restricted to transitive verbs alone suh as *drink* (13) and *wipe* (14) but is also attested with intransitive verbs like *talk* (15) and *run* (16). In such cases, the intransitive verbs involved may extend their valency with the addition of an object which is not possible when they occur in isolation (see (17) and (18)). Similarly to some of the processes of argument reduction described above, causative property resultative constructions have also been claimed to increase their frequency during ModE (Broccias 2008, 51).

(13) And þen ryght as a man leneth to a well and **dryngketh** his body full of watyr.
'And then right as a man leans to a wel and **drinks** his body full of water'.
(ME a1500 (a1415) *Mirk's Festial* (CMMIRK, 32.907); Broccias 2008, 45)

(14) He **wiped** the table clean.	Transitive verb
(15) He **talked** himself hoarse.	Intransitive verb
(16) He **ran** his sneakers threadbare.	Intransitive verb
(17) *He talked himself.	
(18) *He ran his sneakers.	

(Broccias 2008)

Another construction which augments the argument structure of the verb is the cognate object construction as in *The hart lept a great leap* (Horrocks and Stavrou 2010, Lavidas 2018; example (19)). There has been some degree of controversy regarding the status of the object morphologically cognate to the verb. While some linguists claim that the cognate object is like an adverbial (Jones 1988, 93; see also Zubizarreta 1987, Moltmann 1989), others argue that the cognate object is "best characterized as a syntactic direct object which receives a patient theta role from the verb" (Massam 1990, 161; see also Hale and Keyser 1993, Macfarland 1995). This line of argumentation follows from the idea that cognate objects do not behave like normal adverbials as *gruesomely* in *Mordred killed the knight gruesomely* where the adverbial does not have to be adjacent to the verb, or even like nominal adverbials such as *tomorrow* in *Alice will read the book tomorrow* where the nominal adverbial can co-occur with a direct object (*the book*).

(19) The herte **lepte** a grete lepe.
The hart **lept** a great leap.
(1470–1485 Malory, *Morte d'Arthur* (Sommer) III, v; Visser 1963–1973: I, § 424 (b): 416)

Horrocks and Stavrou (2010) provide a useful threefold taxonomy of cognate object constructions depending on the nature of the verb and the morphosyntactic features of the construction: (i) cognate object constructions with transitive verbs (20), (ii) transitivizing cognate object constructions (21), and (iii) aspectual cognate object constructions (22). The main difference between cognate object constructions with transitive verbs and the other two cognate object construction types is that the latter occur with unergative verbs, i.e., intransitive verbs with volitional or experiencer subjects such as the verbs *dream* or *smile* (21)-(22) (Horrocks and Stavrou 2010, 295).[3] Interestingly, cognate object constructions with intransitives were rare in OE, increased their frequency in ME and became numerous in the Modern period, most likely on analogy with cognate object constructions with transitive verbs and also due to the loss of case marking, as some intransitive OE verbs such as *sweltan* ['to die a natural or a violent death', B&T; s.v. *sweltan*], *libban* ['to live'; B&T, s.v. *libban*] and *slepan* ['to sleep'; B&T, s.v. *slépan*] could govern a cognate object in the dative (or instrumental) case (Visser, 1963–1973: I, § 424 (b): 415; also Lavidas 2013, 2014, 2018).

(20) They **drank** their drinks. Transitive verb

(21) She **dreamed** the most wonderful dream. Intransitive verb

(22) She **smiled** an enigmatic smile. Intransitive verb
(Horrocks and Stavrou 2010, 293)

3 van Gelderen (2011) explains that "[t]ypical unergatives involve willed, volitional, controlled acts, i.e. with an Agent central; typical unaccusatives involve change of location or state, i.e. with the Theme central" (van Gelderen 2011, 108). Some examples of the latter type are *arrive*, *appear* and *faint*.

A third example of argument augmentation can be observed in the *way*-construction, which has been argued to be a member of the large family of English resultatives (Levin 1993, 99; Goldberg and Jackendoff 2004; and Mondorf 2011). Like the causative property resultative construction and the cognate object construction discussed above, the *way*-construction not only occurs with transitive verbs, but also has the effect of rendering transitive a previously intransitive structure. As described in Traugott and Trousdale (2013, 76–93), the origins of the *way*-construction lie in the LME period in the use of *wei* with transitive verbs like *nimen* 'take' and *take*, and in the use of *wei* and phrases like *on wei* with intransitive motion verbs such as *go*, *ride*, *wend*, *fare* and *flee*. More recently, the construction has become more fixed in form – since EModE it has been restricted to coreferential possessive determiners and the presence of a directional is now obligatory –, and it has also expanded to an increasing number of verb types, including unergatives such as *work* (23), and modern verbs of sound emission and incidental activity such as *giggle* (1509) in (24).

(23) [S]he . . . encouraged him$_i$ to **work** his$_i$ way to the top of the railroad business$_{\text{DIRECTIONAL}}$.
(COHA, 1920 Alice B. Emerson, *Betty Gordon in Washington*; Mondorf 2011, 398)

(24) She$_i$ **giggled** her$_i$ way up the stairs$_{\text{DIRECTIONAL}}$.
(Israel 1996, 218)

A fourth and last example of valency-increasing construction is the ROC, the main concern of this monograph, and here illustrated in (25)-(29).

(25) She **mumbled** her adoration. (Levin 1993, 98)

(26) Pauline **smiled** her thanks. (Levin 1993, 98)

(27) The door **jingled** a welcome. (Martínez-Vázquez 2010, 555)

(28) Pigs..**squeal** emphatic disapproval of their enforced journey. (OED, s.v. *squeal*, v. 4)

(29) His monocle **gleamed** polite hostility. (Snell-Hornby 1983, 254)

As was the case with the other examples of valency-increasing constructions just described, the ROC shows a discrepancy between the process the verb designates (intransitive) and the type of process profiled by the clause as a whole (transitive, and in the case of the ROC, encoding a communicative act). In Langacker's terminology (2009, 256–257), these structures can be described as *skewing constructions*, "because, by [their] very nature, the construction induces a discrepancy between the meaning of the verb and of the composite expression". It is precisely their condition as skewing constructions that seems to explain the striking similarities (at both a synchronic and a diachronic level) between the ROC, the cognate object construction and the *way*-construction. In fact, the existing studies on the PDE ROC already highlighted the similarities between reaction objects, cognate objects and *way*-objects as nonprototypical objects (Martínez-Vázquez 1998, Felser and Wanner 2001, Mateu 2001, 2014, Mirto 2007, 2017, Kogusuri 2009b, 2011, among others): all three are incompatible with the passive, cannot be topicalized, pronominalized or questioned, and show some restrictions on their form (cf. § 3.2). From a historical perspective, although these three valency-increasing constructions became available in the English language at different points in time, recent studies reveal that they increased in frequency during the ModE period (Israel 1996, Broccias 2008, Traugott and Trousdale 2013, Lavidas 2018). As will be seen, this is also the case of the ROC (see Chapter 5 (§ 5.2) and Chapter 6 (§ 6.3.2)). Such chronological coincidence suggests that these four valency-increasing constructions are part, or result from, the large-scale transitivization process that started in OE times, and that has continued in later stages of English affecting intransitive verbs "that made their first appearance in later English" (Visser, 1963–1973: I, § 132: 99).

1.2 Research questions and hypotheses

The main focus of this monograph is the characterization and diachronic development of the reaction object construction. More precisely, my research questions are the ones specified in (i), for which I put forward the hypotheses in (ii) based on the empirical findings briefly summarized above regarding the nonprototypical features of the PDE ROC (cf. § 3.2.1.3) and the historical development of the cognate object construction (Lavidas 2018) and the *way*-construction (Traugott and Trousdale 2013) (cf. § 5.2.3.1–§ 5.2.3.2). These research questions have been broken down into two sets, the first set concerns the characterization of the ROC from a Construction Grammar perspective, whereas the second set has to do with the evolution of the ROC.

(i) *Research questions*

The nonprototypical features of reaction objects mentioned above (i.e. incompatibility with passivization, topicalization, pronominalization and questioning, alongside with some restrictions in form) reveal that ROCs can be best discussed within the framework of Construction Grammar, a theory of Linguistics that claims that our linguistic knowledge rather than consisting of words and rules is formed *only* by a *large network of constructions* (form-meaning pairings). Thus, two fundamental research questions that are in line with the major tenets of Construction Grammar and that demand answers are the following:

1. How can we account for the *nonprototypical features* of reaction objects from a Construction Grammar perspective?
2. If our linguistic knowledge consists of a *large network of constructions* (form-meaning pairings), then how does the ROC relate to other constructions within the English network?

As for the *evolution* of the ROC, the research questions that this monograph attempts to answer are the following two:

3. *When* does the ROC emerge? Couched in Construction Grammar terms (Traugott and Trousdale 2013),
   — When does the ROC undergo *constructionalization* thus becoming a *new* form-meaning pairing with its own morphosyntactic and semantic constraints?
4. *How* and *why* does the ROC develop? More precisely,
   — What *constructional changes* (i.e. changes in form, function, frequency and distribution) can be identified in its development?
   — Which of these changes qualify as *pre- and post-constructionalization constructional changes*?

— What *mechanisms of change* (e.g. neoanalysis/reanalysis, analogy/analogization, coercion, metaphor, etc.) and *factors* (intralinguistic and/or extralinguistic) have propelled its development?

For the third and fourth research questions concerning the evolution of the ROC, I put forward the hypotheses in (ii) based on findings from Lavidas (2018) and Traugott and Trousdale (2013) for the cognate object construction and the *way*-construction, respectively. Thus, the first hypothesis has to do with the emergence of the ROC as a construction (a *new* form-meaning pairing) with its own morphosyntactic and semantic constraints, whereas the second hypothesis has to do with its development, and in particular with whether the ROC followed the same historical path as other valency-increasing constructions such as the cognate object construction and the *way*-construction, thus occurring first with more transitive-like verbs and then expanding to intransitives.

(ii) *Hypotheses*

Hypothesis 1 is formulated as follows. In ME the *way*-object did not show its modern formal restrictions: the *way*-object did not require the coreferential possessive determiner or the directional that are compulsory in the PDE *way*-construction (e.g. *Bill*$_i$ *belched his*$_i$ *way out of the restaurant*$_{\text{DIRECTIONAL}}$); such restrictions started to apply more strongly in EModE (Traugott and Trousdale 2013, 84). Just like *way*-objects, I hypothesize that the PDE formal restriction of coreferentiality of ROCs as shown in *Pigs*$_i$ *squeal emphatic disapproval*$_i$, and also in Levin's off quoted examples *She*$_i$ *mumbled her*$_i$ *adoration* and *Pauline*$_i$ *smiled her*$_i$ *thanks* also goes back to EModE.

As for *Hypothesis 2*, this is the following. Since the origins of the cognate object construction and the *way*-construction lie in the use of cognate objects and *way*-objects with transitive verbs (Visser 1963–1973: I, § 424: 414–415; Traugott and Trousdale 2013; Lavidas 2018; cf. § 3.2.1.1 and § 3.2.1.2), we may start from the assumption that reaction objects follow the same path of development as these other transitivizing/valency-increasing constructions, occurring first with more transitive-like verbs and then expanding to intransitives.

1.3 Overview of the following chapters

I start in Chapter 2 with a discussion of the process of transitivization that began in OE and led to the development of a number of transitivizing/valency-increasing constructions, and of the ROC in particular, in ModE (§ 2.1 and § 2.2). The chapter concludes with a review of Visser's proposal on the several causes that triggered this large process of transitivization (§ 2.3). The focus of Chapter 3 is on the nonprototypical features of reaction objects, starting from the treatment of the object in historical and contemporary reference grammars (§ 3.1), followed by a discussion on the nonprototypical characteristics of cognate objects, *way*-objects and reaction objects in the more specialized literature (§ 3.2). Chapter 4 provides an overview of the major tenets of Construction Grammar, a theory of linguistic knowledge used here as a heuristic tool to get a better understanding of the idiosyncratic nature and historical development of the ROC.

These introductory chapters on transitivization, reaction objects and Construction Grammar set up the ground for Part II: *Hands-On with Data: A Usage-Based Approach to the History of the ROC*, where the research questions and hypotheses put forward in Part I are subject to investigation. Chapter 5 addresses the first three research questions in § 1.2 above. More specifically, § 5.1 offers a detailed characterization of the modern reaction object construction from the perspective of Construction Grammar, and § 5.2 presents historical evidence, mostly based on the OED, that suggests that the origins of the ROC lie in the LME period and that it followed a similar path of development as other valency-increasing constructions (*Hypothesis 2*). *Hypothesis 1* regarding the configuration of the ROC as a new form-meaning pairing with its formal restriction of coreferentiality, and the fourth research question concerning the development of the ROC are dealt with in Chapters 6 and 7 where I examine the development of the ROC in British and American English. More specifically, Chapter 6 assesses constructional changes in form, function, frequency and distribution (across verbs, time and text types) in British English during the Late Modern English (LModE) period (1710–1920), and Chapter 7 serves to complement Chapters 5 and 6.

It focuses on American English (1810s-2000s) and describes further constructional changes undergone by the ROC during the nineteenth and twentieth centuries that confirm its striking parallel development with the *way*-construction.

PART I
Transitivization, Reaction Objects and Construction Grammar

2. The process of transitivization in the history of English

Verbs' argument structure is usually conceived as a part of grammar that is inherently stable so that verbs are categorized as transitive, intransitive, complex transitive and so on (Huddleston and Pullum et al. 2002, 220), depending on the number and the nature of the arguments they occur with. However, this property of verbs is not as fixed as generally assumed, but is subject to both synchronic and diachronic changes resulting from different types of processes: (a) processes of argument remapping (e.g. ME <u>*me*</u> *liketh* vs. PDE <u>*I*</u> *like*), (b) processes of argument reduction (e.g. *John washed* <u>*himself*</u> > *John washed Ø*), and (c) processes of argument augmentation or transitivization processes (e.g. *Pigs squeal* <u>*emphatic disapproval*</u>). This last type of process is the focus of this chapter, where I will compare Old and Modern English valency paying special attention to the rise of a considerable number of transitive uses of verbs in ModE (§ 2.2), and to some of the possible causes that have led to this large process of transitivization (§ 2.3).

2.1 Old and Modern English valency

Visser (1963–1973: I, § 129: 97) classifies verbs without complement in OE into four main sets, claiming that "similar divisions into four groups can be made of the verbs in the later stages of English". This statement seems to hold true for PDE as well, as can be seen in the comparison of Visser's (1963–1973) classification with Liu's (2008) more recent taxonomy of PDE verbs used without an object. Observe in this regard Tab. 2.1, where both classifications are placed side by side arranged in order of increasing degree of intransitivity, [Type 1] being the most prototypically intransitive type and [Type 4] the least intransitive.

Tab. 2.1: Visser's classification of verbs without complement in OE and Liu's taxonomy of PDE verbs used without an object

Visser's classification of verbs without complement in OE (1963–1973: I)	Liu's taxonomy of PDE verbs used without an object (2008)	
[Type 1] Self-sufficient intransitive verbs (1) OE heo *fordwineþ*[a] PDE she *vanishes* (2) OE we *slapað* PDE we *sleep*	**[Type 1] Pure intransitive verbs** *arrive, come, jog, rise, sleep* also *dream, laugh, live* and *sing* (cognate objects)	Most prototypically intransitive
[Type 2] Double-functioned or amphibious verbs (3) OE heofoncandel *barn* PDE the heavenly candle *burnt*[b] OE Swa fyr wudu *byrneð* PDE As the fire *burns* the wood[c]	**[Type 2] Ergative intransitive verbs** (including **pseudo intransitive verbs)** *break, change, increase, move, open* (**pseudo:** *reads smoothly, spells well*) (4) The window *broke* They *broke* the window	↓
[Type 3] Intransitive verbs construed with an indirect object (in the dative) or with a causative object (in the genitive) (5) OE hit *me-DAT* ne *deraþ* PDE it shall not *hurt me-DAT*[d] (6) OE he *giornade friðes-GEN* PDE he *yearned for peace-GEN*	-------------	↓
-------------	**[Type 3] Transitive-converted intransitive verbs of activity** *eat, drink, hunt, knit, read* (7) Mary *ate a burger* Mary *ate*	↓
[Type 4] Transitive verbs used without the direct object they normally require This 'suppression' of the direct object occurs whenever it is so clear from the **context** or **situation** that the utterance is intelligible without it. (8) OE ic *befrine* PDE I *ask* (9) O.E. Gosp., Mt., II, 7, 'Herodes *befran* hi' PDE Herod *asked* her/them	**[Type 4] Object deleting transitive verbs** (both discourse and situational context warranted) **Discourse:** *accept, ask, deliver, find out, know, promise, see* (10) "Zam, what have you been up to?" "Don't *ask*." **Situational:** *bake, freeze, heat, keep off, shake* (11) *Bake* for 45 minutes. . . (instruction on a cake mix box)	Least prototypically intransitive

a Unless otherwise indicated the translations into PDE are mine. The translations of the OE verbs into PDE are based on Bosworth & Toller's *An Anglo-Saxon Dictionary*.

b Translation provided by Bosworth & Toller's *An Anglo-Saxon Dictionary* (s.v. *beornan*, I. v. n.).

c Translation provided by van Gelderen (2011, 122).

d Translation and example provided by Bosworth & Toller's *An Anglo-Saxon Dictionary* (s.v. *derian*).

Visser's **[Type 1]** consists of self-sufficient intransitive verbs, or intransitive verbs that are never construed with either a direct, an indirect, a prepositional or a causative object, as *fordwínan* 'to dwindle away, vanish' in *heo fordwineþ* (PDE 'she vanishes'), and *slápan* 'to sleep' in *we slapað* (PDE 'we sleep'). **[Type 2]** includes double-functioned or amphibious verbs, which are intransitive verbs which possess an "etymologically related transitive homonym". An example is OE *beornan* (PDE 'to burn, be on fire') which has a transitive homonym, OE *bærnan*, meaning 'to cause to be consumed by fire, burn up', exemplified in *Swa fyr wudu byrneð* (PDE 'As the fire burns the wood'). Regarding double-functioned or amphibious verbs, it is important to point out here that there is no consensus in the literature regarding the use of a particular label. For instance, Visser himself sometimes employs the alternative label 'double-faced verbs', Dixon and Aikhenvald (2000, 4) refer to verbs occurring in either an intransitive or a transitive clause as 'ambitransitive', Huddleston and Pullum et al. (2002, 217 and 298) use the label 'dual-transitivity verbs', and McMillion (2006) and García García (2012) use the term 'labile'. Note that the latter use the term 'labile' in a more restrictive way, namely to refer to those verbs that can function as intransitive and causative with no morphological marking, such as *break* in *The window broke* and *They broke the window*. Visser's **[Type 3]** involves intransitive verbs that are usually construed with an indirect object (in the dative) or with a causative object (in the genitive). This is the case of *derian* 'To injure, hurt, harm, damage' that takes a dative object in *hit me-DAT ne deraþ* (PDE 'it shall not hurt me-DAT'), and *geornan/giornan* 'To desire, beg' that occurs with a genitive object, as shown in *he giornade friðes-GEN* (PDE 'he yearned for peace-GEN'). Finally, Visser's **[Type 4]** is formed by transitive verbs used without the direct object they normally require whenever it is clear from the context or situation that the utterance is intelligible without it (i.e. they are object drop). An example is *befrinan* 'To ask, inquire, learn' in *ic befrine* (PDE 'I ask').

As shown in Tab. 2.1, three out of Visser's four groups of verbs used without a complement in OE are also listed in Liu's taxonomy (2008) of PDE verbs used without an object. Visser's group of self-sufficient intransitive verbs (e.g. *fordwínan* 'to dwindle away, vanish' and *slápan* 'to sleep') corresponds to Liu's class of pure intransitive verbs (e.g.

arrive, come, jog, rise, sleep). Liu (2008, 298 and 305) defines these verbs as inherently intransitive, and explains that they occur with only one argument in the subject position that usually plays the theta role of agent. In addition, they never take an object except for a few of them in very limited situations, as in cognate object constructions (e.g. *dream a bad dream, laugh a good laugh, live a good life* and *sing a song*), and causative transitive constructions (e.g. *walk one's dog, sit someone down*). Visser's [Type 2] involving double-functioned or amphibious verbs (e.g. *beornan* 'to burn, be on fire') matches the group of verbs Liu calls "ergative intransitive verbs" (e.g. *break, change, increase, move* and *open*). This group of verbs occurs with a single argument in the subject position that usually plays the theta role of theme. When these verbs are used transitively, the subject in the ergative intransitive use (e.g. *The window-SUBJECT broke*) becomes the object (e.g. *They broke the window-OBJECT*) (Liu 2008, 298 and 305). Contrary to pure intransitive verbs, which are "inherently intransitive" (Liu 2008, 298), many ergative verbs are opaque when it comes to determining whether they were originally intransitive or transitive (for a similar argument see Möhlig and Klages 2002, 241; see also García García 2012). Finally, Visser's [Type 4] consisting of transitive verbs used without the direct object they normally require (e.g. OE *ic befrine*, PDE 'I ask') perfectly corresponds to Liu's two subtypes of object deleting transitive verbs. Similar to Visser (1963–1973: I, § 129: 97), Liu also focuses on the role of the discourse (e.g. *"Zam, what have you been up to?" "Don't ask."*), and the situational context (e.g. *Bake for 45 minutes… (instruction on a cake mix box)*) to warrant the omission of the object. According to Liu (2008, 304–305), both subtypes of object deleting transitive verbs are characterized by the following features: (i) there is no meaning shift when the verb is used without the object, (ii) there is a specific deleted object which is definite and easily recoverable from the discourse or situational context, and (iii) these verbs cannot function meaningfully without a clear discourse or situational context that allows the recovery of the deleted object as illustrated in the ungrammatical examples (1)-(4).

(1) * I **explained** yesterday. (unless in a discourse context where what was explained was known)

(2) * I will **promise** tomorrow. (unless in a dicourse context)

(3) * Don't **close**. (unless as a sign on a door, window, etc.)

(4) * **Discard** after use. (unless as an instruction on something like plastic gloves)

(Liu 2008, 304)

Despite all these similarities, Visser and Liu's classifications of verbs without an object also show important differences. For instance, Visser's [Type 3] consisting of intransitive verbs construed with an indirect object (in the dative) or with a causative object (in the genitive), is excluded from Liu's classification because this type (e.g. OE *hit me-DAT ne deraþ*, PDE 'it shall not hurt me-DAT') disappeared as a result of the loss of case marking in the late OE period. Additionally, Liu's classification includes two new PDE verb types used without an object. These are (i) pseudo intransitive verbs (e.g. *reads smoothly, spells well*), which are treated as a small group of ergative intransitive verbs – Liu's [Type 2] – , and (ii) transitive-converted intransitive verbs of activity (e.g. *eat*, *drink*, *hunt*, *knit* and *read*). Pseudo intransitive verbs, also referred to as middles in the literature (Möhlig and Klages 2002, 244), are marked by the occurrence of an adverbial (e.g. *reads smoothly, sells well*), or the negator *not* (e.g. *The door won't open*). The main reason why this intransitive use is not distinguished in Visser's classification is because it developed later in the history of English, especially in the nineteenth and twentieth centuries (Denison 1993, 392–393). As for transitive-converted intransitive verbs of activity, this intransitive verb type is usually confused in grammar books with object deleting transitive verbs despite showing clear differences (Liu 2008, 299; see also De Dios 2014, 2015). Contrary to what happens with object deleting transitive verbs, in transitive-converted intransitive verbs of activity (i) there is often a shift in meaning from the object to activity (the verb) when this group of verbs converts from transitive to intransitive; (ii) there is really no specific deleted object, although some grammarians argue that some verbs of this type may assume "a more specific meaning, so a particular kind of object is 'understood' " (Quirk et al. 1985, 1169) as in the intransitive utterance *John drinks heavily*, where *alcohol* is the omitted object; and (iii) these verbs can function meaningfully without a clear discourse or situational context, as shown in examples (5)-(7).

(5) She likes to **read**.

(6) The python has already **eaten**.

(7) She might have been **drinking**.

(Liu 2008, 302)

Interestingly, earlier approaches to transitivization (Jespersen 1909–1949: III, 319–355; see also Deutschbein 1931) did not distinguish either between Liu's transitive-converted intransitive verbs of activity and object deleting transitive verbs. One exception is Möhlig and Klages (2002), who also pointed out that generic uses – which correspond to Liu's transitive-converted intransitive verbs of activity – should be distinguished from absolute uses (i.e. Liu's object deleting verbs). Foreshadowing Liu (2008), Möhlig and Klages (2002) claim that "the objects of generic uses are typically implied by the cultural context (e.g. world knowledge)", whereas the objects of absolute uses are "implied either by the textual or the situational context (e.g. by being anaphorically given or visible in the communication situation)" (239).[4] Importantly, only generic uses are cases of detransitivization, since according to Möhlig and Klages (2002) absolute uses "can occur with any transitive verb in English without changing the verb's transitiveness" (239), mainly because in object deleting transitive verbs there is a specific deleted object which is easily recoverable from the discourse or situational context. The absence of transitive-converted intransitive verbs from Visser's classification may be due to their relatively low frequency in OE in contrast to other periods of English. Note that early instances of this intransitive use for the transitive verbs *drink*, *wash* and *drive* only go back to ModE (examples (8)-(10)), and this intransitive use is missing for most of the transitive verbs analysed by Möhlig and Klages (2002, 239–240) in their famous study on detransitivization in the history of English (e.g. *dress*, *move*, *open*, *break*, *fill*, *tell*, *load* among others).

4 This division seems to correspond to Fillmore's (1986) famous distinction of indefinite null complements (INC) and definite null complements (DNC), respectively: "[w]ith *definite null complements* the missing element must be retrieved from something *given* in the context; with *indefinite null complements* the referent's identity is unknown or a matter of indifference" (Fillmore 1986, 96).

(8) 1640 J. Fletcher & J. Shirley *Night-walker* iv. sig. H2v, Give me the bottle, I can **drink** like a Fish now, like an Elephant. (OED, s.v. *drink*, v.[1] 11. II. a.)

(9) 1697 T. Tryon *Way to Health* (ed. 3) vi. 101 It [*sc.* rain-water] Brews and **Washes** to greater advantage than others. (OED, s.v *wash*, v. I. 2. h.)

(10) 1717 M. Prior *Alma* iii. 140 The man within the coach that sits..Is safer much..than he that **drives**. (OED, s.v. *drive*, v. I. 5. c.)

Although, as has just been seen, Liu's classification of PDE verbs used without an object is basically similar to Visser's, there is no doubt that there have been important changes in verb's argument structure throughout the history of English. Some new intransitive uses have emerged or have become more frequent – for instance, a small group of Liu's [Type 2] pseudo intransitives, and Liu's [Type 3] transitive-converted intransitive verbs of activity –, whereas others have disappeared, namely Visser's [Type 3] intransitive verbs construed with an indirect object (in the dative) or with a causative object (in the genitive). Equally important, there has been a lot of fluctuation in the number of verbs ascribed to each type. For instance, many verbs that were never found with either a direct, an indirect, a prepositional or a causative object in OE – Visser's [Type 1] – came to develop transitive uses in later periods. This meant a significant increase in the number of amphibious or double-functioned verbs and a considerable decrease of self-sufficient intransitive verbs. Visser recognizes this fact in his grammar when he states that double-functioned or amphibious verbs in PDE "far outnumber" those in OE (1963–1973: I, § 132: 99–100). According to Visser, this change in verbs' argument structure involves a large process of transitivization that affected, in particular, verbs expressing motion, and human, animal or other sounds, which were exclusively intransitive in OE. In his own words,

> Historically, the most remarkable fact is that, whereas in Old English the number of double-faced or amphibious verbs was far inferior to that of intransitive verbs, in Pres. D. English amphibious verbs far outnumber the intransitive verbs (of type [I] that is). In other words, transitivation has taken place on a large scale. Thus e.g. almost all **verbs expressing motion** (such as *climb, bolt, bound, burst, creep, dive,flow, glide, run* and *spring*) **or human, animal or other sounds** (such as *bellow, crow, groan, grunt, laugh, lisp, neigh, stammer, weep, whisper* and *whistle*), **which were exclusively intransitive in Old English, are now found construed with a direct object as well**. The process of transitivation started in

> Old English, and went steadily on during the subsequent periods, affecting also the intransitive verbs that made their first appearance in later English (e.g. *bolt, bound* (= *to leap*), *career, crawl, decamp, frisk, coo, creak, croak, drone, gaggle, growl* and many others). (Visser 1963–1973: I, § 132: 99–100; emphasis mine)

Interestingly, Jespersen (1909–1949) argues for a similar process of transitivization affecting "words for producing various sounds":

> Several **words for producing various sounds** are generally used without an object, e.g. *talk, speak, whisper, lisp, whistle*, but they may also be used with an object: *he talks nonsense, speaks his mind, whispers the secret, lisps his consonants, whistles a melody*. Though **historically this is the opposite of what happens with the verbs considered above** [i.e. transitive verbs that show object omission, that is, detransitivization processes], the actual result is practically the same: *he talks*: *he talks nonsense*; *he drinks*: *he drinks whisky*. (Jespersen 1909–1949: III, § 16.1_7: 324; emphasis mine)

Before delving into some of the possible causes that have led to this large process of transitivization, some further clarifications should be made regarding Visser's classification in order to get a better understanding of the dynamics of this process of change that has affected many self-sufficient intransitive verbs throughout the history of English.

2.2 The rise of double-functioned or amphibious verbs

Visser states that the number of double-functioned or amphibious verbs in OE was "considerably less numerous" (98) than the number of self-sufficient intransitive verbs. To illustrate this contrast, he lists 55 amphibious verbs against 223 self-sufficient intransitive verbs[5] and, on the basis of the pre-1933 OED, claims that the large number

5 According to van Gelderen (2011, 118–119), some of these 223 self-sufficient intransitive verbs are not always intransitive and it remains unclear how many of these verbs "are really intransitive and not labile". In her study, van Gelderen (2015) analyses 81 of Visser's list of 223 self-sufficient intransitive verbs, and finds that six of them were not intransitive.

of self-sufficient intransitive verbs available in OE dwindled to 58 in PDE, here represented in (11). However, this reduction of self-sufficient intransitive verbs seems to have been even sharper than suggested by the pre-1933 OED. More specifically, van Gelderen (2011, 119; see also van Gelderen 2018) explains that of these 58 self-sufficient intransitive verbs mentioned by Visser, only 26 remain exclusively intransitive in ModE (those in (12)), 16 verbs have disappeared in non-archaic ModE (those in (13)), and 16 have developed transitive uses, mainly as prepositional verbs (those in (14)). Interestingly, McMillion (2006, 192) also pointed out that the verbs in (15) – also from Visser's list of 58 self-sufficient intransitive verbs – reveal transitive uses in the *British National Corpus* (BNC), although some of these uses are quite unconventional: *crochet a table-cloth, mockery glittered his dark eyes, gyrate her tail, booze him to the devil, gab your ear off* and *migrate data*. After all these verbs' argument structure changes detected by van Gelderen (2011) and McMillion (2006), we are left with a total of just 17 self-sufficient intransitive verbs in PDE (those in (16)). To this short list of intransitive verbs in PDE, van Gelderen (2011, 119) adds a few more, namely *arrive, escape, remain, seem* and *go*. So Visser's original list of 223 self-sufficient intransitive verbs in OE is now diminished to little more than 20 intransitive verbs in PDE (those included here in (17)). Many of these intransitive verbs are unaccusative, that is, verbs that "involve change of location or state" (van Gelderen 2011, 108) such as *appear, arise, arrive, die* and *seem*. Also interesting is the fact that some of them are loanwords (e.g. *appear, arrive, seem* and *exist*) which came to replace native verbs that became obsolete such as OE *bifian*, PDE 'To tremble, shake, be moved' (B&T, s.v. *bifian*), and OE *ablinnan*, PDE 'To cease, desist' (B&T, s.v. *a-blinnan*).

(11) *appear, arise, balbutiate, beetle, blossom, booze, bugle, caper, caterwaul, cleave* (= adhere), *coexist, cohere, coincide, collapse, compete, concur, co-operate, crochet, depend, didder, die, disagree, disappear, elope, exist, exult, lie, gab* (= prate), *gambol, glimpse, glisten, glitter, gruntle, gyrate, halt* (= limp), *interfere, last, limp, lurk, lurch, luxuriate, migrate, prate, pullulate, recur, reluct, result, roister, sally, secede, shimmer, strive, swoon, thrive, ululate, vacillate, wax, yap* → Visser's 58 self-sufficient intransitive verbs in PDE

(12) *appear, arise, blossom, bugle, coexist, collapse, crochet, didder, die, disappear, exist, lie, glisten, glitter, gruntle, gyrate, halt* (= limp), *last, limp, lurk,*

lurch, recur, shimmer, thrive, wax, yap → 26 exclusively intransitive verbs in ModE (van Gelderen 2011, 119)

(13) *balbutiate, beetle, booze, caper, caterwaul, cohere, gab, gambol, glimpse,* [*last*], *prate, pullulate, reluct, roister, sally, swoon* and *ululate* → 16 verbs have disappeared in non-archaic ModE (van Gelderen 2011, 119)[6]

(14) *cleave, coincide, compete, concur, co-operate, depend, disagree, elope, exult,* [*interfere*], *luxuriate, migrate, result, secede, strive* and *vacillate* → 16 have developed transitive uses (van Gelderen 2011, 119)

(15) *beetle, blossom, booze, bugle, cleave, coincide, collapse, crochet, disappear, exult, gab, glitter, gyrate, migrate, shimmer* → These verbs developed unconventional uses (McMillion 2006, 192)

(16) *appear, arise, coexist, didder, die, exist, lie, glisten, gruntle, halt* (= limp), *limp, lurk, lurch, recur, thrive, wax, yap* → 17 self-sufficient intransitive verbs in PDE

(17) *appear, arise,* ***arrive****, coexist, didder, die,* ***escape****, exist, lie, glisten,* ***go****, gruntle, halt* (= limp), *limp, lurk, lurch, recur,* ***remain****,* ***seem****, thrive, wax, yap* → 22 self-sufficient intransitive verbs in PDE (van Gelderen 2011, 119)

As for the category of amphibious or double-functioned verbs, Visser mentions 55, namely those represented in (18). As was the case with the list of self-sufficient intransitive verbs, this list of verbs should be treated with caution. Some linguists have argued that there are more than 55 amphibious verbs in OE (Hermodsson 1952, 196–207), while others disagree with the ascription of some of these verbs to the amphibious class. For instance, OE *beornan* was counted as an amphibious verb by Visser and García García (2012) but according to the OED (OED, s.v. *burn*, v.[1]), OE possessed two distinct verbs, *beornan* (intransitive) and *bærnan* (transitive) which "ran together early in the Middle English period". Although the exact number of amphibious verbs in OE is thus somewhat controversial, what is clear is that these verbs were not as common as they are in PDE. For instance, McMillion (2006, 223–232) lists over 800 PDE labile verbs,[7] and Visser (1963–1973: I,

6 The verb *last* in (12) is erroneously repeated by van Gelderen in (13). The verb *interfere* in (14) is missing from van Gelderen's analysis of Visser's list of self-sufficient intransitive verbs in PDE.

7 In this large list, McMillion (2006, 223–232) includes not only verbs that show causative and inchoative senses, but also a few reflexive verbs such as *wash* and

§ 133: 100–127) provides transitive homonyms for 506 verbs usually marked 'intransitive' in ModE grammars, arguing in this way that the process that lies behind the rise of amphibious verbs in PDE is one of transitivization.[8]

(18) *abrecan* 'break', *abreoðan* 'unsettle/ruin', *acirran* 'turn', *acuman* 'come', *acweccan* 'shake', *acwician* 'quicken/revive', *ætiewan* 'show', *ætstandan* 'stand/remain', *aslacian* 'become/make slack', *baðian* 'bathe', *blawan* 'blow', *blissian* 'be glad/make glad', *brecan* 'break', *bregdan* 'move quickly/shake', *buan* 'live', *byrnan* 'burn', *cierran* 'turn', *clipian* 'speak, cry out', *cwanian* 'lament/mourn', *dragan* 'drag', *dwelian* 'go/lead astray', *dwellan* 'wander/lead astray', *eardian* 'live/inhabit', *fleon* 'fly/flee', *fon* 'take', *geotan* 'pour', *gladian* 'be glad/rejoice', *healdan* 'hold/procede', *hefigan* 'become/make heavy', *hildan* 'lean/hold', *hlænan* 'lean/cause to lean', *hweorfan* 'turn/change', *lacan* 'jump/play', *læstan* 'follow/endure', *langian* 'long for/lengthen', *mierran* 'scatter/disturb', *miswendan* 'err/abuse', *ofergan* 'traverse', *oferfaran* 'traverse', *openian* 'open', *plegan* 'move', *sadian* 'weary', *samnian* 'assemble/meet', *sargian* 'suffer/cause pain', *sarian* 'become painful/feel sorry for', *scotian* 'move rapidly', *spyrian* 'go/pursue', *tolicgan* 'lie/separate', *tostregdan* 'scatter', *tostencan* 'scatter', *tydran* 'produce', *þeostrian* 'darken', *þringan* 'press (on)', *wanian* 'diminish', *wlitigian* 'become/make beautiful'[9]

Fig. 2.1 represents this flux of verbs' argument structure just described, with a sharp increase in the number of amphibious verbs (up to 800), and a comparatively slight decrease in the number of self-sufficient intransitive verbs from OE to PDE (reduced to around 20).

---

stretch. This implies that the existence of over 800 labiles in PDE is not only justified by means of transitivization but, as previously outlined in the introduction, detransitivization or processes of argument reduction such as the development of coreferential intransitive uses (e.g. *John washed* <u>*the clothes*</u> > *John washed* <u>*himself*</u> > *John washed Ø*) also seem to have played a role.

8 Interestingly, this feature of ModE sets it apart from other Germanic languages that did not develop as many amphibious verbs (McMillion 2006, 185; for similar observations see Haspelmath 1993, Möhlig and Klages 2002, Poppe 2009, García García 2012, Mondorf 2016, 88–90).

9 Translations provided by van Gelderen (2011, 120).

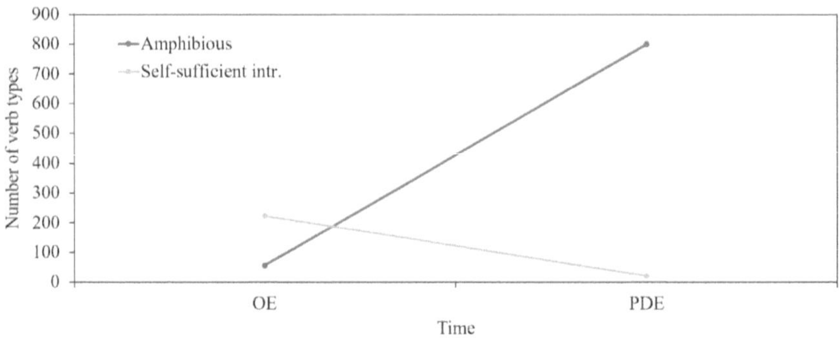

Fig. 2.1: Estimates of amphibious verbs and self-sufficient intransitive verbs in OE and PDE. Based on Visser (1963–1973: I, §§ 130–132), McMillion (2006, 192–193) and van Gelderen (2011, 117–122).

2.3 Causes of the process of transitivization: Visser's proposal

Visser (1963–1973: I, §§ 134–144: 127–135) puts forward a series of internal factors that triggered this broad process of transitivization that started in OE and continued in subsequent periods affecting also intransitive verbs that made their first appearance in later English. These factors can be summarized as follows: (i) the loss of the OE transitivizing/causativizing prefixes (*be-*, *ge-*, Gmc *-j*/*-i*), (ii) the inflectional syncretism which set in late OE, (iii) the complementation changes of a number of intransitive verbs normally construed with a prepositional object, (iv) the two-fold interpretation of the past participle of some verbs, and (v) the LModE fashion of treating verbs expressing human and animal sounds, and verbs of gestures as reporting verbs. In what follows, I will briefly comment on these several factors.

*2.3.1 Loss of OE transitivizing/causativizing affixes (*be-, ge-, *Gmc* -j/-i*)*

OE had an extremely low percentage of loan words and a large number of words created by means of prefixation, suffixation and compounding (Kastovsky 1992, 294). However, the OE system of word formation, was upset by the introduction of many Latin words after the Norman Conquest, and also by the disappearance of many affixes that were too weak phonologically (Marchand 1969, 130). In this section, I will focus on the OE prefixes *be-* and *ge-*, and also on the Germanic affix *-j/-i*, as these affixes have been claimed by some linguists to have functioned as transitivizers of originally intransitive verbs.

2.3.1.1 The prefix *be-* (Marchand 1969)

This prefix is historically the unstressed form of the particle *by*, meaning 'by, around, about, near, etc.', observable in composites such as *before*, *behind*, *beneath*, *benorth*, *beside*, *besouth*, *between*, and *beyond*. As for the functions of the OE prefix *be-*, with some verbs this prefix does not seem to add or have added any nuance to the verb (*betrap* 'catch in a trap', *betoken* 'token, signify'), on other occasions the prefix makes an intransitive verb transitive (i.e. *bemoan*, *bedip*, *begnaw*, *belie*, *besmear*, *beweep*, *becharm*, *besiege*, *besprinkle* and *bewail*), and on others the prefix seemed to have an intensifying function in connection with verbs such as *smear*, *wail* and *weep* (Marchand 1969, 146–147).[10] Regarding the transitivizing function of the prefix *be-*, Visser claims that "the dropping into disuse of almost all the transitive verbs formed by means of the prefix *be-* from intransitive verbs" (Visser, 1963–1973: I, § 144: 134–135) could have played a role in the process of transitivization described in § 2.2. Some examples he mentions of transitive verbs created out of intransitive verbs by means of the prefix *be-* are: *bebark*, *bedwell*, *bechirp*, *beflow*, *befly*, ***begaze***, *beglide*, ***beglitter***, *bego*, *behoot*, *beleap*, *belie*, *bemew*, *berain*, ***beride***, ***berow***, ***beshite***, ***beshriek***, *besit*, *bescramble*, ***bescratch***, *besparkle*, ***beswink***;

10 For similar comments on this prefix see Hiltunen (1983, 48–49) and Kastovsky (1992, 380).

OE ***befaran*** 'To go around, to travel through', ***betihtlian*** 'To accuse, charge', ***betimbran*** 'To build, construct with timber', ***bewitan*** 'To overlook, watch over' and ***bewlatian*** 'To see, look, behold'.[11] On the other hand, amphibious verbs that could have originated by the disuse of this transitivizing prefix are the verbs of sounds *bark*, *chirp*, *hoot* and *mew*, and the verbs of motion *leap* and *glide* (see examples (19)-(24)).[12]

(19) **Bark** (of a dog) (**intr.** c885); tr. (a) (obsol.) c1000 Sax. Leechd. I, 170, Gyf hwa þas wyrte mid him hafað..ne mæg he fram hundum *beon borcen.* | (b) c1440 Morte d'Arth. 1351, *He berkes myche boste.* | 1688 Matth. Prior, Epistle to Fleetwood Shepherd (in: Bickley, Shorter Poems of Prior) 10, Pigs might squeak love-odes, dogs *bark satire.*

(20) **Chirp** (**intr.** 1440); tr. 1614 T. Adams, Devil's Banquet 61, The vncleane Sparrowes, *cherping the voice of Lust* on the house-tops.

(21) **Hoot** (**intr.** a1225); tr. c1200 Ormin 2034, ȝiff mann wollde tælenn þatt. & *hutenn hire.* | a1687 Cotton, Fable (R.), Perched on Parnassus all night long, He [an owl] *hoots a sonnet or a song.*

(22) **Mew** (of a cat) (**intr.** c1325); tr. 1900 Aflalo, in: Cornh. Mag., Nov. 628, The gulls *were mewing their plaintive dirge* over the fishy harbour.

(23) **Leap** (**intr.** Beow.); tr. (a) 1432–50 transl. Higden (Rolls) III, 57, Romulus diede afore thro *lepenge the walles of Rome.* | (b) 1681–6 J. Scott, Chr. Life (1747) III, 355, Those restless Furies... will never cease stimulating and spurring us on... till they have *leapt us* headlong into the everlasting Burnings. | (c) **1530** Palsgr. 606/I, Kepe your horse in the stabyl, for and he *leape a mare* he wyll be the worse to journey a good whyle after.

(24) **Glide** (**intr.** Beow.); tr. 1650 Trapp., Comm. Gen. iv, 17, Silly are they that think *to glide away their groans* with games. | 1893 Gunter, Miss Dividends 128, Ferdie *glides the graceful Louise* through the room in poetic motion.

A glance at the OED (s.v. *be-*, *prefix*, 4) shows that remnants of the transitivizing value of the *be-* prefix still survive in ModE in *begaze*, *behoot* and *beride* (see (25)-(27)). However, none of these verbs is commonly used in PDE. For instance, a quick search in the *Corpus*

11 The meanings of the OE verbs are those provided in Bosworth & Toller's *An Anglo-Saxon Dictionary*. Note also that the intransitive counterparts of the prefixed verbs in bold type are not included in Visser's list of 506 verbs usually marked "intransitive" in ModE grammars which was mentioned in § 2.2 earlier.

12 I cite the transitive uses of these verbs as presented in Visser (1963–1973: I, § 133: 100–127), who follows the pre-1933 OED.

of Contemporary American English (COCA; Davies 2008-) yields no tokens for any of these verbs. Finally, it should be noted that the situation attested in English contrasts sharply with other Germanic languages such as German, or Swedish, in which verbs with the prefix *be-* "are still in extensive use", and their corresponding counterparts without this prefix are rarely used transitively (Visser 1963–1973: I, § 144: 135). This could be one of the reasons why there is no apparent process of transitivization taking place in Swedish, or German, which seem to have about the same number of amphibious verbs as OE (see in this regard McMillion 2006, 194–195).

(25) ***begaze*** v. to gaze at (cf. OED, s.v. *gaze*, v. 1. a. **intr.** c1386)
1802 W. Taylor in J. W. Robberds *Mem. W. Taylor* (1843) I. 411, I could only..**begaze** <u>the site of Lord Nelson's misemployment</u>.

(26) ***behoot*** v. to hoot at (cf. OED, s.v. *hoot*, v. 1. a. **intr.** a1225)
1838 R. W. Emerson *Misc.* 118 It is travestied and depreciated..<u>it</u> is **behooted** and behowled.

(27) ***beride*** v. [Old English *berídan*] to ride beside, to override. (cf. OED, *ride*, v. I. 1. **intr.** a. eOE)
1690 T. D'Urfey *Collin's Walk* ii. 69 Those two that there **beride** <u>him</u>, And with such Graces Prance beside him.

2.3.1.2 The prefix *ge-* (Lindemann 1970)

This prefix can be considered one of the most controversial morphemes in the history of the English language due to its high frequency in OE and also the large number of theories that have been proposed to explain its meanings and functions. For some linguists such as Dorfeld (1885) and Wustmann (1894), *ge-* is the Germanic equivalent of Latin *cum*, meaning 'with, together', whereas for others like Brugmann (1904) and Lindemann (1970), the real origin of *ge-* is in the Indoeuropean demonstrative pronominal stem **gho*, "a highly deictic morpheme stressing the progression of an action from one point forward toward another and as a verbal prefix, capable of expressing such ideas as those inherent in *von, zu, zu-, ver-*" (Lindemann 1970, 25). Generally speaking, in the numerous studies that approach the meaning and function of OE prefix *ge-*, the prefix has been described as being (a) empty, (b) intensifying, (c) transitivizing, (d) completive, and (e) a marker of perfective aspect. Though the claim that this prefix expresses perfective aspect is the most popular interpretation (see for instance Brinton 1988, van Gelderen 2018), this analysis has been challenged by several linguists who have noted that there was no consistent use of *ge-* as a marker of perfective aspect (Lindemann 1970, 8). As for the transitivizing function of *ge-*, Visser (1963–1973: I, § 134: 127) claims that the co-existence of a transitive verb with the prefix *ge-* and an intransitive verb without this prefix was frequent in OE. To support this claim he provides the examples presented in Tab. 2.2 and mentions that the disappearance of the prefix *ge-* after a process of gradual phonological decay (through the stages *ȝe-*, *ȝy-*, *ȝi-*, *y-*, *i-*) led to the sudden emergence of a number of amphibious verbs. In Visser's words, "the verbs with and without *ge-* appeared in an identical form in which the transitive and intransitive characters were seemingly combined" (1963–1973: I, § 134: 127).[13]

2.3.1.3 The Germanic suffix *-*(i)ja*- (García García 2012)

Causative verbs in Germanic such as GER **maltija-* 'melt' (caus.) were productively derived from primary verbs (GER **melta-* 'melt' (intr.)) by means of the suffix *-*(i)ja*-. This word-formation strategy is usually known as the Germanic *jan*-formation, which alludes to the infinitive ending of causative verbs in Gothic (e.g. *kannjan* 'to make known'). OE retains a considerable number of Germanic morphological causatives. García García (2012), for instance, attested 57 OE deverbal *jan*-verbs and pointed out that one of their most relevant developments is the disappearance of the causative opposition because either the intransitive

13 The transitivizing interpretation of the prefix *ge-* was harshly criticized by Lindemann (1970) who argues that this is an "oversimplification that ignores the history of this phenomenon and obscures the role of the prefix" (1970, 47). He opts for its original deictic meaning and on the basis of 45,000 examples of simple and compound verbs claims that "the action of the verb to which it [the prefix *ge-*] is affixed is directed forward *toward* something or *outward*" (1970, 63; emphasis in the original). More recently, Ruiz Narbona (2020) analyses the effects of some OE verbal prefixes on transitivity using Hopper and Thompson's (1980) parameters (i.e. participants, kinesis, aspect, punctuality, volitionality, affirmation, mode, agency, affectedness of object and individuation of object). The results of his analysis show that the prefix *ge-* does not increase the transitivity of the clause whereas the prefix *be-* does indeed show an effect.

Tab. 2.2: Examples of transitive verbs with the prefix *ge-* and intransitive verbs without this prefix in OE. Adapted from Visser (1963–1973: I, § 134: 127)

Transitive	Intransitive
geabydan = to wait for[a]	*abidan* = to remain
geæmtian = to make empty	*æmtian* = to be at leisure
geærnan = to reach, gain by running	*ærnan* = to run
gebirhtan = to make bright	*birhtan* = to shine
geceapian = to buy, purchase	*ceapian* = to bargain
gefeallan = to overthrow	*feallan* = to fall
geferan = to get by going, reach, perform	*feran* = to go
geflowan = to overflow	*flowan* = to flow, be fluid
gegalan = to enchant	*galan* = to be wanton
gegan = to overrun, occupy, subdue	*gan* = to go
gegangan = to overrun, occupy, subdue	*gangan* = to go
gegnigan = to cause to bend	*gnigan* = to descend, sink
gegrowan (of soil) = to produce	*growan* = to sprout, flourish
gehleapan = to leap upon, mount	*hleapan* = to leap, dance
gehliehhan = to deride	*hliehhan* = laugh
gehwelian = to inflame with foul matter	*hwelian* = to suppurate
gehwitian = to make white	*hwitian* = to be(come) white
gehirsumian = to obey, serve	*hirsumian* = to be obedient
geirnan = to run through, reach, obtain	*irnan* = to run
gemanigfealdian = to make numerous	*manigfealdian* = to become numerous
geminsian = to lessen, impair the credit of	*minsian* = to become small
gerestan = to give rest to, lodge	*restan* = to repose
geridan = to ride over, occupy, seize	*ridan* = to ride
geri(g)nan = to wet with rain	*ri(g)nan* = to rain
gesadian = to satiate	*sadian* = to be sated, get wearied
gespringan = to reach by spreading, get by going, cause to spring	*springan* = to leap, burst forth, rise, etc.
gestandan = to cause to stand, place, attend, attack	*standan* = to stand
gestinkan = to perceive by the sense of smelling	*stincan* = to emit a smell
geswætan = to cause to labour (?)	*swætan* = to sweat
gesyngian = to commit sinfully	*syngian* = to sin
geþyldigian = to endure, bear patiently	*þyldigian* = to be patient
gewadan = to traverse, pervade	*wadan* = to go, move, stride
gewarian = to guard, protect, hold, warn	*warian* = to be wary
gewinnan = to obtain by fighting, gain, conquer	*winnan* = to labour, toil

a Translations provided by Visser (1963–1973: I, § 134: 127).

verb or the *jan*-verb adopt an extra valency value. Hence the result is an amphibious (labile) verb that can function both as intransitive and causative. This “syntactic melting” seems to have been initiated in common Germanic as evinced by the intransitive-causative alternation represented in (28) which is not kept in any Germanic language. In general terms, García García’s (2012) findings show that OE causative verb pairs is one of the sources for the rise of labile verbs, and consequently, as suggested by Visser, they played a role in the overall process of transitivization that affected English since OE times (Visser 1963–1973: I, § 134: 131).

(28) GER **brenna*- ‘burn’ (intr.) vs. **brannija*- ‘burn’ (sth)

2.3.2 *Inflectional syncretism followed by reanalysis of the dative/genitive complement*

One significant difference between OE and PDE lies in the number of inflectional endings. Fig. 2.2 illustrates the array of case/number endings of some of the most important noun types in OE (Lass 1992, 103). The endings *-um* and *-es*, for instance, were characteristic of the case/number categories dative plural and the genitive singular (not feminine), respectively.

		a-stem (masc.)	*a*-stem (neut.)	*ō*-stem (fem.)	*u*-stem (masc.)
Singular	nom.	-Ø	-Ø	-u	-u
	gen.	-es	-es	-e	-a
	dat.	-e	-e	-e	-a
	acc.	-Ø	-Ø	-e	-u
Plural	nom.	-as	-u	-a/-e	-a
	gen.	-a	-a	-a/-ena	-a
	dat.	-um	-um	-um	-um
	acc.	-as	-u	-a/-e	-a

		i-stem (fem.)	*n*-stem (masc.)	Consonant-stem (masc.)
Singular	nom.	-Ø	-a	-Ø
	gen.	-e	-an	-es
	dat.	-e	-an	¨-Ø
	acc.	-Ø	-an	-Ø
	nom.	-e/-a	-an	¨-Ø
	gen.	-a	-ena	-a
	dat.	-um	-um	-um
	acc.	-e/-a	-an	¨-Ø

Fig. 2.2: Case/number endings of some of the most important noun types in OE. Adapted from Lass (1992, 103–104).

As explained by Lass (1992, 104), twenty-four noun categories were distinguishable in OE (four cases x two numbers x three genders), and the morphological devices to mark these categories were three: zero, umlaut and the endings *-u*, *-a*, *-e*, *-an*, *-um*, *-as* and *-es*. As shown in Fig. 2.3, these inflectional endings suffered important phonological changes. Baugh and Cable (2002, 159) point out that the earliest changes were (i) the change of final *-m* to *-n* (*muðum* > *muðun*) in the dative plural of nouns and adjectives, and the dative singular (masculine and neuter) of adjectives inflected according to the strong declension, and (ii) the reduction of the vowels in inflectional endings to an intermediate vowel written < e >, sometimes < i, y, u > depending on the dialect.

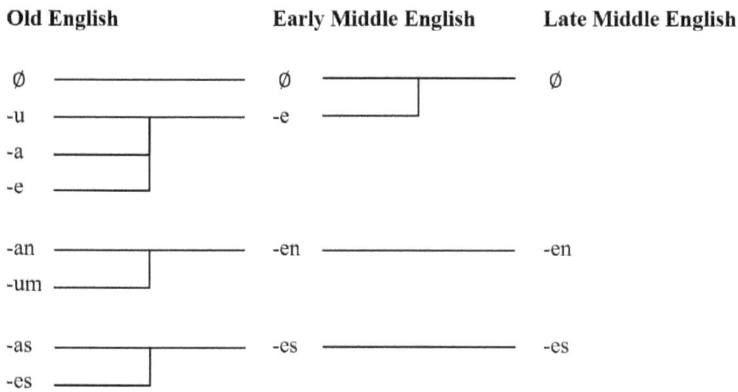

Fig. 2.3: Phonological changes affecting OE inflectional endings. Adapted from Lass (1992, 105).

Importantly, as a result of these phonological changes, the accusative-dative distinction in nouns (also in pronouns; see Lass 1992, 118) was lost and this inflectional syncretism seems to have played a role in the process of transitivization described in § 2.1 and § 2.2. Visser (1963–1973: I, § 134: 128), for instance, argues that the loss of the accusative-dative distinction in ME led speakers to reanalyse the dative objects of OE intransitive verbs (Visser's [Type 3] in Tab. 2.1) as the direct objects of transitive verbs. It is impossible, however, to provide the exact date of when this reanalysis was completed for each individual verb. If one takes a look at the examples provided by Visser (1963–1973: I, § 136: 128–129), we observe that during the ME period verbs such as OE *andswarian* 'to answer' and OE *derian* 'to injure' were used in some cases with the preposition *to* in order to mark explicitly the recipient character of the complement (*he answereþ* to me; and *he dereþ* to me), while others such as OE *helpan* 'to help' and OE *þancian* 'to thank' were construed in the passive (*beon holpenn* 'be helped'; and *þanked be ure louerd* 'be thanked by our Lord'), which can be considered to provide evidence of the conversion of the former dative object into a direct object. Visser (1963–1973: I, § 136: 128–129) argues that this process of reanalysis not only affected verbs of Anglo-Saxon origin (see examples in (29)), but also Old French intransitive verbs adopted into English, which were construed with a dative, or with *à* + noun (see examples in (30)). Finally, a development similar to that affecting the dative object of OE intransitive verbs also applied to those OE intransitive verbs that took a genitive object (see Visser's [Type 3] in Tab. 2.1). However, as explained by Visser, since "nearly all the verbs belonging to this category fell into disuse at an early period, the influence of this phenomenon on later transitivization must have been negligible" (Visser 1963–1973: I, § 136: 128).

(29) *andswarian* 'to answer', *bugan* 'to obey', *cidan* 'to chide', *derian* 'to injure', *forynnan* 'to forerun', *helpan* 'to help', *heorcnian* 'to harken', *hyran* 'to obey' and *þancian* 'to thank'[14]

(30) *avail, agree, displease, fail, please, profit, serve* and *vail* among others

2.3.3 *Twofold interpretation of* be *+ past participle: Perfect and passive*

The twofold interpretation of *be* in combination with the past participle of some verbs could have been another contributing factor to the process of transitivization described in § 2.1 and § 2.2. To express the perfect (completed events with relevance in the present) and the pluperfect (past of the past), OE could employ the simple past, or a periphrasis

14 Translations provided by Visser (1963–1973: I, § 136: 128–129).

with the auxiliary verbs *habban* 'to have' and *beon* 'to be' followed by a lexical verb in the past participle. The constructions involving *habban* occurred with transitive and intransitive verbs, whereas those occurring with *beon* were mainly restricted to mutative verbs, that is, intransitive verbs involving change of place or state such as *faran* 'go', *cuman* 'come', *weaxan* 'grow' and *oðfeallan* 'fall into decay' (Traugott 1992, 190–193). ME continued to make use of the two periphrastic constructions with *habben/hauen* and *be* to express the perfect and the pluperfect. However, the contexts in which the constructions were used became less clear-cut: *habben* was used with some mutative verbs, *be* was attested with some intransitive non-mutatives, and some verbs occurred with both auxiliaries (Fischer 1992, 260). In this complex situation, the auxiliary *have* ended up ousting *be* because *have* was the auxiliary of the perfect with most verb types, and *be* was already used as an auxiliary of the passive and the progressive (Fischer 1992, 261–262). Before this division of labour took place, the use of the auxiliary verb *be* to form the passive and express the perfect seems to have led to the reinterpretation of many intransitive verbs as transitives. In Visser's words (1963–1973: I, § 139: 131),

> It may be assumed that the formal identity of this combination [*be* + past participle] with a passive construction occasionally suggested the operation of an agent, and that this led the way to the transitive use of the verb.

To illustrate this point Visser provides examples of *be* + past participle combinations such as those in (31)-(34) and claims that the pre-1933 OED treats them as the earliest transitive uses of the originally intransitive verbs *congeal*, *clot*, *ferment* and *stagnate*.

(31) 1393 J. Gower *Confessio Amantis* III. 96 So as the fire it hath aneled, Lich unto slime, which ***is congeled***. (OED, s.v. *congeal*, v. I. trans. 1. a.)

(32) 1697 *Countess D'Aunoy's Trav.* (1706) 35 His Hair ***was*** all ***clotted*** together. (OED, s.v. *clot*, v. 4. trans.)

(33) 1673 N. Grew *Idea Phytol. Hist.* iii. 108 The Sap..***is..fermented*** therein. (OED, s.v. *ferment*, v. 2. trans.)

(34) 1693 J. Edwards *Disc. conc. Old & New-Test.* I. iv. 134 Whence gushed out an Inundation of Water, that ***is*** here ***stagnated***, and become a filthy Lake. (OED, s.v. *stagnate*, v. 3. a. trans.)

2.3.4 Changes in the complementation patterns of intransitive verbs normally construed with a prepositional object

Another factor that seems to have contributed to this large process of transitivization was the tendency to use intransitive verbs normally construed with a prepositional object such as *care for*, *boast of*, and *wonder at* with a *that*-clause as direct object without the preposition, as in *I boasted that I did it* and *I wonder that he did not kill you*. The use of *that*-clauses with these prepositional verbs could have been a *bridging context* or *intermediate step* before the adoption of noun phrase objects. Some other verbs provided by Visser that seem to have followed this transitivization path are *brag* (*of*, *about*), *cavil* (*at*, *about*), *complain* (*of*), *deliberate* (*upon*), *dream* (*of*, *about*), *hint* (*at*), *marvel* (*at*), *rejoice* (*at*, *in*) and *yearn* (*after*, *for*).

2.3.5 Use of verbs expressing human and animal sounds and other verbs such as smirk, smile *and* persist *as if they were synonyms of* say

Finally, another factor that may have furthered this process of transitivization is the LModE novelistic fashion of using verbs expressing human and animal sounds (such as *bellow*, *coo* and *groan*) as well as verbs such as *smirk*, *smile* and *persist* as if they were synonyms of *say* by giving them the quoted words as object. Examples of these innovative structures are those in (35) and (36). Regarding these structures, Visser (1963–1973: I, § 142: 133) explains, "[f]rom "She smiled 'I don't believe you' " and "He grunted 'I thank you' " to "She smiled disbelief" and "He grunted his gratitude" was only a step". What Visser seems to be suggesting here is that these innovative reporting speech constructions are somewhat connected with the emergence of ROCs such as *She smiled disbelief* and *He grunted his gratitude*.

(35) She **smiled** 'I don't believe you'.

(36) He **grunted** 'I thank you'.

2.4 Summary

The causes and factors outlined in § 2.3 contributed in different degrees to the large process of transitivization that has affected English since OE times. The loss of transitivizing/causativizing affixes (*be-*, *ge-*, Gmc *-j/-i*) and the inflectional syncretism generalized in ME can be considered as the two major triggering factors of this process. With the loss of affixes, many self-sufficient intransitive verbs (Visser's [Type 1]) became labile, and with the loss of cases, many intransitive verbs followed by an indirect object in the dative or a causative object in the genitive (Visser's [Type 3]) were reanalysed as transitives. These intralinguistic factors were followed in later periods by other processes that further contributed to extending the transitivization process discussed here, such as the twofold interpretation of *be* + past participle, the complementation changes of intransitive verbs usually construed with a prepositional object, and the use of certain intransitive verbs of sound emission and gesture verbs in reporting speech structures.

3. Reaction objects: Review of the literature

The label 'reaction object construction' is first found in Levin's 1993 monograph *English verb classes and alternations*, where she defines reaction objects as "nonsubcategorized objects that express a reaction (an emotion or disposition)" (Levin 1993, 98). This initial consideration of the reaction object as a "nonsubcategorized" type of object leads us to ponder on what object types can be identified in English, and on how nonsubcategorized objects differ from the prototypical direct and indirect object. The purpose of Chapter 3 is to deal with these issues. § 3.1 examines the general treatment of the object in historical and contemporary descriptive reference grammars, whereas § 3.2 zooms in on the nonprototypical features of three types of nonsubcategorized objects recognized in the literature, that is, the cognate object, the *way*-object and the so-called reaction object.

3.1 The object in descriptive reference grammars

3.1.1 Historical grammars

3.1.1.1 Otto Jespersen (1909–1949)

Otto Jespersen (1909–1949, III: 229–248) defines the object as a "primary word (or word-group) which is intimately connected with the verb of a sentence, though less intimately so than the subject" (1909–1949, III: 229). This intimate relation between the object and the verb can be observed in the transitive clause *She eats* <u>*an apple*</u> *every morning*, where the object (*an apple*) answers the basic question "Whom, or What does she eat?". According to Jespersen, the function of the object is "to make the meaning contained in the verb more special, or to limit its sphere of applicability" (1909–1949, III: 230). Although this function applies, if not to all, at least to a wide range of transitive uses, Jespersen himself recognizes that this definition is rather vague as "the notional (or logical) relations between verbs and their objects are so manifold that they defy any attempt at analysis or classification" (1909–1949, III: 230).

Jespersen draws a dividing line between prototypical and non-prototypical objects when he distinguishes between *ordinary objects*, which, as he acknowledges, comprise "the most heterogeneous objects" (1909–1949, III: 230), and *objects of result*, which express what results from the action denoted by the verb (1909–1949, III: 234). This twofold classification of the object is in fact reminiscent of the well-known distinction later established by Fillmore between *affectum* objects, which preexist and are acted upon by the verbal action, and *effectum* objects, which do not exist prior to the verbal action (1968, 4). As prototypical objects of result, Jespersen mentions those in (1)-(5), adding that a chief grammatical point is that some verbs may take both ordinary objects and objects of result "without really changing [their] own signification, though the relation between the verb and the object is entirely different" (1909–1949, III: 232–233). Clear examples of the latter situation are presented in (6)-(9), where the first of the examples is an ordinary object and the second an object of result.

(1) The people **elected** a king.

(2) John **has built** a house.

(3) The girl **paints** flowers.

(4) The dressmaker **made** the dress.

(5) The child **wrote** a letter.

(6) a. I **dig** the ground.
b. I **dig** a grave.

(7) a. She **lights** the lamp.
b. She **lights** a fire.

(8) a. He **painted** the wall.
b. He **painted** a flower on the wall.

(9) a. He **has eaten** an apple.
b. The moths **have eaten** holes in the curtain.

In addition to these prototypical objects of result, Jespersen identifies the following four as special cases of this kind of object: *way*-objects (those involved in the *way*-construction), objects occurring in structures where "a verb assumes the signification 'to express by -ing' " (i.e. reaction objects), objects involved in structures such as *work* *one's hardest*, "where *one's hardest* may be described either as an object of result or as a subjunct" (1909–1949, III: 234), and cognate objects, as *the life of an exile* in *The King lived the life of an exile*. The reason why Jespersen considers these objects in some way different from typical objects of result is that the linguistic structures in which they are involved assume a special signification and/or have some formal marking that distinguishes them from structures featuring the typical objects of result mentioned above (see examples (1)-(5)). For instance, constructions involving *way*-objects acquire the meaning 'to find (or make) one's way by (or while) -ing', and those involving reaction objects can be paraphrased as 'to express by -ing'. As for superlative objects of the type *one's hardest* in *work one's hardest*, these are frequent with verbs "which are otherwise intransitive" (1909–1949, III: 234) and involve an adjective in the superlative form. Finally, cognate objects occur with both transitive (*He has fought the good fight*; see "fight the enemy") and intransitive verbs (*The King lived the life of an exile*) and they add "a descriptive or qualifying trait, which could not conveniently be joined to the verb in the usual way as a subjunct" (1909–1949, III: 235).

Regarding ordinary objects, Jespersen explains, "neither the names given to these objects in German grammars (richtungsobject, or affiziertes object) nor the definitions usually given are comprehensive enough" (1909–1949, III: 230). The definitions Jespersen refers to include, for instance: "the person or thing to which something is done" (Onions), "the receiver of the action" (Kittredge) or "the thing directly affected by the action" (Grattan)" (1909–1949, III: 230). More explicitly, Jespersen argues,

> (...) for while they [these definitions] apply to such examples as these: They *murdered* the chief | John *bought* a house | the girl is *plucking* flowers | the child *broke* his playthings | mother *cut* the pie, etc.—they cannot be applied to a great many cases in which there is no doubt that we have objects: in "the boy *saw* the moon" we must certainly say that the boy is more affected than the moon; cp

further: they *left* London | she *showed* courage | they *parted* company | we *run* a risk, etc. (. . .). (Jespersen 1909–1949, III: 230–231; emphasis in the original)

Also within the group of ordinary objects, Jespersen includes a subtype called the *instrumental object* (1909–1949, III: 236), which in OE was generally marked in the dative case as shown in the instrumental objects exemplified in (10).

(10) teoselum **weorpeþ**[15] 'throws dice' | hit **hagalade** stanum 'it hailed [with] stones' | he ongan **wepan** hluttrum tearum 'he began to weep [with] pure tears' | blode **swætan** 'sweat [with] blood'

Due to case syncretism in ME (cf. § 2.3.2), the instrumental object ceased to be formally distinguished from the ordinary object marked in the accusative. Despite this formal overlapping, Jespersen argues that there are grounds to treat the objects in (11) and (12), as "a separate object of instrument" (1909–1949, III: 237). Note that in the first set (examples in (11)), the objects refer to body parts (head, tail, fingers, shoulders, teeth, feet, hands, eye, forehead and tongue) used as 'instruments' to perform the action denoted by the verb. As for the second set (examples in (12)), these may additionally occur in an alternative construction where the object is introduced by the preposition *with*, as shown in examples (13) and (14). As explained by Jespersen, sometimes it is not clear whether the object of a construction should be regarded as an instrumental object or as an object of result. In examples (15) and (16), for instance, the objects could be treated either as instrumental, if we attend to the way in which they are expressed in OE by means of the dative/instrumental case, or as objects of result, if we interpret the meaning of the objects *blood* and *tears* as results from the actions of *sweating*, *weeping* and *crying*.

(11) She **nods** her head | the dog **wags** his tail | he **snapped** his fingers at it | I only **shrug** my shoulders | Heywood P 901 **gnashynge** hys teeth | Di T 2.237 he **beat** his feet upon the ground | Brontë J 273 Adèle will **clap** her hands | Scott Iv 406 the Grand Master **glanced** his eye slowly round the circle | Benson D 2. 178 the doors were not high enough to enable him to

15 OE *weorpan* (PDE 'throw') can govern an object either in the accusative (what is thrown) or in the dative (instrumental) (Jespersen 1909–1949, III: 236).

pass through them without **hitting** his forehead against the jam | Beresford R 85 Mr. Leaming snorted and **clicked** his tongue.

(12) Galsw MP 54 James **wiped** his napkin all over his mouth | McKenna S 320 "Come along!" he said, **slapping** a cane against his leg

(13) He **wiped** his mouth *with the napkin.*

(14) **Slapping** his leg *with a cane.*

(15) Blode **swætan** 'sweat [with] blood' | he ongan **wepan** hluttrum tearum 'he began to weep [with] pure tears'

(16) Sh Wint V.2 98 my heart **wept** blood | Cowper L 1.187 to have **wept** crocodile tears | Brontë V111 I **cried** hot tears

(Jespersen 1909–1949, III: 236, 237 and 238)

Within this section devoted to the different types of object in English, Jespersen also refers to *objects occurring with the same verb but with totally different significations* (§ 12.5 and § 12.6), *objects after substitutive verbs* (§ 12.7), and *objects after auxiliary verbs* (§ 12.8). A couple of examples of *objects occurring with the same verb but with totally different significations* are in (17) and (18). Regarding the use of *objects after substitutive verbs,* Jespersen employs this label to refer to cases such as (19), in which "[i]t is possible to have an object even if there is no verb, if the verb is easily supplied in the same form from what immediately precedes" (1909–1949, III: 248). He adds that if the verb is necessary in the context for some reason or another, "it is often convenient instead of repeating the same verb to use either *do* or an auxiliary verb (. . .) even if it would not be possible for this substitutive verb in itself to take the same kind of object", as shown in examples (20) and (21) with *do*, and examples (22) and (23) with the auxiliary verb *will*. Finally, the last object subtype mentioned by Jespersen corresponds to those occurring after the auxiliary, 'pre-modal', verbs *can*, *may*, *must*, *will* and *shall*, which in ModE only co-occur with bare infinitives (e.g. *I can sing*), except for isolated uses where these verbs retain their old, full lexical meaning as is the case with the verb *can* in (24).

(17) The verb *walk* in **walk** the streets (usual meaning), and **walk** your horses (causative meaning).

(18) The verb *pay* in **pay** the driver and **pay** five shillings.

(19) Zangwill G 62 He shakes me like a terrier [**shakes**] a rat.

(20) Walton A 27 He never reproved these as he **did** <u>the scribes</u>.

(21) Defoe G 45 I must interrupt you, as you **did** <u>me</u>.

(22) Fielding T 3. 68 This encounter surprised the ladies much more than it **will** <u>the sagacious reader</u>.

(23) Meredith R 147 Even if my father forgives my birth, he **will** not <u>my religion</u>.

(24) Sh I **can** <u>no more</u> (e.g. Haml V. 2331).

(Jespersen 1909–1949, III: 238, 240, 248, 249 and 251)

From Jespersen's taxonomy of the object – summarized in Tab. 3.1 –, we can conclude that a unified definition of this grammatical function is difficult to arrive at. On the one hand, ordinary objects, the category which contains "the most heterogeneous objects" (Jespersen 1909–1949, III: 230), seem to be the most difficult to handle, as Jespersen treats this subtype as a repository bag, where all objects that do not result from the action denoted by the verb are included. This group is therefore quite comprehensive, especially if we take into account the fact that "a great many verbs take totally different objects with totally different significations" (Jespersen 1909–1949, III: 238). On the other hand, the category of objects of result forms a smaller class including both typical objects of result and those special cases where objects assume special significations and/or have some formal marking that distinguishes them from other ordinary object types, as is the case of reaction objects. Apart from his twofold distinction between ordinary objects and objects of result, Jespersen also clarifies that some objects may occur after substitutive verbs – although the verb itself does not take the object in question –, and even after auxiliary, or 'pre-modal', verbs, now restricted to co-occurring with bare infinitives.

Tab. 3.1: Jespersen's taxonomy of the object in ModE. Adapted from Jespersen (1909–1949: III, §§ 12.1–12.8 and §§ 14.1–14.6; pp. 229–252 and pp. 278–287)

Typical objects of result This "kind of object is obvious after verbs like *produce, create, pronounce, construct, manufacture*, etc." (§§ 12.2$_1$–12.2$_2$)	The people **elected** a king John **has built** a house The girl **paints** flowers The dressmaker **made** the dress The child **wrote** a letter (1909–1949, III: 232)
***Way*-object** "One special case of the object of result is *to grope one's way* = 'to find (or make) one's way by (or while) groping'" (§ 12.2$_3$)	Poe 106 I **scrambled** my way through the evergreens Spencer A 1.380 Carlyle never set out from premises and **reasoned** his way to conclusions Shaw 1.202 I'll —er—er—[He **stammers** his way to the porch] Lewis MA 256 This summer Pickerbaugh **had shouted** and **hand-shaken** his way through a brief Chautauqua tour Cp also: **to work** one's passage to America | Wells T 119 we had brought no money **to bribe** a passage north
Reaction object "Another special case is found when a verb assumes the signification 'to express by -ing'" (§ 12.2$_4$)	Harraden D 33 she **laughed** her thanks Austen M 78 Mr. C. **smiled** his acquiescence Shaw C 65 she **smiled** her thanks as she turned away Tylor A 296 Savages and barbarians **dance** their joy and sorrow, their love and rage, even their magic and religion Di D 193 **gesticulating** anything but welcome from the bow-window Morris N 53 I **nodded** a yes Quiller Couch M 189 Sir Cæsar **nodded** approval Austen M 223 Mr. G. **bowed** his thanks Hope R 178 they had withdrawn, **bowing** obedience Norris O 292 Magnus **beamed** satisfaction

Continued on next page

Tab. 3.1: *Continued*

	Housman J 331 the king **breathed** his astonishment Mackenzie S 1. 71 Michael **could only stare** his agreement Jenkins B 53 he **had protested** his innocence **Similar expressions with the verb *look*:** Shaw D 23 he **looked** all wonder Austen M 263 she **looked** the astonishment she felt Tenn 100 **looking** ancient kindness Wells T 22 the gaunt face **looked** interrogation Trollope D 3.170 **looked** daggers at everyone Shaw P 47 She **looks** unutterable reproach at him [also Kipl L143] (1909–1949, III: 234 and 245)
Superlative object *"one's hardest* may be described either as an object of result or as a subjunct" (§ 12.2_5)	**work** one's hardest Carlyle SR 204 while the Beaconfire **blazed** its brightest Trollope D 2.77 **smiling** her prettiest Shaw C 187 they both **looked** their best NP troops can never be expected **to fight** their best on empty stomachs
Cognate object "the King lived *the life of an exile*" (§ 12.3)	Transitive verbs: "he **has fought** the good fight" (cf. "fight the enemy") Intransitive verbs: "I **dreamed** a dream" Malory 104 the herte **lepte** a grete lepe ib 694 she **shalle dye** the moost vylaynous dethe Sh Oth V. 2. 122 a guiltlesse death I **dye**

<table>
<tr><td></td><td>Tp I. 1.72 I would faine **dye** a dry death

Cowper L 1.345 whether we **die** to-day or to-morow, a watery death or a dry one, is of no consequence

ib 2.105 he **lived** the life, and **died** the death of a Christian

Ru Sel 1.243 I never saw a man **die** a violent death

Brontë J 189 she **sighed** a sigh of ineffable satisfaction

Di T 1.50 she said nothing, but **coughed** just one grain of cough

Bennett L 7 Miss Grig **had smiled** her wise, condescending smile

Bennett B 31 he **whistled** a low meditative whistle of satisfaction

Kipl J 1.109 Mowgli **laughed** a little short ugly laugh

Golding SD 96 . . . **died** several deaths of fright. . .

(1909–1949, III: 234–236)</td></tr>
<tr><td>**Ordinary objects**
“the most heterogeneous objects” (§ 12.4)</td><td>“All objects other than those of result we shall here term them *ordinary objects*”

They **murdered** the chief | John **bought** a house | the girl **is plucking** flowers | the child **broke** his playthings | mother **cut** the pie

Cp further: they **left** London | she **showed** courage | they **parted** company | we **run** a risk, etc.

(1909–1949, III: 230)</td></tr>
<tr><td>**Instrumental object**
“A subdivision of the ordinary object” (§ 12.4)</td><td>**Parts of the body:**
she **nods** her head | the dog **wags** his tail | he **snapped** his fingers at it | I only **shrug** my shoulders | Heywood P 901 **gnashynge** hys teeth | Di T 2.237 he **beat** his feet upon the ground | Brontë J 273 Adèle **will clap** her hands | Scott IV 406 the Grand Master **glanced** his eye slowly round the circle | Benson D 2. 178 the doors were not high enough to enable him to pass through them without **hitting** his forehead against the jam | Beresford R 85 Mr. Leaming snorted and **clicked** his tongue</td></tr>
</table>

Continued on next page

Tab. 3.1: *Continued*

	Other examples of instrumental objects: Galsw MP 54 James **wiped** his napkin all over his mouth McKenna S 320 "Come along!" he said, **slapping** a cane against his leg (1909–1949, III: 237)
Object occurring with the same verb but with totally different significations (§§ 12.5–12.6)	"A still better illustration of the essentially vague and indistinct character of the grammatical category 'object' is found, when we see that a great many verbs take totally different objects with totally different significations" **Walk** the streets, a hospital | **Walk** your horses **Pay** the driver | **pay** five shillings | **pay** the bill (1909–1949, III: 238 and 240)
Object after substitutive verbs (§ 12.7)	Zangwill G 62 he shakes me like a terrier [**shakes**] a rat Walton A 27 he never reproved these as he **did** the scribes Defoe G 45 I must interrupt you, as you **did** me Fielding T 3. 68 this encounter surprised the ladies much more than it **will** the sagacious reader Mered R 147 even if my father forgives my birth, he **will not** my religion (1909–1949, III: 248–249)
Object after auxiliary, or 'pre-modal', verbs (§ 12.8)	Sh I **can** no more (e.g. Haml V. 2331) (1909–1949, III: 251)
Indirect object[a] (§§ 14.1–14.9)	he **gave** the boy a shilling (1909–1949, III: 278) **Double object (indirect object + reaction object)** Bennett W 1.119 **kissing** her mother good night (also ib. 1.290, Brontë W 187, Hewlett Q 268, Wells T 103, Williamson S 134, Herrick M 123)

Hankin 2.167 I think I **must kiss** you good- bye (also Wells T 40, Norris P 219, Herrick M 197, 314)

Hardy L 7 he stooped to **kiss** her a farewell

Mackenzie C 196 (he should) **have kissed** her a welcome to the sweet twenties

id SA 174 he **had patted** Mac [a dog] good- bye

Black Ph 98 ready to **smile** us an adieu (1909–1949, III: 298)

Note that Jespersen does not use the labels '*way*-object' or 'reaction object', but simply speaks of 'Object of result' (§ 12.2), 'Cognate Object' (§ 12.3), 'Ordinary Objects' (§ 12.4) and special cases of objects of result (§ 12.2_3; § 12.2_4; § 12.2_5).

a As for the indirect object, Jespersen notes "[w]e shall speak of an "indirect" object only when there are two objects in the same sentence" (1909–1949: III, § 12.1: 231). Interestingly, in the chapter devoted to the direct and the indirect object, Jespersen (1909–1949, III: 278–299) includes an instance of cognate object preceded by the indirect object *her*: Locke HB 272 he kissed her a hearty, unintelligible kiss —the first for twenty years—, and several instances of reaction objects (1909–1949, III: 298).

3.1.1.2 F. Th. Visser (1963–1973)

Visser defines the object as the complement of a non-copula verb, and distinguishes four overarching object types: indirect objects, causative objects, prepositional objects and direct objects (1963–1973: I, § 315: 280). Additionally, he explains (§ 418: 410) that the traditional term 'direct object' is difficult to define, and like Jespersen, he claims that none of the existing definitions are completely satisfactory. In this regard, he provides the three definitions of ordinary objects already adduced by Jespersen (1909–1949, III: 230): "the person or thing to which something is done" (Onions), "the receiver of the action" (Kittredge) or "the thing directly affected by the action" (Grattan)"; to these, he adds two more definitions, one from Curme ("the goal, the object, actually hit or affected by the activity, or the thing representing the goal, the real object of the activity"), and the other from Stokoe ("the sufferer(s) of the action") (Visser 1963–1973: I, § 418: 410). Perhaps the most noticeable characteristic of Visser's taxonomy of the object is his classification of the 'direct object' into many several types, of which the most relevant for our purposes are: direct objects occurring with impersonal verbs in Old and Middle English, objects of result, cognate objects – which can occur with both transitive and intransitive verbs –, instrumental objects, reflexive objects and reciprocal direct objects (1963–1973: I, §§ 418–491: 410–449; see Tab. 3.2). Here we could draw a parallelism with Jespersen's set of ordinary objects, which contains "the most heterogeneous objects". Surprisingly, and contrasting with Jespersen's taxonomy, Visser does not include reaction objects within the category of objects of result. Instead, he adduces clear instances of reaction objects (e.g. *to smile* <u>*one's thanks*</u>, <u>*a welcome*</u>, <u>*disbelief*</u> and *snorting out* <u>*pardons*</u>) within the large list of transitive uses of verbs usually marked 'intransitive' in ModE grammars (1963–1973: I, § 133: 100–127) and which I referred to in § 2.2 when discussing the rise of amphibious verbs in PDE.

Tab. 3.2: Visser's taxonomy of the object. Adapted from Visser (1963–1973: I, §§ 315–673: 280–601)

Indirect object	he **gave** me a book			
Causative object	Ic **gefeah** þæs weorces 'I rejoiced in the work'			(1963–1973, I: 280 and 355)
Prepositional object[a]	*to long for, to laugh at, to see to*			(1963–1973, I: 280)
Direct object "objects that are neither indirect, causative or prepositional objects" (1963–1973, I: 280)	**Impersonal verbs with direct object** (§ 420)	OE hine **hungrede** > ME him **hungered** > PDE he **hungered**[b]		(1963–1973, I: 412)
	Objects of result (§ 421)	*to bore (feel, fight, force, grope, squeeze, push) one's way*: common in ModE the objects of *scieppan* ('to shape, form'), *streonan* ('to gain, acquire'), *erect* and *fabricate* are always objects of result		(1963–1973, I: 412)
	Cognate objects (§§ 422–424)	transitive	**tell** a tale, **do** a deed, **sing** a song	(1963–1973, I: 413)
		intransitive	**die** [a] death, **live** a life, **laugh** a laugh, **fly** a flight, **breathe** a breath, **game** a game, **sigh** a sigh	(1963–1973, I: 413 and 415)
	Instrumental objects (§ 425)	he **beat** his fist on the table (= he beat *with* his fist on the table) he **nodded** his head (= he nodded *with* his head)		

Continued on next page

Tab. 3.2: *Continued*

		ME her hondes **clappe** & with hondes **clap** EModE **clapping** <u>their hands</u> (1963–1973, I: 418–419)
	Reflexive objects[c] (§§ 426–478)	he **gyrede** <u>hine</u> (selfne) ‘he girded himself (with a weapon)’ (1963–1973, I: 439)
	Reciprocal objects (§§ 479–491)	hi **gemetten** <u>hi</u> ‘they met’ we **cyston** <u>us</u> ‘we kissed’ (1963–1973, I: 420)
	Other direct objects taking special forms and combining with other complements (§§ 492–661)	*It* as direct object (e.g. *to hop it, to lord it, to rough it*);[d] heralding objects (e.g. *she told <u>it</u> that she was guilty, I like <u>it</u> better if...*); *so*, as *quasi object*; relative pronouns used as objects; *shall, can, may, will, owe* + direct object; the object used twice, etc.

a Visser’s prepositional objects correspond to Jespersen’s verbs with preposition (1909–1949: III, § 13: 252–277), which I excluded from Jespersen’s taxonomy of the object offered in Tab. 3.1.

b As explained by Visser, “[w]ith those verbs that survived into Middle English *hine* was first replaced by *him* (as everywhere else) and then personal constructions were gradually substituted for the resulting ‘impersonal’ formula” (Visser, 1963–1973: I, § 420: 412).

c Jespersen does not mention reflexive objects and reciprocal objects. In his grammar, he only refers to the omission of reflexive and reciprocal pronouns (§§ 16.2–16.3) when dealing with the issue of transitivity (1909–1949: III, § 16: 319–355).

d This object type has been variously referred to in the literature as ‘pseudo-object’, ‘dummy *it*’, ‘empty *it*’, ‘non-referential *it*’ (Mondorf 2016, 73fn1), and ‘expletive *It* object’ (Postal and Pullum 1988; Levin 1993, 109).

Tab. 3.3: Elements of clause structure. Adapted from Quirk et al. (1985, 49 and 723–732)

Verb	
Subject	
Object	Direct object
	Indirect object
Complement	Subject complement
	Object complement
Adverbial	Optional adverbials
	Obligatory adverbials

3.1.2 Contemporary grammars

3.1.2.1 Quirk et al. (1985)

Moving now onto more recent accounts of the object, Quirk et al. (1985, 49, 720 and 723–732) consider the object as one of the five elements of clause structure, the others being the subject, the verb, the complements and the adverbial.

As shown in Tab. 3.3, Quirk et al. (1985, 726–728) distinguish two main object types: the *direct* and the *indirect* object. These object types are realised by NPs or nominal clauses, they "normally follow the subject and the verb", and "[i]f both objects are present, the indirect object normally comes before the direct object" (1985, 726) as exemplified in *I gave <u>him</u> my address.* Additionally, Quirk et al. mention the following features of the object:

(i) "The object function requires the **objective form for pronouns** that have distinctive case forms" (1985, 726; emphasis mine), as in *They amused <u>me</u>* and *I gave <u>them</u> some chocolate.*

(ii) When the object is coreferential with the subject, a **reflexive pronoun** which agrees with the subject in person is usually required. An example is *I have given <u>myself</u> a treat.*

(iii) The object is generally the subject of its **passive** counterpart: *We have finished the work/The work has been finished* (1985, 727). An exception is *They have a nice house/*A nice house is had* (by them) (1985, 1177).

(iv) The **indirect object** normally corresponds to a **prepositional phrase** placed after the direct object: *I'll send <u>Charles</u> another copy/I'll send another copy <u>to Charles</u>* (1985, 727).

(v) "The **indirect object can generally be omitted** without affecting the semantic relations between the other elements" (1985, 727; emphasis mine): *David saved me a seat/David saved a seat/*David saved me.*

As for the semantic properties of the object, the direct object "typically refers to an entity that is affected by the action denoted in the clause" (1985, 727), as shown in *Norman smashed a window in his father's car.* The indirect object, by contrast, "typically refers to an animate being that is the recipient of the action", as in *I've found you a place* and *We paid them the money.*

In addition to the direct and indirect object distinction, Quirk et al. (1985, 749–755) recognize the existence of a number of objects that semantically differ from the prototypical objects previously described. These are the locative object, the resultant object, the cognate object, the eventive object, the instrumental object, and the affected indirect object. An instance of *locative object* is in (25), where the postverbal NP has a locative role. Examples of *resultant objects* are in (26)-(28), where the referent of the object exists "only by virtue of the activity indicated by the verb" (1985, 749). Example (29) shows a *cognate object*, described as an object similar to a resultant object, where "the noun head is semantically and often morphologically related to the verb" (1985, 750). The *eventive object* is illustrated in (30). This object type "takes the form of a deverbal noun preceded by a common verb of general meaning, such as *do, give, have, make, take*" (1985, 750). The deverbal nature of the eventive object explains why constructions involving this object type can be paraphrased as in (31), where the verb no longer has a general meaning but expresses the same information conveyed by the eventive object in (30). The *instrumental object*, already identified by Jespersen (§ 12.4) and Visser (§ 425), is illustrated in (32), and finally, the *affected indirect object*, represented here in (33), differs from the prototypical indirect object in that it occurs with eventive objects, usually in combination with the verb *give.*

(25) The horse **jumped** the fence.

(26) John has **painted** a new picture.

(27) She **made** a fire.

(28) I'm **writing** a letter.

(29) She **lived** a good life.

(30) They **are having** an argument. [V + eventive object]

(31) They **are arguing**. [Verb only]

(32) He **nodded** his head.

(33) She **gave** me a push. ['She pushed me.']

(Quirk et al. 1985, 749–753)

3.1.2.2 Huddleston and Pullum et al. (2002)

More recently, Huddleston and Pullum et al. (2002, 215) consider the predicator, the complements of the predicator and the adjuncts as the three major constituents in clause structure. They adopt in this way a very broad sense of the term 'complement' if we compare it to Quirk et al. (1985, 49). This is shown in Tab. 3.4.

Tab. 3.4: Comparative table of clause structure. Adapted from Quirk et al. (1985) and Huddleston and Pullum et al. (2002)

Quirk et al. (1985, 49)	Huddleston and Pullum et al. (2002, 215)
Verb	Predicator
Subject	Complements of the predicator
Object	
Complement	
Adverbial	Adjuncts

As explained by Huddleston and Pullum et al. (2002), the most important property of complements is that they "require the presence of an appropriate verb that **licenses** them" (2002, 219; emphasis in the original). This dependence between the complements and their head verbs has been referred to, since the early days of formal grammar, as "subcategorization" (2002, 219), and thus verbs are subcategorized or classified as intransitive, monotransitive, ditransitive, complex transitive, complex intransitive, and so on (2002, 220), depending on the number and the nature of the complements they take. It is worth noting here that although the verb classes just mentioned, "define a large number of different verb subcategories" (2002, 220) "only a few very general ones have established names" (2002, 220). For instance, there is no label yet for verbs like *inquire* and *wonder* that take interrogative clauses as complements (e.g. *He inquired/*believed/*wanted whether it* *was ready*). Moreover, although verbs are often described as belonging to one subcategory or another, "most verbs allow more than one pattern of complementation" (2002, 220 and 296).

The object, as a type of complement, requires the presence of an appropriate verb that licenses it (2002, 219). In contrast to the subject, which is an obligatory element in all English canonical clauses, the object is "permitted – or **licensed** – by some verbs but not by others" (2002, 53; emphasis in the original). Thus, transitive verbs like *eat* and *read* always license an object (be it either overt or covert), while intransitive verbs like *smile* never occur with an object. Similar to Quirk et al. (1985), Huddleston and Pullum et al. (2002) also distinguish two main object types. These are the direct object, which occurs in both monotransitive (*Pat saw Kim*) and ditransitive clauses (*Pat gave Kim the key*) and expresses the patient role; and the indirect object (*I gave Kim the key*), which occurs in canonical clauses only in ditransitives and is characteristically associated with the semantic role of recipient (Huddleston and Pullum et. al. 2002, 244–245).[16]

Huddleston and Pullum et al. (2002) devote § 4.1 of their Chapter 4 to the features of the object in canonical monotransitive clauses where they explain that the prototypical object has the form of an NP and is non-omissible in some clauses (*He accosted her*, *We kept the old battery*, *He delineated the problem* and *I used a knife*). Additionally, the prototypical object corresponds to the subject of a related passive (*Pat overlooked the error*/*The error was overlooked by Pat*), and its position is immediately after the predicator (*He brought the clothes in*/*I returned the books to Jo*/*She rejected the others*). Nonprototypical objects, on the other hand, are discussed by Huddleston and Pullum et al. (2002, 296–321) when dealing with verbs allowing multiple patterns of complementation (i.e. verbs that "occur in two or more constructions differing in respect of the complements"). More specifically, Huddleston and Pullum et al. distinguish three main "patterns of contrasting complementation". These are verbs showing transitive vs. intransitive contrasts, as exemplified

16 The terms 'direct' and 'indirect' are based on the degree of involvement of the object in the process designated by the verb, thus, in ditransitive constructions the indirect object is omissible whereas the direct object is obligatory: *He lent (them) his car* (Huddleston and Pullum et al. 2002, 245).

further below (also known as amphibious verbs or 'dual-transitivity verbs' among other labels; cf. §§ 2.1–2.2), ditransitive vs. monotransitive contrasts (e.g. *I gave her the key* vs. *I gave the key to her*), and verbs showing "further core and non-core contrasts" (e.g. *He supplies arms to the rebels* vs. *He supplies the rebels with arms*).[17] Importantly, cognate objects and reaction objects (the latter referred to as 'objects of conveyed reaction') are discussed under the first group, i.e. verbs that show transitive and intransitive contrasts. As already pointed out in Chapter 2 (§§ 2.1–2.2), PDE has a great number of amphibious verbs, such that these greatly outnumber those that are simply restricted to transitive or intransitive constructions (Visser, 1963–1973: I, § 132: 99–100; Huddleston and Pullum et al. 2002, 298). Given the wide range of verbs that belong to this category, Huddleston and Pullum et al. (2002, 296, 298–308) classify amphibious verbs into four types depending on the kind of contrast they show (examples (34)-(37)).

Type I

(34) a. They **shot** him. — Transitive
b. They **shot** at him. — Intransitive

Type II

(35) a. The sun **radiates** heat. — Transitive
b. Heat **radiates** from the sun — Intransitive

Type III

(36) a. She **drank** some water. — Transitive
b. She **drank**. — Intransitive

Type IV

(37) a. He **broke** the vase. — Transitive
b. The vase **broke**. — Intransitive

17 In Huddleston and Pullum et al.'s framework, core complements have the forms of NPs and non-core complements that of PPs (2002, 216).

In Types I and II, the contrast is between an object (*him*, *heat*) in the transitive construction and a prepositional object (*at him*/*from the sun*) in the intransitive construction while in Types III and IV the contrast is between the presence of an object (*some water*, *the vase*) and its absence. On another dimension, Types I and III show the same subject (*They*, *she*) in both constructions, whereas in Types II and IV, the subject of the intransitive construction (*heat*, *the vase*) corresponds to the object of the transitive construction. According to Huddleston and Pullum et al. (2002), within amphibious verbs of Type III we can distinguish between those contrasts where "the transitive construction is semantically more basic in that the intransitive is interpreted as having an unexpressed object", and those where the intransitive construction "can be regarded as more basic" (2002, 300). As illustrated in examples (38)-(49) in Group 1 and Group 2, the first group of amphibious verbs is comparatively more numerous than the second group.

GROUP 1: Transitive/intransitive contrasts where the *transitive construction* is more *basic*

(38) **Apply** liberally. ("this lotion") [omission of object in instructions]

(39) They **won**. ("the match") [unexpressed definite object]

(40) I must **shave**. ("myself") [unexpressed reflexive object]

(41) We had **met** before. ("one another") [unexpressed reciprocal object]

(42) They **clapped**. ("their hands") [unexpressed body-part object]

(43) That dog **bites**. ("people") [unexpressed human object]

(44) She doesn't **drink**. ("alcohol") [specific category indefinites]

(45) He **read** for a while. ("some reading matter") [normal category indefinites]

GROUP 2: Transitive/intransitive contrasts where the *intransitive construction* is more *basic*

(46) They were **talking** nonsense. [extension of intransitive]

(47) They **pushed** their way to the font. [extension by *way*-object]

(48) He **died** a long and agonising death. [extension by cognate object]

(49) She **smiled** her assent. [extension by object of conveyed reaction = reaction object]

The second group of transitive/intransitive contrasts involves basically intransitive verbs that occur with a narrow selection of object types among which are *way*-objects, cognate objects and reaction objects. Cognate objects are defined as objects "where the head noun is a nominalisation of the verb, as *death* is of *die*" and where "[m]odification of the noun is just about obligatory" (2002, 305). As for reaction objects, they offer the examples in (50) and explain that verbs co-occurring with reaction objects are of two types: nonverbal communication verbs such as *grin*, *laugh*, *nod*, *sigh*, *smile* and *wave*, and manner of speaking verbs such as *mumble*, *roar*, *scream* and *whisper*. According to Huddleston and Pullum et al. (2002), reaction objects that accompany nonverbal communication verbs hardly express an argument of the verb and therefore cannot be made into passive subjects (see (51)), whereas manner of speaking verbs allow a "wider range of objects" (2002, 305) which may in principle undergo passivization (see (52)). As we shall see in § 3.2, there seems to be no complete agreement regarding this property of reaction objects, although Kogusuri (2009b, 2011) convincingly argues that passivization is clearly dependent on factors such as the so-called coreferential constraint and the suspension of this constraint by the elision of the agent in the *by*-phrase, a phenomenon he refers to as "agent-backgrounding" (cf. § 3.2.1.3).

(50) a. He **grinned** <u>his appreciation</u>.
b. I **nodded** <u>my agreement</u>.
c. He **roared** <u>his thanks</u>.

(51) a. She **smiled** <u>her assent</u>. ("She signalled her assent by smiling")
b. *Her assent was smiled.

(52) a. He **roared** <u>the command</u>.
b. On the parade ground commands must be roared, not whispered.

3.1.3 Interim summary

The object is generally conceived in descriptive reference grammars (both historical and contemporary) as a postverbal NP that plays the semantic role of patient or recipient depending on whether there is one or two objects within the clause. However, not all English objects accommodate to this definition, as there is a number of object types that although resembling ordinary objects, exhibit a series of morpho-syntactic and semantic features that clearly set them apart from the prototypical direct and indirect object. As we shall see in § 3.2, these object types have been referred to in the more specialized literature as nonsubcategorized objects (Levin 1993), and clear examples of them are cognate objects, *way*-objects and reaction objects. Importantly, only Jespersen (1909–1949, III: 234) and Huddleston and Pullum et al. (2002, 305) allude specifically to reaction objects, the latter under the label 'objects of conveyed reaction', when they deal with amphibious verbs or verbs showing transitive and intransitive contrasts. By way of conclusion, two features of reaction objects among those mentioned in the previous pages stand out. First, the reaction object is a nonsubcategorized type of object, more specifically a special type of object of result (Jespersen 1909–1949, III: 234) through which basically intransitive verbs, particularly manner of speaking verbs but also nonverbal communication verbs, assume the meaning 'to express by -ing' (Jespersen 1909–1949, III: 234; Huddleston and Pullum et al. 2002, 305). Secondly, the few examples of reaction object constructions mentioned in historical grammars (see Visser, 1963–1973: I, § 133: 100–127), together with the scarce attention given to this linguistic phenomenon, suggest that the reaction object construction is a recent development in the English language, a hypothesis that will be tested in Chapters 5, 6 and 7. These preliminary ideas on reaction objects set up the ground for the following section where I will analyse in detail the nonprototypical features of reaction objects, this time from the perspective of specialized literature, and in relation to other nonsubcategorized objects.

3.2 Reaction object constructions and other related object types

Contrary to other nonprototypical object types such as the cognate object or the *way*-object, the reaction object remained largely unnoticed by linguists until very recently. The label 'reaction object construction' itself stems from Levin's seminal monograph *English verb classes and alternations* (1993, 97), but passing references to this linguistic structure can already be found in Ross (1970a, 239, 266–268fn34) and Levin and Rapoport (1988, 277 and 288).

Ross (1970a) does not use a specific term to refer to the construction, but he clearly has it in mind when he briefly discusses sequences involving verbs of nonverbal communication such as *Tom frowned his displeasure*, which, he adds, "have never been studied by generative grammarians, to the best of [his] knowledge" (267fn34). As a generative linguist, Ross alludes to ROCs as "sentences" or 'krispy clauses' (Perlmutter 1979, 294) with "some strange restrictions on whatever rule it is that produces [them]" (266fn34). In contrast to Ross, Levin and Rapoport (1988) do propose a label for ROCs, namely 'gesture-expression construction' (277), mainly because they treat "verbs of gestures and signs made with the body" as the typical verbs in the construction. Yet despite using this label suggestive of just one particular set of verbs, Levin and Rapoport (1988) also recognize that manner of speaking verbs (Zwicky 1971, Mufwene 1978) can also be found in the construction. In their own words, "[a] similar meaning extension appears to be found with 'manner of speaking' verbs (. . .). Thus She mumbled her adoration means "She expressed her adoration by means of mumbling" (Levin and Rapoport 1988, 288fn2). Interestingly, the label 'gesture-expression construction' was later adopted by Kogusuri (2011, 2012), who attends only to ROCs involving verbs of gestures in order to put forward his arguments on the complex syntactic status of reaction objects (see, in particular, Kogusuri 2009b, 35fn2). More recently, the label 'Expressive Object Construction (EOC)' has been proposed by Martínez-Vázquez (2014a, 172), mainly because these objects apart from describing reactions which are responses to a previous event, may in some contexts denote "an emotional attitude with a possible longer extension over time" (2014a, 172). For instance, the ROC *She mumbled* her adoration (Levin 1993, 98) may imply that "She mumbled that she adores her (and has always adored her)". Though this more overarching label seems to be the most appropriate one to refer to ROCs, here I will retain Levin's as it is the one most generally used in the literature and also because her definition has set the basis for subsequent studies on the ROC.[18] Levin's complete definition (1993, 98) reads as follows,

> Certain intransitive verbs—particularly verbs of manner of speaking and verbs of gestures and signs—take nonsubcategorized objects that express a reaction (an emotion or disposition); possible objects include: *approval*, *disapproval*, *assent*, *admiration*, *disgust*, *yes*, *no*. When these verbs take such objects they take on an extended sense which might be paraphrased "express (a reaction) by V-ing," where "V" is the basic sense of the verb. For instance, *She mumbled her adoration* can be paraphrased as "She expressed/signalled her adoration by mumbling." Most of the verbs that allow such reaction objects name activities that are associated with particular emotions, and the action they name is performed to express the associated emotion. The exceptions are the verbs of emission, which also show this phenomenon to a limited extent. Reaction object constructions do not have passive counterparts.

Taking Levin's definition of the ROC as a starting point, a number of studies dealing with this linguistic phenomenon have seen the light in the last two decades. Some of these studies examine the morphosyntactic and semantic features of reaction object constructions in themselves (Toda 2006, Kogusuri 2009b, 2011, 2012, Haïk 2011), or in relation to other nonprototypical objects (Massam 1990, Martínez-Vázquez 1998, Felser and Wanner 2001, Mateu 2001, 2014, Aue-Apaikul 2006, Mirto 2007, 2012, 2017). Other linguists explore the frequency, productivity and context of occurrence of the ROC in PDE (Martínez-Vázquez 2010, 2014a, 2015, Bouso 2012), and yet others investigate their existence in essentially verb-framed languages such as French (Levin and Rapoport 1988, 280; Dyka, Novakova, and Siepmann 2017), Bangla (Khan 1994, 49), Spanish (Martínez-Vázquez 1998, 2005, 2014b, 2016, 2017, Real Puigdollers 2009, Guerra-García and Sacramento-Lechado 2011, Mateu 2012), Basque (Aldezabal et al.

---

18 Martin Haspelmath (p.c. Leiden 2013) proposes the label 'attitudinal object' and Laura Michaelis the label 'response/quotative object' (p.c. Bangor 2013). Mirto (2017, 546) makes a similar point regarding the unappropriateness of the label 'reaction object' when he notes that some ROCs involve postverbal nouns that describe greetings (e.g. *He smiled a cautious greeting*), and "the referents of the subjects might well act first" and not by way of reaction.

2002, 76–77) and Greek (Horrocks and Stavrou 2010, 300fn18). Interestingly, as recently demonstrated by Martínez-Vázquez (2014b, 2016, 2017), and Dyka, Novakova, and Siepmann (2017), Spanish and French show a quite productive use of the construction despite being Romance languages. Finally, other studies that discuss in passing reaction object constructions are those by Omuro (1995, 1996, 1997, 2000).

The following sections focus on the nonprototypical features of reaction objects in comparison with cognate objects (§ 3.2.1.1) and *way*-objects (§ 3.2.1.2), whereas aspects of the frequency, productivity and context of occurrence of the ROC from a historical perspective will be explored in Chapters 5, 6 and 7.

3.2.1 Nonprototypical objects

3.2.1.1 Cognate objects

Not all scholars agree on the status of cognate objects. While some linguists have claimed that the cognate object is like an adverbial (Jones 1988, 93; see also Zubizarreta 1987, Moltmann 1989), others like Massam (1990) argue that the cognate object is "best characterized as a syntactic direct object which receives a patient theta role from the verb" (Massam 1990, 161; see also Hale and Keyser 1993, Macfarland 1995), among other reasons because they do not behave like normal adverbials, or even like nominal adverbials. Unlike normal adverbials (example (53)), cognate objects must occur adjacent to the verb (examples (54) and (55)), and, unlike nominal adverbials (example (56)), they cannot co-occur with a direct object (examples (57) and (58)). Moreover, following the discussion in Jones (1988), Massam (1990) establishes a distinction between (i) transitivizing objects, as in *Bernadette danced the Irish jig*, and (ii) true cognate objects, as in *Henleigh smiled a wicked smile*. Transitivizing objects display the characteristics of regular/ordinary objects; true cognate objects, by contrast, cannot be passivized (example (6) in Tab. 3.5), topicalized (example (8) also in that table), pronominalized (examples (11) and (12)) or questioned (example (14)). In addition, they show some restrictions on their form since they cannot be preceded by a definite article (examples (16) and (17)),[19] they usually require modification (examples (21), (22) and (23)), and they are morphologically cognate to the verb (examples (24) and (25)).

(53) Mordred **killed** the knight *gruesomely*. [normal adverbial]

(54) Let Ben **run** (*quickly) a little run. [≠ normal adverbials]

(55) Ben **sneezed** (*that way) a glorious sneeze. [≠ normal adverbials]

(56) Alice will read the book *tomorrow*. [nominal adverbial]

(57) *Mordred **killed** *the knight* a gruesome kill. [≠ nominal adverbials]

(58) *Ethel **moved** *her lips* a slight move(ment). [≠ nominal adverbials]

More recently, Horrocks and Stavrou (2010) leave aside the argument/adjunct (object/adverbial) controversy and classify cognate object constructions in English into three types depending on the nature of the verb (transitive or intransitive/unergative), and the morphosyntactic features of the construction. Thus, they distinguish cognate object constructions involving transitive verbs (59), transitivizing cognate object constructions (60), and activity, event-noun cognate object constructions (examples in (61)). The latter are also referred to by Horrocks and Stavrou as aspectual cognate object constructions, to distinguish them from light verb constructions such as *She gave us a grin and left*, which also involve eventive objects (cf. § 3.1.2.1) and denote telic aspect. Note that Horrocks and Stavrou's last two types, namely transitivizing cognate object constructions and aspectual cognate object constructions, correspond to Massam's transitivizing object constructions and true cognate object constructions, respectively (see Horrocks and Stavrou 2010, 287, 293–295).

(59) **Cognate object constructions with transitive verbs**
a. They **drank** their drinks.
b. They want to **write** a writing that will antagonize...

19 Contrary to Jones (1988), Massam (1990, 164fn4) argues that true cognate objects preceded by definite articles are sometimes possible. A clear example she provides is *She smiled the biggest dumbest grin you ever saw* (Massam 1990, 169). Note, however, that in this example the object is not morphologically cognate with the verb, and that it is in a superlative form and modified by a relative clause. This example is reminiscent of the superlative object (cf. Tab. 3.1).

(60) **Transitivizing cognate object constructions**
   a. She **dreamed** the most wonderful dream.
   b. They **danced** all sort of dances at that party.

(61) **Activity, event-noun cognate object constructions** (i.e. aspectual cognate object constructions)
   a. She **smiled** an enigmatic smile.
   b. She **slept** a dreamless sleep.
   c. John **coughed** a sinister cough.

Importantly, Horrocks and Stavrou's three-fold classification of cognate object constructions forms the basis for Lavidas' investigation on the historical development of cognate object constructions in English (2013, 2014, 2018), where he tests Visser's hypothesis (1963–1973: I, § 424 (b): 415) that cognate object constructions involving intransitives developed later in time, probably on analogy with cognate object constructions with transitive verbs, and as a result of the loss of case marking (for discussion cf. § 5.2.3.1).

3.2.1.2 *Way*-objects

Like cognate objects, *way*-objects (*Bill belched his way out of the restaurant*) have been the focus of a number of linguistic studies. Some describe their morphosyntactic features in PDE (Salkoff 1988, Levin and Rapoport 1988, Jackendoff 1990, Massam 1990, Goldberg 1995, to mention a few), while others are concerned with their historical development (Israel 1996, Mondorf 2011, Gisborne and Patten 2011, Traugott and Trousdale 2013, Barðdal and Gildea 2015, Perek 2015b, 2016a, 2018, 2020, McColm 2015, 2019, Fanego 2019), and their use in World Englishes (Brunner and Hoffmann 2020). One of the most influential works on the *way*-construction from a synchronic point of view is Jackendoff (1990), who claims that the *way*-object is not an argument of the preceding verb but rather only "a phrase that happens to be in object position" (1990, 216) (examples (1)-(4) in Tab. 3.6). Jackendoff notes that the non-argument status of the *way*-object is reflected in the fact that the *way*-construction is incompatible with the passive (examples (5) and (6)) and that "the material after the verb [i.e. the *way*-object] does not prepose" (1990, 212) (see example (7)). In addition to these syntactic oddities, as was the case with true cognate objects, *way*-objects cannot

Tab. 3.5: Morphosyntactic features of transitivizing and true cognate objects. Adapted from Massam (1990, 163–166). See also Felser and Wanner (2001), and Horrocks and Stavrou (2010)

FEATURES	Transitivizing objects	True cognate objects
Adjacency condition (insertion test, Verb Object Bonding principle)	YES (1) *Bernadette **danced** *wearily* the Irish jig[a] (my own example)	YES (2) *He **sighed** *wearily* a (heavy) sigh (Felser and Wanner 2001, 109)
Can co-occur with a direct object	NO (3) *Mordred **killed** *the knight* a gruesome kill	NO (4) *Ethel **moved** *her lips* a slight movement
Passive	YES (5) The Irish jig *was* **danced** *by Bernadette*	NO (6) *A silly smile *was* **smiled** *(by Ethel)*
Topicalization (preposing, extraposition, object fronting or extraction test, etc.)	YES (7) The Irish jig, nobody **danced**	NO (8) *A silly smile, nobody **smiled**
Free pronominalization	YES (9) I **sang** the aria then Tosca sang *it* (10) I **sang** an aria then Tosca sang *one*	NO (11) *Maggie **smiled** a silly smile, then her brother smiled *it* (12) ?Maggie **died** a slow death, and her brother died *one* too
Can be questioned	YES (13) *What* did Tosca **sing**?	NO (14) **What* did he **die**?
Definite object possible	YES (15) Fred **danced** *the* slow number	NO (16) ?He **lived** *the* quiet life (17) ?She **smiled** *the* happy smile
Restrictions on form of NP (modification)	NO (18) She **sang** a song/ the *beautiful* song/ the song *you like* (19) Piers **sang** a ballad *from Ireland* (20) She **drank** a *carbonated* drink	YES (21) ?He **died** a death (22) He **died** a *gruesome* death/ a death *a warrior could be proud of* (23) He **smiled** a smile of *peace*/ He **sang** a song of *sixpence*
Object necessarily cognate	NO Cf. examples (5), (7), (9), (10), (15) and (19)	YES (24) *He **died** a *suicide*/ a *murder* (25) *?He **smiled** a silly grin

a Unless stated otherwise the examples provided in Tab. 3.5 are from Massam (1990, 163–166).

Tab. 3.6: Morphosyntactic features of *way*-objects

FEATURES	*Way*-objects
Adjacency condition (insertion test, Verb Object Bonding principle)	YES (1) *Bill **belched** *noisily* his way out of the restaurant[a] (Jackendoff 1990, 212)
Cannot co-occur with a direct object	YES (2) *We **ate** *hot dogs* our way across the U.S. (3) *Sue **whistled** *a tune* her way through the tunnel (4) *Bill **rolled** *the barrel* its way up the alley (Jackendoff 1990, 212)
Passive	NO (5) *His way *was* **belched** out of the restaurant *by Bill* (Jackendoff 1990, 216) (6) *His way *was* **moaned** out the door *by Alfred* (Massam 1990, 180)
Topicalization (preposing, extraposition, object fronting or extraction test, etc.)	NO (7) *His way *out of the restaurant*, Bill **belched** (Jackendoff 1990, 212)
Free pronominalization	**NO** (8) *He **belched** *it* out of the restaurant
Can be questioned	NO (9) **What* did he **belch**?
Definite object possible	NO (10) *He **belched** *the* way out of the restaurant
Restrictions on form of NP (coreferentiality and directional)	YES **[SUB$_i$ [V POSS$_i$** *way*] **(adverb) DIR]** — **COREFERENTIALITY** (11) *Bill$_i$* **belched** *his$_i$* way out of the restaurant

Tab. 3.6: *Continued*

FEATURES	*Way*-objects
	— **DIRECTIONAL**
	(12) Bill **belched** his way **noisily** *out of the restaurant* (Jackendoff 1990, 215)
	(13) I **wormed** my way **quickly** *towards my former servant* (1898 Hope, *Rupert of Hentzau* [CL 3]) (Traugott and Trousdale 2013, 86)
	(14) I was banished the county, **begged** my way **with my poor outcast child** *up to Edinburgh* (1824 Hogg, *Private Memoirs and Confessions of a Justified Sinner* [CL 2]) (Traugott and Trousdale 2013, 86)

a Unless stated otherwise the examples provided in Tab. 3.6 are my own.

be pronominalized (example (8)) or questioned (example (9)).[20] Moreover, like true cognate objects, *way*-objects also show some restrictions on their form, namely, they cannot be preceded by the definite article (example (10)), they have to be coreferential with the subject of the construction (example (11)), and they are always accompanied by a directional (DIR), which can be modified by an adverb of manner (examples (12) and (13)) or accompaniment (example (14)).[21] Finally, *way*-objects, despite their implication of motion and their apparent status as objects,

20 Note that the feature of pronominalization does not apply to all *way*-constructions. As explained by Salkoff (1988, 56), pronominalization is possible with (i) "verbs indicating the manner of locomotion" as in *Max (bicycled, hiked, backpacked, canoed, etc.) (his way, it) across the country*; and (ii) with a "smaller group of verbs appearing in an abstract context", as in *Max (fiddled, improvised) (his way, it) through the dance sequence.*

21 Mondorf (2011, 402) and Traugott and Trousdale (2013) use the term DIR(ectional), as opposed to Salkoff (1988, 49), who refers to this DIR(ectional) as PP, and Jackendoff (1990, 211) who uses the term PP-complement. Goldberg (1995, 199) uses the label OBL, as does Israel (1996, 218). Following Mondorf (2011), Traugott and Trousdale (2013) consider that OBL should be replaced by DIR(ectional) "since direction is crucial to the construction and needs to be distinguished from obliques such as locatives" (2013, 76). In support of this, they note that "the motion subschema without DIR is clearly a marginal member of the construction" (2013, 88).

are, oddly enough, strongly associated with intransitive verbs that do not entail motion (Jackendoff 1990, 212; see also Goldberg 1995, 207).[22] According to Jackendoff (1990, 213), "the verb either is inherently a process verb (e.g. *eat*, *whistle*, *roll*) or else describes a repeated bounded event (e.g. *belch*, *joke*, *homer*)". As in cognate object constructions, the set of verbs involved in the PDE *way*-construction is not limited to intransitives (e.g. *belch*); marginally transitive verbs such as *beg* and *worm* (see (13) and (14) in Tab. 3.6) and ambitransitive verbs like *shoot* may also occur in the construction, as shown in example (62).

(62) and **shot** my way home the next day; having... equally divided the game between the three (1820–2 Hunt, *Memoirs of Henry Hunt* [CL 2]) (Traugott and Trousdale 2013, 87; see also Perek 2018)

It should be noted that some of the morphosyntactic features of *way*-objects just mentioned are essentially a characteristic of ModE and PDE. Following Traugott and Trousdale (2013, 80), the precursors of the PDE *way*-construction lie in ME constructions with *wei* as the object of transitive verbs like *nimen* 'take' and *take*, and in the recurrent use of *wei* and phrases such as *on wei* with intransitive motion verbs such as *go*, *wend*, *fare*, *flee*, some of which, like the verb *ride*, could also specify manner of motion. In ME the *way*-object did not yet exhibit its PDE formal restrictions: as today, it could be premodified by a possessive (see examples (63), (64), (65) and (68)), but it need not (examples in (66) and (67), with a demonstrative and an article respectively); it could be accompanied by a preposition (example (64)), or an adverb (example (65)), and could be pluralized as in example (67). Moreover, the directional, which is nowadays obligatory, was not typically present in the construction, and was in fact often absent with motion verbs (example (63)).

In general terms, Fanego's (2019) most recent historical account of the construction concurs with the one just outlined by Traugott and Trousdale (2013). Yet, the former convincingly demonstrates that the seeds of the *way*-construction must be placed instead in the OE period, and that it is already in ME when the *way*-construction increases its productivity and shows a growing obligatorification of the directional complement. Either way, in both accounts the *fixation* or

22 Jackendoff (1990, 212) points out that a "vast range of intransitive action verbs are acceptable".

conventionalization of the morphosyntactic features of modern *way*-objects (i.e. the obligatory presence of the coreferential possessive determiner as well as the directional) is explained in terms of a gradual process of constructionalization which started at the very earliest in ME (Fanego 2019), and continued in later periods (Traugott and Trousdale 2013, 83).[23] More specific aspects of this gradual and long process will be examined in the forthcoming chapters when dealing with the formation (cf. § 5.2.3.2) and subsequent development of the ROC in American English (cf. § 7.3).

(63) þe kniht tok leue and **wente his wei**. . .
the knight took leave and went his way. . .
(c1390 *St.Greg.* 34 [MED, s.v. *clot*, n. 1. a])

(64) **Ryde on your wey**, for I wille not be long behynde.
Ride on your way for I will not be long behind.
(1485 Malory *Wks* [MED, s.v. *wei*, n. (1) 2b. (d)])

(65) In the see she **dryueth forth hir weye**.
In the sea she drives forth her way.
(c1390 Chaucer, CT *Melibee* B. 875 [MED, s.v. *wei*, n. (1) 2b. (b)])

(66) . . . and to him **þane wei** he **nam**.
. . . and to him that way he took.
(1300 *SLeg.Becket* 713 [MED, s.v. *wei*, n. (1) 2b. (b)])

23 As pointed out by Börjars, Vincent, and Walkden (2015), and Hilpert (2018), the label 'constructionalization', referring to the creation of a *new* form-meaning pairing, is a complex one: its identification is highly dependent on when the analysis starts (see also Flach 2020). If Traugott and Trousdale (2013) had started their analysis in OE rather than in ME they would have probably arrived at the same results as those obtained by Fanego (2019). Still, despite these chronological differences, as we shall see later on, Traugott and Trousdale's account is a solid one with accurate and important insights on the intrincacies of the gradual development of the *way*-construction over the course of the EModE and LModE periods. As Fanego (2019) puts it, Traugott and Trousdale's (2013) "qualitative analysis *usefully* identifies the historical links of the *Way* construction with both the transitive and intransitive constructions. Yet, like Israel before them, their coverage of the construction is limited, since it starts basically from late ME times" (2019, 674; emphasis mine).

(67) And **went the wayes** hym by-fore.
And went the ways him before.
(c1450 *Parl. 3 Ages* 37 [MED, s.v. *wei*, n. (1) 2b. (a)])

(68) As he **wende his wei**, seh þis seli meiden Margarete.
As he went his way, saw this blessed maiden Margaret.
(c. 1225 St. Marg. [MED, s.v. *wei*, n. (1) 2b. (a)])

(Traugott and Trousdale 2013, 80–81; with slight modifications)

3.2.1.3 Reaction objects

As repeatedly mentioned, Levin (1993, 98) defines reaction objects as "nonsubcategorized objects that express a reaction (an emotion or disposition)". Concerning this "nonsubcategorized" nature of the reaction object, Kogusuri (2009b) argues that reaction objects display a complex syntactic behaviour since they exhibit both argument and non-argument properties. The special properties of reaction objects are summarized in Tab. 3.7 and Tab. 3.8, and illustrated with examples from Kogusuri (2009b, 2011) and earlier work on nonprotypical objects such as Ross (1970a), Levin and Rapoport (1988), Massam (1990), Levin (1993), Omuro (1997; see also 1995 and 1996), Martínez-Vázquez (1998), Felser and Wanner (2001), and Huddleston and Pullum et al. (2002).

Reaction objects share some of the features of the prototypical objects given in § 3.1. Thus, they cannot be separated from their verb by a manner adverb (example (1) in Tab. 3.7), they cannot co-occur with a direct object (example (2)), and they can be modified by an attributive adjectival passive (examples (3)-(5)); this last feature, as pointed out by Felser and Wanner (2001, 109; see also Kogusuri 2009b, 38), is usually allowed by direct objects and thus serves to distinguish them from the external argument, i.e. the subject, which does not allow this type of premodification (cf. **a hard-worked lawyer came to visit me*).[24] As regards passivization, which is the feature most commonly associated with objects, it is available only for some reaction objects (examples (6)-(12)) but not for others (examples (13)-(18) in Tab. 3.8). Finally, and contrary to prototypical objects, reaction objects cannot be topicalized (see (19)), pronominalized (examples (22) and (23)) or questioned (example (24)).

24 Like cognate objects, reaction objects cannot co-occur with a direct object either, although like prototypical objects some reaction objects can be accompanied by an indirect object (see Jespersen 1909–1949, III: 298).

Tab. 3.7: Argument properties of ROs

Argument properties (= Prototypical objects)	
Adjacency condition (insertion test, Verb Object Bonding principle)	YES (1) *She **nodded** *gracefully* her approval[a] (Felser and Wanner 2001, 109)
Can co-occur with a direct object	NO (2) *She **nodded** *her head* approval (Felser and Wanner 2001, 109)
Attributive adjectival passive	YES (3) *a half-smiled* **goodbye** (Felser and Wanner 2001, 109) (4) Soon President Lincoln gave him *a nodded* **permission** to accompany the Union armies even on the battlefields (5) . . . just as Lady Macbeth, the fiend-soul of the house, steps from the door, like the speech of the building, with *her falsely smiled* **welcome**? (Kogusuri 2009b, 38)
Passive	YES (6) Warm thanks *were* **smiled** at the audience (Felser and Wanner 2001, 108) (7) On the day of departure, Glyndwr's men assembled, a few mounted, and wagons were ready to roll. Final goodbyes *were* **waved** (8) "You got a smoke?" the young black man asks the older white man who is pulling hard on a cigarette. "This is all I got." "How about a drag?" Without hesitation it's handed over. Thanks *are* **nodded** (9) Unfortunately, just after goodbyes *were* **waved**, the plane ran off the runway and only finally stopped when its tail was high in the air and its nose buried deep in the mud (10) . . . as the time [of fitting out] neared when the last line is cast off, the goodbyes *are* **waved**, the screw makes the water boil under the stern, and the passage to Alaska is under way (11) The lawns in front of the Pequot House were well filled with the guests of the hotel and cottages, and many good-byes *were* **waved** to the yatchtsmen as they sailed away (Kogusuri 2009b, 33, 37 and 50) (12) On the parade ground commands *must be* **roared**, *not* **whispered** (Huddleston and Pullum et al. 2002, 305)

a Unless stated otherwise the examples provided in Tab. 3.7 and Tab. 3.8 are my own.

Tab. 3.8: Non-argument properties of ROs

Non-argument properties (≠ Prototypical objects)	
Passive	NO
	(13) *Her thanks *were* smiled *by Rilla* (Massam 1990, 180) (14) *Grateful thanks *were* smiled *by Rilla* (Massam 1990, 180) (15) *A cheerful welcome *was* beamed *by Sandra* (Levin 1993, 98) (16) *Agreement *was* nodded *by John* (Omuro 1997, 819) (17) *Her adoration *was* mumbled (Martínez-Vázquez 1998, 258) (18) *Her assent *was* smiled (Huddleston and Pullum et al. 2002, 305)
Topicalization (preposing, extraposition, object fronting or extraction test, etc.)	NO
	(19) *Agreement, John **nodded** (Omuro 1997, 822) (20) ?What she **laughed** was her glee (21) *It was his resentment that Jack **grumbled** (Ross 2012)
Free pronominalization	NO
	(22) *Pauline **smiled** thanks and Mary smiled *them*, too (23) *George **nodded** agreement, so I nodded *it*, too (Kogusuri 2009b, 36)
Can be questioned	NO
	(24) **What* did she **smile**?
Definite object possible	NO
	(25) *He **waved** *the* good bye to Hagrid (Kogusuri 2009b, 35) (26) *Pauline **smiled** *the* thanks (Kogusuri 2011, 160)
Restrictions on form of NP (coreferentiality)	YES
	(27) **Tom* **frowned** *Ann's/my* displeasure (28) *Tom$_i$* **frowned/scowled/roared** *(his$_i$)* displeasure (Ross 1970a, 266–267)

When compared with true cognate objects and *way*-objects, reaction objects also show some restrictions on their form. For instance, they cannot be preceded by a definite article (examples (25) and (26); also Martínez-Vázquez 2014a, 175), except when functioning as subjects in passives (example (10) in Tab. 3.7), and they must be coreferential with the subject (example (27) in Tab. 3.8), although it is not necessary for this coreferentiality to be always formally marked by means of a possessive (example (28)). To these various nonprototypical features just mentioned we can add two more recently identified by Mirto (2017, 542): (i) reaction objects can never head a relative clause, and (ii) they can never occur in negative or interrogative sentences.

According to Kogusuri (2009b, 2011), the complex syntactic behaviour of reaction objects just described can be accounted for by their semantics, that is, their character of effected (*effectum*) objects (see Jespersen 1909–1949; Poutsma 1926, 27; and Martínez-Vázquez 1998, 250 and 252). As previously noted in § 3.1.1.1, the label '*effectum* object' comes from Fillmore (1968, 4) and has been widely adopted in the literature in parallel with the term 'objects of result' (Jespersen 1909–1949: III, §§ 12.2–12.3) to refer to objects that "denote entities which come into existence after the activities denoted by the verbs" (Kogusuri 2009b, 39; cf. § 3.1.1.1, § 3.1.1.2 and § 3.1.2.1).

A series of tests – presented here in Tab. 3.9 – have been proposed in the literature to differentiate between ordinary/affected (*affectum*) and effected (*effectum*) objects. Contrary to affected objects, effected objects do not "permit interrogation of the verb with *do to*" (Fillmore 1968, 4) (example (1) in Tab. 3.9), and they are not generally allowed to appear in the subject position of the middle construction (see examples (4) and (5) as opposed to (8) and (9)). Moreover, effected objects cannot occur in resultative constructions such as **John dug the grave rough* and **John painted the portrait impressive and life-like*, where the objects (i.e. *the grave, the portrait*) must be affected by the activity of the verb (Simpson 1983, 146; see also Jackendoff 1990, 230; Kogusuri 2009b, 41).[25] Additionally, as shown in example (17) in Tab. 3.9, sentences with effected

25 Regarding the object in resultatives, Simpson (1983) explains, "the verb must necessarily affect the OBJECT, which is why verbs of contact [e.g. *shot*, *kick*,

objects describe telic events (i.e. events with a definite endpoint), and consequently they only permit a temporal adverbial phrase with *in* (Harley 2005, 43). Finally, effected objects cannot undergo pronominalization, mainly because they refer to entities that belong to the subject of the construction and cannot be created twice (Matsumoto 1996, 208; Kogusuri 2009b, 45). In examples (22) and (23), for instance, the effected objects *house* and *book* created by John and Mary respectively, cannot be recreated by another participant. Tightly related to the lack of pronominalization of effected objects is their general inability to be preceded by a definite article, which, in most cases, implies that the object has been previously created (see examples (28) and (29) against (33) and (34)).

If we now turn to reaction objects, as shown in the relevant literature and in the middle column of Tab. 3.9, reaction objects fulfil the criteria of effected objects all the way down. Regarding the telic status of reaction objects, and in particular those derived from speech act verbs such as *thanks* in example (19), Martínez-Vázquez (2015, 160) specifies the following,

> As resulting objects [i.e. effected objects], these events are frozen into a single resulting act: a personal/individual act linked to the time reference of the verb of the construction. The aspectual status of the nominal is thus limited by the verb of the construction; since both events are causally linked, the noun acquires a telic status.

Finally, with regard to example (32), this adduced by Huddleston and Pullum et al. (2002) as an instance of ROC (cf. § 3.1.2.2), Martínez-Vázquez (2014a, 175) explains that examples like this one "cannot be considered an EOC [i.e. reaction object construction], since its object takes a definite article, which implies a prior mention to this noun; hence, its referent cannot be a product of the verbal action".

---

punch and *beat*] and verbs of change of state [e.g. *freeze*, *melt* and *break*] appear so freely" (146): *I shot/kicked/punched/beat John to death* and *I broke the vase into pieces*. In a similar vein, Jackendoff (1990, 230) states, "[i]t appears to me that the proper role is Patient. Notice that all the direct objects in (37) (38) [instances of resultatives, e.g. *Harry hammered/pounded* *<u>the metal</u>* *flat*] can be construed as Patients of their respective "base forms," as shown by the usual pseudocleft test for Patient" (230): *What Harry did to the metal flat was hammer/pound (on) it.*

Tab. 3.9: Tests to distinguish affected objects from effected objects and ROs. Adapted from Kogusuri (2009b)

TESTS	**Effected objects 'objects of result'**	**Reaction objects**	**Affected objects 'ordinary objects'**
***Do to* test**	NO	NO	YES
	(1) A: *What did John do to the table?*[a] B: *John **built** the table (Fillmore 1968, 4)	(2) A: *What did Mary do to her thanks?* B: *She **smiled** her thanks (Kogusuri 2009b, 40)	(3) A: *What did John do to the table?* B: John **ruined** the table (Fillmore 1968, 4)
Middle subjects (Subject position of the middle construction)	NO	NO	YES
	(4) **These cabinets* **construct/ build** easily (5) **Wool sweater* **knits** easily (Fellbaum 1986, 17)	(6) **Agreement* **nods** easily (7) **Forgiveness* **smiles** easily (Omuro 1997, 819)	(8) *This glass* **breaks** easily (9) *This bread* **cuts** easily (Pinker 1989, 106)
Resultative constructions	NO	NO	YES
	(10) *John **dug** the grave *rough* (11) *John **painted** the portrait *impressive and life-like* (Tanaka 1990, 51)	(12) *He **smiled** his welcome *noticeable* (13) *He **nodded** approval *open* (Tanaka 1990, 50)	(14) John **dug** the ground *rough* (15) John **painted** the door *green* (Tanaka 1990, 51)
Atelic events	NO	NO	YES
	(16) Sue **wrote** *#in five minutes/ for hours* (17) Sue **wrote** a story *in five minutes/ #for hours* (Harley 2005, 43)	(18) She **sang** **in an hour/for an hour* (19) She **sang** her thanks *in an hour/*for an hour* (Aue-Apaikul 2006, 126)	(20) John **painted** the door *in an hour* (21) John **painted** the door *for an hour*

Continued on next page

Tab. 3.9: *Continued*

TESTS	**Effected objects 'objects of result'**	**Reaction objects**	**Affected objects 'ordinary objects'**
Free Pronominal-ization	NO	NO	YES
	(22) *John **built** a house in Boston and Sam **built** *it* in Philadelphia (23) *Mary **wrote** a book for her pleasure and Jane **wrote** *it* for money (Matsumoto 1996, 208)	(24) *Pauline **smiled** thanks and Mary **smiled** *them*, too (25) *George **nodded** agreement, so I **nodded** *it*, too (Kogusuri 2009b, 44)	(26) John **painted** the door and Mary **painted** *it*, too (27) John **dug** the ground, and Mary **dug** *it*, too
Definite object possible	NO	NO	YES
	(28) I **dig** *a* grave *I **dig** *the* grave (29) She **lights** *a* fire *She **lights** *the* fire (Jespersen 1909–1949: III, § 12.2: 233) Cf. § 3.1.1.1	(30) *He **waved** *the* good bye to Hagrid (Kogusuri 2009b, 35) (31) *Pauline **smiled** *the* thanks (Kogusuri 2011, 160) (32) He **roared** *the* command (Huddleston and Pullum et al. 2002, 305; cf. Martínez-Vázquez 2014a, 175)	(33) I **dig** *the* ground (34) She **lights** *the* lamp (Jespersen 1909-1949: III, § 12.2: 233) Cf. § 3.1.1.1

a Unless stated otherwise the examples provided in Tab. 3.9 are mine.

Although the semantics of reaction objects as effected objects can explain why they cannot pronominalize nor be preceded by a definite article, it has to be acknowledged that their semantic status cannot serve to account for unpassivizable reaction objects such as **Her thanks were smiled by Rilla* (for further examples see (13)-(18) in Tab. 3.8 above). Following Zubizarreta (1985, 255–256) and Massam (1990, 180), Kogusuri (2009b, 49) argues that the lack of passivization in such cases is explained by the coreferential relationship existing between the subject and the possessive in the construction (cf. *Rilla*$_i$ *smiled her*$_i$ *thanks*). In Kogusuri's words, for passivization to be possible in cases like **Her thanks were smiled by Rilla*, "the NP in the *by*-phrase cannot establish coreference with (. . .) the subject" (2009b, 47). Even when there is no possessive determiner explicitly marking the coreferential relation between the subject and the NP in the *by*-phrase, passivization is still not possible, as shown by the ungrammaticality of **Grateful thanks were smiled by Rilla* and **A cheerful welcome was beamed by Sandra* in Tab. 3.8 above. As shown in examples (69)-(73), this coreferential constraint not only applies to ROCs but to all constructions where a coreferential relation is established between the subject and the object, such as idiomatic expressions with body-part nouns, as in (69)-(71), or constructions like those in (72) and (73).

(69) *A toe *was* **stubbed** by Philip.

(70) *His toe *was* **stubbed** by Philip.

(71) *His teeth *were* **gnashed** (by Bill).

(72) *His mother *is* **loved** by John.

(73) *His role *was* **played** by John.
(Zubizarreta 1985, 256; Massam 1990, 180; Jackendoff 1990, 216; see also Ross 1970b)

Importantly, this coreferentiality constraint can be solved by eliding the *by*-phrase (Jackendoff 1990, 216 and 298fn3; Kogusuri 2009b; Kogusuri 2011, 159–161). As explained by Kogusuri, "[w]ithout elements describing the agent [i.e. the NP in the *by*-phrase], the semantic relationship between the agent and the entity described by the RO [reaction object] is pragmatically backgrounded, which makes it possible to suspend the coreferential constraint on the ROC" (2009b, 50). Hence passivization is allowed in examples (6)-(12) in Tab. 3.7 above (e.g. *Warm thanks were smiled at the audience* and *Final goodbyes were waved*). Finally, it should be noted that since coreferentiality is also an intrinsic feature of the *way*-construction, the coreferentiality constraint also applies to the unpassivizable cases of *way*-objects in (5) and (6) in Tab. 3.6 (e.g. **His way was belched out of the restaurant by Bill*). In the *way*-construction, however, it is not possible to suspend this constraint because the possessive is an obligatory feature of modern *way*-objects (see Traugott and Trousdale 2013, 83; and § 3.2.1.2).

3.2.2 Concluding remarks

True cognate objects, *way*-objects and reaction objects exhibit a series of morphosyntactic features that clearly set them apart from the prototypical objects described in § 3.1.2.1 and § 3.1.2.2. Contrary to ordinary objects, those three types of nonprototypical objects show restrictions on their form (e.g. modification, the presence of a directional, coreferentiality, etc.) and they cannot be topicalized or questioned. Additionally, they cannot undergo pronominalization nor can they be preceded by a definite article due to their condition as objects of result (Jespersen 1909–1949, Martínez-Vázquez 1998 among others). As regards the lack of passivization, this has to do with the coreferentiality constraint, as discussed by Zubizarreta (1985); this constraint can be suspended, however, when the passive subject lacks the possessive, and the agent *by*-phrase is elided (Kogusuri 2009b, 2011).

A particularly interesting issue discussed in § 3.2.1 of this chapter is Horrocks and Stavrou's (2010) three-fold classification of cognate objects that distinguishes between cognate object constructions with transitive verbs, and cognate objects occurring with intransitive verbs, namely transitivizing cognate object constructions, and aspectual cognate object constructions. This useful classification solves the long-standing controversy concerning the argument/adjunct status of cognate objects, and may also help us to get a better understanding of the development of the reaction object construction. More specifically, since the origins of the cognate object construction, as well as of the *way*-construction, seem to lie with transitive verbs (Visser

1963–1973: I, § 424: 414–415; Traugott and Trousdale 2013; Lavidas 2018; see § 3.2.1.1 and § 3.2.1.2), we may also proceed from the assumption that reaction objects followed the same path of development, occurring first with more transitive-like verbs and then expanding to intransitives.

Finally, what we said in § 3.2.1.2 concerning the fixation of the morphosyntactic features of the *way*-construction in PDE, namely the requirement, especially from ModE onwards, of a coreferential possessive determiner on the *way*-object and of a directional complement (Traugott and Trousdale 2013, 83–84) leads us to wonder whether a similar process may also have been at work with reaction objects at around the same date. The two hypotheses outlined in the preceding paragraphs will be addressed in Part II. Prior to this, Chapter 4 will focus on the theoretical framework adopted for the synchronic and diachronic analysis of ROCs, namely Construction Grammar as developed by Goldberg (1995, 2006) and its application to patterns of language change as formulated in work by Traugott and Trousdale (2013) and Hilpert (2013).

4. Construction Grammar: Synchronic and diachronic perspectives

In this chapter I will provide an overview of a theory of linguistic knowledge known as Construction Grammar, paying attention to its emergence in the late 1980s, the main tenets of constructionist approaches that developed right afterwards, and the application of these postulates to the study of language variation and change. This overview aims at showing how Construction Grammar – from both a synchronic and a diachronic perspective – can help us to get a better understanding of the *nature* and *historical development of the idiosyncratic properties* of the reaction object outlined in Chapter 3. The suitability of this theory of linguistic knowledge for the study of the reaction object construction will be tested empirically by means of the corpus-based studies conducted in Part II.

4.1 Cognitive Linguistics and Construction Grammar

Theories of linguistic knowledge are concerned with what speakers know when they know a language and how this linguistic knowledge is represented in the speaker's mind. In this sense, various theories of Linguistics predating Cognitive Linguistics proper, such as Chomsky's Generative Grammar and its offshoots (see Taylor 2002, 5–6, among many others), can be regarded as 'cognitive' too, in that they consider language as a mental phenomenon. Yet, even though in this respect Generative Grammar can thus be considered part of the cognitive linguistic movement, as a cognitive theory it has to be distinguished from others that treat language as an integral part of cognition. It is for this reason that the term cognitive linguistics (with a small 'c') is generally used to refer to "any linguistic theory which recognizes the fact that language knowledge resides in the mind" (Taylor 2002, 5), whereas Cognitive Linguistics (with a capital 'C') is commonly used to refer to those linguistic theories that consider language as an "integral part of cognition" (Taylor 2002, 8) and therefore, similar to other cognitive abilities such as visual perception and reasoning. According to Croft and Cruse (2004, 1), three major principles or 'hypotheses' guide the Cognitive linguistic approach to knowledge: (i) language is not an autonomous cognitive faculty, (ii) grammar is conceptualization, and (iii) knowledge of language emerges from language use. These three hypotheses are briefly outlined below.

(i) **Language is not an autonomous cognitive faculty**

This hypothesis, which is opposed to Generative Grammar's consideration that language is an autonomous (innate) cognitive faculty, has two major implications: (a) the representation of linguistic knowledge in the speakers' minds is basically the same as the representation of other conceptual structures, and (b) the cognitive abilities and processes that govern language use do not differ significantly from those used in other cognitive tasks such as visual perception, reasoning or motor activity (Croft and Cruse 2004, 1–3).

(ii) **Grammar is conceptualization**

This second major hypothesis, embodied in the title of Langacker's 2000 seminal monograph (Langacker 2000), refers to the notion that conceptual structure cannot be reduced to a "simple truth-conditional correspondence with the world" but is subject to 'construal', that is, to the (varying) conceptualization of the experience to be communicated (Croft and Cruse 2004, 3).

(iii) **Knowledge of language emerges from language use**

This hypothesis assumes that speakers' linguistic categories and structures are built up from their cognition of specific utterances on specific occasions of use, and from an inductive process of abstraction and schematization leading to a model of grammatical representation shaped by language use (Croft and Cruse 2004, 3–4).

Though these three hypotheses are central to Cognitive Linguistics generally, Cognitive Linguistics is not a unified framework but rather a collection of approaches which include Cognitive Semantics (Talmy 1988, 2000), and cognitive research on conceptual metaphor (Lakoff and Johnson 1980, Lakoff 1987) and conceptual blending (Fauconnier and Turner 1998), among many others. My concern here will be with the branch of Cognitive Linguistics known as Construction Grammar, a framework that focuses on the description of grammatical phenomena from a cognitive linguistic perspective.

4.2 The origins of Construction Grammar

Theories of linguistic knowledge have not always had idiosyncratic grammatical phenomena, like the reaction object construction here, as their core subject of investigation. Generative Grammar, for instance, only accounts for what is regular in language. In § 4.2.1, it will be shown that idiomatic units represent a significant subset of any language, and that the Cognitive theory of Construction Grammar, in fact, emerges precisely in order to account for these *idiomatic units*, referred to in this framework as *constructions* or *learned form-meaning pairings*.

4.2.1 From idioms to Construction Grammar

The roots of Construction Grammar as a theory of linguistic knowledge lie in Lakoff's (1987) work on *There*-constructions, and Fillmore, Kay, and O'Connor's (1988) study on the so-called *let alone* construction. The aim of these studies was to demonstrate that *idioms* or *form-meaning pairings* are central to our linguistic knowledge rather than simply an "Appendix to the Grammar" (Fillmore, Kay, and O'Connor 1988, 504). In this regard, Fillmore et al. (1988), for instance, categorized idioms into four main groups: (i) encoding vs. decoding idioms, (ii) grammatical vs. extragrammatical idioms, (iii) substantive vs. formal idioms, and (iv) idioms with and without pragmatic point.

Encoding idioms do not represent the most natural way of expressing a meaning in a particular language, but hearers can figure out their meaning upon hearing them, as in *answer the door* 'open the door in response to someone knocking', *wide awake* 'completely awake', *bright red* 'intense colour' and *spill the beans* 'divulge the information'. *Decoding idioms*, by contrast, cannot be decoded by the hearer; and one of the reasons for this lack of transparency is the mismatch between the literal and the idiomatic meaning of the expression. A couple of examples are *kick the bucket* 'die' and *pull a fast one* 'to successfully deceive someone'.

The second distinction Fillmore et al. make is between *grammatical* and *extragrammatical* idioms. Grammatical idioms are semantically irregular but parsable. The examples above qualify as grammatical idioms; all of them are semantically irregular but they conform to the English syntactic rule that direct objects follow the verb (Croft and Cruse 2004, 233). Extragrammatical idioms, on the other hand, are semantically irregular idioms that cannot be parsed such as *first off, sight unseen, all of a sudden, by and large*, and *so far so good.*

The third contrast is that between *substantive*, or lexically filled idioms, and *formal*, or lexically open idioms. Substantive idioms are those in which "all elements of the idiom are fixed" (Croft and Cruse 2004, 233) as in *It takes one to know one* (**It took one to know one*), whereas formal idioms are those in which "at least part of the idiom can be filled by the usual range of expressions that are syntactically and semantically appropriate for the slot" (Croft and Cruse 2004, 233). An example is *(X) blows X's nose*, which allows the following variations: *I blew my nose*, *Kim blew her nose* and *They all blew their noses.* Finally, Fillmore et al.'s last type is that between *idioms with and without pragmatic point.* The former are used in specific pragmatic contexts such as *Good morning*, *See you later*, *Once upon a time*, and *Him be a doctor?!* An example of the latter is *all of a sudden* which is not tied to any pragmatic context.

As we shall see later, some of these distinctions are still very much alive in the literature on Construction Grammar but with different labels. For instance, the first one between *encoding* and *decoding* idioms is closely related to the notions of *compositionality* (Traugott and Trousdale 2013, 19), *coercion* or *type shifting* (Michaelis 2004), as well as the notion of *accommodation* (Goldberg 1995, 159). The second distinction between *grammatical* and *extragrammatical* idioms is very close to the notion of *analyzability* (Traugott and Trousdale 2013, 19). And, finally, the third contrast between *formal* and *substantive* idioms, the main focus of Filmore et al.'s pioneering study (1988), is tightly related to the crucial notions of *schematicity* and *abstraction* (cf. § 4.3.1).

Fillmore et al.'s study (1988) focuses on a formal (schematic/abstract) idiom involving the lexical item *let alone* in order to demonstrate that it possesses unique "syntactic, semantic and pragmatic properties that cannot be described by the general rules of the language" (Croft and Cruse 2004, 237). From the point of view of syntax, the authors explain that "the phrase *let alone* functions like a coordinating conjunction, in that it occurs in a wide variety of sentential environments where ordinary coordinating conjunctions occur" (1988, 514). Examples of these are those in (1) and (2). *Let alone* also behaves similarly to the comparative conjunction *than* in contexts such as the one in (3), although it differs from this conjunction in other contexts like the one in (4) where the deletion of the verb phrase (excluding the auxiliary) in the second conjunct is not possible.

(1) a. Max won't eat SHRIMP, **let alone** SQUID.
b. We'll need shrimp **and** squid.

(2) a. Max won't TOUCH the SHRIMP, **let alone** CLEAN the SQUID.
b. I want you to cook the shrimp **and** clean the squid.

(3) a. Max won't eat shrimp, **let alone** Rabbi Feldstein.
b. Max ate more shrimp **than** Rabbi Feldstein.

(4) a. Max will eat shrimp more willingly **than** Minnie will.
b. *Max won't eat shrimp **let alone** Minnie will.

(Fillmore, Kay, and O'Connor 1988, 514–516)

From the point of view of semantics, they show that the construction involves two parallel semantic propositions with the same polarity, ranked on a scale, the first proposition being the strongest and the most informative. For instance, in *Max won't eat SHRIMP, let alone SQUID*, the two parallel semantic propositions have negative polarity and the first proposition is stronger and more informative than the second one in that people who would not eat shrimp would not eat squid either, but not the other way around.

Regarding the pragmatics of the construction, the discourse context in which the proposition is felicitous is one in which the second proposition is more relevant (Fillmore, Kay, and O'Connor 1988, 532). In the example above, for instance, what is relevant is whether or not Max eats squid. These semantic and pragmatic features characterize the prototypical *let alone* construction, but as noted by Cappelle, Dugas, and Tobin (2015) there also exist some "illogical" *let alone* constructions that reverse the semantics of the two propositions, with the first proposition being weaker and less informative but more relevant than the second proposition (2015, 79; see also Neels 2015).

Fillmore et al.'s (1988) seminal study on the *let alone* construction inspired a number of linguists such as Michaelis and Lambrecht (1996) and Jackendoff (1997) who some years later uncovered the existence of other similar formal structures with their own syntactic, semantic and pragmatic features. A couple of examples of these are the *nominal extraposition construction*, as in *It's AMAZING* <u>*the odd people my SISTER knows*</u>, and the *time away construction*, as in *Bill slept* <u>*the afternoon away*</u> and *Lois and Clark danced* <u>*two blissful hours away*</u>.

The first one, the nominal extraposition construction, is syntactically characterized by the extraposition of the metonymic NP <u>*the (number/variety of) odd people my SISTER knows*</u>, and semantically by exhibiting the *scalar* interpretation of exclamatives, as in the exclamative paraphrase *My sister knows so* <u>*many*</u> *odd PEOPLE!* In both examples it becomes clear that "the set of odd people known by my sister ranks high on a numerical scale" (Michaelis and Lambrecht 1996, 228–229). The second example, that is, the time away construction, from a syntactic point of view, involves an intransitive verb (*sleep*, *dance*) followed by an NP that functions as direct object (*the afternoon*, *two blissful hours*); semantically, it has a durative meaning (see examples (5) and (6)), as well as a telic meaning since the action denoted by the verb "is understood as occupying a bounded period of time" (Jackendoff 1997, 540).

(5) Bill slept <u>for the (whole) afternoon</u>.

(6) Lois and Clark danced away <u>for two blissful hours</u>.

To sum up, the syntactic structures described in this section no doubt provide further support to the anti-generative idea that linguistic knowledge is highly idiosyncratic and consists of *idioms* or *form-meaning pairings* rather than simply words and rules.

4.3 Construction grammars: Common grounds

In the more than thirty years that Construction Grammar has been around, we have witnessed the emergence of several constructionist approaches that adhere to an integral view of linguistic knowledge not substantially different from the knowledge required for other cognitive tasks (see (i) in § 4.1). Some of these approaches are: Berkeley Construction Grammar (Fillmore, Kay, and O'Connor 1988), Sign-Based Construction Grammar (Boas and Sag 2012), Cognitive Construction Grammar (Lakoff 1987, Goldberg 1995, 2006, 2019), Radical Construction Grammar (Croft 2001) and Cognitive Grammar (e.g. Langacker 1987). Although there are considerable differences among them, Goldberg (2013, 15–31) identifies four major tenets that are shared by all constructionist approaches, and a fifth tenet that is present in most of them (§ 4.3.5). These various tenets are discussed in order in the sections that follow.

4.3.1 Grammatical constructions

One of the major tenets of Construction Grammar is that linguistic knowledge consists of constructions, that is, "conventional, learned form-function pairings at varying levels of complexity and abstraction" (Goldberg 2013, 17). A commonly cited representation of the symbolic structure of constructions is in Fig. 4.1.

As explained by Hoffmann and Trousdale (2013, 1), the term 'construction' in Construction Grammar is understood as an extended version of the Saussurean notion of the linguistic sign. The latter seemingly applies only to words and morphemes whereas the former is

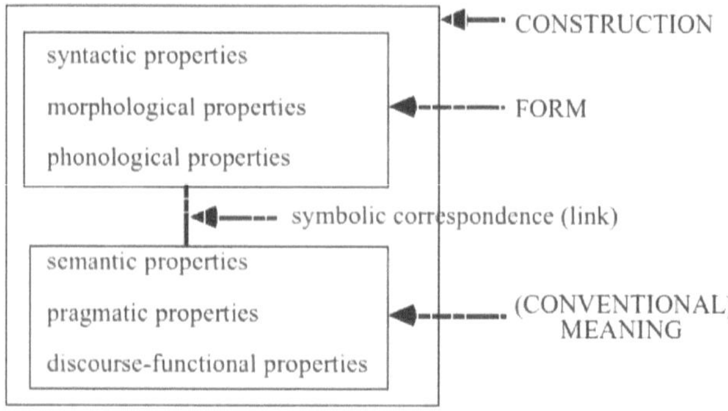

Fig. 4.1: The symbolic structure of a construction. Adapted from Croft and Cruse (2004, 258)

applicable to all levels of grammatical description. As shown in Tab. 4.1, this goes from morphemes, words, and idioms to argument structure constructions such as the ditransitive construction (e.g. *He gave her a fish taco*) and the passive construction (e.g. *The armadillo was hit by a car*). Thus, in contrast to Generative Grammar, Construction Grammar does not make a clear-cut distinction between lexicon and syntax (i.e. between words and rules), but rather posits the existence of a lexicon-syntax continuum (Goldberg and Jackendoff 2004, 532). In Goldberg's (2006) words, "it's constructions all the way down" (18).

In a more precise way, Traugott and Trousdale (2013, 11–13) explain that constructions or "conventional, learned form-function pairings" can be described in terms of three gradient dimensions: size, degree of phonological specificity, and type of concept. As for size, constructions may be classified as (i) atomic or monomorphemic units such as *red* or *-s*, (ii) complex units or units consisting of analysable elements such as *pull strings* or *on top of*, and (iii) intermediate units which are partially analysable such as *bonfire*, where *bon* (< *bone*) is no longer transparent in PDE. Depending on their degree of phonological specificity constructions can be (i) substantive such as the lexical word *dropout*, and the suffix *–dom* in *kingdom*, (ii) schematic such as N (noun) or SAI (subject-auxiliary inversion), and (iii) intermediate when they are partially schematic such as the morphological construction V-*ment* as in *enjoyment* and *employment*, or the *way*-construction which contains the

Tab. 4.1: Constructions at varying levels of complexity and abstraction. Adapted from Goldberg (2013, 17), and Traugott and Trousdale (2013, 13)

Construction	Examples
Morpheme	*-s*
Word	*Iran, another, banana*
Word (partially filled)	*pre*-N, V-*ing*
Idiom (filled)	*Going great guns, give the Devil his due*
Idiom (partially filled)	*Jog* <someone's> *memory*, <someone's> *for the asking*
Idiom (minimally filled) *The* Xer *the* Yer	*The more you think about it, the less you understand*
Ditransitive constructions: Subj V Obj1 Obj2 (unfilled)	*He gave her a fish taco*; *He baked her a muffin*
Passive: Subj aux VP$_{pp}$ (PPby) (unfilled)	*The armadillo was hit by a car*

substantive element *way*. Finally, regarding the third dimension – type of concept – constructions can be (i) contentful ('lexical'), if they can be used referentially as is the case of *red*, and the schematic category *N*, (ii) procedural ('grammatical') if they have a grammatical function such as the atomic construction *-s* which marks the plural in nouns and present tense third person in verbs, or (iii) intermediate if they have both contentful and procedural properties as the *way*-construction: the construction contains the contentful 'lexical' element *way* and with verbs of manner of action or accompanying action such as *giggle* the construction implies iteration (Traugott and Trousdale 2013, 13). These three gradient dimensions of constructions are summarized here in Tab. 4.2.

Tab. 4.2: Dimensions of constructions. Adapted from Traugott and Trousdale (2013, 13)

Size	**Atomic** *red, -s*	**Intermediate** *bonfire*	**Complex** *pull strings, on top of*
Specificity	**Substantive** *dropout, -dom*	**Intermediate** V-*ment*	**Schematic** N, SAI
Concept	**Contentful 'lexical'** *red*, N	**Intermediate** *way*-construction	**Procedural 'grammatical'** *-s*, SAI

It should be noted here that the degree of phonological specificity of a construction is closely related to the notion of linguistic schema. Traugott and Trousdale (2013, 14) define linguistic schemas as "abstractions [i.e. generalizations] across sets of constructions which are (unconsciously) perceived by language-users to be closely related to each other in the constructional network".[26] Linguistic schemas are instantiated by subschemas, and these by specific constructs or micro-constructions. For instance, *may* is a specific construct of the subschema modal and modal is a subschema of the schema auxiliary. As we shall see in Part II, instances such as *Paul kissed her goodbye* and *She kissed her a farewell* are specific constructs of one of the several verb-specific subschemas that conform the more abstract reaction object construction [SUBJ$_i$ [V$_{INTR}$ (OBJ$_1$) (POSS)$_i$ OBJ$_2$]]. These distinctions (i.e. schemas, subschemas and constructs) are by no means absolute and the relations between them may change over time (Traugott and Trousdale 2013). This is one aspect that will be further discussed in § 4.4.2, and illustrated with my historical data in Part II.

4.3.2 Surface generalizations

Unlike generative or lexicalist approaches to grammar (e.g. Levin 1993), which emphasize the role of words (particularly lexical heads) in determining phrasal patterns such as, for instance, (7) and (8), Construction Grammar brings argument structure constructions to the fore. Under a constructionist view, for instance, example (7) patterns syntactically and semantically with the examples represented in (9)-(11) as they all involve subjects, objects and oblique path phrases, and they all express caused motion. They are all instances of the caused motion construction.

(7) Mina sent a book to Mel.

(8) Mina sent Mel a book.

---

26 For Traugott and Trousdale (2013), schemas and subschemas "are not meant to be mental representations" but elements of the linguistic system that "the linguist picks out for discussion and analysis" (14). This does not imply that on some occasions there may be an overlap between the two.

(9) Mina sent a book to Chicago.

(10) Mina sent a book toward the front of the room.

(11) Mina sent a book through the metal detector.

As explained by Goldberg (2013, 20), this approach to grammar allows us to account for the fact that a verb such as *cough*, which does not lexically entail caused motion, can convey such meaning when involved in structures like the one in (12).

(12) "I actually had a moth go up my nose once. I ... coughed him out of my mouth"

(Goldberg 2013, 20)

4.3.3 A network of constructions

Constructions are related to each other in structured networks (Goldberg 2013, 21). This is a view of language structure that is ultimately based on work in cognitive psychology, which regards other aspects of knowledge as being organized as a network. Assuming that our linguistic knowledge is organized in a network, Goldberg (2013) explains that the P[reposition] N[oun] construction (e.g. *She was in prison*, *She was in school*, etc.) inherits its word order from the more abstract Prepositional Phrase (PP) construction, but contrary to the PP construction, it specifies an N instead of an NP (cf. Fig. 4.2). To be more specific, the P N construction involves a preposition and a bare count noun (see examples (13) and (14)), and it carries a special interpretation: the construction implies that a specific activity or role is associated with the nominal referent. For instance, in (13), the nominal referent can only be a prisoner as one does not go to prison as a warden (Goldberg 2013, 17). The same special interpretations have been noted in examples (15) and (16).

(13) She was in prison.

(14) *She went to big bed. (Cf. She went to the big bed)

(15) She was in school.

(16) She came from school.

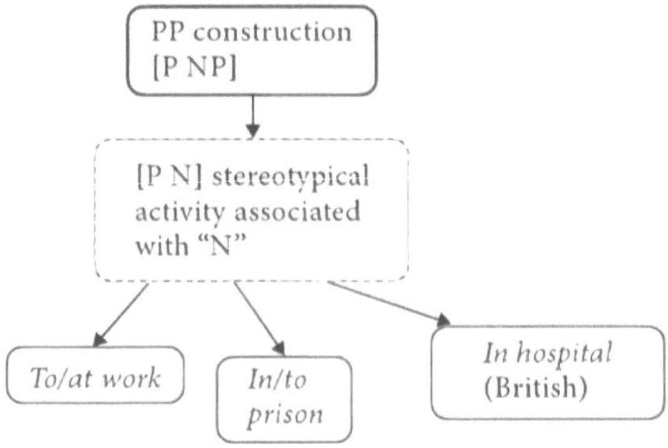

Fig. 4.2: Default inheritance hierarchy that relates the P N construction to the PP construction. Adapted from Goldberg (2013, 21).

Other examples provided by Goldberg (1995, 2013) that serve to illustrate the idea that linguistic knowledge consists of a network of constructions are the intransitive and transitive versions of the resultative construction (see examples (17) and (18)), which are related to each other by a subpart link, with the former being a subpart of the latter. Yet another example is the resultative construction represented in (19), which is related to the caused motion construction in (20) through a metaphorical link. In § 4.4.2, a brief description of the main types of links that can be identified in the network of constructions will be provided.

(17)	The nut broke apart.	Intransitive resultative construction
(18)	She broke the nut apart.	Transitive resultative construction
(19)	She drove him to distraction.	Resultative construction
(20)	She drove him to Detroit.	Caused motion construction

4.3.4 Crosslinguistic variability and generalization

The fourth principle shared by constructionist approaches is the idea that constructions vary crosslinguistically. In Goldberg's words, "[f]inding two constructions in two different languages that are absolutely identical in form, function, and distribution is a rare occurrence outside of cases of shared diachronic history or language contact"

(2013, 23).[27] The crosslinguistic variability of constructions is easily observable in the case of the reaction object construction. As noted in § 3.2, the reaction object construction has not been attested outside of Germanic languages (e.g. Bangla, Basque and Greek) except for Spanish and French, where its use is far more restricted than in English (Martínez-Vázquez 2014b, 2016, Dyka, Novakova, and Siepmann 2017).[28]

4.3.5 Usage-based

Finally, most constructionist approaches are usage-based. This means that they adopt one of the central hypotheses of Cognitive Linguistics, namely that "knowledge of language emerges from language use" (see (iii) in § 4.1): speakers generalize over the instances they hear and at the same time retain large amounts of item-specific knowledge (see Goldberg 2006, 45–65; Goldberg 2013; Diessel and Hilpert 2016; Diessel 2019). This view of linguistic knowledge contrasts with Goldberg's (1995) original definition of constructions, where she only considered learned form-meaning pairings those patterns that were not strictly predictable from their component parts or from other previously established constructions (see (21) for Goldberg's original definition of a construction and (22) for the revised version of it).

27 Apart from cases of shared diachronic history or language contact, there may also be strong universal tendencies across languages, which can be accounted for by "universal functional pressures, iconic principles, and processing and learning constraints" (Goldberg 2013, 23). An example of a strong universal tendency is the expression of actor and undergoer arguments in prominent slots mainly because "human beings' attention is naturally drawn to the actors and undergoers in events" (Goldberg 2013, 25).

28 Martínez-Vázquez (2014b, 214) argues that the Spanish ROC is simply peripheral and "more frequent in certain varieties of American Spanish, where a closer contact with English might favor a process of borrowing". Note however that the productive use of Spanish ROCs with the verb *llorar* 'weep' (e.g. *llorar las penas* 'weep one's sorrows') in contrast to English is a reflection of the cultural rules of each language: "if cultural display rules inhibit emotional display, linguistic expressions about it will also be constrained. Conversely, [their] common use (...) in Spanish suggests that speakers of Spanish are not regulated by such a rigid control of emotions" (Martínez-Vázquez 2017, 11).

Worth of note here is that in her most recent monograph, given the ambiguity of the concept "sufficient frequency" (Goldberg 2006, 5; see (22)), Goldberg solves the controversial issue of "sufficient frequency" introducing the concept of coverage, and characterizes constructions as "emergent *clusters of lossy memory traces* that are aligned within our high-(hyper!) dimensional conceptual space on the basis of shared form, function, and contextual dimensions" (Goldberg 2019, 7; emphasis mine).

(21) C is a CONSTRUCTION iff_{def} C is a form-meaning pair $<F_i, S_i>$ such that some aspect of F_i or some aspect of S_i is not strictly predictable from C's component parts or from other previously established constructions. (Goldberg 1995, 4)

(22) Any linguistic pattern is recognized as a construction as long as some aspect of its form or function is not strictly predictable from its component parts or from other constructions recognized to exist. In addition, patterns are stored as constructions even if they are fully predictable as long as they occur with *sufficient frequency*. (Goldberg 2006, 5; emphasis mine)

As specified in Goldberg's (2006) revised definition of constructions in (22), token frequency is a key factor for the storage of particular linguistic items. This kind of linguistic knowledge is known as item-specific knowledge, and should be distinguished from a more abstract type of knowledge that consists of schematic constructions. For these abstractions to be formed and stored in people's minds they must be productive, a feature that has been defined in the literature as "a function of a construction's type frequency, semantic coherence and an inverse correlation between the two" (Barðdal 2008, 24), that is, the higher the type frequency of a particular construction, the lower the degree of semantic coherence is needed for this construction to be productive and vice versa.

As we shall see in Part II, this monograph promotes a usage-based approach to ROCs. It draws on token frequency and type frequency (i) to make some predictions regarding the levels of specificity of the ROC in people's minds, that is, whether we retain more general, or lower-level ROC verb-specific subschemas (cf. § 6.3.4),[29] and also (ii) to examine changes in its productivity and schematicity (§ 7.3).

29 Though for high-frequency phenomena such as the irregular persons of the verb *be* (*am*, *is*, *are*, *was*, and *were*), their entrenchment in people's minds seems to be indisputable, from a historical perspective and for much less frequent

4.4 Construction Grammar and language change

With the development of constructionist approaches to linguistic knowledge, historical linguists such as Israel (1996), Hollmann (2003), Trousdale (2008a, 2008b), Bergs and Diewald (2008, 2009), Barðdal (2008), Colleman and De Clerck (2011), Patten (2012), Barðdal et al. (2015), Hartmann (2016), Coussé, Andersson, and Olofsson (2018), Hilpert (2019), and Sommerer and Smirnova (2020), among many others, began to apply the postulates of Construction Grammar outlined in § 4.3 to patterns of language change. This new approach has been referred to as Diachronic Construction Grammar (see Noël 2007), and some of its main exponents are Traugott and Trousdale (2013) and Hilpert (2013) who developed in parallel a framework and a methodology to account for language variation and change in a linguistic system formed by constructions. In what follows some of the main ideas outlined in their respective monographs will be summarized, as they set up the ground for the main research questions to be examined in the forthcoming chapters on the formation and subsequent development of the reaction object construction.

4.4.1 Defining constructional change

Traugott and Trousdale (2013) work under the assumptions that: (i) grammar itself is language-specific, (ii) "change is change in usage", and "the locus of change is the construct, an instance of use", and (iii) change is different from innovation: innovation is "a feature of an individual mind", whereas change "must have been replicated across populations of speakers resulting in conventionalization" (2013, 2). As seen in § 4.3.4 and § 4.3.5, assumptions (i) and (ii) are in line with the main tenets of constructionist approaches to grammar.

---

phenomena such as the ROC to make claims regarding their levels/degree of entrenchment is certainly more problematic and "hazardous" (Hilpert 2018; see also Sommerer and Smirnova 2020).

Contrary to other constructionist approaches to language change, Traugott and Trousdale (2013, 1) distinguish between two main types of change: (i) constructionalization, or the creation of a *new* form-meaning pairing; and (ii) constructional changes, or changes that affect features of an existing construction, and that do not necessarily involve the creation of a new form-meaning pairing. Examples of constructional changes involve *semantic changes* (*will-* 'intend' > future), *morphophonological changes* (*will* > *'ll*), *collocational constraints* (expansion of the *way*-construction to include verbs of manner and accompanying action, e.g. *whistle one's way home*), etc.

Within constructionalization, Traugott and Trousdale (2013) also distinguish between *lexical constructionalization* and *grammatical constructionalization* depending on whether the change results in the creation of a contentful 'lexical' new form-meaning pairing or of a procedural 'grammatical' new form-meaning pairing. In line with the gradient dimension of constructions (cf. Tab. 4.2 in § 4.3.1), it may also be the case that the output of this process is an intermediate or hybrid construction which is partly contentful and partly procedural.

An example of lexical constructionalization can be found in the history of the PDE word *cupboard*. This word has undergone semantic and morphological changes that resulted in a new contentful form-meaning pairing. The word originally referred to a piece of wood on which cups were displayed, while now it indicates a closed storage area in a home. As far as form is concerned, this lexical item originally involved two independent words, and now is a compound word that combines the two.

A clear example of grammatical constructionalization is found in the development of English binominal partitives into grammatical quantifiers. For instance, the binominal partitive *a lot of a N* (substitutable by *a unit/piece/share of N*) in example (23) has come to convey in the nineteenth century a quantifier meaning (see 24). There *a lot of* is substitutable by *much* or *many*, that is, it now functions as a modifier as a result of the *neoanalysis* of the head relationship in the original binominal partitive.

(23) ME **binominal partitive** *a lot of a N*
He ne wass nohht wurrþenn mann..Forr to forrwerrpenn ***aniȝ lott Off Moysæsess lare***.

he NEG was nothing become man… for to overthrow any part of Moses' teaching.
'He (Jesus) did not become incarnate … to overthrow any part of Moses' teaching.
(c.1200 *Ormulum*, 15186; [MED, s.v. *lot*, n. (1) 2 (c)]; Traugott and Trousdale 2013, 23)

(24) Nineteenth century **grammatical quantifier** *a lot of a N*
Learning at bottom, physic at top!
Lots of business, ***lots of*** fun,
Jacks of all trades, master of none!
(1833 Daniel, *Sworn at Highgate* [LION: English Prose Drama])

Finally, examples of hybrid constructions that are partly contentful and partly procedural are the *way*-construction and the *give + -ing* construction, the latter instantiated by constructs such as *give someone a kicking* or *give someone a talking to* (Trousdale 2008a, 2013). The *way*-construction involves the contentful element *way*, and with verbs of manner and accompanying action it implies iteration. As for the constructs *give someone a kicking* and *give someone a talking to*, these are partly contentful in that their meaning refers to a physical/verbal assault, but partly procedural in that they imply iteration and denote telic aspect.

Moving now on to constructional changes, or changes that affect one internal dimension of a construction, Traugott and Trousdale (2013, 27) distinguish between: (i) 'pre-constructionalization constructional changes', those changes that "precede and enable or 'feed' constructionalization", and (ii) 'post-constructionalization constructional changes', those further constructional changes that are fed by constructionalization. The former typically involve "expansion of pragmatics, semanticization of that pragmatics, mismatch between form and meaning, and some small distributional changes", whereas the latter typically "involve expansion of collocations, and may also involve morphological and phonological reduction". These can be clearly observed in the development of the grammatical quantifier *a lot of* discussed above, which once constructionalization had occurred expanded its range of collocates and underwent several phonological reductions (e.g. *alotta*, *a lotta*).

Hilpert's (2013) work on constructional change tackles many of the issues discussed by Traugott and Trousdale (2013) though using a slightly different terminology, and offering interesting insights on how corpus-linguistic methodologies can be applied to diachronic corpus data. Contrary to Traugott and Trousdale (2013), Hilpert (2013) does not establish a distinction between constructionalization and constructional change, but rather adopts a broad sense of the term "constructional change" which "operates on a single symbolic unit" (16), and may involve the emergence of a new form-meaning pairing (i.e. Traugott and Trousdale's constructionalization), changes in which a construction is "altered at its functional or at its formal pole" (17), cases in which a construction changes with regard to "any aspect of its frequency" (both text frequency and relative frequency), and/or cases in which a construction changes "its distribution across different groups of speakers or across different genres" (17).

It should be mentioned here that the two constructional approaches to language change just summarized benefit from insights on grammaticalization (Lehmann 1995, Hopper and Traugott 2003, Himmelmann 2004, Brinton and Traugott 2005). However, none of these approaches equate constructionalization and/or constructional change with grammaticalization. As is well known, this is commonly defined as "the process whereby lexical items and constructions [i.e. syntactic units] come in certain linguistic contexts to serve grammatical functions, and, once grammaticalized, continue to develop new grammatical functions" (Hopper and Traugott 2003, xv). More precisely, in Hilpert's work (2013, 8–9), constructional change involves changes that are characteristic of grammaticalization such as reanalysis, fixation, host-class expansion, and morphological and phonological reduction, but also some other types of changes not covered by grammaticalization such as lexicalization and frequency changes. Also, Hilpert's constructional change does not include some aspects of grammaticalization such as paradigmatization or "the tendency of grammaticalizing constructions to form paradigms or to become integrated into already existing paradigms" (Hilpert 2013, 11; Lehmann 1995). Tab. 4.3 aims to summarize these differences and correspondences.

Locus of change → Constructions		**Locus of change → Lexical and syntactic units**
Traugott and Trousdale (2013)	**Hilpert (2013)**	**Lehmann (1995), Hopper and Traugott (2003), Himmelmann (2004), and Brinton and Traugott (2005)**
Grammatical constructionalization creation of a form$_{new}$-meaning$_{new}$ pairing → grammatical 'procedural'		**Grammaticalization** (reanalysis, fixation, host-class expansion, morphophonologial reduction, etc.)
Lexical constructionalization creation of a form$_{new}$-meaning$_{new}$ pairing → lexical 'contentful'	**Constructional change**	
Constructional change changes in *meaning* and/or *form*		
+ frequency + distribution in the linguistic community		+ paradigmatization

Tab. 4.3: Constructionalization, constructional change(s) and grammaticalization

4.4.2 Dynamic network of constructions: Links, gains, losses and reconfigurations

In connection with the construction grammar idea that linguistic knowledge consists of a network of constructions shaped by language use (§ 4.3), Traugott and Trousdale (2013) explore in their monograph how this network of constructions grows, contracts and reconfigurates by means of constructional changes and cases of grammatical and lexical constructionalizations. Following Goldberg (1995, 74–81), Traugott and Trousdale (2013), and also Hilpert (2019), distinguish several kinds of links among constructions which are relevant to understanding this dynamic network of constructions. These are: inheritance, polysemy, metaphorical extension, subpart and instance links.

Inheritance links represent taxonomic constraints and categorizations at varying levels of generality. These links, as defined by Goldberg (1995, 67), imply that "relations between constructions may be partially arbitrary but also partially predictable" (Traugott and Trousdale 2013, 61). An example of an inheritance link is the one represented in Fig. 4.2 in § 4.3.3 above with the P N construction (e.g. *She was in prison*, *She was in school*, etc.) and the more general PP construction (e.g. *She went to the big bed*).

The second in the list is the polysemy link. This is a type of semantic relation that connects "the prototypical sense of a construction and its extensions" (Traugott and Trousdale 2013, 59). The linked constructions show the same syntax but slightly different semantics. Goldberg (1995, 75–77) illustrates the polysemy link with the ditransitive construction, and the caused motion construction. The ditransitive construction, for instance, has the syntax [SUBJ V OBJ_1 OBJ_2], the central sense [X CAUSES Y to RECEIVE Z], and the semantic extensions specified in (25) (Goldberg 1995, 38). Though considerably less numerous, the *way*-construction and the ROC also involve a number of polysemy links (for the *way*-construction see Goldberg 1995, Israel 1996, Perek 2015b, 2016a, 2018). These polysemy links will be referred to as frames/subsenses/interpretations/subschemas in Chapters 5, 6 and 7.

(25) **The polysemy links of the ditransitive construction**
A. **'X CAUSES Y to RECEIVE Z'** (central sense)
Example: Joe gave Sally the ball.
B. **Conditions of satisfaction imply 'X CAUSES Y to RECEIVE Z'**
Example: Joe promised Bob a car.
C. **'X CAUSES Y not to RECEIVE Z'** (blocked transfers)
Example: Joe refused Bob a cookie.
D. **'X ACTS to CAUSE Y to RECEIVE Z at some future point in time'** (future transfers)
Example: Joe bequeathed Bob a fortune.
E. **'X ENABLES Y TO RECEIVE Z'** (enabled transfers)
Example: Joe permitted Chris an apple.
F. **'X INTENDS to CAUSE Y to RECEIVE Z'**
Example: Joe baked Bob a cake.

A third type is one in which there is a metaphorical mapping involved. For instance, the resultative construction as in *She drove him to distraction* is related to the caused motion construction as in *She drove him to Detroit* via a metaphorical link in that a change of state (e.g. *distraction*) can be metaphorically interpreted as a change of location. This has been previously mentioned in § 4.3.3 above, and is shown again here in examples (26) and (27) with the resultative construction *Joe kicked Bob* black and blue, and the caused motion construction *Joe kicked the bottle* into the yard. Also, the ditransitive construction (e.g. *Joe gave Sally the ball*) is related to the communicative construction (e.g. *She wired Jo a message* or *Pat faxed Bill the letter*) just in the same way, with information interpreted as a type of transfer travelling from speaker to hearer (Goldberg 1995, 131; and Reddy 1979).

(26) Joe kicked Bob black and blue. (Resultative construction)

(27) Joe kicked the bottle into the yard. (Caused motion construction)

Another type of relation mentioned by Goldberg (1995) is the instance link which connects structures in which "a particular construction is a *special case* of another construction" (Goldberg 1995, 79; emphasis in the original). A clear example is the verb *drive* when used in the resultative construction where this verb can only occur with a limited set of nouns involving negative or idiomatic semantics (e.g. *drive someone* crazy, nuts, or up the wall).

The last type is the so-called subpart link which relates constructions, one of which is larger and exists independently from the other, smaller one. For instance, in § 4.3.3, I mentioned the intransitive and transitive versions of the resultative construction (e.g. *The nut broke apart* and *She broke the nut apart*). Another example can be found in the intransitive motion construction in relation to the transitive/caused motion construction in examples (28) and (29) from Traugott and Trousdale (2013, 60).

(28) The toddler walked to the door.

(29) She walked the toddler to the door.

Particularly relevant in this last type of relation is the concept of 'multiple inheritance' (see Petré 2012, De Smet, Ghesquière, and Van de Velde 2013, Hilpert 2019), which occurs when a construction inherits features from several constructions. This term is usually applied to intermediate or hybrid constructions like the gerund which inherits features from nouns and verbs (e.g. *having* in *We were talking about Mary's* having *a beautiful garden*, where *having* takes a subject in the possessive case but governs an object), or the *give + -ing* construction instantiated by *give someone a kicking* or *give someone a talking to*, which inherits features from the ditransitive construction, the composite predicate construction (as in *Bob gave John a kick*) and the *-ing* construction (Trousdale 2008a, 508; Trousdale 2013). As we shall see in § 5.1.2, the ROC also qualifies as a syntactic amalgam or multiple inheritance construction in that it seems to inherit features from several well-established constructions.

Before concluding this section, it should be mentioned here that in this highly interconnected network of constructions, the links among constructions may break due to the marginalization or obsolescence of particular constructions or subschemas, some new links may arise when grammatical or lexical constructionalization occurs, and some links within the network may be reconfigurated. Examples of gains within the network are the development of the modal auxiliary schema which did not exist in OE (e.g. *could*, *might*, *should*, *can*, *may* and *shall*), and the gradual constructionalization of the *way*-construction, which I briefly mentioned earlier in Chapter 3 (§ 3.2.1.2) and I will discuss further in Chapter 5 because of its close connection with the ROC.

An example of a radical loss within the network is the demise of the OE and ME impersonal construction, which in the literature is usually understood as one lacking a nominative NP argument and having a verb inflected for the third person singular (Méndez-Naya and López-Couso 1997; see also Trousdale 2008b, 305), as in ME <u>*me*</u> *liketh* '[it] pleases me' > ModE <u>*I*</u> *like*. As can be seen in the example just mentioned, impersonal constructions prototypically involve experiencer verbs. In the transition from ME to EModE, structures of this kind fell gradually into disuse as speakers of English came to increasingly code object experiencers by means of transitive constructions with experiencer subjects, as in *I like all this teaching in every way* (see (30) in opposition to (31); see also Traugott and Trousdale 2013, 69–70)).

(30) ME Al this sentence <u>me</u> **liketh** euery del.
NOM-Source **DAT-Exp**
((c1395) Chaucer *CT.WB.*(Manly-Rickert) D.162; MED, s.v. *everi-dēl*, n. & adv.)
PDE All this teaching <u>me</u> **likes** ('pleases') in every way.

(31) PDE <u>I</u> **like** all this teaching in every way.

Finally, a case of reconfiguration of links has been attested in the long history of the ditransitive construction. Rohdenburg (1995, 2007) observes that the ditransitive construction has lost the subschemas formed by verbs of banishment (e.g. *banish*, *dismiss*, *expel*) and dispossession (e.g. *bereave*, *rob* and *deprive*) as well as the subschema formed by verbs denoting "directive" acts (e.g. *command*), and concludes that the verb types associated with the present-day ditransitive construction have been reduced to verbs of giving and related verb classes.

In a more recent study, Colleman and De Clerck (2011) confirm Rohdenburg's (1995, 2007) observations on the basis of LModE data (*Corpus of Late Modern English Texts*; CLMET; De Smet 2005). The authors argue for a process of *semantic specialization* of the ditransitive construction, mainly because there are no important uses of the construction in PDE which were not present in the eighteenth century (the exception is the class of verbs of instrument of communication such as *fax*, *e-mail*, *radio*, *cable*, etc.), and important uses of the eighteenth century ditransitive construction have disappeared or been radically reduced in PDE. These obsolete, marginalized subschemas of the ditransitive construction Colleman and De Clerk (2011) refer to involve: (a) Rohdenburg's verbs of banishment such as *discharge*, *dismiss*, *expel*, *forbid* and *banish*; (b) verbs of pure benefaction, that is, verbs that do not involve a subsequent transfer of possession and in which there is no intended recipient of an object which is created or obtained for their sake (examples of such verbs are *hold*, *flower* and *vote*); (c) verbs of manner of speaking or communication verbs (this class includes Rodhdenburg's verbs denoting "directive" acts) such as *shout*, *whisper*, *mumble*, etc. (for PDE negative evidence see Stefanowitsch 2006); and (d) verbs concerned with feelings and attitudes such as *envy*, *forgive* and *intend*, which are on their way to disappearing (see statistical evidence provided by Colleman and De Clerck 2008). Some specific examples of these four marginalized uses of the PDE ditransitive (Colleman and De Clerck 2011, 193–201) are provided in (32)-(35).[30]

30 The third marginalized subschema mentioned by Rohdenburg is formed by verbs of dispossession such as *bereave*, *rob* and *deprive*. This subschema was already quite rare at the beginning of the LModE period, hence relevant examples are absent from Colleman and De Clerck's (2011) eighteenth century data. More recently, Zehentner (2019) shows that the spread of the *to*-NP paraphrase during

(32) **Verbs of banishment** (e.g. *discharge, dismiss, expel, forbid* and *banish*)
I will put it entirely into your power to **discharge** her the house, if you think proper. (Richardson 1740)

(33) **Verbs of pure benefaction** (e.g. *hold, flower* and *vote*)
. . . so snatching out his pocket-book, and the young Benedictine **holding** him the torch as he wrote, he set it down as a new prop to his system of Christian names. (Sterne 1767)

(34) **Verbs of manner of speaking or communication verbs** (e.g. *shout, whisper, mumble*)
At her departure she took occasion to **whisper** me her opinion of the widow, whom se called a pretty idiot. (Fielding 1751)

(35) **Verbs concerned with feelings and attitudes** (e.g. *envy, forgive* and *intend*)
And I did not in haste **intend** you the mortification of being undeceived. (Richardson 1740)

4.5 Concluding remarks

This chapter shows how Construction Grammar, as a theory of linguistic knowledge that considers language as an "integral part of cognition" (Taylor 2002, 8), emerged to account for idiosyncratic linguistic expressions that generative grammarians had relegated to the lexicon, as they were not considered to be part of the 'grammar' of a language. In particular, attention has been paid (i) to the main tenets of constructionist approaches to linguistic knowledge – linguistic knowledge is similar to other cognitive abilities and consists of a network of stored form-meaning pairings shaped by language use –; and (ii) to how

---

ME played a significant role in the marginalization of nonprototypical uses of the ditransitive construction – or uses which had resulted from the erosion of the case marking system – such as the dispossession one.

language variation and change can be understood and explained from the perspective of Construction Grammar (Hilpert 2013, Traugott and Trousdale 2013). Though the two approaches that have been discussed here have benefitted from insights from grammaticalization and lexicalization theory, they consider the construction as the locus of change, and propose a battery of concepts and a terminology to account for constructions on their various dimensions.

Like the constructions mentioned at the end of this chapter (i.e. the *way*-construction, the impersonal (experiencer) construction, and the ditransitive construction), the reaction object construction is a constructional idiom (Kogusuri 2011) or form-meaning pairing (Martínez-Vázquez 2010, Bouso 2012, Martínez-Vázquez 2014a, 2015). As such it is part of the English dynamic network of constructions and consequently subject to the properties and changes characteristic of this network: emergence, marginalization, obsolescence, and reconfiguration. Thus, aspects of the ROC that deserve investigation from the perspective of Diachronic Construction Grammar, and which will be addressed in Part II are the following: (i) *how* does the ROC relate to other constructions within the English network?, (ii) *when* does the ROC emerge, in other words, when does the ROC undergo constructionalization and becomes a new form-meaning pairing with its own morphosyntactic and semantic constraints?; and (iii) *how* and *why* does it develop?, more precisely, what constructional changes (i.e. changes in form and/or function, in frequency and distribution) can be identified in its development? which of them qualify as pre- and post-constructionalization constructional changes?, and finally, what mechanisms of change (e.g. neoanalysis/reanalysis, analogization/analogy, coercion, metaphor, etc.) have played a role in its development?

PART II
Hands-On with Data: A Usage-Based Approach to the History of the ROC

5. The formation of ROCs

As repeatedly noted, ROCs have not been the subject of investigation until quite recently, a lack of attention which is partly justified by the fact that this type of structure cannot be easily explained under a modular theory of linguistic knowledge such as Generative Grammar and its various offshoots (see Ross 1970a). With the emergence of Construction Grammar (Lakoff 1987, Fillmore, Kay, and O'Connor 1988), and most specially following Goldberg's major publications in the field (1995, 2006), a number of idiosyncratic structures, including the reaction object construction, were brought to the fore and became an object of attention. They served as a major motivation for the continued development of the theory (see Goldberg 1995, 10) and demonstrated its utility to account for aspects of the grammar that had previously been neglected. It is therefore the aim of this chapter and the following ones to delve into the reaction object construction from the perspective of Construction Grammar, and to offer a detailed synchronic and historical analysis that provides tentative answers to the research questions presented at the end of the preceding chapter: (i) how does the ROC relate to other constructions within the network of English constructions? (§ 5.1), (ii) when does the ROC emerge? (§ 5.2), and (iii) how and why does it develop? This last research question will be the concern mainly of Chapters 6 and 7.

5.1 Characterization of the ROC

5.1.1 The modern reaction object construction: An overview

Examples of the modern reaction object construction, some of which were adduced already in Chapter 3 above, include the following:

(1) Pauline smiled her thanks. (Levin 1993, 98)

(2) Linda winked her agreement. (Levin 1993, 220)

(3) Paul kissed her$_{REC}$ (a) goodbye. (Martínez-Vázquez 2010, 559; with slight modifications)

(4) She mumbled her adoration. (Levin 1993, 98)

(5) The audience roared their approval. (Martínez-Vázquez 2014a, 176)

(6) The door jingled a welcome. (Martínez-Vázquez 2010, 555)

(7) Pigs squeal emphatic disapproval. (OED, s.v. *squeal*, v. 4; with slight modifications)

(8) I honk good-bye to Charles and Faye. (Martínez-Vázquez 2010, 555)

In each of the examples in (1)-(8), the event structure of the verb undergoes a process of argument augmentation taking on the extended sense "express/communicate/signal a reaction or an attitude while/by V-ing". For instance, in (1) Pauline expressed/communicated her thanks by smiling, and in (6) the door expressed/signalled a welcome by jingling. This process of argument augmentation is attested in other related constructions that also allow paraphrases "in which the base verb of the sentence is no longer the main verb" (Levin and Rapoport 1988, 280).[31] Examples of such related constructions have been mentioned in the introduction and they include the aspectual cognate object construction (see example (19) there), the *way*-construction (example (23)), and the causative property resultative construction (example (13) also in that chapter).

The modern reaction object construction can be described as a construction in its own right in the traditional Goldbergian sense:

31 Under a lexico-semantic perspective, this process of argument augmentation has been referred to as 'lexical subordination' (Levin and Rapoport 1988). From a typological point of view, Talmy (1985, 2000) speaks of a process of conflation by which a verb lexicalizes a number of components of meaning. Given the constructionist approach adopted here we will refer to processes of argument augmentation. Other related terminology used in the literature to refer to similar processes are: 'syntactic condensation' (Martínez-Vázquez 2015, 151), and 'fusion' (Gross 1981, 45–48).

> C is a CONSTRUCTION iff_{def} C is a form-meaning pair <F_i, S_i> such that some aspect of F_i or some aspect of S_i is not strictly predictable from C's component parts or from other previously established constructions. (Goldberg 1995, 4)

This is evidenced by (i) its unusual syntax/argument structure consisting of SUBJ_i, an (INTR) V, an optional indirect object, and a (POSS)_i OBJ (expressive message), (ii) its lack of compositionality as the meaning of the construction X_i EXPRESS [Y_i BY V] is not strictly predictable from the component parts of the construction: the verbs involved in the construction do not have an expressive/communicative meaning as their core sense, and the argument structure that these verbs can be expected to have on the basis of their core meaning does not include an object participant, and (iii) its productivity, as the construction occurs with a considerable number of predicates in PDE (Martínez-Vázquez 2014a, 184). According to Fillmore et al.'s (1988) typology of idioms described in § 4.2.1, the ROC qualifies as:

(a) Grammatical: it is semantically irregular but parsable.
(b) Encoding: it does not represent the most natural way of expressing the meaning intended.
(c) Formal: a part of the ROC can be filled by the range of expressions syntactically and semantically appropriate for the slot.

In the terminology of the founder of Cognitive Grammar (Langacker 1987), the ROC can also be described as a *skewing construction*, "because, by its very nature, the construction induces a discrepancy between the meanings of the verb and of the composite expression" (Langacker 2009, 256–257). This discrepancy in the ROC is between the process the verb designates (intransitive) and the type of process (transitive, and encoding a communicative/expressive act) profiled by the clause as a whole. A common label used in the literature to refer to this kind of discrepancy is *coercion*, which as we shall see in greater detail in Chapter 7 is one of the mechanisms at play in the development of the ROC: "[i]f a lexical item is semantically incompatible with its morphosyntactic context, the meaning of the lexical item conforms to the meaning of the structure in which it is embedded" (Michaelis 2004, 25).

In a more precise way, the ROC can be defined as a *valency-increasing argument structure construction* which expresses an attitude or emotion of the subject through a nonprototypical type of object that *results* from the action denoted by the verb. This consideration of the ROC implies that instances where the object is preceded by a definite article like *He roared the command* (Huddleston and Pullum et al. 2002, 305) are not generally considered as pertaining to the ROC (see Kogusuri 2009b, 35fn2; and Martínez-Vázquez 2014a; cf. also Tab. 3.9 in Chapter 3 and comments therein). The object here despite being emotional "has a generic reference" (Martínez-Vázquez 2014a, 175) and consequently it does not necessarily express an attitude of the subject.

Typical verbs involved in the ROC are the intransitive manner of speaking verbs *mumble* and *mutter*, and the verbs of gestures and signs *smile*, *wink* and *kiss*, some of which most naturally occur in a ditransitive pattern (e.g. *Paul kissed her a goodbye*). Verbs of sounds, which are also essentially intransitive (Levin and Song 1997), have also been shown to occur in the modern reaction object construction, these being used metonymically as manner of speaking verbs as in *The audience roared their approval* (example (5) above), metaphorically with inanimate subjects, as the verb *jingle* in *The door jingled a welcome* (example (6)), or simply as verbs of animal sounds describing the emotions of animals as in the *The pigs squeal emphatic disapproval* (see example (7)). As revealed by Martínez-Vázquez (2014a and elsewhere) the array of predicates involved in the construction in PDE is diverse; from the results adduced in her research these verbs seem to be mostly restricted to the following verb classes: manner of speaking verbs, verbs of sounds, verbs of gestures and signs, verbs of bodily processes (verbs of inhalation, substance emission, etc.) and verbs of light emission (see Levin 1993 for exhaustive lists of these verb classes).

As for the reaction object itself, this has been defined by Felser and Wanner (2001) as consisting of "abstract nouns, expressing an attitude which can be made visible by the action denoted by the verb" (117). More recently, Martínez-Vázquez (2015) further refined Felser and Wanner's definition by characterizing reaction objects as "expressive speech acts resulting from a gesture or sound performed by the subject of the construction, who expresses a mental state towards an antecedent event" (152). Although not syntactically licensed by the verb, the reaction object in some cases matches so well the verb's semantics that becomes highly redundant (Martínez-Vázquez 1998; see also Felser and Wanner 2001; Martínez-Vázquez 2010; and Kogusuri 2009b and elsewhere). For instance, the act of nodding, defined as the act of making "a brief inclination of the head, esp. in salutation, assent, or command (. . .)" (cf. OED, s.v. *nod*, v. 1. a.) mostly occurs in PDE with reaction objects describing assent or understanding: *nod assent*, *approval*, or *agreement* (see Martínez-Vázquez 2015, 148). This semantic feature of some reaction objects makes them semantically similar to cognate objects as these are "etymologically and semantically related to the verb" (Visser 1963–1973: I, § 422: 413; cf. § 3.2.1.1). Note however that the verb *nod* may also be accompanied by other reaction objects that do not match its meaning so well but are still pragmatically compatible with it. In example (9), for instance, the reaction object *surrender* is not related at all to the core meaning of the verb *nod*.

(9) With a resigned droop of her shoulders, Cardenas **nodded** her surrender.

(COCA, 2001, FIC, Analog; Martínez-Vázquez 2015, 149)

On top of all these features, Martínez-Vázquez (2015) importantly argues that reaction objects can be treated as nominalized expressive acts "involving a recategorized component" (147), that is, that the recategorized component is a communicative act converted into a nominal (152). Based on extensive data from COCA, she proposes a useful three-fold classification of reaction objects on the basis of their derivational status and their morphosyntactic properties, namely delocutive nouns, deverbal illocutionary nouns, and predicative expressive nouns. In what follows each type will be described and illustrated with my own data from the LModE period as extracted from the *Corpus of Late Modern English Texts, version 3.0* (CLMET3.0; De Smet, Diller, and Tyrkkö 2011).

As its very name indicates, delocutive reaction objects derive from locutions, that is, "independent utterances associated with specific conventional situations" (Martínez-Vázquez 2015, 153).[32] Some instances

32 The label 'delocutive noun' for this type of nominalization is adopted by Martínez-Vázquez from Benveniste (1966 [1958], 277).

of delocutive nouns are given in (10) and (11), where the conventional independent utterances *Welcome!* and *Adieu!* have been recategorized as NPs in the reaction object construction. In connection with this, note that two different categories of conventional independent expressions have been distinguished in the literature: interjections (e.g. *wow!*), and routines or formulae (e.g. *thank you*). The main difference between these is that interjections are "*spontaneous* immediate *responses* to situations" (Ameka 1992, 109; emphasis mine), whereas routines or formulae are "*intentional and (socially) expected reactions* to situations" (Ameka 1992, 109; emphasis mine). Following Ameka's definition, the reaction objects *welcome* and *adieu* in (10) and (11) would be regarded as routines or formulae as they are not spontaneous but rather intentional and somehow expected in the context in which they occur. Another difference between formulae and interjections is that formulae "may have addressees" (see example (10) where the addressee is Mr Haredale; and example (11) where the addressee is Rebecca's husband), whereas interjections "are not addressed to specific people" as evinced, for instance, in example (12) (Martínez-Vázquez 2015, 153; see also Ameka 2012).

(10) 'Haredale, my dear fellow, I am extremely glad to see you. How very much you have improved in your appearance since our last meeting! I never saw you looking better. HOW do you do?' Mr Haredale$_{REC}$ turned his eyes towards the casement whence the voice proceeded, though there was no need to do so, to recognise the speaker, and Mr Chester waved his hand, and **smiled** a courteous welcome.

CLMET3.0 1841, Dickens; *Barnaby Rudge*

(11) And Rebecca, as we have said, wisely determined not to give way to unavailing sentimentality on her husband's departure. She **waved** him$_{REC}$ an adieu from the window, and stood there for a moment looking out after he was gone.

CLMET3.0 1847–48, Thackeray; *Vanity Fair*

(12) I felt sick with the idea. But the next moment I **was shouting** hurrah! they are all right, thank goodness, they were saved.

CLMET3.0 1855, Baker; *Eight Years' Wanderings in Ceylon*

The second type of reaction object identified by Martínez-Vázquez is that of deverbal illocutionary nouns. These derive from speech act verbs, that is, verbs that express or manifest *mental states* of certain psychological modes (Vanderveken 1990, 117) such as assertives (e.g. *assert* and *suggest*), commissives (e.g. *commit* and *promise*), directives (e.g. *warn* and *advise*), declaratives (e.g. *declare* and *disclaim*), and expressives (e.g. *approve* and *praise*).[33] As explained by Vanderveken (1990, 213), expressive speech act verbs, also known as expressive illocutionary verbs, like those in (13), "express (...) mental states of the speaker such as joy, approbation or discontent". Though all reaction objects express mental states by definition, contrary to delocutive nouns, and predicative expressive nouns (the third reaction object type), deverbal illocutionary nouns commit the speaker to a particular decision or statement.[34]

(13) *approve, compliment, praise, laud, extol, plaudit, applaud, acclaim, brag, boast, complain, disapprove, blame, reprove, deplore, protest, grieve, mourn, lament, rejoice, cheer, boo, condole, congratulate, thank, apologize, greet* and *welcome.*

Clear examples of deverbal nouns in my own material are for instance *acquiescence* and *assent* in examples (14) and (15), which derive from the expressive illocutionary verbs *acquiesce* and *assent.* Taking these examples as prototypical of this category we can describe the main features of deverbal illocutionary nouns as follows:

---

33 For an analysis and extensive lists of English speech act verbs see Wierzbicka (1987) and Vanderveken (1990).

34 Note here that mental states can be manifested *verbally*, for instance, by means of expressive illocutionary verbs such as *approve* and *praise*, and *nonverbally* as in the case of many ROCs involving nonverbal communication verbs where human beings can "express their happiness by smiling and laughing, and their sadness by crying" (Vanderveken 1990, 213; cf. § 6.3.1.2). This is the reason why Martínez-Vázquez (2015, 152) decides to leave out the label 'illocutionary', and refer instead to reaction objects in general, simply as *nominalized expressive acts* or *expressive nominals.* Cf. OED, s.v. *illocution*, v. (1955) "*Philos.* An act such as ordering, warning, undertaking, performed in **saying** something" (emphasis mine).

(i) Deverbal illocutionary nouns describe individual acts performed by the subject of the construction (Martínez-Vázquez 2015, 159). Thus, in example (14), the Chief Justice smiled and *acquiesced*, and in (15) Tristram nodded and *assented*.
(ii) These individual acts result from the event denoted by the verb (Martínez-Vázquez 2015, 159), for instance, the act of *acquiescence* in (14) results from the event of *smiling*, and the individual act of *assent* in (15) results from the event of *nodding*.
(iii) These acts are addressee-oriented and "they are interpreted as a decision or declaration made by the speaker, or expresser, in response to a previous situation" (Martínez-Vázquez 2015, 154). In (14) the Chief Justice's act of *acquiescence* is addressed to the Englishman and refers anaphorically to the Englishman's request that the Chief Justice arrest a man who had cheated him; in (15) Tristram's declaration of *assent* is a response to Herne's order "Proceed to the cave... and remain there till I join you".

(14) I knew an Englishman$_{REC}$, who went to the Chief Justice (he told me, that not then understanding the ways of the place, he trembled as he entered the room), and said, "Sir, I have come to offer you two hundred (paper) dollars (value about five pounds sterling) if you will arrest before a certain time a man who has cheated me. I know it is against the law, but my lawyer (naming him) recommended me to take this step." The Chief Justice **smiled** acquiescence, thanked him, and the man before night was safe in prison.

CLMET3.0 1839, Darwin; *The Voyage of the Beagle*

(15) "You must go, girl," cried Tristram angrily. "I will not leave you to Henry's lawless passion." Meanwhile, Herne had passed into one of the large embrasures, and opened, by means of a spring, an entrance to a secret staircase in the wall. He then beckoned Tristram towards him, and whispered some instructions in his ear. "I understand," replied the old man. "Proceed to the cave," cried Herne$_{REC}$, "and remain there till I join you." Tristram **nodded** assent. "Come, Mabel!" he cried, advancing towards her, and seizing her hand. "Away!" cried Herne in a menacing tone.

CLMET3.0 1843, Ainsworth; *Windsor Castle*

The third and final type of reaction objects identified by Martínez-Vázquez (2015) are predicative expressive nouns that describe a "state of mind or feeling of the subject" (Martínez-Vázquez 2015, 160) which "is perceived as a [transitory] *reaction* to a contextual element" (160; emphasis mine). Contrary to deverbal illocutionary nouns, which describe acts, predicative expressive nouns "denote the *result of a process* undergone by the *expresser*" (2015, 161; emphasis mine). For instance, the subjects in (16), (17) and (18) *become* discontent, disdainful and dissatisfied, respectively. Semantically, predicative expressive nouns can be classified into positive or negative (Martínez-Vázquez 2015, 161): examples of the former would be *delight*, *joy* and *satisfaction*; of the latter nouns like *discontent* and *disdain* among others.

Also worthy of note is that ROCs involving predicative expressive nouns mostly "denote *solitary* situations, where an expresser releases a strong or repressed feeling" (Martínez-Vázquez 2015, 161–162; emphasis mine).[35] This explains the almost complete absence of overt recipients (i.e. indirect objects) in ROCs involving predicative expressive nouns in my LModE data (examples (16)-(18)) and in the PDE examples provided by Martínez-Vázquez (2015) (examples (19)-(20)). As shown in (21)-(23), the insertion of a recipient in the form of an NP or a PP in these examples results in odd sentences, whereas the insertion of a *goal* or a *stimulus* in the form of a PP is grammatically possible as shown in (19) and (20) from COCA.

(16) Dumouriez, conquering Holland, **growls** ominous discontent, at the head of Armies.

CLMET3.0 1837, Carlyle; *The French Revolution*

(17) I heard them [the poor animals] **snort** disdain; and I saw them lift the hoof against the very benefactor, who put on their shoes, and gave the vigour to kick.

CLMET3.0 1779, Pratt; *Shenstone-Green*

35 This means that this reaction object is associated to the transitive use of the ROC described later on in § 5.1.2, in which there are no *intended* recipients; instead, the expressers themselves – and if present the people surrounding these expressers – become *accidentally* the recipients of their own expressed emotions.

(18) Pitt, who is well, is married, is dissatisfied--not with his bride, but with the Duke of Newcastle; has twice **thundered out** his dissatisfaction in Parliament, and was seconded by Fox.

CLMET3.0 1735–69, Walpole; *Letters*

(19) Mistress Grofe sat at her end of the table and **glared** her anger at all of us_{GOAL}.

(COCA, 1990, FIC, BkSF:LensWorld; Martínez-Vázquez 2015, 160)

(20) Max **chuckled** his delight at her $\text{ingenuity}_{\text{STIMULUS}}$.

(COCA, 1991, FIC, BkSF:RobinHood; Martínez-Vázquez 2015, 161)

(21) a. *Dumouriez **growls** them_{REC} ominous discontent.
b. *Domuriez **growls** ominous discontent to them_{REC}.

(22) a. *I heard them **snort** me_{REC} disdain.
b. *I heard them **snort** disdain to me_{REC}.

(23) a. *Pitt has **thundered out** them_{REC} his dissatisfaction in Parliament.
b. *Pitt has **thundered out** his dissatisfaction in Parliament to them_{REC}.

The three types of reaction objects just described differ mainly with regard to their morphosyntactic properties: delocutive nouns "are derived from locutions" (Martínez-Vázquez 2015, 153), deverbal nouns are derived from speech act verbs – particularly expressive illocutionary verbs such as *assent* and *approve* –, and predicative expressive nouns exhibit adjectival features, in that these nouns describe "a state of mind or feeling of the subject" (160) rather than describe actions.

However, as Martínez-Vázquez (2015) herself recognizes, the boundary between these three types of reaction objects is not as straightforward as it appears to be. This becomes clear in instances such as *She smiled a welcome*, where *welcome* can be interpreted as deriving from a formula (OED, s.v. *welcome*, n.[1], adj., int.), or from an expressive illocutionary verb (OED, s.v. *welcome*, v.[1]). Classifying them correctly is therefore no easy matter. In the case of *welcome*, as also in the case of *thanks* (OED, s.v. *thank*, v. and OED, s.v. *thank*, n.), the fact that both may occur in isolation and as quotes (e.g. *'Welcome', she said*) is one of the reasons that led Martínez-Vázquez (2015, 156–157) to ascribe them to the category of delocutive nouns, because neither deverbal illocutionary nouns (e.g. *acquiescence* or *assent*) nor predicative expressive nouns (e.g. *discontent*, *disdain* or *dissatisfaction*) can occur independently. Finally, it should also be noted that when delocutive nouns are partially integrated into the construction within quotation marks with manner of speaking verbs, as in *She murmured "thanks"*, the boundary between ROCs and less constrained communicative constructions involving verbs of saying such as *say* or *tell* followed by direct speech becomes somewhat blurred (Martínez-Vázquez 2014a, 183; see examples (24) and (25) from Martínez-Vázquez 2015, 155).

(24) He shouts «hello» and the echo responds «hello.» (COCA, 1992, ACAD, LatAmPopScult)

(25) Hannah murmured good-bye. (COCA, 2006, FIC, Bk: NightSins)

Turning now to the difference between deverbal illocutionary nouns and predicative expressive nouns, Martínez-Vázquez argues that although both object types designate mental states, they can be teased apart through the "doing" test, which is only possible with deverbal illocutionary nouns such as *acquiescence* in (26). This is so because, as previously mentioned, deverbal illocutionary nouns describe actions, whereas predicative expressive nouns, as in (27), describe the result of processes undergone by the expresser.

(26) <u>The Chief Justice</u> **smiled** <u>acquiescence</u>.
What did the Chief Justice do?
The Chief Justice acquiesced.

(27) <u>The philosophers</u> **muttered** <u>their sage contempt</u>.
What did the philosophers do?
*The philosophers contempted.

To conclude this overview of the features of reaction objects in PDE, a few comments are in order concerning two additional morphosyntactic features, namely, premodification by a possessive, and presence or absence of an indirect object within the clause. With respect to premodification by a possessive, as already noted, PDE reaction objects are often introduced by a possessive determiner that is coreferential with the subject of the construction. Since coreferentiality between the reaction object and the subject of the ROC is an intrinsic feature of the construction in PDE, the pattern with a possessive determiner could in principle be considered as the prototypical one for the construction. Yet the fact is that other alternatives can be found which are far more frequent than the pattern with a possessive, as will be seen when I present in Chapter 6 the data from CLMET3.0. But despite the absence of a possessive, these alternative patterns nevertheless imply a coreferential relation, as can be seen in (28)-(30). In (28) and (29), the reaction object is introduced by an indefinite article, but the reference to the clause subjects *Bruno* and *You* is clear. The same applies to (30), in which the reference of *approval* to *Henry* is contextually obvious despite the lack of any determiner.

Finally, it was noted earlier that the reaction object construction may also involve a recipient which is either retrievable from the context as shown in examples (10), (14) and (15) above, or formally specified by means of an NP or a PP headed by the prepositions *to* or *at*, as shown in (28), (29) and (30). Examples (10), (14) and (15) are instances of definite null complement constructions (Michaelis p.c. Bangor 2013; Fillmore 1986, Ruppenhofer and Michaelis 2010) in which the addressees are left uninstantiated but are easily retrievable from the context (e.g. Mr Haredale, the Englishman, and Herne, in examples (10), (14) and (15), respectively).

(28) Yes, once, just before I quite lost sight of them, Bruno half turned his head, and **nodded** me$_{REC}$ a saucy little good-bye over one shoulder.

CLMET3.0 1889, Carroll; *Silvye and Bruno*

(29) You **wave** an airy adieu to the boys$_{REC}$ on shore, light your biggest pipe, and swagger about the deck as if you were Captain Cook, Sir Francis Drake, and Christopher Columbus all rolled into one.

CLMET3.0 1889, Jerome; *Three Men in a Boat*

(30) "Do not appeal to me, Wolsey," said Henry, **smiling** approval at Anne$_{REC}$.

CLMET3.0 1889, Jerome; *Windsor Castle*

5.1.2 The reaction object construction in the network of English constructions

This section offers an overview of the different subtypes of ROC that can be identified today, and tries to show their connections with other constructions existing in the language: (i) the experiencer construction (*Bob likes Sue, I fear the messengers*); (ii) the ditransitive construction (*Joe gave Sally the ball*); (iii) the communicative construction (*She wired Joe a message*); and (iv) the large family of English resultative constructions. This last type is discussed in detail in Goldberg and Jackendoff (2004) and is formed by structures such as *Joe kicked Bob black and blue*, *She kissed him unconscious* or *The pond froze solid*, where the adjective phrases (*black and blue*, *unconscious* and *solid*) denote the state resulting from the action of the verbs.

The first subtype of ROC that I will consider comprises examples such as *They sigh out* *their thankful relief* (31), *The poor animals snort* *disdain* (32) and *The first train stood whistling* *its triumph* (33). As noted by Martínez-Vázquez (2010 and elsewhere), these ROCs exalt the release of a strong or repressed feeling via a gesture or a sound produced by a human being, as in (31), an animal (32), or an inanimate object, as in (33).

(31) She slept a natural sleep; and they stole about on tip-toe, and spoke low, and softly, and hardly dared to breathe, however much they longed to **sigh out** their thankful relief.

CLMET3.0 1848, Gaskell; *Mary Barton*

(32) The poor animals whom—to carry on the allusion—you had taken from the barren heath (where they were starving upon thistles) to place, of a sudden, in the luxuriant pasture, where the corn and grass came mantling to their chests—were turned too rapidly loose to become steady. They first grew fat, then indolent, next restive, and last vicious. I heard them **snort** disdain; and I saw them lift the hoof against the very benefactor, who put on their shoes, and gave the vigour to kick.

CLMET3.0 1779, Pratt; *Shenstone-Green*

(33) The first train had crawled over the new bridge, and stood **whistling** its triumph in the station.

CLMET3.0 1920, Bagnold; *The Happy Foreigner*

In such cases, the reaction object construction adjusts to the schematic representation [SUBJ$_i$ [V → [(POSS)$_i$ message] (OBL)] (Martínez-Vázquez 2014a, 185) and involves two participants: an experiencer subject or sentient agent, and an internal cause/source which is an emotion or mental state that leads the experiencer to assume a particular facial expression (see example (31)), or emit a particular sound (see examples (32) and (33)). In this sense, this first subtype of ROC turns out to be quite similar to the experiencer construction as in *Bob likes Sue* (Trousdale 2008b, 315). Both construction types have the surface structure of a transitive construction [SUBJ V OBJ] and, semantically, involve experiencers (i.e. sentient agents) and indicate a cause/source, which is *internal* in the case of the ROC, and *external* in the case of the experiencer construction. In Fig. 5.1, the internal cause of the ROC *I sighed relief* is the emotion or mental state of relief, whereas the external cause of the experiencer construction *Bob likes Sue* is *Sue* herself. It should be noted here that this subtype of ROC apart from the internal cause (emotion or mental state) that leads the experiencer to assume a facial expression or emit a particular sound, may additionally indicate the external cause that triggers such emotional state by means of a PP. This is what happens, for instance, in examples such as (19), *Mistress Grofe glared her anger* at all of us, and (20), *Max chuckled his delight* at her ingenuity.

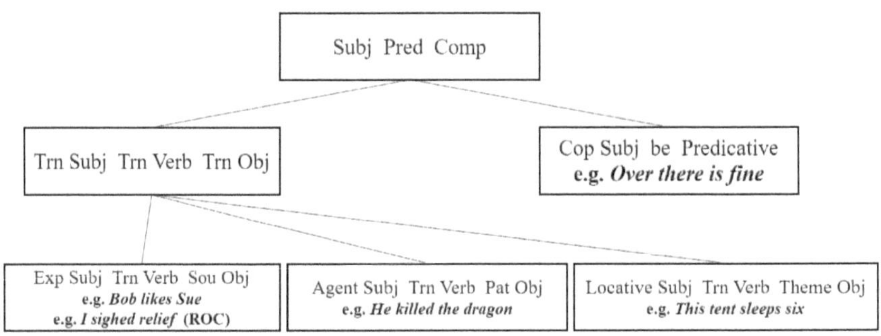

Fig. 5.1: A partial constructional taxonomy illustrating subjects and transitivity in ModE. Adapted from Trousdale (2008b, 315).

A second subtype of ROC, rather than highlighting the release of a strong feeling, foregrounds the transfer of an expressive message from an experiencer to a recipient. In such cases the ROC has three participants rather than two: an experiencer or sentient agent, a theme or emotional *response*, and an intended recipient, which is sometimes covert but easily retrievable from the context. Examples of this second subtype of ROC are *The Chief Justice smiled acquiescence* (at the Englishman) and *Tristram nodded assent* (at Herne); for the complete quotations see examples (14) and (15) above, respectively. This ROC pattern with an intended recipient accommodates to the syntactic structure [SUBJ$_i$ [V → **OBJ** [(POSS)$_i$ message] (OBL)] (Martínez-Vázquez 2014a, 185) and it shows clear similarities with the communicative construction as in *She wired Joe a message* (Martínez-Vázquez 2005, 84; see also Sams 2008, Boas 2010, Colleman and De Clerck 2011, De Clerck et al. 2011). First, the ROC and the communicative construction share the same surface structure, that of the more basic ditransitive construction [SUBJ OBJ1 OBJ2]; they also have similar semantics consisting of an agent (in the case of the ROC an experiencer or a sentient agent), a recipient, and a theme. Second, both the communicative construction and the ROC involve a metaphorical kind of transfer: a neutral message, or an expressive message in the case of the ROC, is viewed as "*traveling across* from the stimulus to the listener" (Goldberg 1995, 148; emphasis in the original).

Following Goldberg (1995), the communicative construction and the ditransitive reaction object construction subtype are related to the more general and basic ditransitive construction through a metaphorical link, by which communication – neutral or expressive – has been metaphorically interpreted as a kind of transfer (see also Rudzka-Ostyn 1988, Grady 1998, Martínez-Vázquez 2005 and elsewhere). Using Goldberg's formalisms (1995, 88 and 142), the metaphorical relationship between the ditransitive construction and the ditransitive ROC subtype can be represented as shown in Fig. 5.2. In each construction R stands for 'relation' – this referring to the type of relation between the verb and the construction –, and the dashed line indicates that the argument (in this case the recipient) is provided by the construction (Goldberg 1995, 51). Shaded in grey are those elements that distinguish the ditransitive reaction object construction from the more general

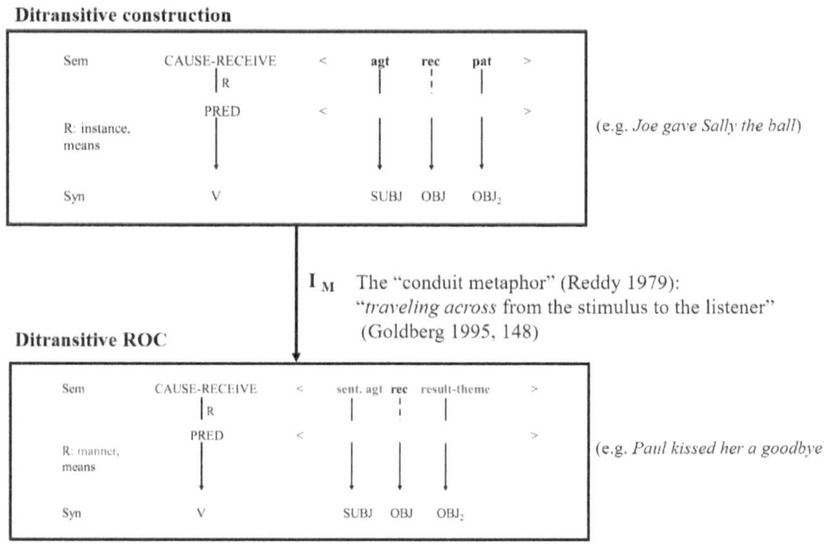

Fig. 5.2: Metaphorical relationship between the ditransitive construction and the ditransitive ROC

ditransitive construction (i.e. sent. agt. and result-theme). Note also that the semantic role of patient in the ditransitive construction could be better treated as a 'theme' or "argument which undergoes a change of state or location" (Ron Vaz 2003, 88fn6).

It should be noted here that the link between the ditransitive construction and a number of ROC ditransitive subschemas with manner of action verbs such as *nod* or *kiss* is not so obvious in PDE. These verb-specific subschemas of the ROC show a tendency to leave out the indefinite article that provides the reaction object with its unambiguous nominal status (Martínez-Vázquez 2015, 155). For instance, Martínez-Vázquez (2014a, 182) notes that constructs with a bare noun object like *nod yes*, *nod agreement* and *kiss good-bye* have, in PDE, "lexicalized into semi-fixed collocations". Interestingly, an informal search in Google Books n-grams shows that the construct with a bare noun (e.g. ***kissed*** *her*$_{REC}$ *Ø farewell*) is far more frequent nowadays than the more ditransitive-like construct ***kissed*** *her*$_{REC}$ *a farewell*, where the reaction object is a full NP.[36] Importantly, the lower frequency in PDE of ditransitive-like constructs for these ROC subschemas with gesture verbs links well with the ongoing semantic specialization or narrowing of the ditransitive construction, briefly summarized in § 4.4.2.[37] At the same time, the increasing frequency in PDE of these bare nouns might be interpreted as bringing this ROC subtype closer to the larger system of English resultatives. The *kiss* ROC subschema ***kissed*** *her*$_{REC}$ *Ø farewell* is clearly reminiscent of the *kiss* subschema of the resultative construction *She kissed him*$_{REC}$ *unconscious* (Goldberg 1995, 3): both constructions have a layer of resultative meaning and the difference between them lies in the grammatical status of the element that comes after the personal pronoun, which in the case of the resultative is an adjective and in the case of the ROC is a bare delocutive noun (OED, s.v. *farewell*, int., n. (and adj.) and adv.). This might serve therefore as further evidence that the relations between constructions (the ditransitive construction and the ROC, in this case) are subject to change (Traugott and Trousdale 2013, 16; § 4.4.2).

I turn now to a number of other important properties shared by the two subtypes of ROC discussed so far, that is, the monotransitive ROC subtype, which highlights the release of a strong or repressed feeling via a gesture or a sound, and the ditransitive ROC subtype, which foregrounds the transfer of an expressive message from an experiencer to a recipient. Both subtypes impose a number of *constraints*, or *requirements*, on the overall construction, as follows:

(i) An *expressive meaning*, which arises naturally from the construction and involves sentient agents or experiencers as subjects. This expressive meaning becomes perhaps more obvious in the monotransitive ROC subtype (*I sighed relief*), which is closer to the experiencer construction (*Bob likes Sue*, *I fear the messengers*) in form and meaning. As mentioned above, the monotransitive ROC subtype and the experiencer construction have the surface structure of

36 Search conducted in August 2020.

37 Historical examples of ditransitive-like constructs where the reaction object is headed by an indefinite article are shown in Tab. 3.1 in § 3.1.1.1.

a transitive construction [SUBJ V OBJ]; semantically, they involve *experiencers* (i.e. sentient agents) and indicate the *cause/source of a particular expression*, which as previously mentioned, is *internal* in the case of the ROC (*relief*), and *external* in the case of the experiencer construction (*Sue* and *messengers* in the examples just given).

(ii) An *animacy constraint*, as inanimates by definition cannot be experiencers/sentient agents. This constraint is sometimes solved via metonymy, personification and metaphor, as happens in cases like (6) and (33) above: *The door jingled a welcome*, and *The first train stood whistling its triumph*, where the door expresses/signals a welcome by jingling, and the first train expresses/signals its triumph by whistling, respectively.

(iii) A *coreferentiality constraint*, already discussed in § 3.2.1.3. In other words, the reaction object is coreferential with the subject of the construction; such coreferentiality is often marked by the presence of a possessive determiner (*They sigh out their relief*), but not necessarily (*John smiled approval*). This constraint blocks passivization, as shown in the ungrammatical examples **Her thanks were smiled by Rilla*, **Grateful thanks were smiled by Rilla* and **A cheerful welcome was beamed by Sandra*. However, as noted in § 3.2.1.3, the restrictions on passivization can be solved if the agent is backgrounded as in *Warm thanks were smiled at the audience* and *Final goodbyes were waved* (for further examples see Tab. 3.7).

(iv) An implication of *resultative* and *aspectual meaning*, as already briefly discussed in § 3.2.1.3. In this section, it was explained that reaction objects fulfil the criteria of *effected objects* (objects of result) all the way down. Among the several criteria mentioned there were (a) the resultative meaning of the reaction object (the reaction object is the result of the action denoted by the verb), and (b) its telic status, already identified by Martínez-Vázquez (2015, 160) (cf. § 3.2.1.3). The resultative meaning of reaction objects links this construction to the larger family of English resultative constructions. This comprises the causative property resultative construction (*He **wiped** the table clean*) and the *way*-construction (*She **giggled** her way up the stairs*), among many other subtypes (see Levin and Rapoport 1988, Levin and Song 1997, Goldberg and Jackendoff 2004). The link between the ROC and the family of resultative constructions becomes even more evident when we compare intransitive resultatives such as *The pond **froze** solid* (34) and ROCs involving predicative expressive nouns such as *disdain* in (35). In both cases the postverbal elements qualify as resultative predicative complements, where the pond becomes/gets solid and the poor animals become disdainful. To be more precise, resultative predicative complements are defined by Huddleston and Pullum et al. (2002, 251; emphasis mine) as follows: "[t]he resultative PC [predicative complement] typically occurs with verbs that denote a change of state. The PC denotes the state of the predicand argument *at the end of the process*."

(34) The pond **froze** solid.

(Goldberg and Jackendoff 2004, 536)

(35) The poor animals **snort** disdain.

(adapted from example (32), from CLMET3.0 1779, Pratt; *Shenstone-Green*)

(v) A *manner* and/or a *means interpretation*. Across languages, complex verbal events are often expressed preferably by means of two separate clauses; for instance, *John smiled, and thereby he expressed his approval*. But some languages, including English, have the ability to express and compress two separate events within a single clause. Among the best known examples of this process, which is usually referred to in the literature with Talmy's term *conflation* (Talmy 1985, 2000), are motion expressions such as *The knight clanked into the hall*, with the meaning 'the knight walked into the hall and his armour clanked as he walked' or *She crawled in our direction*, which conflates two separate conceptual events, one denoting the motion, and the other the means or manner of that motion: 'She moved in our direction', 'She did so by crawling' (for discussion see Fanego 2012, 2017; also Slobin 2006, and Sandford 2016 for manner of speaking verbs). In the same way, as has been made abundantly clear in this research, event conflation is a fundamental characteristic of the reaction object construction: *Max chuckled his delight at her ingenuity* is simply the conflation of the more extended sequence 'Max was delighted at her ingenuity and he expressed this by chuckling'. Importantly, it is precisely this requirement that ROCs must conflate a means or manner component which makes this construction fundamentally different from clauses with ordinary transitive communication verbs such as *announce* or *communicate*: *Jack announced his displeasure*, *Peter communicated his disapprobation*, etc. Despite closely resembling ROCs at the surface, such clauses are fully compositional, as shown by the fact that paraphrases with 'express X by V-ing' are unacceptable: *?Jack expressed his disapproval by announcing, ?Peter expressed his disapprobation by communicating*, etc.

In light of the previous discussion, I propose the schematic representation in (36) for the PDE ROC (see also Fig. 5.3 later on). This schematic representation is partly based on Traugott and Trousdale's (2013, 79) formalism for the *way*-construction, as given in (37), but with some adaptation to render the notation more perspicuous. This representation reflects the following properties of ROCs: the subject is an experiencer or sentient agent, as derived from the expressive meaning of the ROC as a whole; OBJ2, the reaction object proper, is an object of result which is coreferential with the subject; OBJ1 represents the recipient, which does not need to be always explicit, hence the notation in parentheses. Finally, V is an intransitive verb coding means or manner.

(36) **Syntax:** $SUBJ_i$ [$V_{INTRmanner/means}$ (OBJ1) $OBJ2_i$]. Where OBJ2 = $(POSS)_i$ NP
Semantics: 'Sentient $agent_i$ cause Y_i become expressed while/$by_{manner/means}$ doing V'

(37) [[SUBJ$_i$ [V POSS$_i$ *way*] DIR] ↔ ['SEM$_i$ traverse the path PP while/by doing V']][38]

Cf. Traugott and Trousdale (2013, 8 and 79)

The features represented in this schema reflect the hybrid nature of the ROC in PDE. As becomes evident from the various constraints discussed in this section, the ROC qualifies as a multiple inheritance construction, a syntactic amalgam that inherits features from, or shares features with: (i) the experiencer construction as in *Bob likes* Sue (Trousdale 2008b, 315) and *I fear* the messengers (van Gelderen 2014, 104); (ii) the resultative construction as in *Joe kicked Bob* black and blue, *She kissed him* unconscious and *The pond froze* solid, where the adjectives (i.e. *black and blue*, *unconscious* and *solid*) denote the state resulting from the action denoted by the verbs (Goldberg and Jackendoff 2004); and (iii) the ditransitive and communicative constructions, as in *Joe gave Sally the ball* and *She wired Jo a message* (Goldberg 1995, 3, 50, 127–128 and 148). This proposed hybrid nature of the ROC is explicitly illustrated in Fig. 5.3, where I use Goldberg's formalisms to indicate the specific features shared by the ROC with each of the other three constructions, namely the sentient agent with the experiencer construction, the resultative meaning with the resultative construction and the communicative meaning with the ditransitive construction. Space reasons impede us here to keep on exploring further the hybrid nature of the ROC. This will be left for future research alongside the issue of whether there exist other constructions in the network that could have shaped somehow its diachronic development.

Having offered a detailed characterization of the modern reaction object construction and explained how the PDE ROC relates to other constructions within the English network of constructions, in the following section I will discuss the second one of the three main research questions posited at the end of Chapter 4, i.e. when does the ROC emerge. The data sources and the methodology used for this first historical study on the English ROC are discussed in § 5.2.1 and § 5.2.2,

38 Since the DIR(ECTIONAL) is obligatory in the construction (see Tab. 3.6 in § 3.2.1.2) I have omitted the parentheses present in the original.

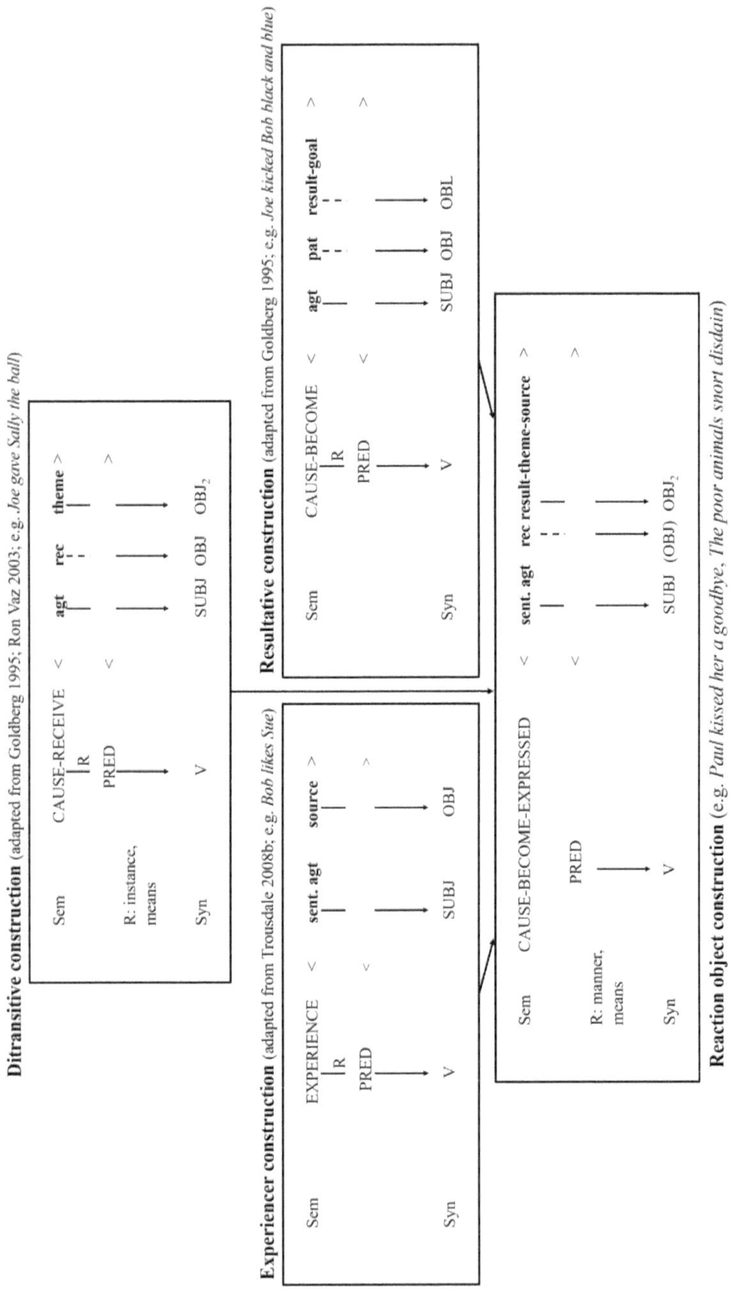

Fig. 5.3: Proposed hybrid nature of the ROC

while § 5.2.3 and § 5.2.4 provide the results and some first concluding remarks that determine the course of Chapter 6.

5.2 On the emergence of the ROC

5.2.1 Data sources

As a heuristic strategy to investigate when and how the ROC emerged in the history of English, and identify its early instances, I first compiled a list of 645 verbs taken from the catalogues of verbs in two historical grammars, namely Jespersen (1909–1949, III: 234, 245 and 298) and Visser (1963–1973: I, § 133: 100–127), and in Levin's seminal monograph on PDE verbs classes (1993, 98). The data obtained from these various sources is summarized in what follows.

5.2.1.1 Jespersen (1909–1949)

Jespersen's list (1909–1949, III: 234, 245 and 298) of reaction object constructions was given in Tab. 3.1. The total number of different verb types mentioned by Jespersen is twelve (*beam*, *bow*, *breathe*, *dance*, *gesticulate*, *kiss*, *laugh*, *look*, *nod*, *pat*, *smile* and *stare*). As we shall see in § 5.2.2, two of these verbs (*smile* and *nod*) are also mentioned in Levin (1993, 98) and Visser (1963–1973: I, § 133: 100–127), and one more (*laugh*) in Levin (1993, 98). The nine verbs occurring in the ROC which are exclusively listed in Jespersen are detailed in Tab. 5.1. For two of these verbs (namely *breathe* and *look*) the OED records earlier examples of their occurrence in the ROC. Note also that in Tab. 5.1 I have added information on whether the reaction objects in question are delocutive, deverbal or predicative expressive nouns.

5.2.1.2 Visser (1963–1973)

Visser's list (1963–1973: I, § 133: 100–127) of 506 transitive homonyms of verbs usually marked 'intransitive' in ModE grammars was mentioned in passing in § 2.2 when I discussed the sharp rise of

Tab. 5.1: Earliest ROCs for the verbs exclusively listed in Jespersen (1909–1949, III: 234, 245 and 298) [dates shown are those of the *first* edition of each work]

Verb type	Date of first attestation as a transitive/ intransitive verb	Date of first attestation in the reaction object construction		Example
(1) *Breathe*, v. (a1300)	I. intr. †1. To exhale, steam, evaporate. Obs.	1535	12. To give utterance to: b. To utter with vehemence or passion. Also with *out*.	*Bible* (Coverdale) Acts ix. A, Saul was yet **breathinge out** threatnynges and slaughter agaynst the disciples of the Lorde. *threatnynges* = deverbal
(2) *Bow*, v.1 (c893)	†3. a. To have a curved direction, to lie or proceed in a curve; to curve, to be deflected. Obs.	1814		Austen M 223 Mr. G. **bowed** his thanks *thanks* = delocutive
(3) *Kiss*, v. (c900)	1. a. trans. To press or touch with the lips (at the same time compressing and then separating them), in token of affection or greeting, or as an act of reverence; to salute or caress with the lips; to give a kiss to.	1847		Brontë W 187 **kissing** her mother good night *good night* = delocutive
(4) *Look*, v. (eOe)	I. To direct one's sight, and related senses. * General senses. 1. a. intr. To direct one's sight; to use one's ability to see. Hence (contextually): to conduct a visual inspection, examination, or search. Also of the eye: to be directed so as to see. Also in extended use and in figurative contexts.	1867	I. 1. e. trans. To express by a look or glance, or by one's countenance; to cast looks conveying (an emotion or question), threatening (a punishment), etc. to look daggers: see *dagger* n.1 3b.	1867 *Good Words* May 335/2, I was obliged to be contented with **looking** my pleasure. *pleasure* = predicative expressive

Tab. 5.1: *Continued*

Verb type	Date of first attestation as a transitive/ intransitive verb	Date of first attestation in the reaction object construction	Example
(5) *Dance*, v. (c1300)	1. intr. To leap, skip, hop, or glide with measured steps and rhythmical movements of the body, usually to the accompaniment of music, either by oneself, or with a partner or in a set.	1881	Tylor A 296 Savages and barbarians **dance** <u>their joy and sorrow, their love and rage,</u> even their magic and religion *joy, sorrow, love* and *rage* = predicative expressive
(6) *Beam*, v. (c1430)	I. From the 'beam' of light. †1. trans. To shed light upon, irradiate, illumine.	1901	Norris O 292 Magnus **beamed** <u>satisfaction</u> *satisfaction* = predicative expressive
(7) *Pat,* v.1 (1533)	1. trans. †a. To hit or strike (a person or thing) with a flat or blunt implement or with the hand. Obs. (in later use Brit. regional).	1912?	id SA 174 he had **patted** Mac [a dog] <u>good-bye</u> *good-bye* = delocutive
(8) *Gesticulate*, v. (1609)	1. intr. To make lively or energetic motions with the limbs or body; esp. as an accompaniment or in lieu of speech.	1849–1850	Di D 193 **gesticulating** anything but <u>welcome</u> from the bow-window *welcome* = delocutive
(9) *Stare*, v. (OE)	1. a. intr. To gaze fixedly and with eyes wide open. Said also of the eyes. Const. in mod. use chiefly *at* (also in indirect passive), *in* (a person's face), and occas. *after, into, through;* formerly (now arch.) *on, upon*. Also with advs. *about, around*, or advb. phr. denoting direction.	1913–1914	Mackenzie S 1. 71 Michael could only **stare** <u>his agreement</u> *agreement* = deverbal

double-functioned or amphibious verbs in ModE, and again in § 3.1.1 when analysing the references to reaction objects in historical grammars. The dates and quotations of the earliest transitive uses of these verbs are mainly based on the pre-1933 OED and therefore should be checked against the current online version.

Visser's list provides one example for each transitive homonym of his 506 originally intransitive verbs, except where the verb in question developed more than one transitive sense, in which case he gives instances of the various transitive uses attested. Thus, for the originally intransitive verb *yelp*, v. (c888), Visser (1963–1973: I, § 133: 127) mentions the following transitive uses: a reaction object construction (example (38)), a variant of the cognate object construction involving a hyponym of a cognate object (example (39)), and a caused motion construction (example (40)). Interestingly, some of Visser's originally intransitive verbs are recorded in transitive use exclusively in the reaction object construction, a piece of evidence which suggests that the reaction object might have played a role in the process of transitivization of at least some English verbs.

Yelp, v. (c888) I. †1. a. intr. To boast, speak vaingloriously. Const. of (= Old English gen.). Obs.[39]

(38) c1400 *Laud Troy Bk.* 13520 And he myȝt not him selff helpe; His sorwe coude he to no man **ȝelpe**. (Reaction object construction)

(39) 1654 W. Price in C. Wase tr. Gratius *Cynegeticon* Illustr. 70 There lurks the pride o' th' woods, the Lyon fell, At whose decease our troops [of hounds] shall **yelpe** a knell. (Cognate object construction)

(40) 1711 E. Budgell *Spectator* No. 116. 6 A raw Dog..might have **yelped** his Heart **out**, without being taken notice of. (Caused motion construction)

5.2.1.3 Levin (1993)

The last data source I employed as a starting point for my own investigation was Levin's list (1993, 98) of verbs occurring in the construction in PDE. Levin's monograph (1993) is built on the assumption that "the behavior of a verb, particularly with respect to the expression and

39 Definition provided for the first attestation of this verb in English (c888).

interpretation of its arguments, is to a large extent determined by its meaning" (Levin 1993, xviii). In accordance with this, her monograph "presents a large number of semantically coherent classes of verbs whose members pattern in the same way with respect to [a range of] diathesis alternations and other properties" (1993, 17). More specifically, she identifies a total of 127 verbs which are capable of occurring in the reaction object construction, and classifies them into the following verb classes: verbs of nonverbal expression (*smile*), wink verbs (*blink*) and verbs of manner of speaking (*chatter*). These various classes and their members are listed in Tab. 5.2 and Tab. 5.3.

It should be noted that when Levin (1993) published her monograph, corpora were not as readily available as today. This means that to compile her different verb listings she used the *Oxford Advanced Learner's Dictionary* in electronic form, dictionaries in printed form such as *The Collins-Robert English-French Dictionary*, *The Collins COBUILD English Language Dictionary*, *The Longman Dictionary of Contemporary English*, and *The Longman Lexicon of Contemporary English* (Levin 1993, xviii), and crucially, also her own intuitions (p.c.). This may explain why my searches for reaction object constructions in several large historical corpora and in the OED turned out to be unsuccessful for many of Levin's verbs. In fact, I was able to find clear instances of ROCs only for 51 out of the total of 127 verbs Levin mentions as capable of occurring in the construction (cf. § 5.2.2). As pointed out by Levin herself, her monograph has clear limitations as "continuing work has uncovered more and more properties of verbs and the various constructions they appear in that suggest many refinements to what is there" (p.c.). Yet despite these limitations Levin's work has proved to be an excellent starting point for my research, as also for earlier research on the reaction object construction such as Martínez-Vázquez (see Martínez-Vázquez 2005, 2010, and elsewhere).

To sum up so far, the total number of verbs gleaned from Jespersen, Visser and Levin initially came to 645, but as we shall see in § 5.2.2 and § 5.2.3, a number of verb types had to be left out for various reasons, so the group of verbs finally considered in this research was substantially smaller.

Tab. 5.2: Verbs of nonverbal expression and wink verbs (Levin 1993, 98)

Verbs of nonverbal expression (Number of verbs: 41)				**Wink verbs (Number of verbs: 9)**
beam	glare	moan	snivel	blink (eye)
cackle	glower	pout	snore	clap (hands)
chortle	goggle	scowl	snort	nod (head)
chuckle	grimace	sigh	sob	point (finger)
cough	grin	simper	titter	shrug (shoulders)
cry	groan	smile	weep	squint (eyes)
frown	growl	smirk	whistle	wag (tail)
gape	guffaw	sneeze	yawn	wave (hand)
gasp	howl	snicker		wink (eye)
gawk	jeer	sniff		
giggle	laugh	snigger		

Tab. 5.3: Verbs of manner of speaking (Levin 1993, 98)

Verbs of manner of speaking (Number of verbs: 77)						
babble	chant	gabble	lilt	scream	squeak	wheeze
bark	chatter	gibber	lisp	screech	squeal	whimper
bawl	chirp	groan	moan	shout	stammer	whine
bellow	cluck	growl	mumble	shriek	stutter	whisper
bleat	coo	grumble	murmur	sing	thunder	whistle
boom	croak	grunt	mutter	snap	tisk	whoop
bray	croon	hiss	purr	snarl	trill	yammer
burble	crow	holler	rage	snuffle	trumpet	yap
cackle	cry	hoot	rasp	splutter	twitter	yell
call	drawl	howl	roar	squall	wail	yelp
carol	drone	jabber	rumble	squawk	warble	yodel

5.2.2 Methodology

My analysis started from a detailed examination of Visser's list of 506 transitive homonyms of verbs usually marked 'intransitive' in ModE grammars (1963–1973: I, § 133: 100–127). This extensive list includes verbs of many different types, among which stand out verbs expressing motion such as *bolt, bound, burst, climb, creep, dive, flow, glide, run* and *spring*, and most interestingly for the emergence of the reaction object construction, verbs expressing sounds, whether human, animal or other; examples of these include *bellow, crow, groan, grunt, laugh, lisp, neigh, stammer, weep, whisper* and *whistle*.

Out of the transitivized uses attested in Visser's long list, only 24 could finally be considered as instances of the construction under discussion, since they were the only ones to clearly conform to the meaning required, i.e. ['Sentient agent_i cause Y_i become expressed while/ $\text{by}_{\text{manner/means}}$ doing V']. It will thus be evident from this much smaller figure of 24 verb types that very many of the transitive uses attested in Visser's list had to be discarded, since they did not fulfil the relevant criteria. Tab. 5.4 provides details on some of the transitivized verb classes in Visser that were left out; among these, class 12 (message objects) at the very end of the table merits special attention. At the surface, sequences such as *The Rauen (. . .)* ***croakes*** *<u>the fatall entrance of Duncan</u>* closely resemble constructions with reaction objects, but such similarity is only apparent, as shown, inter alia, by the lack of an appropriate paraphrase; cf. **The raven expresses the fatal entrance of Duncan by croaking*; see also § 6.1 later.

Tab. 5.4: Some of the transitive uses discarded from Visser's list (1963–1973: I, § 133: 100–127)

Transitive use	Verb[a]	Example
1 Goal complements	*Bark*, v.1 (c885)	c1000 Sax. Leechd. I. 170 Gyf hwa þas wyrte mid him hafað..ne mæg <u>he</u> fram hundum **beon borcen**. [PDE 'If someone has this plant with him. . . <u>he</u> cannot **be barked at** by dogs.']
2 Direct speech complements	*Wheeze*, v. (a1500)	1849 C. J. Lever *Confess. Con Cregan* xiv, <u>'If you'll look in that glass yonder, which is opposite the mirror, you'll soon see!'</u> **wheezed out** the old man, maliciously.
3 Sentential relative clauses	*Tattle*, v. (1481)	1594 Shakespeare *Titus Andronicus* iv. ii. 167 Then let the Ladies **tattle** <u>what they please</u>.
4 Complement clauses	*Trumpet*, v. (1530)	a1616 Shakespeare *Othello* (1622) i. iii. 250 <u>That I did loue the Moore</u>,..My..scorne of Fortunes, May **trumpet** to the world.

(*Continued on next page*)

Tab. 5.4: *Continued*

Transitive use	Verb[a]	Example
5 Pronominal items functioning as direct and indirect objects or passive subjects: *hire, what so, hem, hym, what, whatsoever, the same, what, him, me, some idle thing, them, . . .*	*Brawl*, v.1 (?a1400)	1474 Caxton tr. *Game & Playe of Chesse* (1883) ii. iv. 47 **Brawlynge** and betynge hym as his seruant. [PDE '**Scolding** and beating him ...'] **Indirect object**
	Caw, v.1 (a1586)	1616 B. Holyday tr. Persius *Sat.* 323 [Thou] Hoarsly crow-like **caw'st out** some idle thing. **Direct object**
	Jabber, v. (1499)	1532 T. More *Confut. Tyndale* in *Wks.* 665 Whatsoeuer the Iewes would **iaber** or iangle agayn. **Direct object**
	Whisper, v. (c950)	1562 *Reg. Privy Council Scotl.* I. 209 It is **quhisperit** and murmurrit that sum suld forgett thair devoyr. **Passive subject**
6 Hyponyms of cognate objects (see Felser and Wanner 2001, 106; e.g. *She danced a piece from Swan Lake*)	*Bark*, v.1 (c885)	c1440 *Morte Arth.* 1351 He **berkes** myche boste. [Literal translation: 'He **barks** a great boast'] [Free translation: 'he speaks/shouts menancingly'; cf. MED, s.v. *bōst* (n.) 5.]
	Gobble, v.2 (1680)	1774 O. Goldsmith *Hist. Earth* V. 181 He.. struts about the yard, and **gobbles out** a note of self-approbation.
	Whoop, v. (a1400)	1575 G. Gascoigne *Noble Arte Venerie* xlii. 127 When the Harte is kylled, then all the huntesmen..shall blowe a note, and **whoupe** also a deade note.
7 Objects designating bodily parts	*Nod*, v. (c1390)	1553 T. Wilson *Arte of Rhetorique* iii. f. 118, Some **noddes** their head at euery sentence.
	Twinkle, v. (c888)	1591 R. Percyvall *Bibliotheca Hispanica* Dict. at *Parpadear*, **To twinkle** the eies.
8 Other nonprototypical object types: objects involved in resultative constructions, time away constructions, . . .	*Sigh*, v. (13..)	1600 Shakespeare *Much Ado about Nothing* i. i. 190 Thou wilt needes thrust thy necke into a yoke,..and **sigh** away sundaies.
	Snivel, v. (c1325)	1668 R. L'Estrange tr. F. G. de Quevedo y Villegas *Visions* (1702) 268 To **snivel** and sneeze himself into another World.

Tab. 5.4: *Continued*

Transitive use	Verb[a]	Example
9 Semantically unrelated transitive uses	*Flag*, v.1 (154a0)	1602 J. Marston *Antonios Reuenge* iii. iii. sig. F2^{v}, O, for thy sisters sake, I **flagge** reuenge. "To allow or cause to become languid; to be tardy in prosecuting (a purpose); to deprive of vigour, animation, or energy; to depress, enfeeble. Obs." (OED, s.v. *flag*, v.[1] †5. trans. b.).
	Glister, v. (c1380)	a1586 Sir P. Sidney *Arcadia* (1590) iii. x. sig. Oo1, With eies which **glistered forth** beames of disdaine. "To send forth with glitter." (OED, s.v. *glister*, v. †c. quasi-trans.)
	Scowl, v. (1340)	1667 Milton *Paradise Lost* ii. 491 As when.. the dusky clouds..o'respread Heav'ns chearful face, the lowring Element **Scowls** ore the dark'nd lantskip Snow, or showre. "To send forth with a scowl; to express with a scowl." (OED, s.v. *scowl*, v. 3. trans.)
10 Idiomatic transitive uses of verbs	*Weep*, v.	1597 Shakespeare *Richard III* i. iv. 234 *Clar.* Bid Glocester thinke of this, and he will **weepe**. *Am.* I, milstones as he lessond vs to weepe. [Cf. i. iii. 351 Your eies drop milstones when fooles eies drop tears.] (OED, s.v. *weep*, v. 7. †c)
11 A misinterpreted intransitive use by Visser and the OED	*Cough*, v.1 (c1325)	c1450 J. Myrc *Instr. to Par. Priests* 891 **Koghe** thow not thenne thy thonkes. **Misinterpretation**: "To express or utter by coughing" (s.v. *cough*, v.[1] 2. a. trans.) **Correct interpretation**: 'Do not **cough**, willingly, nor wring (twist/ contract) your shanks' 'Don't **cough**, if you will/please, don't contract your shanks' Cf. MED, s.v. *thank*, n. 5. a. (a) Gen. **thankes** used adverbially: **here (his, oure**, etc.) **thankes**, willingly, voluntarily;?also with a play on **stink** n. or **stench** n. [quots. c1250 & c1300 vr.]; also, by its nature, of itself [quot. c1450] Cf. OED, *wring*, v., II. intr., †12.b. a1450 J. Myrc *Instr. to Par. Priests* 780 **Koghe** þow not þenne, þy þonkes, Ny wrynge þou not wyth þy schonkes.

Continued on next page

Tab. 5.4: *Continued*

Transitive use	Verb[a]	Example
12 Message objects	*Bawl*, v. (1556)	1600 Shakespeare *Henry IV, Pt. 2* ii. ii. 22 + 1 Those that **bal out** the ruines of thy linnen.
	Chuckle, v. (1598)	1820 M. R. Mitford in A. G. L'Estrange *Life M. R. Mitford* (1870) II. v. 120 Whatever you praise to Jeffrey he directly **chuckles out** some error which you did not perceive.
	Complain, v. (c1374)	1509 A. Barclay *Brant's Shyp of Folys* (Pynson) f. cxxvi^{v}, Suche oft **complayne** the charge of pouerte.
	Croak, v. (a1500)	a1616 Shakespeare *Macbeth* (1623) i. v. 38 The Rauen himselfe is hoarse, That **croakes** the fatall entrance of Duncan.
	Hiccup, v. (1580)	1788 C. Dibdin *Musical Tour* vi. 20 Convivial lords..**hiccup out** *non nobis domine*.
	Sigh, v. (13..)	1553 T. Wilson *Arte of Rhetorique* 117 b, Some **sighes out** their woordes. Some synges their sentences.
	Whisper, v. (c950)	1597 Shakespeare *Richard II* ii. iv. 11 Leane-lookt prophets **whisper** fearefull change. (*whisper* = 'announce')
	Wink, v.1 (c897)	1918 *Glasgow Herald* 22 Nov. 5 Their flagship's great..eye of flame **winking out** a message.

a The dates and the examples have been checked in the OED online and conveniently updated whenever necessary. As previoulsy noted, Visser's list is based on a pre-1933 version of the OED.

Tab. 5.5 displays the 24 examples of ROCs attested in Visser (1963–1973: I, § 133: 100–127) chronologically by date of attestation, rather than in alphabetical order. As previously mentioned, some intransitive verbs in Visser's list show transitive uses only when involved in the ROC, pointing to the fact that the reaction object may have played a direct role in the process of transitivization of some English verbs. These verbs, which are shaded in grey in Tab. 5.5, are, in order of appearance, the following: *bray*, *buzz*, *pant*, *neigh*, *drone*, *giggle*, *lour/lower*, *gabble*, *growl*, *whimper*, *grumble* and *low*. Additionally, in Tab. 5.5, for those verbs that show more than one transitive use, I have also shaded in grey those examples involving reaction objects that antedate other transitive uses mentioned in Visser's list (cf. Tab. 5.4 for examples of such transitive uses); this applies to the following verbs: *yelp*, *rave*, *snort* and *trumpet*.

Finally, Tab. 5.6 displays seven verbs in Visser's list which I have excluded from my group of 24 verbs unambiguously taking reaction objects, but which nevertheless merit attention on different grounds. The seven verbs in question are: *froth*, *foam*, *resound*, *grin*, *bark*, *squeak* and *coo*. In examples (1) and (2) with *froth* and *foam*, the coreferential relationship between the apparent reaction objects (*confusiouns*) and the higher subjects is not 100 % clear, as the objects might refer either to the *wawis of the woode see* 'waves of the raging sea' or to the *see* 'sea'; in this latter case they might indeed be considered as genuine reaction objects. Examples (5) and (6) involve the verbs *bark* and *squeak* and show the meaning ['Sentient agent_i cause Y_i become expressed $\text{while/by}_{\text{manner/means}}$ doing V'], but the objects *satire*, and *love-odes* do not belong to any of the reaction object types previously described: they are not delocutive, deverbal or predicative expressive nouns. Examples (3), (4) and (7) are also exceptions to the criteria I have recognised. As previously mentioned, coreferentiality is an intrinsic feature of ROCs in PDE. Still, I find it relevant to include here these examples despite the fact that the objects are not coreferential with their subjects: (i) the clauses show the meaning ['Sentient agent cause Y become expressed $\text{while/by}_{\text{manner/means}}$ doing V'], (ii) they involve the deverbal illocutionary noun *praise*, and (iii) these are the earliest transitive examples provided by Visser for these originally intransitive verbs (i.e. *resound*, *grin* and *coo*). Noncoreferential instances like these might have been transitional in the development of the construction, just as the requirement of coreferentiality which now applies to the *way*-construction is essentially a modern development (for discussion, cf. § 3.2.1.2). It deserves mention, too, that the verbs *grin* and *coo* developed ROC uses at a later stage (see example (9) in Tab. 5.7 for the verb *grin* (1732) and example (24) in Tab. 5.8 for the verb *coo* (1834)).

Tab. 5.5: ROCs in Visser's list of transitivized verbs (1963–1973: I, § 133: 100–127)

Verb type		Date of first attestation as a transitive/intransitive verb	Date of first attestation in the reaction object construction		Example[a]
(1)	*Bray*, v.1 (a1300)	†1. a. intr. To cry out, to utter a loud harsh cry; esp. of grief or pain. Obs.	c1400 (?c1380)	4. a. trans. To utter harshly (cries, sounds, etc.). Often with *out*.	*Pearl* l. 346 Braundysch & **bray** þy braþez breme. [PDE 'struggle and **cry out** your terrible agony'] [PDE 'writhe and moan in agony'][b] (*braþez* = "anger, rage"; MED, s.v. *bratthe* (n.)) *braþez* = predicative expressive **Another interesting example provided by Visser:** 1860 *Sat. Rev.* 10 421 A Brass band **brayed** welcome at the terminus. *welcome* = delocutive
(2)	*Yelp*, v. (c888)	I. †1. a. intr. To boast, speak vaingloriously. Const. *of* (= Old English gen.). Obs.	c1400	II. 2. †b. trans. To call out, utter. Obs.	*Laud Troy Bk.* 13520 And he myȝt not him selff helpe; His sorwe coude he to no man **ȝelpe**. [PDE 'He could not **yelp** his sorrow to any man'] *sorwe* = predicative expressive
(3)	*Buzz*, v.1 (1398)	1. intr. To make the humming sibilant sound characteristic of bees and other insects; to fly out, in, etc. with such a sound.	1583	4. trans. To tell in a low murmur or whisper, to communicate privately and busily. (Occas. with noun-sentence as obj., introduced by *that*.) arch.	P. Stubbes *Anat. Abuses* sig. Civ, **Hauing buzzed** his venemous suggestions into their eares. *suggestion* = deverbal

(4)	*Chat*, v.1 (c1440)	†1. intr. To talk idly and foolishly; to prate, babble, chatter. Obs.	1596	†4. trans. To speak familiarly of, talk of, tell as gossip. Obs.	W. Smith *Chloris* (1877) 11 When to my flocke my daily woes I **chate**. *woe* = delocutive
(5)	*Rave,* v.1 (a1325)	1. intr. a. Originally: †to be mad, to show signs of madness or delirium (obs.). Later: to speak or declaim wildly, irrationally, or incoherently. Also occas.: to talk loudly or boisterously; to shout, bawl (now chiefly Eng. regional). Also with *on.*	1602	3. trans. a. To utter in a frenzied, enthusiastic, or uncontrollably angry manner. Also with *out.* Now usu. with direct speech as object.	J. Marston *Antonios Reuenge* iv. v. sig. I, Like to some boy, that actes a Tragedie,..and **raues out** passion. *passion* = predicative expressive
(6)	*Weep,* v. (c897)	II. trans. 6. To shed tears over; to lament with tears.	1602	II. trans. 7. d. To declare, express, utter with lamentation. Also with *forth.* rare (chiefly poet.).	J. Marston *Hist. Antonio & Mellida* v. sig. H3, Ile **weepe** my passion to the senselesse trees. [PDE 'I will **weep** my passion to the senseless trees'] *passion* = predicative expressive
(7)	*Pant,* v. (c1350)	1. intr. a. To breathe hard with quick, short breaths, as from exertion, heat, or agitation; to gasp for breath.	1608	4. trans. To utter gaspingly or breathlessly.	Shakespeare *King Lear* vii. 210 Came there a reeking Post,..halfe breathles, **panting [1623 painting] forth** From Gonorill his mistris, salutations. (*Salutation* = The action, or an act, of saluting; a manner of saluting; an utterance, form of words, gesture, or movement, by which one person salutes another; OED, s.v. *salutation*, n. 1. a.) (Cf. Shakespeare 1997c, 1318) *salutation* = deverbal

Continued on next page

Tab. 5.5: *Continued*

	Verb type	Date of first attestation as a transitive/intransitive verb	Date of first attestation in the reaction object construction		Example[a]
(8)	*Blush*, v. (?a1400)	†1. intr. To shine forth. (in allit. poetry.) Obs.	a1616	3. c. trans. With extended force: To express, exhibit, make known by blushing. Chiefly poetic.	Shakespeare *Winter's Tale* (1623) iv. iv. 584 Ile **blush** you Thanks. **Context** Camillo. I cannot say 'tis pity/She lacks instruction, for she seems a mistress/To most that teach. Perdita. Your pardon, sir; for this/ I'll **blush** you thanks. (Shakespeare 1997d, 1643) = "I will express thanks to you by blushing." *thanks* = delocutive
(9)	*Neigh*, v. (OE)	1. intr. a. Of a horse, etc.: to make a loud or high whinnying sound. Also with *out*.	1624	2. trans. Of a horse: to communicate (something) by neighing. Of a person: to utter, voice, or express with a sound resembling or suggestive of a horse's neigh. Freq. with adverbs, esp. *out*.	P. Massinger *Bond-man* iv. ii. sig. H2, The noble horse..**Neigh'd** courage to his Rider. *courage* = predicative expressive
(10)	*Drone*, v.1 (?a1513)	1. intr. To give forth a continued monotonous sound; to hum or buzz, as a bee or a bagpipe; to talk in a monotonous tone.	1631	2. trans. To utter or emit in a dull, monotonous tone. Also with *out*.	B. Jonson *Bartholmew Fayre* i. iii. 89 in *Wks*. II, A drie grace, as long as thy Tablecloth? and **droan'd out** by thy sonne. (*Grace* = A short prayer or blessing offered in thanks before or after eating; OED, s.v. *grace*, n. II. The giving or an expression of thanks; gratitude. 11.)

					(*Grace* = (a) Grace before or after meals; --usually pl.; (b) thanks, a prayer of thanksgiving; --usually pl.; don (yelden) ~, to give thanks (to God, a person); ~ doinge, thanksgiving.; MED, s.v. *grāce* (n.), 6.) (*Grace* = To thank.; OED, s.v. *grace*, v. †1. trans.) *grace* = deverbal
(11)	*Snort*, v. (a1366)	†1. intr. Of the nose: To turn up, as in sniffing.	a1635	6. trans. a. To utter with a snort; to give out, drive away, etc., by snorting (†for snoring).	T. Randolph *Muses Looking-glasse* iv. iii. 78 in *Poems & Muses Looking-glasse* (1638), Your pittifull Worship **snorting out** pardons To the despairing sinner. *pardon* = delocutive
(12)	*Giggle*, v.1 (1509)	a. intr. To laugh continuously in a manner not uproarious, but suggestive either of foolish levity or uncontrollable amusement. Cf. *snigger* v.1, *titter* v.1 Also with *on*, *out*.	a1657	b. quasi-trans. To utter with a giggle. Also to giggle out (time): to waste in giggling. to giggle away: to do away with by giggling.	G. Daniel *Trinarchodia* in *Poems* (1878) III. To Rdr. 128 These pass the glass about; the Conclave set, **Giggle** applause. (*Applause* = Approbation loudly expressed; acclamation; OED, s.v. *applause*, n. 1) *applause* = deverbal
(13)	*Nod*, v. (c1390)	1. a. intr. To make a brief inclination of the head, esp. in salutation, assent, or command, or to draw attention to something.	1713	1. d. trans. To signify or express (assent, salutation, etc.) with a nod.	R. Steele *Englishman* No. 8. 50 Ay, ay **nodded** the Porter; but, Sir, whom must I say I came from? (*Ay, ay* = aye, but. . . Indicating provisional assent to a statement for the sake of rebutting it.; OED, s.v. *aye* / *ay*, int. (and adv.) and n. 2. b.) *ay, ay* = delocutive

Continued on next page

Tab. 5.5: *Continued*

Verb type		Date of first attestation as a transitive/intransitive verb	Date of first attestation in the reaction object construction		Example[a]
(14)	*Trumpet*, v. (1530)	1. a. intr. To blow or sound a trumpet.	1729	2. trans. a. To sound on a trumpet; to utter with a sound like that of a trumpet.	Young *Merchant* ii. ix, She **trumpets** shrill her dread command. *command* = deverbal
(15)	*Lour*, *lower*, v. (c1290)	1. a. intr. Of persons, their eyes, countenances, etc.: To frown, scowl; to look angry or sullen. †Also, to be depressed or mournful. Const. *at*, *on*, *upon*; rarely in indirect passive.	1746	1. b. quasi-trans. To express by frowning.	J. Wesley *Wks*. (1872) II. 21 The other part [of the crowd] remained a little way off, and **loured** defiance. (*Defiance* = Declaration of aversion or contempt; rejection. Obs. rare—1.; OED, s.v. *defiance*, n. †5) *defiance* = predicative expressive
(16)	*Gabble*, v. (1577)	1. intr. To talk volubly, inarticulately and incoherently; to chatter, jabber, prattle. Also, to read so fast as to be unintelligible.	1758	2. trans. To utter rapidly and unintelligibly. Also with *over*.	*Monthly Rev*. 308 **Gabbling** infidelity and laughing at the religion of his country. (*Infidelity* = In general sense: Disbelief, incredulity.; OED, s.v. *infidelity*, n. 2) *infidelity* = predicative expressive
(17)	*Growl*, v.3 (c139.)	1. intr. †a. Of the bowels: to rumble; = *gurl* v. Cf. *grolling* n. Obs. rare—1.	1759	2. Of persons: b. trans. To utter or express with a growl or in a growling manner: with simple nouns, quoted words, or clause as obj. Also with *out*.	Johnson *Idler* 21 Apr. 121 She **grouls out** her discontent. *discontent* = predicative expressive

(18)	*Frown,* v. (c1386)	1. a. intr. To knit the brows, especially by way of expressing displeasure or (less frequently) concentration of thought; to look sternly. Said also of the brow. †Also (rarely), to sneer.	1775	3. quasi-trans. b. To enforce, express, produce, etc. by a frown.	R. B. Sheridan *Rivals* Epil., She smiles preferment, or she **frowns** disgrace. *disgrace* = predicative expressive
(19)	*Whimper,* v. (1513)	1. a. intr. To utter a feeble, whining, broken cry, as a child about to burst into tears; to make a low complaining sound.	1785	1. c. trans. To utter or express in a whimper.	W. Cowper *Task* iv. 429 But poverty, with most who **whimper forth** Their long complaints, is self-inflicted woe. *complaint* = deverbal
(20)	*Smile,* v. (a1300)[c]	I. intr. a. Of persons: To give to the features or face a look expressive of pleasure or amusement, or of amused disdain, scorn, etc.	1814	8. b. To exhibit, indicate, or express by smiling; to grant, bestow, etc., with a smile; with direct speech as obj., to say with a smile. Also fig. and with *in* (quot. 1860).	to smile one's thanks, a welcome, disbelief' 1814 Byron *Lara* ii. xvii. 1072 He..sadly **smiles** his thanks to that dark page. *thanks* = delocutive 1853 E. K. Kane U.S. *Grinnell Exped.* (1856) xlvi. 423 They cannot be said to **smile** a welcome upon the navigator. *welcome* = delocutive 1880 *Daily Tel.* 21 Feb. She **smiled** disbelief. *disbelief* = predicative expressive

Continued on next page

Tab. 5.5: *Continued*

Verb type		Date of first attestation as a transitive/intransitive verb	Date of first attestation in the reaction object construction		Example[a]
(21)	*Grumble*, v. (a1586)	1. intr. a. Of persons and animals: To utter dull inarticulate sounds; to mutter, mumble, murmur; to growl faintly.	1824	3. trans. a. To express or utter with mumbling, muttering, or complaining. Also with *out*.	in *Spirit of Public Jrnls.* (1825) 285 He..**grumbled out** good night, and departed to his domus. *good night* = delocutive
(22)	*Sneeze*, v. (1493)	1. a. intr. To drive or emit air or breath suddenly through the nose and mouth by an involuntary and convulsive or spasmodic action, accompanied by a characteristic sound.	1851	4. To utter with a sneeze. Also with *out*.	Tennyson *Edwin Morris* 80 Shall not Love to me, As in the Latin song I learnt at school, **Sneeze out** a full God-bless-you, right and left? *God-bless-you* = delocutive[d]
(23)	*Grunt*, v. (c725)	1. a. intr. Of a hog: To utter its characteristic low gruff sound. Also of other animals and of persons (with conscious allusion to the pig): To utter a sound resembling this.	1875	2. b. trans. To utter or express with a grunt; to breathe out with a grunt.	F. T. Buckland *Log-bk.* 100 He only **grunted** his gratitude. *gratitude* = predicative expressive

(24)	*Low*, v.1 (OE)	1. intr. a. Of a cow or other bovine animal: to make its characteristic deep, resonant vocal sound; to moo.	1876	3. trans. Of a cow or other bovine animal: to make (a sound) or communicate (something) by lowing. Of a person: to utter or express with a sound resembling or suggestive of the lowing of a cow, esp. by making a long low melancholic sound. Freq. with adverbs, esp. *out*.	'A. Thomas' *Blotted Out* iii. 27, I shudder under the conviction that she is going to **low** reproof at me, and so she does. *reproof* = predicative expressive

a Unless stated otherwise, translations are mine.

b Modern translation provided by Stanton (1995).

c Though not explicitly mentioned in the OED, this verb shows an earlier transitive use with a reaction object in *She* ***smiles*** *preferment, or she frowns disgrace*, a verse fragment attested in the eighteenth century comedy of manners *The Rivals: A Comedy* (1775) by Sheridan (see example (18) above in this table).

d The construction *sneeze (a) bless you* is discussed by Claridge and Arnovick (2010, 178 and 184) who hypothesize that *bless you* became a polite formula through a process of 'discursisation': superstitious blessing > wish > polite formula.

Tab. 5.6: Discarded marginal examples from Visser (1963–1973: I, § 133: 100–127)

Verb type		Date of first attestation as a transitive/intransitive verb	Date of first attestation in the reaction object construction		Example
(1)	*Froth*, v. (1382)	1. intr. To emit froth or foam; to foam at the mouth. Of liquids: To gather or throw up froth; to run foaming away, by, over.	1382	2. trans. To emit or send forth in or like froth or foam. Now only with *out*.	*Bible* (Wycliffite, E.V.) Jude ii. 13 **Frothinge out** her confusiouns. [1611 *King James Bible*, 'Raging waues of the sea, **foming out** their owne shame, wandring stars, to whom is reserued the blacknesse of darkenesse for euer.']
(2)	*Foam*, v. (c950)	1. a. intr. To emit foam; esp. to froth at the mouth; also with *out*. Often as a hyperbolical description of vehement rage or wrath. Also of a horse, etc.: To be covered with foam (of perspiration). Cf. *foam* n. 1b.	1388	5. trans. To send forth or emit in or like foam; to pour out with rage and violence. Chiefly fig.	*Bible* (Wycliffite, L.V.) Jude 13 These ben..wawis of the woode see, **fomynge [1382 frothinge] out** her confusiouns. [1611 *King James Bible*, 'Raging waues of the sea, **foming out** their owne shame, wandring stars, to whom is reserued the blacknesse of darkenesse for euer.']
(3)	*Resound*, v.1 (c1405)	1. a. intr. Of a place: to ring or re-echo with sound.	1561	3. c. trans. To proclaim, repeat loudly (a person's praises, etc.); to celebrate. Also with complement: to proclaim (a person) to be something.	B. Googe tr. 'M. Palingenius' *Zodiake of Life* (new ed.) sig. a5, If Homere here might dwell, Whose praise the Grekes **resounde**. [PDE 'The Greeks **proclaimed** Homer's praise'

(4)	*Grin*, v.2 (OE)	1. intr. Of persons or animals: To draw back the lips and display the teeth: a. generally, or as an indication of pain or †anger; † also to grin with the teeth. Const. *at*, †*on*, †*upon*. Said also of the jaws or teeth.	1681	2. a. trans. To express by grinning	N. Lee in *Dryden's Wks.* (1701) III. p. vii, Even the Phanaticks.. Bow in their own despite, and **grin** <u>your Praise</u>.
(5)	*Bark*, v.1 (c885)	1. intr. To utter a sharp explosive cry. (Orig. of dogs, hence of other animals, and spec. of foxes at rutting-time.) Const. *at* (*on*, *upon*, *against*, obs.).	1688	5. trans. or with subord. clause (also bark out, bark forth): To utter or give forth with a bark; to break out with, burst forth with.	Matth. Prior, *Epistle to Fleetwood Shepherd* (in: Bickley, Shorter Poems of Prior) 10, Pigs might squeak love-odes, dogs **bark** <u>satire</u>.
(6)	*Squeak*, v. (1387)	1. intr. To emit a short or slight sound of a thin high-pitched character.	1688	a. trans. To utter, sing, or play in a squeaking manner or with a squeaky voice. Usu. derisively. Freq. without.	Matth. Prior, *Epistle to Fleetwood Shepherd* (in: Bickley, Shorter Poems of Prior) 10, Pigs might **squeak** <u>love-odes</u>, dogs bark satire.
(7)	*Coo*, v. (1672)	1. a. intr. To make the soft murmuring sound or note characteristic of doves and pigeons.	1798	4. trans. a. To utter or express by cooing.	B. Johnson *Orig. Poems* 73 No longer now he..**cooes** <u>the praise of ev'ry fair</u>.

After having examined Jespersen and Visser's lists of verbs, I went on to follow the same procedure as other diachronic studies on argument structure such as McMillion (2006), Mantlik (2011), Lavidas (2013), van Gelderen (2014), Siemund (2014), Mondorf (2016), Fanego (2017) among many others. In other words, I used the OED to check the first transitive use attested for Levin's 127 verbs taking reaction objects (see Tab. 5.2 and Tab. 5.3). Only 51 of them, however, turned out to be recorded in the OED with unambiguous instances of ROCs; 16 of these were already included in Jespersen and Visser's lists of verbs (cf. Tab. 5.9 in § 5.2.3). The remaining 76 verbs in Levin's list will be explored in future research. For the time being, I believe Levin's sample of 51 verb types attested with reaction objects in the historical records, plus the verb types collected from Jespersen and Visser, should suffice to make some initial predictions regarding when and how the ROC emerged.

Tab. 5.7 and Tab. 5.8 provide chronological information on the 51 verbs gleaned from Levin, following the same procedure as in Tables 5.5 and 5.6. Tab. 5.7 relates to nonverbal expression and wink verbs; Tab. 5.8 to manner of speaking verbs.

Tab. 5.7: Historical evidence on Levin's nonverbal expression and wink verbs

	Verb type	Date of first attestation as a transitive/intransitive verb	Date of first attestation in the reaction object construction		Example
(1)	*Moan*, v. (a1325)	1. trans. a. To complain of, lament; to bemoan, bewail. Now rare.	a1325	1. trans. a. To complain of, lament; to bemoan, bewail. Now rare.	(c1250) *Gen. & Exod.* (1968) l. 180 He pine man wid sorwe and dred, And don h[i]m [*MS* hem] **monen** his sinfulhed. [PDE 'He afflicts man with sorrow and death, and makes him **moan** his sinfulness'][a] (*Sinfulness* = The state or character of being sinful; wickedness, iniquity.; OED, s.v. *sinfulness*, n.) [Latin: (Gen 6, 6) *paenituit Dominum quod hominem fecisset in terra. Et tactus dolore cordis intrinsecus*; Literal translation: 'It repented him that he had made man on the earth. And being touched inwardly with sorrow of heart' Translation taken from the Challoner revision of the Douay-Rheims Bible (1899)]
				5. trans. To utter with a moan or moans, or in a moaning voice. Freq. with direct speech as object.	a1822 Shelley *Dirge* in *Posthumous Poems* (1824) 219 Rough wind, that **moanest** loud Grief too sad for song.
(2)	*Clap*, v.1 (c1300)	III. Of actions incidentally accompanied by the noise. 6. trans. To strike, hit, knock, beat, with sounding blows. Obs. or arch. (To clap a dish (quot. 1670): cf. *clap-dish* n.)	1591	II. Of making the noise by particular actions. 5. †d.	R. Greene *Second Pt. Conny-catching* sig. A3, He.. bargained, & bought him..and that the horse-stealer **clap** him good lucke.

Continued on next page

Tab. 5.7: *Continued*

Verb type		Date of first attestation as a transitive/intransitive verb	Date of first attestation in the reaction object construction		Example
(3)	*Weep*, v. (c897)	II. trans. 6. To shed tears over; to lament with tears.	1602	7. d. To declare, express, utter with lamentation. Also with forth. rare (chiefly poet.).	J. Marston *Hist. Antonio & Mellida* v. sig. H3, Ile **weepe** my passion to the senselesse trees. [PDE 'I'll **weep** my passion to the senseless trees']
(4)	*Groan*, v. (7..)	1. a. intr. To breathe with a deep-toned murmur; to utter a low deep sound expressive of grief or pain.	1609	3. trans. a. To utter with groans; with an exclamation or sentence as obj. Also with *out*.	Shakespeare *Troilus & Cressida* iii. i. 122 So dying loue liues still..O ho **grones out** for ha ha ha. (*O ho* = Expressing surprise, mockery, exultation, etc. Also formerly used to attract attention. Cf. *ho* int.[1]; OED, s.v. *oho*, int.) (Cf. Shakespeare 1997a, 502)
(5)	*Laugh*, v. (eOE)	1. a. To make the spontaneous sounds and movements of the face and body usual in expressing joy, mirth, amusement, or (sometimes) derision; to have the same reaction in response to being tickled; to emit laughter. Also in extended use: to feel joy, mirth, amusement, or derision without such accompanying sounds and movements. (a) intr. Without construction. †(b) trans. With the thing laughed at as object. Obs. rare. In Old English with genitive of object. (c) intr. With preposition (esp. *at*, *over*) indicating the object of laughter.	1609	4. trans. a. To say or express with a laugh; (also) to utter as a laugh. Chiefly with *that*-clause or direct speech as object.	Shakespeare *Troilus & Cressida* i. iii. 163 The large Achilles..**laughs out** a lowd applause. (*Applause* = Approbation loudly expressed; acclamation; OED, s.v. *applause*, n. 1) (Cf. Shakespeare 1997a, 490)

(6)	*Snort*, v. (a1366)	†1. intr. Of the nose: To turn up, as in sniffing.	a1635	6. trans. a. To utter with a snort; to give out, drive away, etc., by snorting (†or snoring).	T. Randolph *Muses Looking-glasse* iv. iii. 78 in *Poems & Muses Looking-glasse* (1638) Your pittifull Worship **snorting out** pardons To the despairing sinner.
(7)	*Giggle*, v.1 (1509)	a. intr. To laugh continuously in a manner not uproarious, but suggestive either of foolish levity or uncontrollable amusement. Cf. *snigger* v.1, *titter* v.1 Also with *on*, *out*.	a1657	b. quasi-trans. To utter with a giggle. Also to giggle out (time): to waste in giggling. to giggle away: to do away with by giggling.	G. Daniel *Trinarchodia* in *Poems* (1878) III. To Rdr. 128 These pass the glass about; the Conclave set, **Giggle** applause. (*Applause* = Approbation loudly expressed; acclamation; OED, s.v. *applause*, n. 1)
(8)	*Nod*, v. (c1390)	1. a. intr. To make a brief inclination of the head, esp. in salutation, assent, or command, or to draw attention to something.	1713	1. d. trans. To signify or express (assent, salutation, etc.) with a nod.	R. Steele *Englishman* No. 8. 50 Ay, ay **nodded** the Porter; but, Sir, whom must I say I came from? (*Ay, ay* = aye, but. Indicating provisional assent to a statement for the sake of rebutting it.; OED, s.v. *aye / ay*, int. (and adv.) and n. 2. b.)
(9)	*Grin*, v.2 (OE)	1. intr. Of persons or animals: To draw back the lips and display the teeth: a. generally, or as an indication of pain or †anger; † also to grin with the teeth. Const. *at*, †*on*, †*upon*. Said also of the jaws or teeth.	1732	2. a. trans. To express by grinning.	Ld. Lansdowne *Ess. Unnat. Flights* 62 He **grins** defiance at the gaping crowd. (*Defiance* = Declaration of aversion or contempt; rejection. Obs. rare—1.; OED, s.v. *defiance*, n. †5)
(10)	*Sob*, v.1 (a1200)	1. a. intr. To catch the breath in a convulsive manner as the result of violent emotion, esp. grief; to weep in this fashion. Also in figurative contexts.	1748	3. trans. a. To send out, bring up, etc., by sobbing or with sobs.	S. Richardson *Clarissa* V. xii. 130 He **sobb'd up** his grief.

Continued on next page

Tab. 5.7: *Continued*

Verb type	Date of first attestation as a transitive/intransitive verb	Date of first attestation in the reaction object construction		Example
(11) *Growl*, v.3 (c138.)	1. intr.†a. Of the bowels: to rumble; = *gurl* v. Cf. *grolling* n. Obs. rare—1.	1759	2. Of persons: b. trans. To utter or express with a growl or in a growling manner: with simple noun, quoted words, or clause as obj. Also with *out*.	Johnson *Idler* 21 Apr. 121 She **grouls out** her discontent.
(12) *Frown*, v. (c1386)	1. a. intr. To knit the brows, especially by way of expressing displeasure or (less frequently) concentration of thought; to look sternly. Said also of the brow. †Also (rarely), to sneer.	1775	3. quasi-trans. b. To enforce, express, produce, etc. by a frown.	R. B. Sheridan *Rivals* Epil., She **smiles** preferment, or she **frowns** disgrace.
(13) *Wave*, v. (c1000)	†6. intr. To make a movement to and fro (with the hands). Only OE.	1810	10. a. To signify (something) by a wave of the hand or arm. Also with dative of person.	Scott *Lady of Lake* ii. 51 Perchance the maiden smiled to see Yon parting lingerer **wave** adieu.
(14) *Sigh*, v. (13..)	1. a. intr. To emit, give, or heave a sigh.	1811	3. trans. a. To speak or utter (words, etc.) with a sigh. Chiefly with advs., as *forth* and *out*.	J. Austen *Sense & Sensibility* III. i. 28 Marianne **sighed out** her similar apprehension. (*Apprehension* = Fear as to what may happen; dread.; OED, s.v. *apprehension*, n. II. 12)
(15) *Smile*, v. (a1300) See example (12)	I. intr. 1. a. Of persons: To give to the features or face a look expressive of pleasure or amusement, or of amused disdain, scorn, etc.	1814	8. b. To exhibit, indicate, or express by smiling; to grant, bestow, etc., with a smile; with direct speech as obj., to say with a smile. Also fig. and with in (quot. 1860).	Byron *Lara* ii. xvii. 1072 He..sadly **smiles** his thanks to that dark page.

(16)	*Cough*, v.1 (c1325)	1. a. intr. To expel the air from the lungs with a more or less violent effort and characteristic noise, produced by the abrupt forcible opening of the previously closed glottis; usually in order to remove something that obstructs or irritates the air-passages.	1837	3. d. To utter or express with a cough.	E. Howard *Old Commodore* I. ix. 293, I **coughed out** my gratitude.
(17)	*Guffaw*, v. (1721)	a. intr. To laugh loudly or boisterously; to laugh coarsely or harshly.	1865	b. trans. To say with a guffaw; to express by means of a guffaw.	J. Hatton *Bitter Sweets* viii, Mat shrugged his shoulders and **guffawed** his satisfaction.
(18)	*Sniff*, v. (c1340)	1. a. intr. To draw air through the nose with short or sharp audible inhalations; to clear the nose in this way, esp. when under the influence of emotion.	1865	7. To utter with a (scornful) sniff; to express by means of a sniff.	A. Smith *Summer in Skye* i. 24 Fastidious Edinburgh **sniffs** disdain.
(19)	*Cackle*, v.1 (?c1225)	1. a. intr. To make a noise as a hen, especially after laying an egg; also to make a noise as a goose (which is more specifically to *gaggle* n.).	1880	3. trans. To utter with or express by cackling.	W. D. Howells *Undiscov. Country* i. 28 The ladies.. now rose..and joyously **cackled** satisfaction.
(20)	*Wink*, v.1 (c897)	†1. a. intr. To close one's eyes. (Also in fig. context: cf. 5, 6) Obs.	1919	9. d. To give (a signal), express (a message), etc. by means of flashlights.	Glasgow *Herald* 21 Apr. 7 H.M.S. Glory..**winked** us welcome from the mast-head.

a Interestingly, the earliest attested ROC in Spanish with the verb *llorar* 'weep' – which is a verb semantically related to *moan* as shown in (3) in this table – also goes back to the ME period. More specifically, regarding the ROC *llorando sus peccados* 'weeping their sins', Martínez-Vázquez (2014b, 207) explains the following, "[t]his metonymic usage is highly entrenched and can be traced back to, at least, the thirteenth century, with an example by the Spanish poet Gonzalo de Berceo (c.1198 – c.1264)".

Tab. 5.8: Historical evidence on Levin's manner of speaking verbs

Verb type		Date of first attestation as a transitive/intransitive verb	Date of first attestation in the reaction object construction		Example
(1)	*Bray*, v.1 (a1300)	†1. a. intr. To cry out, to utter a loud harsh cry; esp. of grief or pain. Obs.	c1400 (?c1380)	4. a. trans. To utter harshly (cries, sounds, etc.). Often with *out*.	*Pearl* l. 346 Braundysch & **bray** þy braþez breme. [PDE 'struggle and **cry out/bray** your terrible agony'] [PDE 'writhe and moan in agony'][a] (*braþez* = "anger, rage"; MED, s.v. *bratthe* (n.)) **Another interesting example provided by the OED:** 1667 Milton *Paradise Lost* vi. 209 Arms on Armour clashing **bray'd** Horrible discord.
(2)	*Yelp*, v. (c888)	I. †1. a. intr. To boast, speak vaingloriously. Const. of (= Old English gen.). Obs.	c1400	II. †2. †b. trans. To call out, utter. Obs.	*Laud Troy Bk.* 13520 And he myȝt not him selff helpe; His sorwe coude he to no man **ȝelpe**. [PDE 'He could not **yelp** his sorrow to any man']
(3)	*Roar*, v.1 (OE)	1. intr. a. Of a large (typically wild) animal (esp. a lion): to utter a loud deep cry. Also with *out*.	c1450	5. trans. a. To utter or express (something) loudly; to state boldly; to shout out. Freq. with direct speech or that-clause as object. Also fig.	C. d'Orleans *Poems* (1941) 219 (MED), Mi bollid hert doth so his sikis **rore** That mawgre me hit doth my wele biwray. [PDE 'My bold heart **roars** its suffering so, that in spite of myself, it betrays my happiness'] **Marginal example provided by the OED:** a1616 Shakespeare Henry VI, Pt. 1 (1623) iii. i. 40 That..makes him **rore** these Accusations **forth**.[b]

(4)	*Mumble*, v. (c1325)	1. a. intr. To eat slowly and ineffectually; to chew tentatively with or as with toothless gums. Now rare.	1534	3. trans. b. With †*forth*, *out*, *over*, †*up*.	tr. Erasmus *Enchiridion Militis Christiani* (new ed.) vii. sig. Hvi, Thou in the meane space **momblest vp** thy prayer vnto god. [Latin: *tu interim preculis tuis Deo* ***obmurmuras***; Literal translation: 'You, meanwhile, **murmur** to God with your little prayers'] Originally written in Latin by Desiderius Erasmus (1501) and published in English by William Tyndale (1533)
(5)	*Thunder*, v. (c888)	1. intr. a. Impersonally: it thunders, thunder sounds, there is thunder.	1548	3. fig. b. trans. To utter or publish in the way of terrible threatening, denunciation, or invective; also simply, to utter loudly, shout out, roar.	N. Udall et al. tr. Erasmus *Paraphr. Newe Test.* I. Matt. xii. 74 Do not **thunder** sore threatenings. [Latin: *non* ***intono*** *saeuas minas*; Literal translation: 'I do not **intone/thunder** cruel threats'] Cf. Erasmus (1544 [1467–1536], 187) Originally written in Latin by Desiderius Erasmus, and published in English in 1548 in the *The First tome or volume of the Paraphrase of Erasmus upon the new testament* edited by Nicholas Udall (Devereux 1968, 24)
(6)	*Shriek*, v. (1567)	1. intr. To utter a loud sharp shrill cry. b. of the characteristic cry of certain animals, spec. of the badger in rutting-time (cf. *shrike* v.).	1597	2. trans. To utter (a shriek); to utter (words) with a shriek or shrieks.	M. Drayton *Lover's Compl.* 18 Often reading what contents it bears; As often **shrieking** undistinguish'd woe.[c]

Continued on next page

Tab. 5.8: *Continued*

Verb type		Date of first attestation as a transitive/intransitive verb	Date of first attestation in the reaction object construction		Example
(7)	*Shout*, v. (c1374)	2. b. With clause or quoted words as object.	a1616	2. a. trans. To utter (something) with a loud voice.	Shakespeare *Coriolanus* (1623) i. i. 212 They threw their caps As they would hang them on the hornes a'th Moone, **Shooting** their Emulation. a1616 Shakespeare, *Coriolanus* I.i. 212: they threw their caps As they would hang them on the horns a' th' Moone, **Shouting** their emulation. (Shakespeare 1997b, 1447) (*Emulation* = 1. The endeavour to equal or surpass others in any achievement or quality; also, the desire or ambition to equal or excel. In early use the word is perh. more freq. applied to the mental emotion; OED, s.v. *emulation*, n.)
(8)	*Drone*, v.1 (?a1513)	1. intr. To give forth a continued monotonous sound; to hum or buzz, as a bee or a bagpipe; to talk in a monotonous tone.	1631	2. trans. To utter or emit in a dull, monotonous tone. Also with *out*.	B. Jonson *Bartholmew Fayre* i. iii. 89 in *Wks*. II, A drie grace, as long as thy Tablecloth? and **droan'd out** by thy sonne. (*Grace* = A short prayer or blessing offered in thanks before or after eating; OED, s.v. *grace*, n. II. The giving or an expression of thanks; gratitude. 11.) (*Grace* = (a) Grace before or after meals; --usually pl.; (b) thanks, a prayer of thanksgiving; --usually pl.; don (yelden) ~, to give thanks (to God, a person); ~ doinge, thanksgiving.; MED, s.v. *grāce* (n.), 6.) (*Grace* = To thank.; OED, s.v. *grace*, v. †1. trans.)

(9)	*Murmur*, v. (c1390)	1. a. intr. To complain in low muttered tones; to give voice to an inarticulate discontent; to grumble. Freq. with *at*, against. Now rare.	1637	3. trans. a. To utter (sounds, words) in a subdued or indistinct voice. Formerly also: †to put about, whisper (a rumour, etc.) (obs.). Also with clause as object.	Milton *Comus* 10 Fell Charybdis **murmur'd** <u>soft applause</u>. (*Applause* = Approbation loudly expressed; acclamation; OED, s.v. *applause*, n. 1)
(10)	*Snuffle*, v. (1583)	I. intr. †1. To show dislike or disdain by snuffing; to sniff at a thing in contempt. Obs.	1641	II. trans. 7. a. To utter, say, declare, etc., in a snuffling or nasal tone.	in J. Nalson *Impartial Coll. Affairs State* (1683) II. 809 Those That **snuffle** <u>their unlearned Zeal</u> in Prose. (*Zeal* = In a specialized sense: Ardent love or affection; fervent devotion or attachment (to a person or thing). Obs. or merged in sense 4.; OED, s.v. *zeal*, n. †2) **Another interesting example provided by the OED:** 1837 T. Carlyle in *London & Westm. Rev.* Jan. 429 Even the old Marquis **snuffles** <u>approval</u>.
(11)	*Whisper*, v. (c950)	1. a. intr. To speak softly 'under one's breath', i.e. without the resonant tone produced by vibration of the vocal cords; to talk or converse in this way, esp. in the ear of another, for the sake of secrecy. (See also 4a.)	1697	2. a. trans. To say, tell, communicate, utter, or express by whispering. (With simple obj. or obj. clause; often with the actual words uttered as obj.) See also 4b.	Dryden tr. Virgil *Æneis* xii, in tr. Virgil *Wks.* 587 <u>Rising Fears</u> **are whisper'd** thro' the Crowd. [Latin: *serpitque per agmina murmur* Virgil *Æneis* xii, 239; Literal translation: 'and a murmur snakes through the crowd'] Originally written in Latin by the Roman poet Virgil and translated into English by the English poet Laureate and dramatist John Dryden. Observe the use of the reaction object *fear* and the native manner of speaking verb *whisper* in Dryden's translation, both of them absent in the Latin original

Continued on next page

Tab. 5.8: *Continued*

Verb type		Date of first attestation as a transitive/intransitive verb	Date of first attestation in the reaction object construction		Example
(12)	*Whine*, v. (c1275)	1. intr. To utter a low somewhat shrill protracted sound or cry, usually expressive of pain or distress; to cry in a subdued plaintive tone: also occasionally merely referring to the tone. a. of persons.	1702	3. trans. b. To utter in a whining tone.	C. Beaumont *J. Beaumont's Psyche* (new ed.) i. ccxxiv. 13 To sigh, and weep, and **whine Out** long complaints.
(13)	*Mutter*, v.1(a1325)	†1. intr. Of a goat: to bleat. Obs.	1724	3. trans. a. To utter indistinctly and in a low tone. Also: to say (a thing) covertly or in secret.	A. Ramsay *Vision* in *Ever Green* I. ix, Revenge **is muttert** be ilk clan.
(14)	*Trumpet*, v. (1530)	1. a. intr. To blow or sound a trumpet.	1729	2. trans. a. To sound on a trumpet; to utter with a sound like that of a trumpet.	Young *Merchant* ii. ix, She **trumpets** shrill her dread command.
(15)	*Purr*, v. 2 (1620)	1. intr. a. Of a cat or another feline animal: to make a low, continuous, vibratory sound taken to be expressive of satisfaction or pleasure.	1748	3. trans. To utter or express by purring; to say in a low, soft voice.	T. Gray *Ode Death Favourite Cat* ii, in R. Dodsley *Coll. Poems* II. 268 She [sc. the cat] saw; and **purr'd** applause.

(16)	*Gabble*, v. (1577)	1. intr. To talk volubly, inarticulately and incoherently; to chatter, jabber, prattle. Also, to read so fast as to be unintelligible.	1758	2. trans. To utter rapidly and unintelligibly. Also with *over.*	*Monthly Rev.* 308 **Gabbling** infidelity and laughing at the religion of his country. (*Infidelity* = In general sense: Disbelief, incredulity.; OED, s.v. *infidelity*, n. 2)
(17)	*Warble*, v.1 (a1400–50)	†1. b. trans.? To proclaim by flourish of trumpets;? to sound (a trumpet). Obs.	a1771	3. trans. a. To sing with quavering trills and runs, to utter melodiously, to carol. Also to warble forth, out, over. 3. trans. b. To express or celebrate in song or verse. Also with *forth*, †*out*.	T. Gray *Ode* in W. Mason *Mem. Life & Writings* (1775) 236 The Sky-Lark **warbles** high His trembling thrilling extacy. **Another interesting example provided by the OED:** 1868 L. M. Alcott *Little Women* I. ii. 32 Having **warbled** his thanks..Hugo departed.
(18)	*Hiss*, v. (c1400)	1. intr. To make the sharp spirant sound emitted by certain animals, as geese and serpents, or caused (e.g.) by the escape of steam through a narrow aperture, or uttered in the pronunciation of 's'. (Latin *sibilāre.*) Also in Electricity (cf. *hissing* arc n.).	1775	5. To utter or express by hissing or with a hiss, esp. as expressive of intense anger or hate.	Johnson *Taxation No Tyranny* 78 One of the threats **hissed out** by the Congress.

Continued on next page

Tab. 5.8: *Continued*

Verb type		Date of first attestation as a transitive/intransitive verb	Date of first attestation in the reaction object construction		Example
(19)	*Whimper*, v. (1513)	1. a. intr. To utter a feeble, whining, broken cry, as a child about to burst into tears; to make a low complaining sound.	1785	1. c. trans. To utter or express in a whimper.	W. Cowper *Task* iv. 429 But poverty, with most who **whimper forth** Their long complaints, is self-inflicted woe. **Another interesting example provided by the OED:** 1820 J. Hogg *Allan Gordon* in *Tales & Sketches* (1837) I. 314 The generous animal whined and **whimpered** her joy.
(20)	*Bark*, v.1 (c885)	1. intr. To utter a sharp explosive cry. (Orig. of dogs, hence of other animals, and spec. of foxes at rutting-time.) Const. *at* (*on*, *upon*, *against*, obs.).	1821	5. trans. or with subord. clause (also bark out, bark forth): To utter or give forth with a bark; to break out with, burst forth with.	J. Clare *Village Minstrel* II. 33 The dog **bark'd** a welcome.
(21)	*Twitter*, v.1 (c1374)	1. a. intr. Of a bird: To utter a succession of light tremulous notes; to chirp continuously with a tremulous effect.	1821	2. a. trans. Of a bird: To utter or express by twittering.	J. Clare *Village Minstrel* II. 105 Linnets,..**twittering** their welcomes to the day's return.

(22)	*Whoop*, v. (a1400)	1. a. intr. To utter a cry of 'whoop!' or a loud vocal sound resembling this; to shout, hollo (as in incitement, summons, exultation, defiance, intimidation, or mere excitement).	1821	2. intr. To hoot, as an owl. Also trans. as in 1b – 1d. 1. b. trans. with cognate obj. (either a n. or the actual words), or indef. it: to utter with a whoop; to express by whooping.	J. Clare Village Minstrel II. 33 The owl..**whoop'd** a 'good-night'. 1865 F. Parkman *Huguenots* iv, in Pioneers of France in New World 44 An Indian chief..ran to meet them, **whooping** and clamoring welcome.
(23)	*Grumble*, v. (a1586)	2. To utter murmurs expressive of discontent; hence gen., to complain. Const. *about*, *at*, *over*, occas. *for* (a desired object), with inf., or clause.	1824	3. trans. a. To express or utter with mumbling, muttering, or complaining. Also with *out*.	in *Spirit of Public Jrnls.* (1825) 285 He**..grumbled out** good night, and departed to his domus.
(24)	*Coo*, v. (1672)	1. a. intr. To make the soft murmuring sound or note characteristic of doves and pigeons.	1834	4. trans. a. To utter or express by cooing.	*Fraser's Mag.* 10 444 A pair of turtle-doves lived in one nest, and **cooed** their love on the same branch.
(25)	*Bellow*, v. (c1000)	1. a. prop. To roar as a bull, or as a cow when excited. (Ordinarily, a cow lows.)	1852	4. b. With obj.: To give forth, emit, utter, or proclaim with loud noise.	Tennyson *Ode Wellington* 66 His captain's-ear has heard them boom, **Bellowing** victory, bellowing doom. **Less clear example provided by the OED:** 1603 R. Knolles Gen. Hist. Turkes 663 **Bellowing out** certaine superstitious charmes.[d] (OED, s.v. *bellow*, v. 3. b. trans. To utter (words or cries) in a loud and deep voice; frequently with *out*, *forth*).

Continued on next page

Tab. 5.8: *Continued*

Verb type	Date of first attestation as a transitive/intransitive verb	Date of first attestation in the reaction object construction		Example
(26) *Jabber*, v. (1499)	1. a. intr. To talk rapidly and indistinctly or unintelligibly; to speak volubly and with little sense; to chatter, gabble, prattle. Often applied, in contempt or derision, to the speaking of a language which is unintelligible to the hearer.	1854	2. trans. To speak or utter rapidly and indistinctly; to express by jabbering. Often contemptuously = to speak (a foreign language), with the implication that it is unintelligible to the hearer.	H. Miller *Schools & Schoolmasters* (1856) xviii. 383 A poor idiot,..used to come every day to the churchyard, to..**jabber** in broken expressions his grief.
(27) *Bleat*, v. (OE)	1. a. intr. To cry, as a sheep, goat, or calf.	1871	1. b. trans. (with cognate object.) Also to bleat out: to give forth with a bleat.	B. Taylor tr. Goethe *Faust* I. v. 104 An old he-goat.. Should his good-night in lustful gallop **bleat** her! Originally written in German by Johann Wolfgang von Goethe and translated into English in the original metres by Bayard Taylor.
(28) *Squeal*, v. (a1300)	1. intr. To utter (or give out) a more or less prolonged loud sharp cry, esp. by reason of pain or sudden alarm; to scream shrilly: a. Of persons.	1871	4. trans. To utter or produce with a shrill, grating, or squeaking sound. Also with *out*.	L. Stephen *Playground of Europe* (1894) xii. 294 Pigs..**squeal** emphatic disapproval of their enforced journey.

(29)	*Grunt*, v. (c725)	1. a. intr. Of a hog: To utter its characteristic low gruff sound. Also of other animals and of persons (with conscious allusion to the pig): To utter a sound resembling this.	1875	2. b. trans. To utter or express with a grunt; to breathe out with a grunt.	F. T. Buckland *Log-bk.* 100 He only **grunted** his gratitude.
(30)	*Snap*, v. (1530)	I. 1. a. intr. Of animals: To make a quick or sudden bite at something; to feed on in this way.	1888	I. 2. b. trans. To utter (words) in an angry, sharp, or peevish manner or tone. c. Similarly with *out*.	F. Hume *Madame Midas* i. ii. 26 Slivers was just going to **snap out** a refusal. **Another interesting example provided by the OED:** 1897 'O. Rhoscomyl' *White Rose Arno* xxviii. 298 He tore into the long reaches behind, **panting** and **snapping** curses.
(31)	*Hoot*, v. (?c1200)	2. a. trans. To assail with shouts or sounds of disapproval, contempt, or derision.	1989	b. trans. Of the driver of a motor vehicle or (occas.) transf. of the vehicle itself: to sound (a horn); to transmit or express by making such a sound. Cf. *honk* v.1 3c.	*Independent* 27 Nov. 1/6 Passing cars, many adorned with the national flag or red, white and blue ribbons, **hooted** their support.

a Modern translation provided by Stanton (1995).

b Note that the object in this case is preceded by a demonstrative determiner.

c I reproduce the OED's entry verbatim, but note that the authorship of the narrative poem *A Lover's Complaint*, though doubtful, is most commonly attributed to Shakespeare. Older editions of the OED also attribute the citation to Shakespeare.

d Note that the object in this case is preceded by a determiner.

5.2.3 Results

The procedure detailed in § 5.2.1 and § 5.2.2 allowed me to identify a total of 87 tokens of reaction object constructions in my historical data sources. They involve 69 different verb types, which were collected from Jespersen, Visser and Levin, and finally checked in the OED. Of these 69 verbs, nine were found in Jespersen, another nine in Visser, and 35 in Levin. The remaining 16 verbs up to the total of 69 occurred in more than one source list, as shown in Tab. 5.9.

Tab. 5.9: Distribution of verbs and ROCs across the data sources

	Number of verbs initially investigated	**N° of ROCs**	**Breakdown of verbs taking ROs per data source**
Jespersen (1909–1949)	12	12	9
Visser (1963–1973)	506	24	9
Levin (1993)	127	**51 (20 with nonverbal expression verbs; 31 with manner of speaking verbs)**	35
Levin & Jespersen	-	-	1
Levin & Visser	-	-	13
Levin, Jespersen & Visser	-	-	2
TOTAL	645	87	69

Tab. 5.10 provides the complete list of 69 verb types attested with reaction objects in the historical record (the arrangement here is chronological by date of first attestation in the ROC).

My next step was examining the distribution across time of the 51 reaction object constructions attested with Levin's verbs; this is shown in Fig. 5.4.[40] It reflects well that the construction gradually expanded

40 The graph takes into account the eighteenth century example of ROC involving the verb *smile* (see examples (12) and (15) in Tab. 5.7).

Tab. 5.10: Verb types attested with ROs in the historical record, in chronological order

	Verb type	**First attestation in the ROC**	**Source**
1	*Moan*, v. (a1325)	a1325	(Levin)
2	*Bray*, v.[1] (a1300)	c1400 (?c1380)	(Levin & Visser)
3	*Yelp*, v. (c888)	c1400	(Levin & Visser)
4	*Roar*, v.[1] (OE)	c1450	(Levin)
5	*Mumble*, v. (c1325)	1534	(Levin)
6	*Breathe*, v. (a1300)	1535	(Jespersen)
7	*Thunder*, v. (c888)	1548	(Levin)
8	*Buzz*, v.[1] (1398)	1583	(Visser)
9	*Clap* v.[1] (c1300)	1591	(Levin)
10	*Chat*, v.[1] (c1440)	1596	(Visser)
11	*Shriek*, v. (1567)	1597	(Levin)
12	*Rave*, v.[1] (a1325)	1602	(Visser)
13	*Weep*, v. (c897)	1602	(Levin & Visser)
14	*Pant*, v. (c1350)	1608	(Visser)
15	*Groan*, v. (7..)	1609	(Levin)
16	*Laugh*, v. (eOE)	1609	(Levin & Jespersen)
17	*Blush*, v. (?a1400)	a1616	(Visser)
18	*Shout*, v. (c1374)	a1616	(Levin)
19	*Neigh*, v. (OE)	1624	(Visser)
20	*Drone*, v.[1] (?a1513)	1631	(Levin & Visser)
21	*Snort*, v. (a1366)	a1635	(Levin & Visser)
22	*Murmur*, v. (c1390)	1637	(Levin)
23	*Snuffle*, v. (1583)	1641	(Levin)
24	*Giggle*, v.[1] (1509)	a1657	(Levin & Visser)
25	*Whisper*, v. (c950)	1697	(Levin)
26	*Whine*, v. (c1275)	1702	(Levin)
27	*Nod*, v. (c1390)	1713	(Levin, Jespersen and Visser)
28	*Mutter*, v.[1] (a1325)	1724	(Levin)
29	*Trumpet*, v. (1530)	1729	(Levin & Visser)
30	*Grin*, v.[2] (OE)	1732	(Levin)
31	*Lour, lower*, v. (c1290)	1746	(Visser)
32	*Purr*, v.[2] (1620)	1748	(Levin)
33	*Sob*, v.[1] (a1200)	1748	(Levin)
34	*Gabble*, v. (1577)	1758	(Levin & Visser)

Continued on next page

Tab. 5.10: *Continued*

	Verb type	First attestation in the ROC	Source
35	*Growl*, v.[3] (c138.)	1759	(Levin & Visser)
36	*Warble*, v.[1] (a1400–50)	a1771	(Levin)
37	*Frown*, v. (c1386)	1775	(Levin & Visser)
38	*Hiss*, v. (c1400)	1775	(Levin)
39	*Whimper*, v. (1513)	1785	(Levin & Visser)
40	*Wave*, v. (c1000)	1810	(Levin)
41	*Sigh*, v. (13..)	1811	(Levin)
42	*Bow*, v.[1] (c893)	1814	(Jespersen)
43	*Smile*, v. (a1300)	1814	(Levin, Jespersen and Visser)
44	*Bark*, v.[1] (c885)	1821	(Levin)
45	*Twitter*, v.[1] (c1374)	1821	(Levin)
46	*Whoop*, v. (a1400)	1821	(Levin)
47	*Grumble*, v. (a1586)	1824	(Levin & Visser)
48	*Coo*, v. (1672)	1834	(Levin)
49	*Cough*, v.[1] (c1325)	1837	(Levin)
50	*Kiss*, v. (c900)	1847	(Jespersen)
51	*Gesticulate*, v. (1609)	1849–1850	(Jespersen)
52	*Sneeze*, v. (1493)	1851	(Visser)
53	*Bellow*, v. (c1000)	1852	(Levin)
54	*Jabber*, v. (1499)	1854	(Levin)
55	*Guffaw*, v. (1721)	1865	(Levin)
56	*Sniff*, v. (c1340)	1865	(Levin)
57	*Look*, v. (eOe)	1867	(Jespersen)
58	*Bleat*, v. (OE)	1871	(Levin)
59	*Squeal*, v. (a1300)	1871	(Levin)
60	*Grunt*, v. (c725)	1875	(Levin & Visser)
61	*Low*, v.[1] (OE)	1876	(Visser)
62	*Cackle*, v.[1] (?c1225)	1880	(Levin)
63	*Dance*, v. (c1300)	1881	(Jespersen)
64	*Snap*, v. (1530)	1888	(Levin)
65	*Beam*, v. (c1430)	1901	(Jespersen)
66	*Pat*, v.[1] (1533)	1912	(Jespersen)
67	*Stare*, v. (OE)	1913–1914	(Jespersen)
68	*Wink*, v.[1] (c897)	1919	(Levin)
69	*Hoot*, v. (?c1200)	1989	(Levin)

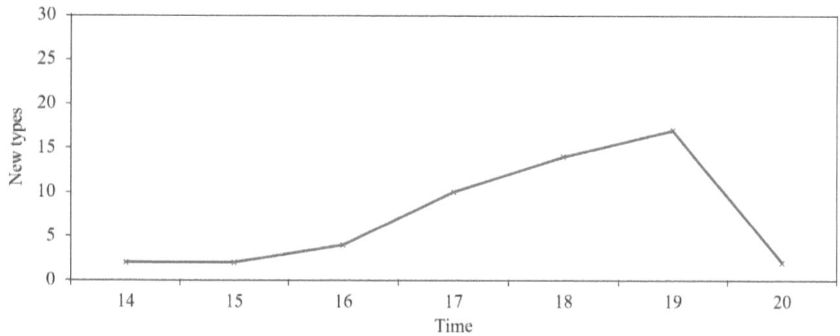

Fig. 5.4: Accumulation of new verb types entering the ROC by century (I). Based on Levin's list and the OED. No. of verbs: 51.

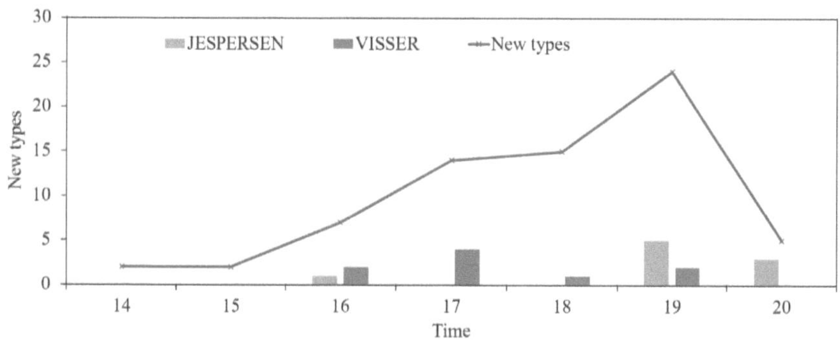

Fig. 5.5: Accumulation of new verb types entering the ROC by century (II). Based on Jespersen, Visser, Levin and the OED. No. of verbs: 69.

to an increasing number of verb types, starting approximately in the fourteenth century, and reaching a significant peak in the nineteenth century. If we include the 18 additional verb types from Jespersen and Visser, the picture does not differ significantly. As shown in Fig. 5.5, ROCs accumulate during the Early and Late Modern English periods (16th - 20th centuries).

For the nineteenth century I decided to conduct a search on the string 'express by' employing the advanced search tool of the OED. This method enabled me to retrieve 12 new verbs also recorded in the ROC, in addition to the 69 verbs above mentioned. These 12 new verbs are *bay, beck, colour, curtsy, droop, lute, ooh, score, slob, thump, whinny* and *yowl.* The ROCs in question are shown in chronological order in Tab. 5.11, whereas Fig. 5.6 reflects the distribution of these new verb types over time. The data confirms my previous findings: the earliest examples of ROCs with these new verbs concentrate mostly in the nineteenth century.

Tab. 5.11: New verb types attested with ROs in the OED, in chronological order. Data retrieved using the search string 'express by'

Verb type	Date of first attestation as a transitive/ intransitive verb	Date of first attestation in the reaction object construction		Example
(1) *Lute*, v.1 (1377)	b. quasi-trans. with cognate obj. or quoted words: To express by means of the lute.	1377	b. quasi-trans. with cognate obj. or quoted words: To express by means of the lute.	Langland *Piers Plowman* B. xviii. 423 Thanne **luted** Loue in a loude note, Ecce quam bonum et quam iocundum, etc. [PDE 'then **luted** Love in a loud note, Behold, how good and joyful a thing it is' (to live together in unity.) *Psalm* 133:1][a]
(2) *Droop*, v. (c1330)	5. To flag in spirit or courage; to become dejected, dispirited, or despondent.	1605	6. †b. nonce use with out: To express by drooping.	*Hist. Tryall Cheualry* sig. F2v, Why wither not these trees..And euery neighbour branch **droup out** their grief?
(3) *Curtsy | curtsey*, v. (a1556)	1. a. intr. To make a curtsy; to do reverence to; now, like the n., said only of women.	a1817	2. b. To give or express by curtsying.	J. Austen *Northanger Abbey* (1818) II. vii. 128 She **curtesied** her acquiescence.
(4) *Beck*, v. (a1300)	1.a. intr. To make a mute signal, or significant gesture, as by nodding, shaking the fore-finger, etc.	1821	1. b. trans. To express by a beck.	J. Clare *Village Minstrel* II. 72 While turning nods **beck** thanks for kindness done.
(5) *Colour | color*, v. (a1325)	I. 1. a. trans. To impart colour to; to impregnate with colour. In early use usu. in pass. to be coloured: to be of the specified colour.	1824	I. 3. †c. trans. To express by blushing. Cf. *blush* v. 3c. Obs. nonce-use.	S. E. Ferrier *Inheritance* I. xiv. 151 'You understand the difference, don't you, Miss St. Clair?' who only **coloured** a reply.

Tab. 5.11: *Continued*

Verb type	Date of first attestation as a transitive/ intransitive verb	Date of first attestation in the reaction object construction		Example
(6) *Yowl*, v. (a1225)	1. a. intr. To cry out loudly from pain, grief, or distress; also said of the howling of dogs and various wild animals, the 'wauling' of cats, and (formerly) of the hooting of owls, the cooing of doves.	1842	2. trans. To express by yowling; to utter with a yowl.	J. Wilson *Recreations Christopher North* I. i. 13 The chained mastiff in the yard **yowls** his admiration.
(7) *Bay*, v.1 (1399)	2. fig. Applied (depreciatively) to the noise of human assailants.	1856	4. To give forth, utter, or express by baying.	E. K. Kane *Arctic Explor.* I. xxii. 279 These faithful servants generally **bayed** their full-mouth welcome from afar off.
(8) *Whinny*, v. (1530)	1. intr. Of a horse: To neigh, esp. in a low or gentle way; also occasionally of other animals, as calves or certain birds, or of inanimate objects making a similar noise.	1888	2. trans. To utter with a whinnying sound; to express by whinnying.	A. C. Gunter *Mr. Potter* iv. 45 The donkeys.. **whinny** their pleasure as they drink.
(9) *Thump*, v. (c1537)	1. a. trans. To strike or beat heavily, as with the fist, a club, or any blunt instrument, producing a dead, dull, somewhat hard sound; also, without reference to the sound produced, to hammer, pound, knock forcibly.	1928	1. e. To express by thumps.	Manch. *Guardian Weekly* 26 Oct. 335/3 His [sc. a dog's] tail..**thumped** a welcome.
(10) *Ooh*, v. (1930)	1. intr. To say 'ooh'. Esp. in to ooh and ah (cf. *ah* v.).	1970	2. trans. a. To express by making the sound 'ooh'. rare.	G. Corso *Elegaic Feelings Amer.* iii. 9 How we knew to feel each dawn, **to ooh and aah** each golden sorrow and helplessness coast to coast.

Continued on next page

Tab. 5.11: *Continued*

Verb type	Date of first attestation as a transitive/ intransitive verb	Date of first attestation in the reaction object construction		Example
(11) *Score*, v. (c1386)	III. To record by scores. 10. a. To record (debts) by means of notches on a tally; hence to write down as a debt. Also with *up*.	1607	3. To produce (marks, figures, etc.) by cutting. Also (with allusion to sense 10), to record or express by cuts or notches.	1607 B. Jonson *Volpone* iii. ii. 67 Draw your iust sword, And **score** your vengeance, on my front, and face.
(12) *Slob*, v. (1887)	*Slobbed* adj. 1887 W. D. Parish & W. F. Shaw *Dict. Kentish Dial.* 152 Slobbed, slopped, spilt.	1918	trans. To slop (out); to express by slobbering.	a1918 W. Owen *Poems* (1963) 69 Drooping tongues from jaws that **slob** their relish.

a Modern translation provided by Byram-Wigfield (2006, 214).

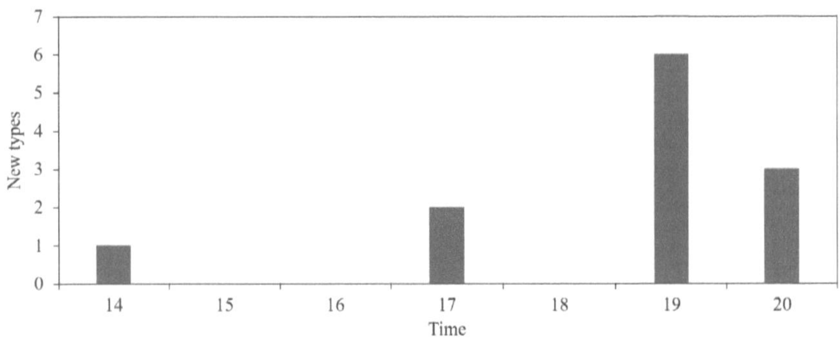

Fig. 5.6: Accumulation of new verb types attested with ROs in the OED. Data retrieved using the search string 'express by'.

Some prior research, most notably Cortés-Rodríguez and González-Orta (2006, 272), has claimed that the reaction object construction already existed in OE. However, my findings do not support this claim, despite the fact that 20 out of the 69 verb types displayed in Tab. 5.10 go back to the OE period, namely *bark*, *bellow*, *bleat*, *bow*, *grin*, *groan*, *grunt*, *kiss*, *laugh*, *look*, *low*, *neigh*, *roar*, *stare*, *thunder*, *wave*, *weep*, *whisper*, *wink* and *yelp*. It has to be acknowledged, though, that my data on reaction objects is ultimately based on the OED, which contains less than half a million words for OE (see Hilpert 2013, 121). Further research should therefore be conducted in the future using the *Dictionary of Old English Web Corpus* (600–1150; DOE Web Corpus; Healey et al. 2009), which contains around three million running words of OE.

If we normalize per one million words the data on the 51 ROCs represented in Fig. 5.4 above, the graph preserves roughly the same camel shape (cf. Fig. 5.7), though the peak now coincides with the eighteenth century rather than with the nineteenth. This finding is interesting if we bear in mind that there is evidence (see Algeo 1998, 63–64, Hoffmann 2004, Hilpert 2013, among others) that the OED's compilers were inconsistent in the thoroughness with which they gathered citations; the eighteenth century, for example, is seriously underrepresented, in terms of number of citations, with respect to the nineteenth and twentieth centuries, as shown in Fig. 5.8 adapted from Hilpert (2013, 121).[41] The peak of ROCs in the eighteenth century is thus specially noteworthy and confirms that the expansion of the construction is essentially a LModE development, as I have pointed out earlier.

I have to admit here that I cannot yet offer a clear explanation for the apparent absence in the OED of new verb types used in the ROC during the twentieth century, as this century is not one of those underrepresented in the dictionary (see Hilpert 2013, 121). For the time being, what we can affirm is that the ROC is a low-frequency

41 Hoffmann (2004, 26) argues that "normalized frequency counts might suggest an inappropriate level of precision" as "20 per cent of all its [OED] quotations have been shortened". Hilpert (2013), however, manages to show the reliability of normalized frequencies to examine the development of morphological constructions such as the V-*ment* construction, based on data from the OED (see Hilpert 2013, 120 ff).

construction, and thus its occurrences may have escaped the eye of the editors and readers of the dictionary. We know, though, that new verbs have continued to enter the construction in recent times. Thus, a search in Google, for instance, yielded uses in the ROC for the Anglo-Saxon manner of speaking verb *call*, as in (41). Martínez-Vázquez likewise identifies nonce verbs in the construction such as the verb of sound emission *tut-tut* (cf. OED, *tut*, v. 1832) in (42). Yet another verb class not mentioned by Levin (1993, 98) but which appears to be of very recent occurrence involves verbs of light emission such as *gleam* and *shine* in examples (43) and (44). As shown by Faber and Mairal (1999, 261), this verb class is closely connected with emotional meanings, and therefore their attestation in the ROC should not come as a surprise.

(41) The bird **called** its displeasure as the revenant cut again and again.

2013, FanFiction; *A Smoked Glass Crow*. Cf. OED, *call*, v. (OE)

(42) I have great respect for the work you are doing. Seed **tut-tuts** his thanks.

(Martínez-Vázquez 2010, 555)

(43) His monocle **gleamed** polite hostility; his naked eye was evasive and shifty.

1935, Isherwood, *Mr Norris Changes Trains* (cited in Snell-Hornby 1983). Cf. OED, *gleam*, v.[1] (a1225)

(44) Around the last bend of the driveway, the lights of the house **shone** their welcome.

(COCA, 2011, FIC, Bk:WhenSparrowsFall; Martínez-Vázquez 2015, 168)

The results presented so far suggest that, despite being a rare construction in terms of type frequency, the ROC is still on the rise, an aspect of the construction that will be examined later on in Chapter 7. On the other hand, my data shows that the ROC has proliferated in the Late Modern English period. This finding is particularly relevant, since it suggests a path of development for the ROC which is parallel to that followed by other valency-increasing constructions involving a process of transitivization such as the cognate object construction, the *way*-construction, and the dummy *it* object construction, which acquired prominence during the LModE period (approx. 1700–1925; see Israel 1996, Mondorf 2016, Lavidas 2018). If this is actually the case, we would be facing here a systemic change in the English language (see Mondorf 2016), since these argument structure changes seem to be running in parallel. In the following sections common aspects of the development of these valency-increasing constructions will be briefly outlined.

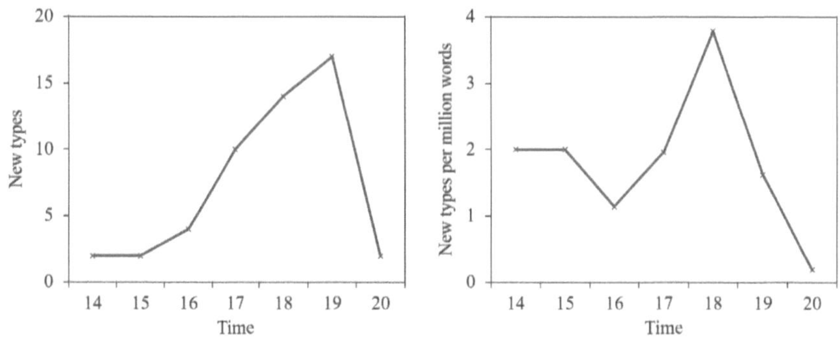

Fig. 5.7: Accumulation of new verb types entering the ROC by century (III)

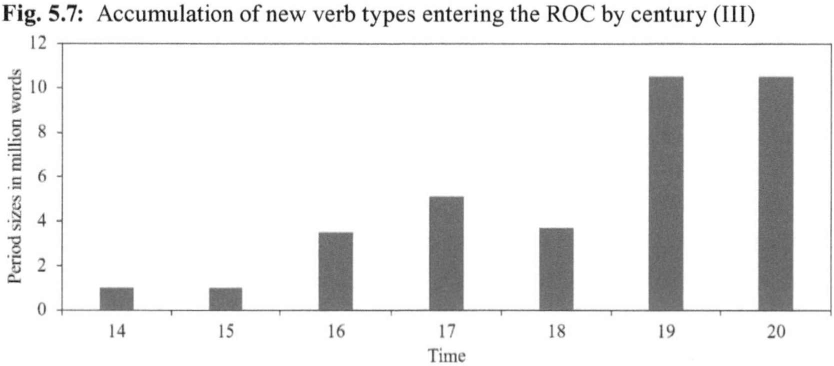

Fig. 5.8: Approximate period sizes of the OED from the 14th to the 20th centuries. Adapted from Hilpert (2013, 121)

5.2.3.1 The ROC and the cognate object construction

According to Visser, cognate object constructions (COCs) involving intransitive verbs such as *fly a flight*, *breathe a breath*, *game a game*, *sigh a sigh*, *die a death*, *sleep a sleep*, and *live a life* were rare in OE, increased their frequency in ME, and became numerous in the Modern period, where their usage "remains confined to literary diction" (Visser 1963–1973: I, § 424 (b): 415). Visser also hypothesizes that these constructions could have been formed on analogy with cognate object constructions involving transitives, or due to the loss of case marking that became general in ME – in OE some intransitive verbs could govern a cognate noun in the dative, as already mentioned in passing in the introduction and also at the end of § 3.2.1.1–.

Following a similar procedure to the one used here for the study of the formation of ROCs, Lavidas (2013, 2014, 2018) tests Visser's hypothesis. He collected a sample of 59 verbs for which "there is a clear description (or example) of the **first** appearance of their cognate construction in the OED" (Lavidas 2013, 79; emphasis in the original). Some of these intransitive verbs are the following: *dance*, *fight*, *fly*, *grin*, *know*, *labor*, *laugh*, *limp*, *live*, *love*, *mean*, *name*, *pick*, *play*, *quack*, *quadrille*, *rede*, *shoot*, *sleep*, *slush*, *smile*, *snore*, *spang*, *stand*, *steer*, *strike*, *strive*, *sup*, *vote*, *vow*, *war* and *yawn* (p.c.). The results of this study show precisely what Visser had predicted: cognate object constructions involving intransitives are rare in OE (only 5.1 %), increased their frequency in ME (35.6 % of the data), and became quite numerous in the Modern period (59.3 %). Tab. 5.12 shows these findings. Note that Lavidas uses the chronological periods of the York, Helsinki, and Penn-Helsinki corpora, which are distributed as shown in Tab. 5.13.

In Fig. 5.9, I merged these different subperiods into four so as to compare Lavidas' data with my own data for the ROC: Old English (850–1150), Middle English (1150–1500), Modern English (1500–1914), and Present Day English (1914-onwards). As can be seen, in both the COC and the ROC, there is a peak in type frequency in the Modern English period. However, there is an important difference between the two graphs when it comes to ME. The increase in types in the ROC

Tab. 5.12: Accumulation of new verb types entering the COC per period (based on the OED). Adapted from Lavidas (2013, 79)

O2	O3	O4	M1	M2	M3	M4	E1	E2	E3	MBE
0	**0**	**3/59** (5.08 %)	**0**	**7/59** (11.86 %)	**8/59** (13.56 %)	**6/59** (10.17 %)	**1/59** (1.69 %)	**7/59** (11.86 %)	**8/59** (13.56 %)	**19/59** (32.20 %)

Tab. 5.13: Chronological periods of the York, Helsinki, and Penn-Helsinki corpora. Adapted from Lavidas (2013, 74fn11)

Corpus	Period		Time span
The York-Toronto-Helsinki Parsed Corpus of Old English Prose (YCOE)	Old English	O2	850–950
		O3	950–1050
		O4	1050–1150
The Penn-Helsinki Parsed Corpus of Middle English (PPCME2)	Middle English	M1	1150–1250
		M2	1250–1350
		M3	1350–1420
		M4	1420–1500
The Penn-Helsinki Parsed Corpus of Early Modern English (PPCEME)	Early Modern English	E1	1500–1570
		E2	1570–1640
		E3	1640–1710[a]
The Penn-Helsinki Parsed Corpus of Modern British English (PPCMBE)	Modern British English	MBE	1700–1914

a There is an overlap of ten years between the EModE period (1640–1710) and the Modern British period (1700–1914).

is only very slight, as opposed to the COC. This could be explained by the later emergence of most of the verbs featuring in the ROC. As represented in Fig. 5.10 further, out of the 69 verbs attested in the ROC, 20 verbs go back to the OE period (up to 1100), 35 became part of the English language in ME (1100–1500), and 14 are new formations (1500–1925): *coo, drone, gabble, gesticulate, giggle, grumble, guffaw, pat, purr shriek, snap, snuffle, trumpet,* and *whimper.* Interestingly, 11 of these new formations belong to the class of sound emission verbs (i.e. *coo, drone, gabble, giggle, grumble, guffaw, purr, shriek, snuffle, trumpet,* and *whimper*), a finding that reinforces Fanego's claim that this particular verb class became prominent in type and token frequency during ModE (Fanego 2017, 65–66). In this regard, Fig. 5.10 also shows that out of the 67 verbs Fanego attested in the subschema of the intransitive motion construction involving sound emission verbs (e.g. *The trolley rumbled through the tunnel*), 27 were documented as sound emission verbs in OE and ME, while 36 were new formations.[42] This time I am using the slightly different temporal distribution represented in Tab. 5.14.

42 Four verbs of uncertain origin in Fanego's 2017 list have been excluded from this count: *quethir(en)* 'to whizz, whirr', *swalter* 'to slosh through water', *splodge*

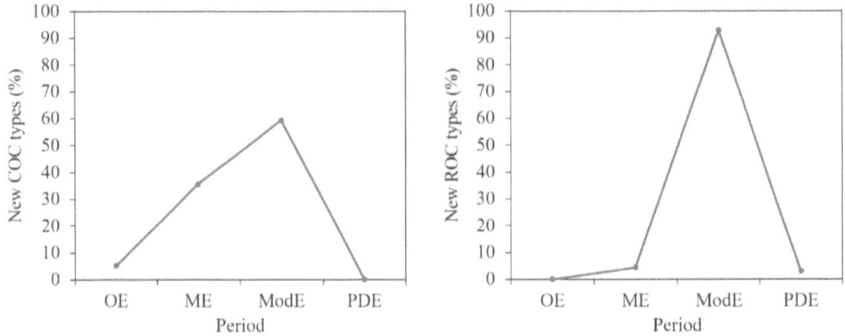

Fig. 5.9: Accumulation of new verb types per period in the COC and the ROC. Based on Lavidas (2013) and on 69 ROCs.

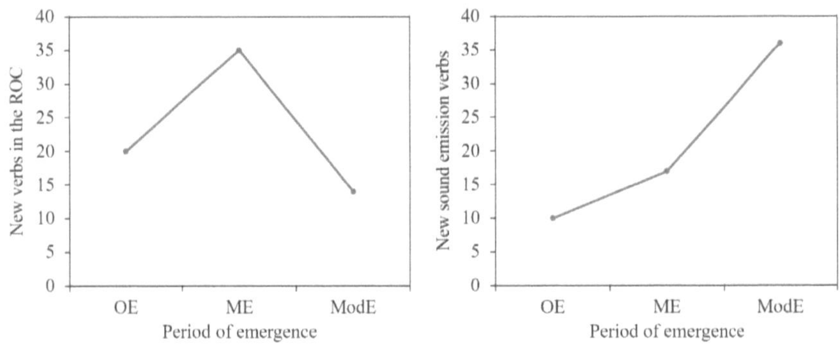

Fig. 5.10: Periods of emergence of 69 verbs attested in the ROC, and of 63 sound emission verbs

Tab. 5.14: Historical periods of English. Adapted from Fanego (2017)

Period		**Time span**
Old English	OE	up to 1100
Middle English	ME	1100–1500
Modern English	ModE	1500–1925

'to trudge or plod splashily through mud or water', and *swoosh* 'to move with a noise like that of the syllable swoosh'.

Lavidas' work focuses only on two of the three types of cognate object constructions recognized by Horrocks and Stavrou (2010, 263), namely transitivizing cognate object constructions (e.g. *She dreamed the most wonderful dream*) and aspectual cognate object constructions (e.g. *She smiled an enigmatic smile*). As described in § 3.2.1.3, reaction objects display the morphosyntactic features of the latter, which could be an additional reason why these two constructions became prominent during the same period. The nonprototypical features of the ROC and the aspectual cognate object construction might explain why neither of them have been found in languages which are typologically different from English such as Modern Greek, as shown by (45) and (46) from Horrocks and Stavrou (2010, 300). In the well-known typology of languages proposed by Talmy (1985, 2000), English is 'satellite framed' and shows a high degree of syntactic flexibility which makes it 'constructionally tolerant' (for this label, see Perek and Hilpert 2016); Modern Greek, by contrast, is essentially a verb-framed language.

(45) She **smiled** <u>her approval</u>.
Mod. Gr.: *Xamo'jelase tin 'engri'si tis.
smiled-pfve the approval of-her

(46) S/he **smiled** <u>a disarming smile</u>.
Mod. Gr.: *Xamo'jelase 'ena afoplisti'ko xa'mojelo.

5.2.3.2 The ROC and the *way*-construction

The ROC does not only show striking similarities with the history of the cognate object construction but also with the *way*-construction. This construction has been examined from a historical perspective by Israel (1996), Mondorf (2011), Gisborne and Patten (2011), Traugott and Trousdale (2013), Barðdal and Gildea (2015), Perek (2015b, 2016a, 2018, 2020), Perek and Hilpert (2017), McColm (2015, 2019), and more recently by Fanego (2019). As noted in the introduction, and also in § 3.2.1.2, Traugott and Trousdale (2013) claim that the *way*-construction emerged in ME out of two different sets of verbs: an intransitive motion set involving verbs such as *go*, *wend*, *fare*, *flee* and *ride*, and a transitive set of verbs involving the verbs *nimen* 'take' and *take*. Over the ME period, the *way*-construction as we know it in PDE with its formal constraints (§ 3.2.1.2) was not solidly formed yet (i.e. [SUB_i [V $POSS_i$ *way*]

DIR]; what we have instead is, in Traugott and Trousdale's words, "only constructs that were instances of an intransitive motion construction and a transitive acquisition construction, some of which happened to include the lexical/referential construction *wei*" (Traugott and Trousdale 2013, 82).

As we enter the EModE period (sixteenth and seventeenth centuries), data from the *Middle English Dictionary* (1100–1500; MED; Kurath, Sherman and Robert 1952–2001) and the *Helsinki Corpus of English Texts* (c.730–1710; HC; Rissanen et al. 1991) reveals that the *way*-construction starts to take on some shape. During this period, the intransitive pattern becomes mainly restricted to deictic motion verbs like *go* and *come* whereas the transitive variant of the construction expanded to new verb types such as *make* and *pave*, and some verbs of obstruction such as *fight*, *battle*, *force*, *push*, *drag* and *dig*. At this point, the formal side of the *way*-construction also becomes quite fixed, i.e. possessive rather than an article or a demonstrative, *wei* instead of *ways*, DIR "becomes distinctly preferred" (2013, 84), and no prepositions or adverbs (cf. § 3.2.1.2). This means that we have, on the one hand, an emergent subschema consisting of an intransitive deictic motion verb + POSS + *way* (without DIR) meaning 'go along a path' and, on the other, a second subschema consisting of a transitive verb + POSS + *way* with the meaning 'cause to traverse a path'. Following Traugott and Trousdale (2013), this process of formation of the *way*-construction as a pairing of form and meaning during the EModE period was preceded by some pre-constructionalization constructional changes: (i) the *neoanalysis* of *way* as a complement of the motion verb (i.e. the interpretation of *way* as a fake object possibly by *analogy* with the transitive acquisition subschema), (ii) the *routinization* or *fixation* of its morphosyntactic features, and (iii) the *host-class expansion* of POSS *way* to new transitive verbs such as *make*, *pave* and some other verbs denoting obstruction such as *force* and *dig*.

From the end of the seventeenth century, the transitive subschema expands to more new verb types semantically similar to *force* and *dig* in that they indicate manner to some degree. These are manner of action verbs like *beg*, *worm* and *elbow*, which are marginally transitive and do not entail motion. By the early nineteenth century, the *way*-construction expands to verbs denoting accompanying action such as *shoot*, and *plash*. Some of these new verbs are *intransitive* (cf. *plash*, v.[2] 2. intr. “To strike and break the surface of water with a splashing sound; to move through water splashily; to splash about”.), while others such as *shoot* can be either transitive or intransitive (cf. OED, s.v. *shoot*, v.). In this respect, Traugott and Trousdale (2013) hypothesize that these amphibious verbs “may have been transitional types enabling intransitive verbs of manner to be recruited into the construction [e.g. *plash*]” (2013, 87). As previously seen in Fig. 5.10 (§ 5.2.3.1), verbs of sounds such as *plash* increased their type and token frequency during ModE, a fact that explains part of the development of this particular dimension/sense/subschema of the *way*-construction. A graphic representation of the development of the *way*-construction as described in Traugott and Trousdale (2013, 76–93) is in Fig. 5.11 below.

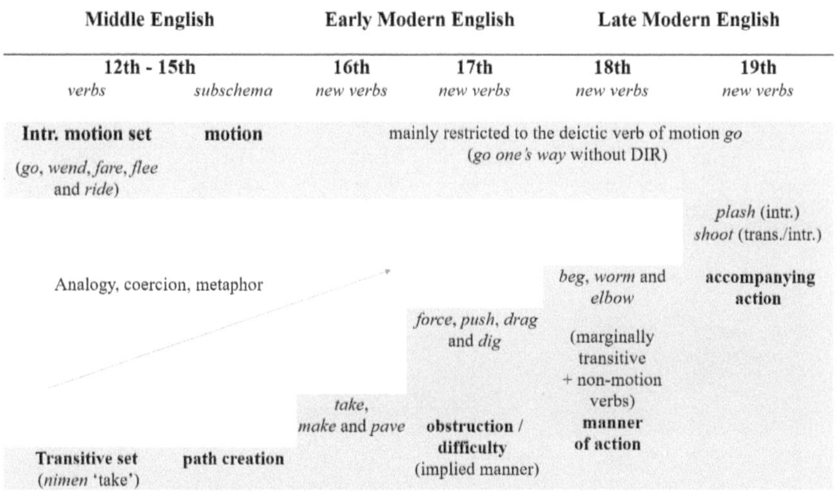

Fig. 5.11: Historical development of the *way*-construction. Traugott and Trousdale’s account (based on MED, HC and CLMET-EV) concurs with Israel’s (1996) historical study (mostly based on the OED) regarding the periods in which verb types begin to occur in the construction. Traugott and Trousdale (2013) and Israel (1996) also agree on the occurrence of *go* in the construction in PDE contra Goldberg (1995, 199).

The extension of the *way*-construction to new verb types was gradual and constant over the centuries (Israel 1996, 226; Traugott and Trousdale 2013, 79) until it became grammatically stable around the nineteenth century. This also seems to have also been the case with the reaction object construction. As shown in Fig. 5.11 and Fig. 5.12, transitive-like verbs seem to have taken the lead in the development of both the *way*-construction and the ROC. In the case of the *way*-construction, as repeatedly noted, these are the verbs *nimen* 'take' and *take*, and in the case of the reaction object construction, as shown in Fig. 5.12, these are the manner of speaking verbs *bray*, *yelp*, *roar* (~ *cry out*) and the nonverbal expression verbs *moan*, *weep*, *clap* and *laugh*, which had an original transitive meaning (the case of *moan* and *weep* ~ *lament*, and *clap* "To strike, hit, knock, beat, with sounding blows"), or held a genitive object in OE (the case of *laugh*). As in the *way*-construction, in the ROC transitional verb types allowing for both a manner of speaking and a nonverbal interpretation such as *groan*

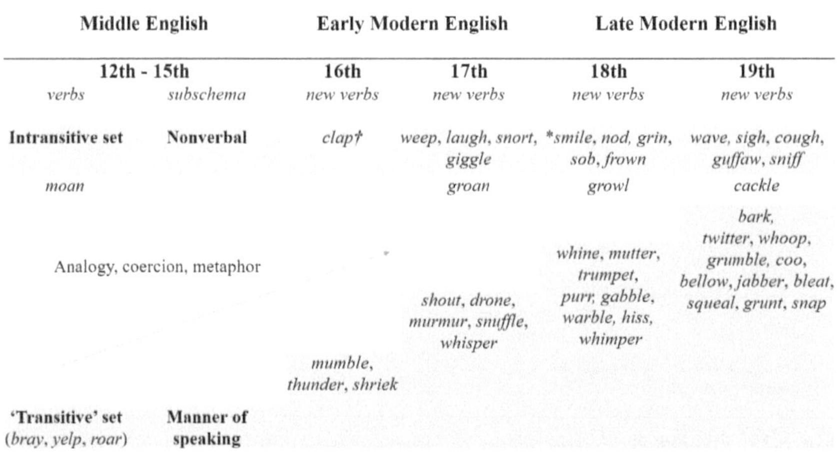

Fig. 5.12: Historical development of the ROC. Based on Visser (1963–1973: I, § 133: 100–127) and the OED. To keep it simple, I excluded the verbs attested exclusively in Visser and Jespersen (18 in total), and the two verb types found in the twentieth century from Levin's list of verbs (i.e. *hoot* and *wink*). Also, I am considering here Sheridan's eighteenth century example of *smile*.

(out) and *growl (out)*, could have facilitated the Late Modern English extension of the ROC to originally intransitive verbs of sounds such as *purr* and *coo* by means of analogy, coercion, and metaphor.

5.2.3.3 The ROC and the dummy *it* object construction

Finally, the modern dummy *it* object construction is exemplified in (47) and (48), where the *it* object is a non-referential one.

(47) Highway panic as snake **legs** it to freedom. (*The Guardian*, 2000; Mondorf 2016, 96)

(48) The stunning Barahona coastline is ... perfect for independent travelers willing to **rough** it a bit. (OED; *Rough Guide Caribbean*, 2002; Mondorf 2016, 75)

The dummy *it* object construction seems to have been "a common feature of the English language in all its stages" (Visser 1963–1973: I, § 492: 449). However, according to data provided by Visser (1963–1973: I, § 497: 453), clear dummy *it* object constructions involving intransitive verbs such as "And I can *loke* it lordly" (PDE 'And I can look it lordly') are not attested until the sixteenth century (see also Mondorf 2016, 74fn2). This suggests that the construction most likely developed during the LModE period (approx. 1700–1925) alongside the other valency-increasing constructions previously discussed. Interestingly, the path of development of the construction seems to be somehow analogous to that followed by the COC, the *way*-construction and the ROC. According to the OED compilers, the developmental path of the dummy *it* construction was characterized by occurring first with transitive verbs (e.g. *fight* as in *fight it out*), and later on with intransitives (e.g. *king* as in *king it*) via ambitransitives (e.g. *flaunt* as in *flaunt it*). As evinced by instances such as *fight it out*, during its period of emergence, dummy *it* was also supported by a particle which, in Mondorf's (2016) words "operates somewhat like a directional in the sense of Goldberg (1996, 1999) or a measuring-out phrase in the sense of Tenny (1994, 11)" (92).

The idea that the origins of the dummy *it* object construction are to be found in the use of transitive verbs accompanied by particles needs further support from the data, since, as Mondorf acknowledges, "historical data are far too sketchy" (Mondorf 2016, 92), but is nevertheless very attractive. Curiously enough, we find a similar tendency in the earliest data for the ROC: 14 of the 51 earliest attested instances of

ROCs from Levin's list feature the particles *forth*, *out*, and *up*, which in some way reassures the transitivizing power of these particles (Dehé et al. 2002, Los 2004, Los et al. 2012).

5.2.4 Concluding remarks

This chapter has dealt with the idiomatic status of the ROC within the framework of Construction Grammar (Fillmore et al. 1988, Goldberg 1995, 2006). We have seen that the ROC is not a basic construction but rather a hybrid that inherits features from several well-established constructions in the English language (i.e. the experiencer construction, the resultative construction, and the ditransitive communicative construction), thus qualifying as a clear case of multiple inheritance construction (Traugott and Trousdale 2013; Hilpert 2019). On a historical dimension, this hybrid construction seems to have originated in the LME period but has only become fairly frequent in the nineteenth century. Finally, and perhaps most importantly, the ROC seems to have followed a path of development similar to other valency-increasing constructions discussed in this chapter (COC, *way*-construction and the dummy *it* object construction) occurring first with more transitive-like verbs, namely the manner of speaking verbs *bray*, *yelp* and *roar* (~ *cry out*), and the nonverbal expression verbs *moan* and *weep* (~ *lament*), *clap* ("To strike, hit, knock, beat, with sounding blows") and *laugh* (+ genitive object), and expanding later on to more intransitive-like ones, i.e. verbs of nonverbal expression like *smile* (a1300), *grin* (OE) and *frown* (c1386), and the modern verbs of sound emission *purr* (1620) and *coo* (1672).

6. Development of the ROC in British English

This chapter is devoted to the study of the development of the ROC, with a focus on the LModE period (1710–1920), the period at which the ROC proliferates (§ 5.2.3), and on British English, since most of the earliest examples of ROCs attested in the OED come from British authors. More specifically, the main aims of this chapter are to assess the frequency, distribution (across verbs, time and text types), form and function of the ROC using data from the largest corpus available for Late Modern British English, that is, the *Corpus of Late Modern English Texts, version 3.0* (CLMET3.0; De Smet, Diller, and Tyrkkö 2011).

The chapter adopts a bottom-up approach similar to the one used in Chapter 5. This was regarded as the best approximation to the study due to a number of reasons. Firstly, due to the exploratory nature of the work it is crucial to detect the different formal variants of the construction in earlier stages of the language. Furthermore, a perfect exhaustive search of the construction in the corpus is impossible since, as also happens with the cognate object construction (Höche 2009), the ROC is a highly schematic construction that does not specify any particular lexical item (§ 4.3.1). The bottom-up approach will allow us to assess the overall frequency and distribution of the construction with particular verb types so as to identify which verbs occurring in the construction functioned as prototypes paving the way for the development of the ROC during the LModE period, and ultimately, to make some predictions regarding its levels of specificity (§ 4.3.5).

The structure of this chapter is as follows. First, I provide a more precise description of the data sources and the methodology used (§ 6.1), then the focus zooms into the typical verbs of the ROC (§ 6.2), and then into the distribution of the ROC across verb classes (§ 6.3.1), time periods (§ 6.3.2) and text types (§ 6.3.3).

6.1 Data sources and methodology

The historical findings in Chapter 5 showed that the ROC proliferates in the Late Modern English period, thus my study of the frequency, distribution, form and function of the construction is based on data extracted from CLMET3.0. Apart from being the largest multigenre corpus available which is exclusively devoted to Late Modern British English (1710–1920), CLMET3.0 has a strong emphasis on narrative texts, as opposed to other text-types with a higher degree of orality such as drama or letters. This makes it ideal for the study of the ROC, as the vast majority of contemporary ROCs analysed in Bouso (2012) and Martínez-Vázquez (2015) occur in fiction. To give the curious reader an idea, out of the more than 923 tokens attested by Martínez-Vázquez (2015) in COCA for the verb *kiss*, the most frequent ROC verb type in her findings, only 121 ROCs belong to the spoken component of the corpus (Martínez-Vázquez 2015, 163).

CLMET3.0 is the latest version of a collection of texts extracted from various online archiving projects covering the period 1710–1920. Among these online repositories are the *Project Gutenberg*, the *Oxford Text Archive* and the *Victorian Women Writers Project*. This version of the corpus contains approximately thirty-four million words of running text, which makes it large enough to explore rare linguistic structures such as the ROC. The texts have been written by British authors (male and female) who are native speakers of English and belong to various social classes. Importantly, no more than three texts belong to the same author and the texts within each subperiod have been written by authors born within a correspondingly restricted time-span. This is shown in Fig. 6.1. The aim of this parameter is to "increase the homogeneity within each sub-period" and to avoid that the same author "be represented in two subsequent sub-periods" so as to identify historical trends more clearly (De Smet 2005, 70).

Contrary to previous versions of the corpus such as the *Corpus of Late Modern English Texts* (CLMET; De Smet 2005) or the *Corpus of Late Modern English Texts (extended version)* (CLMET-EV; De Smet 2006; Diller, De Smet, and Tyrkkö 2010), the texts in CLMET3.0 are more or less evenly distributed across three 70-year subperiods.

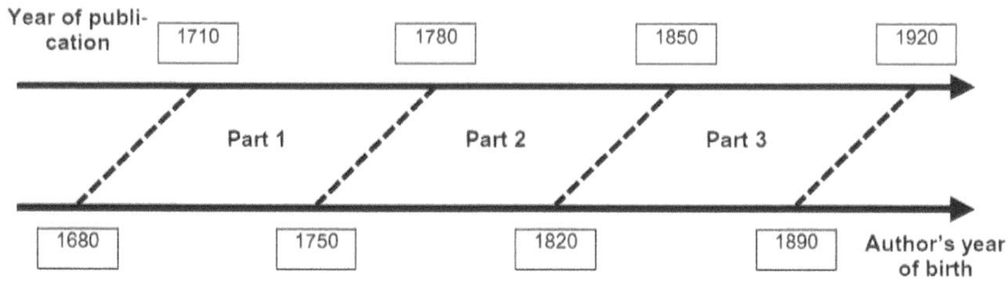

Fig. 6.1: Corpus subperiods of CLMET, CLMET-EV and CLMET3.0. Adapted from De Smet (2005, 70).

Tab. 6.1: The Corpus of Late Modern English Texts (extended version)

Subperiod	Number of authors	Number of texts	Number of words
1710–1780	23	32	3,037,607
1780–1850	46	64	5,723,988
1850–1920	51	80	6,251,564
TOTAL	120	176	**14,970,622**

Tab. 6.2: The Corpus of Late Modern English Texts, version 3.0

Subperiod	Number of authors	Number of texts	Number of words
1710–1780	51	88	10,480,431
1780–1850	70	99	11,285,587
1850–1920	91	146	12,620,207
TOTAL	212	333	**34,386,225**

Compare in this regard Tab. 6.1 and Tab. 6.2. This is important, since preliminary studies of the construction based on CLMET-EV showed hardly any instances of the construction for subperiod one (Bouso 2014a, 2014b, 2014c).

Other improvements of CLMET3.0 with regard to previous versions include (i) genre classification of texts, those shown in Tab. 6.3 (narrative fiction, narrative non-fiction, drama, letters, treatises and other), (ii) the addition in the corpus files of standardized text headers with descriptive meta-data (author, genre, sub-genre, author's gender, author's year of birth, date of text, etc.), and (iii) part-of-speech tagging,

Tab. 6.3: Genre-division per subperiod in CLMET3.0

Genre	1710–1780	1780–1850	1850–1920
Narrative fiction	4,642,670	4,830,718	6,311,301
Narrative non-fiction	1,863,855	1,940,245	958,410
Drama	407,885	347,493	607,401
Letters	1,016,745	714,343	479,724
Treatise	1,114,521	1,692,992	1,782,124
Other	1,434,755	1,759,796	2,481,247
TOTAL	**10,480,431**	**11,285,587**	**12,620,207**

which permits the application of collostructional analysis (Stefanowitsch and Gries 2003, Gries and Stefanowitsch 2004b, Stefanowitsch and Gries 2005, Stefanowitsch 2013).

The sample of verbs selected for analysis (40 in all) is shown in Tab. 6.4. It comprises all nonverbal expression verbs from Levin's list attested with ROCs in the OED (16 in total) (those included in Tab. 5.7 in § 5.2.2), a heterogeneous sample of 19 manner of speaking verbs (Levin 1993, 98) denoting sounds typically emitted by human beings (e.g. *chant*), animals (e.g. *bellow*), and inanimate objects (e.g. *thunder*), and a sample of five verbs (marked with an asterisk) that allow for both a manner of speaking and a nonverbal interpretation according to Levin (1993, 98).

For the retrieval of the data, I used the plain version of the corpus and the search engine *WordSmith Tools version 6* (Scott 2012), entering

Tab. 6.4: Sample of 40 verbs selected for analysis in CLMET3.0. Classification based on Levin (1993, 98)

Verbs of nonverbal expression/communication	clap, cough, frown, giggle, grin, guffaw, laugh, nod, sigh, smile, sniff, snort, sob, wave, weep and wink
Manner of speaking verbs	bellow, bray, chant, coo, drone, gabble, grunt, hiss, mumble, murmur, mutter, roar, shout, shriek, snuffle, thunder, trumpet, whisper and yelp[a]
Both interpretations (*)	*cackle, *groan, *growl, *moan and *whistle

a Except for *chant* (manner of speaking) and **whistle* (manner of speaking and nonverbal interpretation), all verbs selected for analysis show instances of ROCs in the OED.

the different word forms of the 40 verbs selected. For instance, for the verb *smile*, the search string *smile/smiles/smiling/smiled/smil'd* was used. Though, as we shall see in the results section, these verbs do not occur very frequently in the ROC, some of them are quite prolific in other constructions, sometimes yielding more than 7,000 hits in CLMET3.0, as is the case of the verb *smile*. Thus, after searching for all forms of the verbs selected, manual pruning of the data (43,491 tokens) was necessary. The focus of attention was on the uses in which these 40 verbs were followed by an NP.[43]

It should be noted here that some manner of speaking verbs show a considerable number of transitive uses involving *message objects* in the form of NPs. This is mainly because manner of speaking verbs are semantically related to speech and consequently, they tend to show a similar syntactic behaviour to prototypical "verbs of communication" such as *say* or *tell* (Levin 1993, 202–212; see also Boas 2010).[44] An effort has been made here to differentiate ROCs from these formally similar but functionally different constructions. For instance, I discarded:

(i) *Neutral communicative constructions* involving prototypical metalinguistic nouns such as *words*, *messages* and *opinion*. These metalinguistic nouns summarize and/or introduce, gloss the whole or part of the content of what is being communicated; these are exemplified in: *the Gloucester men* ***shouted*** <u>*messages*</u> *to their wives, she longed to* ***shout*** <u>*the words*</u>*: "It is all right (. . .)"*, and *she took occasion to* ***whisper*** *me* <u>*her opinion of the widow,*</u> *whom she called a pretty idiot*).

43 The methodology used here has been tested and validated first in a previous corpus-based study (Bouso 2017).

44 Other labels used to refer to 'verbs of communication' in the literature are: 'verba dicendi', 'verbs of saying/utterance', 'reporting verbs', 'linguistic action verb(ial)s' (Verschueren 1985; see also Dirven et al. 1982), 'verbs of speaking'(Lehrer 1988), 'quotative verbs' (Amberber 1996, 3), and 'metapragmatic descriptors' (Collins 2001, 304fn9). Martínez-Vázquez (2005, 2014a) also noticed the similarities between prototypical verbs of communication and manner of speaking verbs, and on a theoretical level, she argued for a SOUND FOR SPEECH (MANNER FOR ACTION) metonymy that permits verbs that only involve the emission of sounds to be used as verbs of communication (2014a, 174; Martínez-Vázquez 2005).

(ii) *Coercive communicative constructions* (this label suggested by Hilpert p.c.). By coercive communicative constructions I refer to those that consist of: (a) *message abstract nouns* that are metonymically construed as communicative acts as is the case of the noun *success* in the construction *my heart* ***whispers*** *me* <u>*success*</u> (meaning → my heart is suggesting/telling me that I will be successful); and (b) *message abstract nouns that depict a quality of the subject of the construction.* An example is *imprisonment* in the construction *tight mounds bonded with sticks, which* **shout** <u>*imprisonment*</u> *in the ears* (meaning → the tight mounds seem like prisons).

As in Chapter 5, I stored in my database of ROCs those instances that show the constructional meaning ['Sentient agent$_i$ cause Y$_i$ become expressed while/by$_{manner/means}$ doing V'], and occur with one of the three types of reaction objects distinguished by Martínez-Vázquez (2015). Although as mentioned there in Chapter 5, reaction objects are commonly introduced by an indefinite article or a possessive determiner, in the present corpus-based study I have also considered twelve ROCs involving a reaction object introduced by the following determiners: *some*, *certain*, *another*, *sundry*, *a few* and *one of* + *possessive*. These are exemplified in (1), (2) and (3). Eleven of these occur with the manner of speaking verbs *mutter*, *whisper*, and *thunder*, and one of them with the verb of nonverbal communication *sigh* (see example (3)).

(1) This letter sharpened Lord Vargrave's anxiety and resolve; nay, it seemed almost to sharpen his sharp features as <u>he</u> **muttered** *sundry* <u>denunciations</u> on Messrs.

CLMET3.0 1838, Bulwer-Lytton; *Alice*

(2) <u>He</u> let go, **thundering** *one of his* <u>horrid curses</u>, and I galloped home more than half out of my senses.

CLMET3.0 1847, Emily Brontë; *Wuthering Heights*

(3) (...) <u>she</u> rested to take a retrospect of the garden, and to **sigh forth** *another* <u>adieu</u>.

CLMET3.0 1794, Radcliffe; *The Mysteries of Udolpho*

In addition to these twelve reaction objects introduced by these determiners, I also included in my database of LModE ROCs examples involving emotional abstract nouns such as *love* (x4), *comfort* (x2), *courage* (x2), *longing* (x2), *sweetness* (x3) and *blessedness* (x1). Like other reaction objects these emotional abstract nouns describe a "state of mind or feeling of the subject" which "is perceived as a [transitory] reaction to a contextual element" (Martínez-Vázquez 2015, 160). However, as opposed to predicative expressive nouns, which "denote the result of a process undergone by the expresser" (Martínez-Vázquez 2015, 161), such as *discontent* in (4), the subjects of ROCs involving these emotional abstract nouns, do not *get* or *become* loved, comfortable, courageous, longing, sweet or blessed but rather communicate their own feelings of love, comfort, courage, longing, sweetness, and blessedness (= felicity; beatitude; OED, s.v. *blessedness*, n. a.). This is shown in examples (5)-(8). Such emotional abstract nouns are clearly reminiscent of Levin's off quoted ROC example *She mumbled her adoration* (Levin 1993, 98) where the experiencer subject also *communicates* her adoration rather than *gets* or *becomes* adoring (*adoration* = Deep respect or affection; fervent admiration or love; cf. OED, *adoration*, n. 2.).

(4) Dumouriez, conquering Holland, **growls** ominous discontent, at the head of Armies.

CLMET3.0 1837, Carlyle; *The French Revolution*

(5) James, with full heart, **murmured out** his ardent love, his sense that no captive had ever been so generously treated as he.

CLMET3.0 1870, Yonge; *The Caged Lion*

(6) Perhaps, the very notion of returning as a suspected criminal to that part of the country where a portion of his youth had been passed, was sufficient to disquiet and deject him. All this while his poor Madeline seemed actuated by a spirit beyond herself; she would not be separated from his side—she held his hand in hers—she **whispered** comfort and courage at the very moment when her own heart most sank. The magistrate wiped his eyes when he saw a creature so young, so beautiful, in circumstances so fearful, and bearing up with an energy so little to be expected from her years and delicate appearance. Aram said but little; he covered his face with his right hand for a few moments, as if to hide a passing emotion, a sudden weakness.

CLMET3.0 1832, Bulwer-Lytton; *Eugene Aram*

(7) There was something so unobtrusive in her sympathy, that Olive felt inclined to open her heart to the gentle Meliora. "I can't tell you all," she said, "I think it would not be quite right;" and, trembling and hesitating, as if in the confession were something of shame, she **whispered** her longing for that great comfort, money of her own earning. "You, my dear, you want money!" cried Miss Meliora, who had always looked upon her new iniate, Mrs. Rothesay, as a sort of domestic gold-mine. But she had the delicacy not to press Olive farther.

CLMET3.0 1850, Craik; *Olive*

(8) I saw her clearer than at noon Day, by the Light which she cast with Profusion abroad. Every Feature and former Trace seemed heightened into a Lustre without a Loss of the least Similitude. She **smiled** ineffable Sweetness and Blessedness upon me.

CLMET3.0 1765–70, Brooke; *The Fool of Quality*

Finally, structures with the meaning ['Sentient agent$_i$ cause Y$_i$ become expressed while/by$_{manner/means}$ doing V'] and involving the particles *forth*, *off*, *out*, *over* and *up* followed by a reaction object were also considered for analysis. This is mainly because there is solid evidence that these particles "affect the valency of the verb as [they] may transitivize an intransitive verb or intransitivize a transitive one" (Los 2004, 85).[45] For instance, in examples (9)-(12), the particles *out*, *down*, *up* and *off* clearly function as transitivizers of the unergative verbs *play* and *work*. More importantly, these particles seem to have played a role in the emergence of some ROCs, to judge from the considerably large number of early instances of ROCs containing these particles (18 out of the 69 ROCs attested in the OED) (see Chapter 5).

To summarize, the focus of this corpus-based study was on linguistic instances that follow the pattern in (13), which can be regarded as the skeleton upon which a family of ROCs is being built.

(9) Handel. . . asked the organist to permit him to **play** the people *out*. (OED 1823)

45 Regarding the role of the particles *out* and *forth* in communicative constructions see Rudzka-Ostyn (1988).

(10) They accused the minister of **playing** *down* the number of the unemployed.

(11) He **worked** his way *up*.

(12) Ten great places to **work** *off* weight.

(Los 2004, 86; see also Dehé et al. 2002 and Los et al. 2012)

(13) **SUB**$_i$ **V**$_{\text{INTR manner/means}}$ (*forth/off/out/over/up*) **OBJ**$_i$ (delocutive, deverbal, predicative expressive nouns, and emotional abstract nouns)

6.2 Frequency of occurrence and prototypical verbs in the construction

The aim of this section is to assess the overall frequency and distribution of the ROC with particular verb types so as to identify which verbs of the construction functioned as prototypes paving the way for the grammatical constructionalization of the ROC schema. As suggested by the exploration based on the OED (Chapter 5), the data extracted from CLMET3.0 confirms that the ROC is a very low-frequency construction: only 305 examples of ROCs were attested for the 40 verbs selected for analysis, and only 26 of these 40 verbs analysed show instances of ROCs. Despite the fact that 305 is clearly a low figure considering the size of CLMET3.0 (more than 34 million words), this figure goes hand in hand with the general low frequency of the PDE ROC (Martínez-Vázquez 2014a, 173), and also the scarce frequency of other similar transitivizing constructions such as the LModE *way*-construction (Mondorf 2011, 401). This is shown in Fig. 6.2 where I compare, on the one hand, the overall frequency of nine nonverbal expression verbs in the ROC in my LModE data and in Martínez-Vázquez' PDE data,[46] and on the other, the overall frequency of the LModE ROC for the ten most frequent verbs in the construction in my data, with the overall

46 As previously mentioned, I analysed a total of 16 nonverbal expression verbs. However, only nine of these nonverbal expression verbs were among those analysed by Martínez-Vázquez (2014a, 180) in PDE.

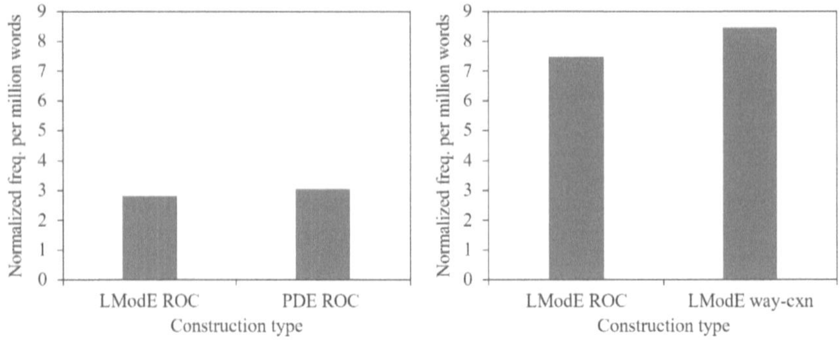

Fig. 6.2: Comparison of the overall frequency of the ROC and the *way*-construction

frequency of the LModE *way*-construction for the ten verbs analysed by Mondorf (2011, 405). Tab. 6.5 further below specifies the verbs taken

Tab. 6.5: Verbs and corpora compared in Fig. 6.2

Nine nonverbal expression verbs analysed in the LModE and the PDE ROC	**Ten verbs analysed in the LModE *way*-construction (Mondorf 2011, 405)**	**Ten most frequent verbs in the LModE ROC**
Number of tokens attested for the LModE ROC: 96 Number of tokens attested for the PDE ROC: 1,369 (see Martínez-Vázquez 2014a, 180)	Number of tokens attested: 355	Number of tokens attested: 257
clap, *frown*, *nod*, *sigh*, *smile*, *snort*, *wave*, *whistle* and *wink*	*cut*, *drink*, *eat*, *fight*, *grope*, *hit*, *wind*, *work*, *worm* and *wriggle*	*mutter*, *murmur*, *nod*, *shout*, *sigh*, *smile*, *thunder*, *wave*, *weep* and *whisper*
CLMET3.0 (1710–1920) 34,386,225 words **COCA Corpus (1990–2013)**	**British English Historical Corpora (1700–1900). See Mondorf (2011, 401)** *Eighteenth-Century Fiction* (5,000,000 words) *Nineteenth-Century Fiction* (37,000,000 words)	**CLMET3.0 (1710–1920)**
450,000,00 words	42,000,000 words	34,386,225 words

into account in Fig. 6.2, their frequency in the corresponding construction, and number of words of the corpora compared.

The verbs with the highest token frequency in the LModE ROC are the manner of speaking verbs *mutter*, *murmur* and *whisper* followed by the nonverbal expression verbs *smile* and *nod*. As shown in Fig. 6.3 the rest of the verbs analysed rank very low on the scale of frequency, either with less than 20 tokens per verb (see the verbs *shout*, *wave*, *thunder*, *weep*, *sigh*, *sob*, *mumble*, *growl*, *roar*, *shriek*, *bellow*, *groan*, *hiss*, *laugh*, *frown*, *grin*, *snort*, *chant*, *grunt*, *whistle* and *wink*), or not occurring at all in the ROC in CLMET 3.0, although they feature in the ROC in the OED quotation database, namely the verbs *bray*, *cackle*, *clap*, *coo*, *cough*, *drone*, *gabble*, *giggle*, *guffaw*, *moan*, *sniff*, *snuffle*, *trumpet* and *yelp*.

The raw frequencies presented in Fig. 6.3 can be further refined by a collexeme analysis. This is one of a family of statistical methods known under the cover term collostructional analysis which allows us to identify those elements that co-occur in a construction more frequently than expected (Stefanowitsch and Gries 2003, 214; Hilpert 2014a, 392). In § 6.2.1 I will describe some methodological considerations, present the results and offer some discussion of the results obtained. The section concludes with a summary.

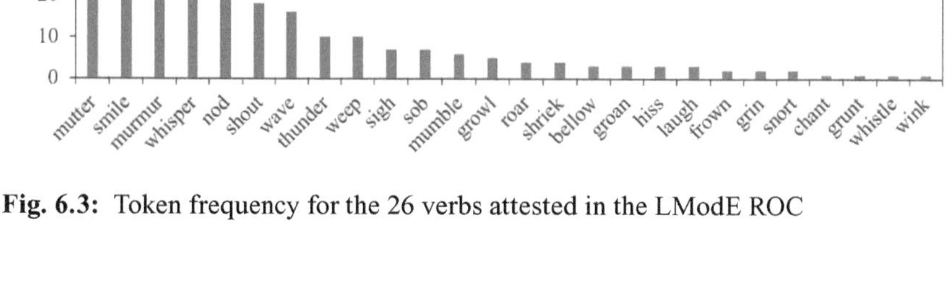

Fig. 6.3: Token frequency for the 26 verbs attested in the LModE ROC

6.2.1 A collexeme analysis of ROCs: Identifying typical verbs in the construction

6.2.1.1 Some methodological considerations

As explained by Gries and Stefanowitsch, collostructional analysis (Stefanowitsch and Gries 2003, Gries and Stefanowitsch 2004a, 2004b, Stefanowitsch and Gries 2005, Stefanowitsch 2013, Stefanowitsch and Flach 2020) was developed as a way of overcoming the shortcomings of traditional collocational analysis in corpus linguistics approaches to language. Two of these shortcomings are: the lack of discrimination between relevant and accidental results (Stefanowitsch and Gries 2003, 214), and the fact that traditional collocational analyses do not take into account the overall frequency of the words in the corpus (Stefanowitsch and Gries 2003, 216).[47]

Collostructional analysis differs from other collocational analyses in that it "always starts with a particular construction [a form-meaning pairing]" (Stefanowitsch and Gries 2003, 214), and takes into account a number of frequencies other than those of the collocates. More specifically, in order to perform any collostructional analysis four frequencies are necessary: (i) the frequency of L (lexeme) in C (construction), (ii) the frequency of L in all other constructions (these constructions are referred to in Tab. 6.6 as ¬[construction]), (iii) the frequency of C with lexemes other than L (these other lexemes are referred to in Tab. 6.6 as ¬lexeme), and (iv) the frequency of all other constructions with lexemes other than L. These four frequencies are then entered in a 4-by-4 table, like the one shown in Tab. 6.6, and submitted to some distributional statistics such as the Fisher exact test. Though computationally costly, the Fisher exact test seems to be always a good option when dealing with linguistic data because it "neither makes any distributional assumptions, nor does it require any particular sample size" (Stefanowitsch and Gries 2003, 218).[48] On the basis of the four frequencies previously

47 For an overview of the advantages and disadvantages of using collostructional analysis in usage-based linguistics see Gries (2012).

48 As is well known, many linguistic phenomena, including word frequencies, show a Zipfian distribution (Zipf 1935). As explained by Cantos-Gómez (2013), "Zipf observed the distribution of word frequencies in English and found that

Tab. 6.6: Crosstabulation of *accident* (= L) and the [N *waiting to happen*] construction (e.g. *it was an accident waiting to happen*). Adapted from Stefanowitsch and Gries (2003, 219)

	accident	¬*accident* (other lexemes than *accident*)	**Row totals**
[N *waiting to happen*]	**14**	21	**35**
¬[N *waiting to happen*] (other constructions than [N *waiting to happen*])	8606	10197659	10206265
Column totals	**8620**	10197680	**10206300**

Tab. 6.7: Collexemes most strongly attracted to the [N *waiting to happen*] construction. Adapted from Stefanowitsch and Gries (2003, 219)

Collexeme (n)	**pFisher exact (collostruction strength)**
accident (14)	2.12E-34
disaster (12)	1.36E-33
welkom (1)	4.46E-05
earthquake (1)	2.46E-03
invasion (1)	7.10E-03
recovery (1)	1.32E-02
revolution (1)	1.68E-02
crisis (1)	2.21E-02
dream (1)	2.45E-02
it (sex) (1)	2.83E-02
event (1)	6.92E-02

mentioned, the Fisher exact test calculates the p-values that indicate the strength of association between each lexeme and the construction (see Tab. 6.7).

In order to identify which verbs (of those 26 attested in my LModE data) occur in the ROC more often than expected, I performed collexeme

(. . .) the frequency of any word is inversely proportional to its rank in the frequency table (. . .)" (2013, 180): the most frequent word will occur twice as often as the second most frequent word, three times as often as the third most frequent word, and so on.

analysis on the 305 ROCs extracted from CLMET3.0. For this purpose, I used the open source software R (R Core Team 2019), and a script taken from Stefan Th. Gries' collostructional analysis website (Gries 2014). This script prompts the user for the following information:

(i) The kind of collostructional analysis we wish to perform: collexeme analysis, distinctive collexeme analysis or co-varying collexeme analysis. Since I am investigating which verbs are most strongly attracted by a particular slot in the ROC, I selected here collexeme analysis. Distinctive collexeme analysis is used to contrast two or more constructions, whereas co-varying collexeme analysis examines the dependencies between two lexical items in a construction (for further information regarding these analyses see Hilpert 2014a).

(ii) The name of the construction (without spaces), in this case "roc".

(iii) The size of the corpus, or as Hilpert (2014a, 395) puts it, "the combined frequency of all potential collexemes", i.e. potential "[l]exemes that are attracted to a particular construction" (Stefanowitsch and Gries 2003, 215). In the ROC, this number would be the combined frequency of all verbs in CLMET3.0 that may potentially enter the construction. Thus, I searched for the actual number of all verbal constructions in CLMET3.0 (34,386,225 words). This search calculated a total of 5,329,179 verbal constructions using the vector myverbs<-c("_V"). This figure constitutes approximately the 16 % of the words in CLMET3.0.

(iv) The frequency of the construction in the corpus we investigate. In the case of the ROC this frequency is 305, i.e. the number of examples that were retrieved from the corpus. Though this number does not correspond with the total frequency of ROCs in CLMET3.0, collexeme analysis would tell us *for the verbs in our subset* which ones are most strongly attracted. One should bear in mind that the searches in CLMET3.0 are restricted to 40 verbs, and there could be examples of ROCs depending on verbs which were not considered. The retrieval of all the instances of ROCs in the corpus would imply reading and manually scanning all the texts in the corpus. Automatic searches are not feasible given the absence of any formal cues that would allow us to keep track of all instances of the ROC (see Höche 2009, for similar methodological problems with the cognate object construction).

(v) The next piece of information we are requested to specify by the script is the index of association strength that we want to apply to our data. The choices given by the script are: -log10 (Fisher-Yates exact, one-tailed), log-likelihood, Mutual Information, Chi-square and log10 of odds ratio (adds 0.5 to each cell). The one selected here is the Fisher-Yates exact test, which, as previously mentioned, does not make any distributional assumptions on the data and does not require any particular sample size (Stefanowitsch and Gries 2003, 218).

(vi) And finally, in the last step before performing collexeme analysis we are requested to upload a txt file that specifies in a table with three columns the frequency of each ROC verb both in the corpus and in the construction (cf. Tab. 6.8). The frequencies of the verbs in the corpus were retrieved by using the following vector: myverbs<-c (e.g. "^mutter.*_V", "^smil.*_V", etc.). On the basis of the information specified in (i)-(vi) above, the R program (R Core Team 2019) performs the Fisher's exact test on a 4-by-4-table for the 26 verbs attested in the construction. For the verb *smile* see the figures represented in Tab. 6.9.

6.2.1.2 Results and discussion

Tab. 6.10 lists the results of collexeme analysis for the 26 verbs under study. The results included in the 'coll.strength' column are presented with four decimals and in the form of the negative logarithm to the base of ten of the p-value. If one wishes to translate these figures into p-values, they should be interpreted according to the following correspondences (Gries 2014):

Tab. 6.8: Frequency of each ROC verb in the corpus and in the construction

verb	corpus_frequency	construction_frequency
mutter	516	65
smile	3644	43
murmur	690	36
whisper	1627	28
nod	469	24
shout	1284	18
wave	940	16
thunder	170	10
weep	691	10
sigh	1186	7
sob	520	7
mumble	79	6
growl	193	5
roar	233	4
shriek	182	4
bellow	97	3
groan	419	3
hiss	141	3
laugh	4466	3
frown	138	2
grin	436	2
snort	33	2
chant	340	1
grunt	56	1
whistle	621	1
wink	122	1

Tab. 6.9: Crosstabulation of the verb *smile* and the ROC

	smile	*¬smile*	**Row totals**
ROC	**43**	262	**305**
¬ROC	3600	5325273	5328873
Column totals	**3644**	5325535	**5329179**

Tab. 6.10: The 26 collexemes attracted to the ROC

words (i.e. verbs)	exp. freq	relation	coll. strength	words (i.e. verbs)	exp. freq	relation	coll. strength
1 mutter (65/516)[a]	0.0295	attraction	195.3804	14 shriek (4/182)	0.0104	attraction	9.3358
2 murmur (36/690)	0.0394	attraction	93.4484	15 roar (4/233)	0.0133	attraction	8.9045
3 smile (43/3644)	0.2085	attraction	83.5879	16 bellow (3/97)	0.0055	attraction	7.5644
4 nod (24/469)	0.0268	attraction	62.1744	17 hiss (3/141)	0.0080	attraction	7.0737
5 whisper (28/1627)	0.0931	attraction	59.0428	18 snort (2/33)	0.0018	attraction	5.7640
6 shout (18/1284)	0.0734	attraction	36.5168	19 groan (3/419)	0.0239	attraction	5.6536
7 wave (16/940)	0.0537	attraction	33.8784	20 frown (2/138)	0.0078	attraction	4.5128
8 thunder (10/170)	0.0097	attraction	26.8642	21 grin (2/436)	0.0249	attraction	3.5163
9 weep (10/691)	0.0395	attraction	20.6966	22 laugh (3/4466)	0.2555	attraction	2.6419
10 mumble (6/79)	0.0045	attraction	17.0331	23 grunt (1/56)	0.0032	attraction	2.4948
11 sob (7/520)	0.0297	attraction	14.4455	24 wink (1/122)	0.0069	attraction	2.1574
12 sigh (7/1186)	0.0678	attraction	11.9432	25 chant (1/340)	0.0194	attraction	1.7150
13 growl (5/193)	0.0110	attraction	11.9040	26 whistle (1/621)	0.0355	attraction	1.4569

a In parentheses the frequency of the verb in the construction (i.e. observed frequency) and in the corpus, in this order.

- Coll.strength > 1.30103 = p <0.05
- Coll.strength > 2 = p <0.01
- Coll.strength > 3 = p <0.001

The order of the results obtained from collexeme analysis does not differ greatly from the previous results based on raw frequency counts (the observed frequency is specified in Tab. 6.10 between parentheses). As shown in Fig. 6.4 these values are positively correlated (*r* = 0.985462923) as the higher the observed frequency, the more attracted the verb is to the construction (i.e. the higher the index of association strength is).

Contrary to raw frequency analyses, what collexeme analysis does is to establish the threshold between those verbs which are attracted to a construction (a value greater than 0) and those which are not (a value of less than 0).[49] In this particular case, the method

49 Note that 1.3 is the threshold value for significance (Coll.strength> 1.30103 = p<0.05). That which is attracted to the construction will have a value greater than 0, that which is repelled by the construction will have a value of less than zero, and any word that has a value with an absolute value greater than 1.3 is significantly attracted or repelled. It may be the case that the analysis returns an

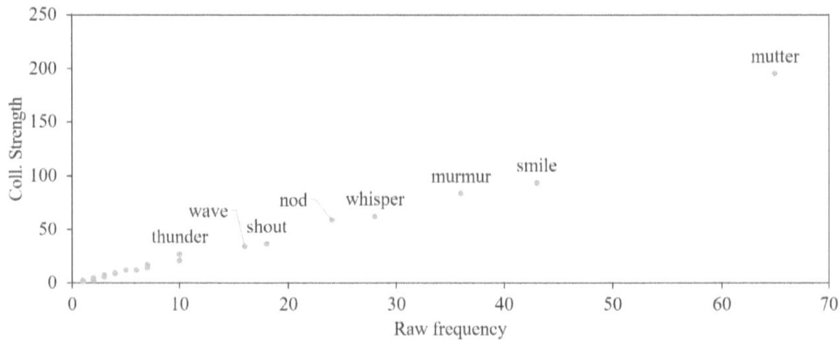

Fig. 6.4: Correlation between diverging values of collostruction strength and raw frequency

cannot detect such a barrier, as even verbs that occur only once in the ROC, such as *grunt* or *wink*, show attraction to the construction at a significant level (coll.strength > 1.30103 = p <0.05). The analysis is still worth doing because not all verbs show the same degree of attraction to the ROC, and differences with respect to raw frequency counts can still be detected, particularly for the four most strongly attracted verbs (see Tab. 6.11).

As just seen, in either case, the prototypical verbs of the LModE ROC are the manner of speaking verbs *mutter* and *murmur*, and the nonverbal expression verb *smile*. Such finding contrast with the one major study that exists on ROCs in PDE (Martínez-Vázquez 2014a) where the vast majority of the ROCs involve gesture verbs: over 2,433 tokens of the more than 3,000 examples collected from COCA; see Tab. 6.12 for details on how these examples are distributed across these verbs (Martínez-Vázquez 2015, 162; see also Martínez-Vázquez 2014a, 180).

infinitely strong value of collostructional strength (this indicated as "infinite"), which is an issue that arises in low type frequency constructions. This is the case of the shell noun construction (Schmid 2000, Schmid and Mantlik 2015) which, as rightly pointed out by Hilpert (2014a, 397), forms a "small and relatively closed set": *N+BE+that*-construction as in *the talk is that.*

Tab. 6.11: Comparison between the results obtained from collexeme analysis (most strongly attracted verbs) and raw frequency counts (most frequent verbs)

Most strongly attracted verbs	**Most frequent verbs (raw frequencies)**
mutter	mutter
murmur	smile
smile	murmur
nod	whisper

Tab. 6.12: Most frequent gesture verbs in ROCs in COCA. Adapted from Martínez-Vázquez (2014a, 180)

Most frequent gesture verbs	**Tokens**	**Percentage share**
kiss	926	5.10
nod	693	2.19
wave	507	3.28
hug	103	1.20
smile	92	0.20
snort	26	0.97
sigh	25	0.21
shrug	15	0.12
glare	10	0.24
blink	10	0.14
whistle	9	0.28
frown	7	0.10
wink	5	0.18
clap	5	0.14

6.2.1.3 Summary

From a Construction Grammar perspective the fact that there are no repelled verbs and that some verbs are more attracted to the ROC than others leads us to identify two different degrees of specificity of the ROC: the more general schema of the ROC and the two main subschemas pertaining to manner of speaking verbs (manner subschema) on the one hand, and nonverbal communication verbs (means subschema) on the other. More specifically, the results from collexeme analysis applied to the 26 verbs attested in the construction in CLMET3.0 suggest that the manner subschema involving the verbs *mutter* and *murmur*, as well as the means subschema involving the verbs *smile*, *nod* and *wave* are possible candidates for entrenchment in people's minds. As the most strongly attracted verb types to the LModE ROC, these verbs function as prototypes paving the way for the grammatical constructionalization of the ROC and its two main subschemas over the LModE period (1710–1920).

The strong association between these verbs (*mutter*, *murmur*, *smile*, *nod* and *wave*) and the ROC is further evidenced by my historical data from the OED and also by my historical data from *Early English Books Online* (cf. § 6.3.1.2.5), where I found that the attestation of most of these verbs in the ROC goes back to the EModE period (1474–1700). The strong association between these verbs and the ROC is additionally supported by the fact that analysts continuously refer to them. This applies most particularly to the nonverbal communication verb *smile*, which has been mentioned in every single work on the construction since Jespersen's times (cf. § 3.1.1.1), and to other verbs of nonverbal communication such as *nod* and *wave*, which have also been included within the list of most frequent gesture verbs in the PDE ROC (cf. Tab. 6.12 above). These findings prepare the ground for the following section where I provide a fine-grained analysis of the distribution of the ROC across different verb classes (§ 6.3.1).

6.3 Distribution and function

6.3.1 Distribution of reaction objects across verb classes

6.3.1.1 Verbs of manner of speaking

Out of the 24 manner of speaking verbs selected for analysis only 15 show instances of ROCs in CLMET3.0.[50] This figure contrasts with

50 For comparison purposes I include in this count the five verbs that allow for interpretation as both, verbs of nonverbal expression and manner of speaking (i.e. *cackle*, *groan*, *growl*, *moan* and *whistle*). See Tab. 6.4 in § 6.1.

the list of 58 manner of speaking verbs attested in the ROC in PDE (Martínez-Vázquez 2014a, 175), among which are the 15 manner of speaking verbs I found in the ROC in CLMET3.0. The number of manner of speaking verbs involved in the LModE ROC and the PDE ROC is probably higher in both periods than the figures in Tab. 6.13 show. Among other reasons, this is mainly because as Levin herself notes (1993, 205–206; see also Martínez-Vázquez 2014a, 175), her list of manner of speaking verbs is cross-listed under other lists of verb classes such as verbs of sounds made by animals (Levin 1993, 212) and general verbs of sound emission (Levin 1993, 234).

Manner of speaking verbs – and related verb classes – have been addressed by a considerable number of linguists. Some of them have been concerned with the morphosyntactic and semantic properties of this verb class (Zwicky 1971, Mufwene 1978, Atkins and Levin 1991, Tanaka 1991, Levin 1991, Omuro 1995, 1996, 2000, Levin and Song 1997, Urban and Ruppenhofer 2001, Kogusuri 2009a), others have discussed manner of speaking verbs when building up a lexicon of English verbs in PDE and in OE (Faber and Martínez 1990, Faber and Mairal Usón 1999, Cortés-Rodríguez and González-Orta 2006), and others have approached them from a theoretical, literary, cross-linguistic and cognitive perspective (Snell-Hornby 1983, Mastrofini 2014, Vergaro et al. 2014, Rojo and Valenzuela 2005, Ruano San Segundo 2016, 2017, 2018a, 2018b, Caballero 2015, 2016, Sandford 2016, among many others).

Perhaps for being the earliest, the most famous study on manner of speaking verbs is the one by Zwicky (1971), where he identifies twenty properties characteristic – though not exclusive – of this verb class (see Mufwene 1978). Zwicky (1971) defines manner of speaking verbs as "verbs referring to intended acts of communication by speech [i.e. verbally] and describing physical characteristics of the speech act" (223; emphasis mine). Among the twenty properties of these verbs mentioned by Zwicky (1971), two stand out: the typically human subject of these verbs (1971, 224), and their ability to be interpreted noncommunicatively when they are used intransitively without an object (1971, 225).

Tab. 6.13: Manner of speaking verbs attested in the LModE ROC and the PDE ROC

LModE ROC	PDE ROC
15 verbs attested in the ROC in CLMET3.0 *bellow, chant, groan, growl, grunt, hiss, mumble, murmur, mutter, roar, shout, shriek, thunder, whisper, whistle*	**58 verbs attested in the ROC in PDE (Martínez-Vázquez 2014a, 175)** *babble, bark, bawl, bellow, bleat, boom, bray, burble, chant, chatter, chirp, cluck, coo, croak, croon, crow, cry, drawl, groan, growl, grumble, grunt, hiss, holler, hoot, howl, lisp, moan, mumble, murmur, mutter, purr, rage, rasp, roar, rumble, scream, screech, shout, shriek, sing, snarl, squeal, stammer, stutter, thunder, trill, trumpet, wail, wheeze, whimper, whine, whisper, whistle, yap, yell, yelp, yodel* **20 verbs in common with the 24 verbs analysed in CLMET3.0**[a] *bellow, bray, chant, coo, groan, growl, grunt, hiss, moan, mumble, murmur, mutter, roar, shout, shriek, thunder, trumpet, whisper, whistle, yelp* **15 verbs *attested* in the ROC in CLMET3.0 and in PDE** *bellow, chant, groan, growl, grunt, hiss, mumble, murmur, mutter, roar, shout, shriek, thunder, whisper, whistle*

a Of those 24 verbs, those not analysed by Martínez-Vázquez (2014a) are *cackle, drone, gabble* and *snuffle.*

Though not included in Zwicky (1971) – mostly because this is more a feature of verbs of sound emission in general –,[51] an interesting aspect of manner of speaking verbs is that some of them are conventionally associated with particular emotions or attitudes (Levin 1991, 1993; Levin and Song 1997, 53). For instance, the verb *whistle* may indicate surprise or admiration, the verb *hiss* is typically associated with anger (Levin 1991, 213), the verb *squeal* with pain or pleasure (Snell-Hornby 1983, 174 ff), the verb *hoot* with ridicule and enthusiasm, and the verb *groan* with pain or disappointment (Levin and Song

51 Note here that manner of speaking verbs are regarded in the literature as essentially intransitive verbs of sound emission (Martínez-Vázquez 2005, 90–98; see also Levin and Song 1997, 37).

1997, 36).[52] Having discussed the features of manner of speaking verbs, in what follows I will focus on the distribution of the different types of reaction objects (delocutive, deverbal, predicative expressive nouns and emotional abstract nouns) across the 15 manner of speaking verbs attested in the LModE ROC.

As previously mentioned, in my CLMET3.0 data the manner of speaking verbs *mutter* and *murmur* are the strongest collocates of the LModE ROC (cf. Tab. 6.10 in § 6.2.1.2) and they function as prototypes for the consolidation of the manner subschema of the ROC. Like prototypical manner of speaking verbs, they typically occur with *human subjects* describing *verbal messages* in the form of *deverbal illocutionary nouns* (see examples (14) and (15)), though note that they do not seem to show restrictions with regard to the kinds of reaction objects they collocate with. These verbs freely occur with delocutive nouns such as *farewell* and *thanks* in examples (16) and (17), predicative expressive nouns such as *contempt* in (18), and emotional abstract nouns such as *love* in example (19). Tab. 6.14 illustrates the total number of reaction object types attested with *mutter* and *murmur* in my LModE data.

(14) The Cornet scowled, and many of my comrades looked black, and **muttered** dissent; but no one seemed inclined to debate the question.

CLMET3.0 1820–2, Hunt; *Memoirs of Henry Hunt*

(15) The Dudgeons all **murmur** assent, except Christy, who goes to the window and posts himself there, looking out. [Stage direction]

CLMET3.0 1897, Shaw; *The Devil's Disciple*

(16) **Muttering** a farewell that was not complimentary, Mr Carker pursued his way; but as he turned out of that place, and looked over his shoulder at the root of the old tree, he could yet see the finger pointing before him, and thought he heard the woman screaming, 'Go and meet her!'.

CLMET3.0 1844, Dickens; *Dombey and Son*

52 A similar claim regarding verbs of light emission (e.g. *gleam* and *shine*) and the expression of emotions has been made by Faber and Mairal Usón (1999, 259–263). They mention the following: "[a]greeable types of light emission (*sparkle, twinkle, glow*) are characteristic of positive emotions such as happiness and amusement, whereas more disagreeable types of light emission (*glitter, glint, blaze*) translate into more negative emotions such as anger".

(17) Richards deferred to these compliments by curtseying and **murmuring** her thanks; but finding it quite impossible to recover her spirits from the disorder into which they had been thrown by the image of her son in his precocious nether garments, she gradually approached the door and was heartily relieved to escape by it.

CLMET3.0 1844, Dickens; *Dombey and Son*

(18) 'When he thus spoke, the long-pent murmur went forth, and the philosophers that were mingled with the people, **muttered** their sage contempt; there might you have seen the chilling frown of the Stoic, and the Cynic's sneer; and the Epicurean, who believeth not even in our own Elysium, muttered a pleasant jest, and swept laughing through the crowd: but the deep heart of the people was touched and thrilled; and they trembled, though they knew not why, for verily the stranger had the voice and majesty of a man to whom "The Unknown God" had committed the preaching of His faith.'

CLMET3.0 1834, Bulwer-Lytton; *The Last Days of Pompeii*

(19) '(...). Pardon me, Jamie; but I have not kept you out of malice, such as man must needs renounce on his death-bed. I trust to John, and to the rest, for giving you freedom at such time as you can safely return to be such a king indeed as we have ever hoped to be. Do you pardon me, James, for this, as for any harshness or rudeness you may have suffered from me?' James, with full heart, **murmured out** his ardent love, his sense that no captive had ever been so generously treated as he.

CLMET3.0 1870, Yonge; *The Caged Lion*

As shown in Tab. 6.15, the manner of speaking verbs *mumble*, *growl* and *groan* – though much less frequent in my data – behave similarly to *mutter* and *murmur* in that they also occur with the three types of RO: delocutive nouns (i.e. *amens*, *'No'* and *thanks*), deverbal nouns (i.e. *acceptance*, *curse*, *excuses*, *prayer* and *responses*), and predicative expressive nouns (i.e. *discontent*, *joy*, *misery* and *satisfaction*).

Other manner of speaking verbs such as *whisper*, *chant*, *grunt* and *whistle* are mainly associated with positive attitudes such as *approval*, *comfort*, or *compliments* (cf. Tab. 6.16); while the manner of speaking verbs *thunder*, *shriek* and *hiss* mainly occur with reaction objects denoting negative emotions such as *curse* or *dissatisfaction* (cf. Tab. 6.17). The last set of manner of speaking verbs attested in the ROC (i.e. *shout*, *roar* and *bellow*) denote loud, penetrating sounds (Snell-Hornby 1983, 174) and are typically associated with highly emotional nouns such as *applause*, *astonishment*, *hurrah!*, *huzza*, *Bravo*, *acclaim* and *'ahoy!'*

(see Tab. 6.18). This finding concurs with Rosca's (2011, 36–37, and 41) hypothesis that the higher the intensity of a sound the higher the intensity of the emotion expressed.

Tab. 6.14: RO types with *mutter* and *murmur*

Mutter (65 ROCs; 34 RO types)			Murmur (36 ROCs; 33 RO types)		
adjuration	denunciations	lamentations	adieux	gaiety	request (x2)
affirmative (x2)	dissent	maledictions (x2)	apology	good-night	salutation
answer	ejaculation(s) (x3)	oath (x5)	applause	gratitude	suggestion
apology	encouragements	objurgation	assent	interjection	sympathy
assent	exclamation	prayer(s) (x8)	assurances	invocation	'thank you'
Ave	excuse(s) (x2)	promises	blessing(s) (x2)	joy	thanks (x4)
censure	execrations	remark(s) (x2)	complaint	love	thanksgiving
charm(s) (x4)	farewell	reply (x3)	congratula-tions	prayer (x2)	threats
(C)omplaint(s) (x2)	imprecations (x4)	suspicion	curses	questions	vengeance
conjurations	incantations (x2)	vengeance	encourage-ments	remon-strance	
contempt	invocations		entreaties	reply	
(C)urse(s) (x7)	judgment		fears	reproaches	

Tab. 6.15: RO types with *mumble*, *growl* and *groan*

Mumble (6 ROCs; 5 RO types)	Growl (5 ROCs; 5 RO types)	Groan (3 ROCs; 3 RO types)
excuses	acceptance	amens
'No'	curse	conviction
prayer (x2)	discontent	misery
responses	joy	
thanks	satisfaction	

Tab. 6.16: Manner of speaking verbs *mainly* associated with positive emotions (shaded)

Whisper (28 ROCs; 24 RO types)					Chant (1 ROC)	Grunt (1 ROC)	Whistle (1 ROC)
adieus	disbelief	good-night	persuasion	*surprise*	*thanks-giving*	*approval*	*triumph*
apprehen-sions	discontent	*hope(s)* (x6)	*pleasure*	suspicion(s) (x2)			
comfort (x2)	enquiries	longing (x2)	request	*tenderness*			
compliments	fears	*love*	revenge	warning			
courage (x3)	*gladness*	*peace*	salutations				

Tab. 6.17: Manner of speaking verbs *mainly* associated with negative emotions (shaded)

Thunder (10 ROCs; 8 RO types)	Shriek (4 ROCs; 5 RO types)	Hiss (3 ROCs; 2 RO types)
command(s) (x2)	advice	declarations
conviction	cautions	*defiance (x2)*
curse(s) (x2)	*curses*	
dissatisfaction	*discord*	
love	*imprecations*	
menaces		
question		
salutes		

Tab. 6.18: Manner of speaking verbs *mainly* associated with highly emotional nouns (shaded)

Shout (18 ROCs; 14 RO types)			Roar (4 ROCs; 4 RO types)	Bellow (3 ROCs; 3 RO types)
adieus	consolation	luck	*applause*	*acclaim*
applause (x4)	greetings	prayers	*Bravo*	*'ahoy!'*
approval	grievances	promises	orders	orders
astonishment	*hurrah!* (x2)	welcome (x2)	welcome	
blessings	*huzza*			

Finally, out of the 188 ROCs attested for the 24 verbs of manner of speaking analysed, 27 ROCs occur with subjects that correspond to *animals* or *inanimates*. At least 12 of them describe nonverbal messages and therefore conform to the means subschema of the ROC [‘Sentient agent_i cause Y_i become expressed by_{means} doing V’]) rather than to the manner subschema ([‘Sentient agent_i cause Y_i become expressed $\text{by}_{\text{manner}}$ doing V’]). These are shaded in grey in Tab. 6.19.

The 27 ROCs with animal or inanimate subjects concern the verbs *growl* (example (1) in Tab. 6.19), *grunt* (example (2)), *hiss* (examples (3)-(5)), *murmur* (examples (6)-(8)), *mutter* (examples (9)-(11)), *roar* (example (12)), *shout* (example (13)), *thunder* (examples (14)-(16)), *whisper* (examples (17)-(26)), and *whistle* (example (27)). In such constructions the writer *reports* on the feelings or attitudes of animals (e.g. *the old sow* in example (2) and *flocks of geese* in examples (4) and (5)), and via metaphor *expresses* the attitudinal messages suggested/signalled by a wide range of inanimates (e.g. *beam* in (3), or *waters* in (8)). Some other inanimate subjects occurring with manner of speaking verbs involve personification rather than metaphor, as *Patriotism* in (1). Yet other inanimate subjects are metonymic human beings (e.g. *every tongue* (example (9)). As explicitly shown in Tab. 6.19, most of the ROCs just described involve metaphors, personifications and metonymies, which lends support to the literary and poetic side of the ROC which will be discussed in § 6.3.3.

Tab. 6.19: Manner of speaking verbs with animal and inanimate subjects

(1) Nay here comes a second Committee-reporter, Deputy Mailhe, with a Legal Argument, very prosy to read now, very refreshing to hear then, That, by the Law of the Country, Louis Capet was only called Inviolable by a figure of rhetoric; but at bottom was perfectly violable, triable; that he can, and even should be tried. This Question of Louis, emerging so often as an angry confused possibility, and submerging again, has emerged now in an articulate shape. Patriotism **growls** indignant joy. The so-called reign of Equality is not to be a mere name, then, but a thing! Try Louis Capet? scornfully ejaculates Patriotism: Mean criminals go to the gallows for a purse cut; and this chief criminal, guilty of a France cut; of a France slashed asunder with Clotho-scissors and Civil war; with his victims 'twelve hundred on the Tenth of August alone' lying low in the Catacombs, fattening the passes of Argonne Wood, of Valmy and far Fields; (...).

CLMET3.0 1837, Carlyle; *The French Revolution*

PERSONIFICATION

(2) A pig-sty is not, perhaps, a strictly eligible seat, but there were special reasons, of which you shall hear something later, for sitting on this particular pig-sty. The old sow was within, extended at full length. Occasionally she **grunted** approval of what was said, but, beyond that, she seemed to show but a faint interest in the proceedings. She had been a witness of similar gatherings for some years, and, to tell the truth, they had begun to bore her, but, on the whole, I am not prepared to deny that her appreciation was an intelligent one.

CLMET3.0 1890; *Punch, Vol. 99*

approval = deverbal noun (OED, s.v. *approve*, v.1)

(3) Drury Lane! Drury Lane!
Drury Lane! Drury Lane!
They shout and they bellow again and again.
All, all in vain!
Water turns steam;}
Each blazing beam}
Hisses defiance to the eddying spout;}
It seems but too plain that nothing can put it out!}
Drury Lane! Drury Lane!
See, Drury Lane expires!

CLMET3.0 1812, James Smith and Horace Smith; *Rejected Addresses, or the New Theatrum Poetarum*

METAPHOR

Tab. 6.19: *Continued*

(4) Flocks of geese, arising from damp repose upon the ragged autumn turf, **hissed forth** futile declarations of war.

CLMET3.0 1901, Kingsley; *The History of Sir Richard Calmady*

declaration = deverbal noun (OED, s.v. *declare*, v.)

(5) The single street, sun-covered, sleepy, empty save for a brewer's dray and tax-cart or two standing before the solid Georgian portals of the White Lion Inn, for a straggling tail of children bearing home small shoppings and jugs of supper beer, for a flock of gray geese proceeding with suggestively self-righteous demeanour along the very middle of the roadway and lowering long necks to **hiss** defiance at the passer-by, and for an old black retriever dozing peacefully beneath one of the rustling sycamores in front of Josiah Appleyard, the saddler's shop—all these, as she looked at them, became uncertain in outline, reeled before Honoria's eyes.

CLMET3.0 1901, Kingsley; *The History of Sir Richard Calmady*

(6) He raises his huge stature, he shakes his huge black head, fire flashes from the eyes of him,—piercing to all Republican hearts: so that the very Galleries, though we filled them by ticket, **murmur** sympathy; and are like to burst down, and raise the People, and deliver him!

CLMET3.0 1837, Carlyle; *The French Revolution*

METONYMY

(7) THE EARTH:
I spin beneath my pyramid of night,
Which points into the heavens dreaming delight,
Murmuring victorious joy in my enchanted sleep;}
As a youth lulled in love-dreams faintly sighing,
Under the shadow of his beauty lying,
Which round his rest a watch of light and warmth doth keep.}

CLMET3.0 1820, Shelley; *Prometheus Unbound*

PERSONIFICATION

(8) It is all very pretty to see the trees big with their hopes of another year, though dumb as yet on the subject, and the waters **murmuring** gaiety, and the banks spread out with comfort; but a boy takes none of this to heart; unless he be meant for a poet (which God can never charge upon me), and he would liefer have a good apple, or even a bad one, if he stole it.

CLMET3.0 1869, Blackmore; *Lorna Doone*

METAPHOR

Continued on next page

Tab. 6.19: *Continued*

(9) Many of those who surrounded the Bassa were sent only to watch and report his conduct: every tongue **was muttering** censure, and every eye was searching for a fault.

CLMET3.0 1759, Johnson; *Rasselas, Prince of Abyssinia*

METONYMY

censure = deverbal noun (OED, *censure*, v.)

(10) Every great tradition has its own way of dying; and the classical tradition died of timidity. It grew afraid of the flesh and blood of life; it was too polite to face realities, too elevated to tread the common ground of fact and detail; it would touch nothing but generalities, for they alone are safe, harmless, and respectable; and, if they are also empty, how can that he helped? Starving, it shrank into itself, **muttering** old incantations; and it continued to mutter them, automatically, some time after it had expired. But, in the heyday of the age of Louis XIV, literature showed no signs of such a malady—though no doubt it contained the latent germs of the disease; on the contrary, the masterpieces of that epoch are charged to the full with vitality and force.

CLMET3.0 1912, Strachey; *Landmarks in French Literature*

PERSONIFICATION

incantation = deverbal noun (OED, *incant*, v.)

(11) Soon, however, a noise of striving urchins arose, and **muttered** encouragements from the neighbouring boys of "Go it, Tadpole!" "Now, young Green!" "Haul away his blanket!" "Slipper him on the hands!" Young Green and little Hall, commonly called Tadpole, from his great black head and thin legs, slept side by side far away by the door, and were for ever playing one another tricks, which usually ended, as on this morning, in open and violent collision; (...).

CLMET3.0 1857, Hughes; *Tom Brown's Schooldays*

METONYMY

encouragement = deverbal noun (OED, *encourage*, v.)

(12) Then a voice **roared** orders, half a dozen shots sang about the fugitive, and there were galloping horses quickly in pursuit.

CLMET3.0 1910, Brebner; *The Brown Mask*

METONYMY

order = deverbal noun (OED, *order*, v.)

(13) All these have been tried, cast,--the Galleries **shouting** approval; and handed over to the Realised Idea, within a week.

CLMET3.0 1837, Carlyle; *The French Revolution*

METONYMY

approval = deverbal noun (OED, s.v. *approve*, v.[1])

Tab. 6.19: *Continued*

(14) These men, like the owners of negro ships, never smell on their money the blood by which it has been gained, but sleep quietly in their beds, terming such occupations lawful callings; yet the lightning marks not their roofs to **thunder** conviction on them "and to justify the ways of God to man."

[= These men are so untouched by consciousness that not even the thunder could make any aware of awaking them]

CLMET3.0 1796, Wollstonecraft; *Letters on Sweden, Norway and Denmark*

METAPHOR

conviction = deverbal noun (OED, s.v. *convict*, v.)

(15) He exulted in his power: and well he might, for after the cannon **had thundered** indefinite salutes, no fewer than 100,000 armed men defiled to the music of the war-drums and the ombyas before the famous Black Flag.

CLMET3.0 1899, Churchill; *The River War (unabridged edition)*

METAPHOR

salute = deverbal noun (OED, s.v. *salute*, v.)

(16) "I see what you are: you are too proud, but you are fair. My lord and master loves you. Oh, such a love could but be recompensed though you were crowned the queen of beauty; for Orsino loves you with adoration and with tears, with groans that **thunder** love, and sighs of fire."

CLMET3.0 1807, Lamb; *Tales from Shakespeare*

METAPHOR

(17) SPIRIT:

On the brink of the night and the morning}
My coursers are wont to respire;
But the Earth **has just whispered** a warning}
That their flight must be swifter than fire:
They shall drink the hot speed of desire!

CLMET3.0 1820, Shelley; *Prometheus Unbound*

PERSONIFICATION

warning = deverbal noun (OED, s.v. *warn*, v.[1])

(18) 'Since thou leftst me so abruptly,' said Olinthus, 'hast thou been happy? has thy heart found contentment under these priestly robes? hast thou, still yearning for the voice of God, heard it **whisper** comfort to thee from the oracles of Isis? (...)'.

CLMET3.0 1834, Bulwer-Lytton; *The Last Days of Pompeii*

METONYMY

Continued on next page

Tab. 6.19: *Continued*

(19) My soul **whispers** hope, it sweeps exultingly beyond the boding hour, it revels in the future- its own courage is its fittest omen.

CLMET3.0 1834, Bulwer-Lytton; *The Last Days of Pompeii*

METONYMY

(20) I know not how this may be; but I have, ere now, heard a voice break so upon the silence, To angels' 'twas most like, and charm the moonlight air with its balmy essence, that the budding leaves trembled to its accents. Would I might have heard it once more **whisper** peace and hope (as erst when it was mingled with the breath of spring), and with its soft pulsations lift winged fancy to heaven.

CLMET3.0 1821–2, Hazlitt; *Table-Talk: Essays on Men and Manners*

METONYMY

(21) But thou, oh Hope! with eyes so fair,
What was thy delighted measure?}
Still it **whisper'd** promised pleasure,}
And bade the lovely scenes at distance hail!

CLMET3.0 1821–2, Hazlitt; *Table-Talk: Essays on Men and Manners*[a]

METAPHOR

(22) The shock that crushed her heart with the tidings that Glaucus loved, had at first only saddened and benumbed – by degrees jealousy took a wilder and fiercer shape; it partook of hatred – it **whispered** revenge.

CLMET3.0 1834, Bulwer-Lytton; *The Last Days of Pompeii*

METAPHOR

(23) He did not speak, as though fearing to destroy by sound or motion the happiness of that moment, when her soft hand's touch thrilled through his frame, and her silvery voice **was whispering** tenderness in his ear.

CLMET3.0 1848, Gaskell; *Mary Barton*

METONYMY

(24) In my heart nevertheless there was a reserve of wonderment at his apparent astuteness and resolution, and my old love for him **whispered** disbelief in his having disgraced me.

CLMET3.0 1870, Meredith; *The Adventures of Harry Richmond*

METAPHOR

(25) Some of his remarks partly swayed me, in spite of my seeing that they were based on the supposition of an 'all for love' adventure of a mad princess. They **whispered** a little hope, when I was adoring her passionately for being the reverse of whatever might have given hope a breath.

CLMET3.0 1870, Meredith; *The Adventures of Harry Richmond*

METONYMY

Tab. 6.19: *Continued*

(26)	But the couplet, 'My undissuaded heart I hear **Whisper** courage in my ear,' is exactly what I want for the thought, and to me seems very energetic as speech, if not as verse. CLMET3.0 1868–94, Stevenson; *Letters of Robert Louis Stevenson*[b] **METONYMY**
(27)	The first train had crawled over the new bridge, and stood **whistling** its triumph in the station. CLMET3.0 1920, Bagnold; *The Happy Foreigner* **METAPHOR**

a Stanza from "The Passions. An Ode for Music" (Collins 1746) included in Hazlitt's treatise. In this ode, "delighted measure" refers to "a piece of music" and "promised pleasure" refers to hope or faith/optimism in the future.

b The ROC attested in Stevenson's letters belongs to his poem "Our Lady of the Snows".

6.3.1.2 Verbs of nonverbal communication

As for the 16 verbs of nonverbal communication analysed from Levin's list (1993, 98), only 11 of these verbs were attested in the ROC in CLMET3.0. This figure contrasts with the 20 verbs of this class found in the ROC in COCA (Martínez-Vázquez 2014a, 179–180). The verbs in question are specified in Tab. 6.20.

Tab. 6.20: Verbs of nonverbal communication attested in the LModE ROC and the PDE ROC

LModE ROC	PDE ROC
16 verbs analysed in CLMET3.0 *clap, cough, frown, giggle, grin, guffaw, laugh, nod, sigh, smile, sniff, snort, sob, wave, weep, wink* **11 verbs attested in the ROC in CLMET3.0** *frown, grin, laugh, nod, sigh, smile, snort, sob, wave, weep, wink*	**20 verbs attested in the ROC in COCA (Martínez-Vázquez 2014a, 179–180)** *blink, bob, bow, chortle, chuckle, clap, cough, frown, glare, hug, kiss, nod, shrug, sigh, smile, snort, wag, wave, weep, wink*

Tab. 6.21 lists the overall types of verbs of nonverbal communication analysed for both periods with their corresponding frequencies (raw and normalized). Note here that only seven of these 26 verb types

have been attested in both periods, namely the verbs *frown*, *nod*, *sigh*, *smile*, *snort*, *wave* and *wink*. These are shaded in grey.

Tab. 6.21: Frequencies of the verbs of nonverbal communication analysed in the literature

	Verb	Raw frequencies in CLMET3.0	Normalized freq. pmw in CLMET3.0 (1710–1920) (34,386,225 words)	Raw frequencies in COCA. Based on Martínez-Vázquez (2014a, 179–180)	Normalized freq. pmw in COCA[a] (1990–2013) (450,000,000 words)
1	*Blink*	Not analysed	-	10	0.02
2	*Bob*	Not analysed	-	Less than 5 occurr.	-
3	*Bow*	Not analysed	-	Less than 5 occurr.	-
4	*Chortle*	Not analysed	-	Less than 5 occurr.	-
5	*Chuckle*	Not analysed	-	Less than 5 occurr.	-
6	*Clap*	0	0	5	0.01
7	*Cough*	0	0	Less than 5 occurr.	-
8	*Frown*	2	0.06	7	0.02
9	*Giggle*	0	0	Not analysed	-
10	*Glare*	Not analysed	-	10	0.02
11	*Grin*	2	0.06	Not analysed	-
12	*Guffaw*	0	0	Not analysed	-
13	*Hug*	Not analysed	-	103	0.23
14	*Kiss*	Not analysed	-	926	2.06
15	*Laugh*	3	0.09	Not analysed	-
16	*Nod*	24	0.70	693	1.54
17	*Shrug*	Not analysed	-	15	0.03
18	*Sigh*	7	0.20	25	0.06
19	*Smile*	43	1.25	92	0.20
20	*Sniff*	0	0	Not analysed	-
21	*Snort*	2	0.06	26	0.06
22	*Sob*	7	0.20	Not analysed	-
23	*Wag*	Not analysed	-	Less than 5 occurr.	-
24	*Wave*	16	0.47	507	1.13
25	*Weep*	10	0.29	Less than 5 occurr.	-
26	*Wink*	1	0.03	5	0.01

a When the searches were conducted, the corpus contained 450 million words (Martínez-Vázquez 2014a, 173fn1). The compilers add approximately 25 million words each year. Nowadays it contains more than one billion words (August 2020).

As previously seen in § 6.2.1.2 the verbs s*mile*, *nod* and *wave* are the strongest collexemes of the LModE ROC for the class of verbs of nonverbal communication, and they function as prototypes for the consolidation of the means subschema of the ROC during the LModE period. Interestingly, these verbs also seem to be the ones that show the most dramatic frequency changes across time. The verb *smile*, for instance, becomes much less frequent in the PDE ROC, and the verbs *nod* and *wave* considerably increase their frequency in PDE. The frequency of the rest of the verbs of nonverbal communication *attested* in the ROC in both LModE and PDE (i.e. *frown*, *sigh*, *snort* and *wink*) remains more or less constant. Fig. 6.5 illustrates this point.

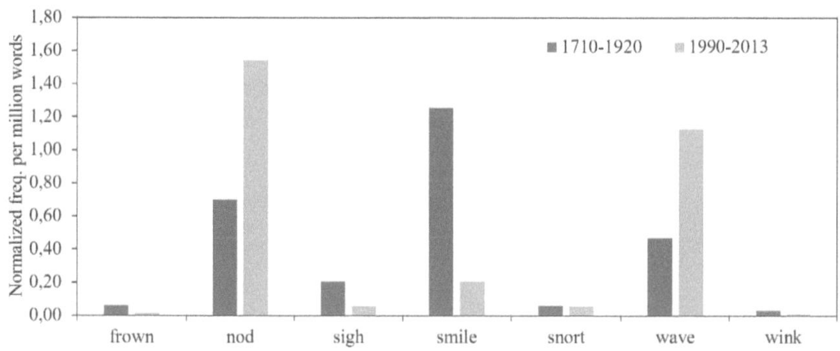

Fig. 6.5: Frequencies for seven nonverbal communication verbs attested in the LModE and the PDE ROC

6.3.1.2.1 The verb smile

The verb *smile* shows a wide range of reaction objects in LModE. As seen in Fig. 6.5, this variation, however, seems not to be a feature of PDE, when the verb *smile* decreases in frequency in the ROC and shows a restriction in RO types. As shown in Tab. 6.22 at the end of this section, in LModE the verb *smile* collocates with delocutives (i.e. *"God bless you"*, *farewell*, *good luck*, *goodbye*, *good-morning*, *thanks* and *welcome*), deverbal nouns indicating agreement (i.e. *acknowledgment(s)*, *acquiescence*, *appreciation*, *approbation*, *approval*, *assent*, *consent* and *encouragement*), and expressive nouns such as *negative*, *invitation*, *perferment*, *reproach*, *Sweetness* and *Blessedness*. ROCs with these expressive nouns bring about idiosyncratic examples such as those in (20)-(25), where context turns out to be crucial for their precise decoding.

In example (20), the reaction object *negative* apparently contradicts the inherent positive prosody of the verb *smile*. In example (21) there is no such contradiction but the coerced meaning of the ROC *his gracious sovereign smiles invitation* [= welcome] *upon him* would not be properly understood if given out of this context. Similarly, the ROC examples with *smile* in (22) and (23) are written in verse and the selection of these reaction objects is highly dependent on poetic licence. Finally, examples (24) and (25) involving the reaction objects *Sweetness* and *Blessedness* belong to Brooke's sentimental novel entitled *The Fool of Quality* (1765–70). The attestation of several ROCs in this novel (a total of six ROCs, specified in (24)-(29)), and other sentimental novels such as Richardson's *Clarissa* (1748) and Dickens' *Dombey and Son* (1844) suggest that ROCs come in especially handy for writers of that particular genre. This aspect will be briefly discussed later on in § 6.3.3.2.

(20) 'Well, I'll be moving on,' was Mr Sampson Levi's next remark. 'Good day, and thank ye. *I suppose you aren't doing anything in Kaffirs*?' Mr Racksole **smiled** a negative.

CLMET3.0 1902, Bennett; *The Grand Babylon Hotel*

(21) Think for a moment of the clattering of porter-pots, and the scream of my goodly hostess. Imagine that the blazing fire smiles through the impenetrable window, and that the kitchen shakes with the peals of laughter. These are temptations, my lord, that no mortal porter can withstand. When the unvaried countenance of his gracious sovereign **smiles** invitation upon him from the weather beaten sign-post, what loyal heart but must be melted into compliance. From all these considerations, my lord, I would advise you to write with invisible ink. Milk I believe will serve the purpose, though I am afraid, that the milk that is hawked about the streets of London, has rather too much water in it. The juice of lemon is a sovereign recipe. There are a variety of other preparations that will answer the purpose.

CLMET3.0 1783–4, Godwin; *Four Early Pamphlets*

(22) EPILOGUE
(. . .)
The servile suitors—watch her various face,}

She **smiles** perferment—or she frowns disgrace,}
Curtsies a pension here—there nods a place.}

CLMET3.0 1796, Sheridan; *The Rivals*

(23) MERCURY
Crouch then in silence.
Awful Sufferer!
To thee unwilling, most unwillingly
I come, by the great Father's will driven down,
To execute a doom of new revenge.
Alas! I pity thee, and hate myself
That I can do no more: aye from thy sight
Returning, for a season, Heaven seems Hell,
So thy worn form pursues me night and day,
Smiling reproach. Wise art thou, firm and good,
But vainly wouldst stand forth alone in strife
Against the Omnipotent; as yon clear lamps
That measure and divide the weary years
From which there is no refuge, long have taught
And long must teach. (. . .)

CLMET3.0 1820, Shelley; *Prometheus Unbound*

(24) My Mind notwithstanding, at the Time, seemed more awake and more alive to Objects than ever. In an Instant she stood visible and confessed before me. I saw her clearer than at noon Day, by the Light which she cast with Profusion abroad. Every Feature and former Trace seemed heightened into a Lustre without a Loss of the least Similitude. She **smiled** ineffable Sweetness and Blessedness upon me. And stooping down, I felt her Embrace about my Heart and about my Spirit, while, at the same Time, I saw her bent in Complacence before me.

CLMET3.0 1765–70, Brooke; *The Fool of Quality*

(25) The Moor, hereat, **smiled** celestial Sweetness, and Joy beamed from his Eyes and throughout his dimpling Aspect.

CLMET3.0 1765–70, Brooke; *The Fool of Quality*

(26) They **murmured** their applause of that Virtue which they could not but revere, even in Enemies.

CLMET3.0 1765–70, Brooke; *The Fool of Quality*

(27) Their Mouth is first to be bridled, they must not dare to speak or even **mutter** their Complaints; and, after being laden with all Kinds of Grievances and Oppressions, they are to be led to the gloomy Receptacles of their insulting Proprietor, there to be further dealt with according to his Pleasure.

CLMET3.0 1765–70, Brooke; *The Fool of Quality*

(28) Poor Peter, finding himself thus between two Fires, gave a slight Trip to his male Assailant who, instantly, fell with his Shoulder against the Pavement, and, rising with Difficulty, limped homeward, **muttering** Curses all the Way.

CLMET3.0 1765–70, Brooke; *The Fool of Quality*

(29) With Respect to such Obligations I am indeed a beggar'd Insolvent. But, my Heart is pleased with the Thought, that the Connection between us, of Creditor on your Part and of Debtor on mine, should remain on Record to all Eternity. Here, the worthy Meekly became oppressed under Sensations of grateful Recollection, and, putting his Handkerchief to his Eyes, he **sobbed out** his Passion.

CLMET3.0 1765–70, Brooke; *The Fool of Quality*

Tab. 6.22: RO types with *smile*

Smile (43 ROCs; 22 RO types)	
"God bless you"	good luck
acknowledgment(s) (x2)	goodbye
acquiescence	good-morning
appreciation	*invitation*
approbation (x3)	*negative*
approval (x5)	*perferment*
assent (x8)	*reproach*
*Blessedness**	salutation
consent	*Sweetness (x2)*
encouragement	thanks (x2)
farewell (x2)	**welcome (x6)**

* Shaded in grey ROs where context plays a crucial role for their precise decoding

6.3.1.2.2 The verb **nod**

In LModE the verb *nod* only occurs with formulae (e.g. *"Good bye!"*, *adieu*, *farewell*, *good-bye*, *good-night*) and deverbal nouns indicating some type of agreement (e.g. *acquiescence*, *affirmative*, *approval* and *assent*). By contrast, in PDE this verb allows for a great deal of variation: it occurs with 41 RO types against the nine RO types attested in LModE (see Tab. 6.23).

As explained by Martínez-Vázquez (2014a, 2015), this variation in PDE with *nod* is possible because context supplies the necessary information for the correct interpretation of the ROC. For instance, in example (30) the linguistic context reveals that the ROC stands for a message of confirmation, and in example (31) the adequate interpretation of the ROC depends on: (i) the polar question formulated by the first participant, and (ii) the information provided by the expresser right afterwards. Interestingly, among the 41 reaction object types attested in PDE with the verb *nod*, Martínez-Vázquez (2015) mentions a couple of examples involving the negative locution *no*, which goes against the usual positive prosody of this verb (see examples (32) and (33)).

Tab. 6.23: RO types with *nod* in the LModE and the PDE ROC

LModE ROCs with *nod* (24 ROCs; 9 RO types)	**PDE ROCs with *nod* (693 ROCs; 41 RO types) (Martínez-Vázquez (2014a, 181; 2015, 164–165)**		
"Good bye!"	acceptance	confirmation	lie
acquiescence	acknowledgment	congratulations	no
adieu (x2)	acquaintances	consent	permission
affirmative (x3)	acquiescence	disinterest	recognition
approval	affirmation	dismissal	recrimination
assent (x12)	agreement	dreads	reply
farewell	answer	encouragement	satisfaction
good-bye (x2)	apology	farewell(s)	support
good-night	appreciation	forgiveness	surrender
	approval (x130)	go-ahead	**thanks/thank-you (x72)**
	assent (x42)	good-bye(s)	**understanding (x39)**
	awareness	gratitude	welcome
	compliance	greeting	**yes (x280)**
	comprehension	hello	

(30) With a resigned droop of her shoulders, Cardenas **nodded** her surrender.

(COCA, 2001, FIC, Analog; Martínez-Vázquez 2015, 149)

(31) You're still a virgin, aren't you? For several reasons I lacked the heart to tell him about my latest discovery . . . so I **nodded** a lie.

(COCA, 2011, FIC, Bk:NobleNorfleet; Martínez-Vázquez 2015, 165)

(32) He motions to her two top buttons of her blouse. She **nods** no. Austin nods yes. She sheepishly undoes them.

(COCA, 1997, FIC, Mov: AustinPowers; Martínez-Vázquez 2015, 164)

(33) You like hiking? (Erica nods no) Fishing? (Erica **nods** no) Sailing? (Erica **nods** no) What do you like? # ERICA # Boys.

(COCA, 1992, FIC, Mov: KnightMoves; Martínez-Vázquez 2015, 164)

6.3.1.2.3 The verbs **wave, frown, snort** *and* **wink**

The most typical reaction objects occurring with the verbs *smile* and *nod* in LModE are redundant with the verb's (emotional) meaning: *smile assent* (x8), *smile a welcome* (x6), *smile approval* (x5), *nod assent* (x12). This semantic matching is also observable in LModE ROCs involving the verbs *wave*, *frown*, *snort* and *wink*. The latter (i.e. *wink*) is a hapax in my historical data, the verb *wave* only seems to accept formulae (e.g. *"good-byes"*, *adieu(s)* (x6), *cheer*, *farewell(s)* and *good-bye*), and the verbs *frown* and *snort* only blend with reaction objects describing negative emotions such as *defiance* (examples (34) and (35)), *disgrace* (example (36)), and *disdain* (example (37)). Tab. 6.24 shows the complete distribution of reaction objects with these verbs.

(34) Silent, lonely, and sublime, it [the whole edifice] seemed to stand the sovereign of the scene, and to **frown** defiance on all, who dared to invade its solitary reign.

CLMET3.0 1794, Radcliffe; *The Mysteries of Udolpho*

(35) 'Except some ordinary preparation at home, and from this lady,' replied Mr. Dombey, introducing Mrs. Pipchin, who instantly communicated a rigidity to her whole muscular system, and **snorted** defiance beforehand, in case

the Doctor should disparage her; 'except so far, Paul has, as yet, applied himself to no studies at all.'

CLMET3.0 1844, Dickens; *Dombey and Son*

(36) EPILOGUE
(. . .)
The servile suitors—watch her various face,}
She smiles perferment—or she **frowns** disgrace,}
Curtsies a pension here—there nods a place.}

CLMET3.0 1796, Sheridan; *The Rivals*

(37) I heard them [the poor animals] **snort** disdain; and I saw them lift the hoof against the very benefactor, who put on their shoes, and gave the vigour to kick.

CLMET3.0 1779, Pratt; *Shenstone-Green*

Tab. 6.24: RO types with *wave*, *frown*, *snort* and *wink*

Wave (16 ROCs; 6 RO types)			Frown (2 ROCs; 2 RO types)	Snort (2 ROCs; 2 RO types)	Wink (1 ROC)
"good-byes"	cheer	good-bye	approbation	defiance	approbation
adieu(s) (x6)	**farewell(s) (x6)**	greeting	disgrace	disdain	

As shown in Tab. 6.25, the collocates of the verbs *wave* and *frown* remain more or less constant in the PDE ROC. This is particularly interesting in the case of *wave*. As previously noted, its frequency in the ROC has increased dramatically over the last couple of centuries (it went up from 16 ROCs in LModE to 507 ROCs in PDE; cf. Fig. 6.5 above for normalized frequencies), however, this increase in frequency is not reflected in width of collocation.

Perhaps the most interesting example of these PDE ROCs with *wave* and *frown* involves the verb *frown* and the reaction object *agreement* (38) where there is an apparent mismatch between the semantics of the verb and that of the reaction object. As with some idiosyncratic reaction object types occurring with the verb *smile* in LModE (examples (20)-(25)) and *nod* in PDE (examples (30)-(33)), context here plays a crucial role for its proper decodification.

(38) He stares right at me. "Clears two or three murders, bitch thinks she's a dick." Our Watch LT **frowns** agreement and checks the camera. (Martínez-Vázquez 2014a, 179)

Tab. 6.25: RO types with *wave* and *frown* in the LModE and the PDE ROC

LModE ROCs with *wave* (16 ROCs; 6 RO types)	**PDE ROCs with *wave* (507 ROCs; 5 RO types) (Martínez-Vázquez 2015, 166)**	**LModE ROCs with *frown* (2 ROCs; 2 RO types)**	**PDE ROCs with *frown* (7 ROCs; 5 RO types) (Martínez-Vázquez 2014a, 179)**
"good-byes"	goodbye (x401)	defiance	agreement
adieu(s) (x6)	hello (x52)	disgrace	annoyance
cheer	farewell (x22)		confusion
farewell(s) (x6)	greeting (x19)		disapproval
good-bye	thanks (x13)		displeasure
greeting			

6.3.1.2.4 The verbs sigh, sob, weep, grin *and* laugh

The rest of the verbs of nonverbal communication attested in the LModE ROC (i.e. *sigh*, *sob*, *weep*, *grin* and *laugh*) are treated here together because of their low frequency in the ROC. As can be seen in Tab. 6.26,

Tab. 6.26: RO types with *sigh*, *sob*, *weep*, *grin*, and *laugh*

Sigh (7 ROCs; 6 RO types)	**Sob (7 ROCs; 7 RO types)**	**Weep (10 ROCs; 7 RO types)**	**Grin (2 ROCs; 2 RO types)**	**Laugh (3 ROCs; 3 RO types)**
adieu (x2)	complaints	affliction	assent	impertinence
apprehension	denial	farewell (x3)	defiance	welcome
farewell	entreaty	repentance		yahyah[a]
love	grief	shame (x2)		
relief	Passion	thankfulness		
sweetness	terror	thanks (x3)		
	thanks	woe		

a "An exclamation of disgust, aversion, or malicious defiance. Also used loosely as a vague or meaningless exclamation." (OED, s.v. *yah*, int.[1] (and n.[1]))

sigh, *sob* and *weep* occur with a higher number of different RO types than *grin* and *laugh*, which are far more restricted in this respect.

Here again context plays an important role in both the *formation* and *decodification* of these LModE ROCs. For instance, ROCs involving the verb *sigh* and the expressive nouns *adieu*, *love* and *sweetness*, have been attested in excerpts written in verse, and having inanimates as subjects of the construction: one holding a metonymic human subject (*this trembling heart* in (39)) and the other two involving metaphorical mappings (*the land, the sea, and heaven* in (40); and *soft west winds* in (41)). These examples are similar to those attested for the verb *smile* (cf. 6.3.1.2.1) and to those analysed at the end of § 6.3.1.1 for manner of speaking verbs with subjects that correspond to animals or inanimates.

(39) FLORIDOR. SONG.
Tho' honour loudly strikes my ear,
The softer notes of love prevailing,
Every sense assailing,
Swell with hope, or sink with fear!
Who for the goal of glory start,}
To love, as honour true,}
Would ne'er forbid this trembling heart,}
To **sigh** a last adieu!}
I go—my faith and truth to prove,
Valour ne'er was foe to love; I will,
I must obey the call,
Love's triumphant over all!

CLMET3.0 1770, Garrick; *A Christmas Tale*

(40) CHAPTER VI.
IT seemed the laurel chaste and stubborn oak,
And all the gentle trees on earth that grew,
It seemed the land, the sea, and heaven above,}
All breathed out fancy sweet, and **sighed out** love.}

Fairfax's Tasso

CLMET3.0 1838, Bulwer-Lytton; *Alice*

(41) She could not tell why, but thinking of him now, her whole world seemed to change and sublimate into content. He was coming back! With him came spring and sunshine, youth and hope! It was yet early in the year. The little crocuses peeped out--the violets purpled the banks. Now and then came soft west winds,

> **sighing** <u>sweetness</u> over the earth. Not a breeze passed her by--not a flower sprang in her sight--not one sunny day dawned to ripen the growing year, but Olive's heart leaped within her; for she said, "He will come with the spring--he will come with the spring!" How and with what mind he would come,--whether he would tell her he loved her, or ask her to be his wife,--she counted none of these things. Her love was too unselfish, too utterly bound up in him.
>
> CLMET3.0 1850, Craik; *Olive*

6.3.1.2.5 Structural variation with **nod** *and* **wave**

The data analysed in the last four sections (§ 6.3.1.2.1–§ 6.3.1.2.4) demonstrates the existence of a number of idiosyncratic ROCs, which in LModE apply most particularly to those ROCs attested with the nonverbal communication verbs *smile* and *sigh*. In addition to these idiosyncratic ROCs there is also evidence of a number of semi-fixed ROC constructs which are highly redundant with the verb's meaning, namely those attested with the verbs of nonverbal communication *nod* and *wave* (e.g. *nod* + *assent* (x12), *wave* + *adieu(s)* (x6), *wave* + *farewell(s)* (x6)), but also some with the verb *smile* (e.g. *smile* + *assent* (x8), *smile* + *welcome* (x6), *smile* + *approval* (x5)). From a Construction Grammar perspective, these semi-fixed constructs point out to another level of specificity in the ROC network. In the following lines, I will briefly comment on the variation of the ROC subschemas with *nod* and *wave*; in particular on whether the reaction objects involved in these verb-specific subschemas are preceded by a possessive determiner, an indefinite article or a zero determiner.

As shown in Tab. 6.27, in LModE the ROC subschema with *nod* shows a great deal of variation. Although this subschema has a slight preference for zero determiners in terms of token frequency, these tokens are basically restricted to the reaction object types *assent* and *"Good bye!"*.

A glance at the EModE period using the *Early English Books Online* corpus (525 million word corpus; 1474–1700; EEBO; Petré 2016) also shows some variation. Only four ROCs were attested with *nod*, and these occur with both indefinite articles (see examples (42) and (43)), and zero determiners (see examples (44) and (45)).[53]

53 1,837 tokens analysed using the regular expression: \bnodd?s?([ei']d)?([iy]ng(e)?)?\b.

Tab. 6.27: Structural distribution of ROs in LModE ROCs with *nod*

Reaction object	**possessive determiner**	**indefinite article**	**Ø determiner**
"Good bye!"	0	0	1
acquiescence	1	0	0
adieu (x2)	1	1	0
affirmative (x3)	0	3	0
approval	0	1	0
assent (x12)	2	0	10
farewell	0	1	0
good-bye (x2)	0	2	0
good-night	0	1	0
TOTAL	4	9	11
%	17 %	38 %	46 %

*ROC tokens with *nod*: 24

(42) It is all one if a man lies, whether it be by word or by deed. A man may *look a lie*, and **nod** a lie, and *smile a lie.*
EEBO 1660, Jeremy Taylor (1613–1667); *Ductor Dubitantium, or, The Rule of Conscience in all her Generall Measures Serving as a Great Instrument for the Determination of Cases of Conscience: In Four Books*

(43) Curiosity invited many Spectators, and Courtesy some of Quality to be my Harbingers at my Lodgings; which at my return I found pestered, as I had the Streets all the way I came: They were very Civil, making no Intrusion before they had requested leave; and then interrogating the State of Europe, the Government, Policy, and Learning; **nodding** a satisfaction in the account I gave them: Nor were they less communicative in their Relations, of those Occurrences which wheeled in their Sphere, being highly concerned to shew they had Book-men as well as Sword-men.
EEBO 1698, John Fryer (d. 1733); *A New Account of East-India and Persia, in Eight Letters Being Nine years Travels Begun 1672 and Finished 1681: Containing Observations Made of the Moral, Natural and Artifical Estate of Those Countries ... /by John Fryer ... ; Illustrated with Maps, Figures and Useful Tables*

(44) Enter the Imaginary Queen, her Gentleman Usher bare headed leads her, her Page holds up her Train, her Woman follows her, and that is all her Train, a Company of people flock to see her, and kneel to kiss her hand, she brideling in her Chin, as thinking that doth advance her state, they kneeling she gives them her hand to kiss, they pray God bless her Royalty, she **nods** them$_{\text{REC}}$ **Ø** thanks, and then passes away.

EEBO 1662, Margaret Cavendish, Duchess of Newcastle (1624?-1674); *Playes Written by the Thrice Noble, Illustrious and Excellent Princess, the Lady Marchioness of Newcastle*

(45) A SATYR AGAINST Common-Wealths.

(1)
I'LE not forbear---for who can longer stay}
When Loyal Muses bid me not delay}
But **nodding Ø** promise an auspicious way?}
Thus Caesar once Heaven's anger to attone
Beck'nd to, by a God, pass'd Rubicon,
To scourge his own Republick, haughty Rome.
A Commonwealth! curse on that nauseous name
Which from the Devil with damnation came;
He first set up the curs'd reforming Trade,
And boldly sought Heaven's Empire to invade;
Till blasted by Joves Thunder, down he fell,
State-holder to the Commonwealth of Hell.

EEBO 1684, H. P.; *A Satyr against Common-wealths*

With regard to PDE, Martínez-Vázquez (2014a, 182) shows that for the ROC subschema with *nod* there are far more reaction object types and tokens occurring with zero determiners (61 % of the data) than with indefinite articles (only 2 % of her data). This is shown in Tab. 6.28.

Tab. 6.28: Structural distribution of *the most frequent ROs* in PDE ROCs with *nod*

Reaction object	possessive determiner	indefinite article	Ø determiner
yes	0	7	273
agreement	71	2	70
approval	79	2	39
thanks	51	1	20
assent	20	0	21
understanding	35	0	4
TOTAL	256	12	427
%	37 %	2 %	61 %

As for the ROC subschema with *wave*, in LModE we observe that there is also some variation, but only with its most frequent RO types, i.e. *adieu(s)* and *farewell(s)*. These may be preceded by a possessive determiner, an indefinite article or a zero determiner. Beyond these RO types, *wave* shows a clear preference in type and token frequency for reaction objects preceded by indefinite articles. These account for 50 % of the overall data – against the 31 % and 19 % of the bare and possessive patterns respectively (see Tab. 6.29). For this verb no PDE data is presented in Martínez-Vázquez (2014a).

Tab. 6.29: Structural distribution of ROs in the LModE ROC subschema with *wave*

Reaction object	possessive determiner	indefinite article	Ø determiner
"good-byes"	0	0	1
adieu(s) (x6)	1	3	2
cheer	0	1	0
farewell(s) (x6)	2	2	2
good-bye	0	1	0
greeting	0	1	0
TOTAL	3	8	5
%	19 %	50 %	31 %

*ROC tokens with *wave*: 16

To sum up, in LModE the ROC subschemas with *nod* and *wave* show an overall preference for reaction object types headed by indefinite articles. In addition to this, the following can also be pointed out:

(i) During the LModE period the bare construct *nod assent* was already semi-fixed and over time it could have attracted other reaction object types with similar semantics to the bare pattern of the ROC subschema with *nod*. In particular, I am referring here to the bare constructs *nod yes*, *nod agreement* and other reaction object types shown in Tab. 6.28.

(ii) Though in LModE *wave* has a clear preference for RO types headed by indefinite articles (50 % of the data vs 31 % with zero determiners), this subschema also involves some variation with its most frequent reaction object types, i.e. *adieu(s)* and *farewell(s)*. This variation may end up in PDE with a preference for the bare pattern by analogy with the PDE ROC subschema with *nod*: *wave an adieu > wave Ø adieu*; *wave a farewell > wave Ø farewell*. This trend of leaving out the indefinite determiner in some ROC subschemas could be described as a post-constructionalization constructional change. As explained by Traugott and Trousdale (2013, 27), this type of change involves, among other aspects, "morphological and phonological reduction":

> In turn, constructionalization may feed further constructional changes. Such **'post-constructionalization constructional changes'** (PostCxzn CCs for short) typically involve expansion of collocations, and may also involve **morphological and phonological reduction**. For example, once the micro-construction [[a lot of] ↔ [large quant]] had come into existence its collocates expanded exponentially and it has recently been subject to various phonological reductions (Traugott and Trousdale 2013, 27; emphasis mine).

(iii) Apart from those semi-fixed bare constructs in the LModE ROC subschemas with *nod* and *wave* (i.e. *nod assent* (x10), and *wave adieu(s)* (x2) and *farewell(s)* (x2)), the only bare constructs attested with *nod* and *wave* in LModE involve reaction objects between inverted commas (*nod + "Good bye!"* and *wave + "good-byes"*). This is reminiscent of Visser's hypothesis that the ROC is historically networked with innovative reporting speech structures of the type *He grunted "I thank you"* (cf. § 2.3.5, and § 6.3.3.2).

(iv) The lack of quantitative data at this point on the structural variation of PDE ROC subschemas with *wave* and other high-frequency verbs of nonverbal communication such as *smile*, keeps us from making comparisons with their corresponding LModE ROC subschemas. This aspect will therefore be left for future investigations on the ROC.

(v) Finally, a last comment that should be included here is that the four ROCs with *nod* attested in EEBO date from the second half of the seventeenth century. The verb *wave* was also analysed in EEBO,[54] but only one clear ROC was attested,

54 8,812 tokens using the regular expression: \bway?ve?s?([ei']d)?([iy]ng(e)?)?\b.

also from the seventeenth century; this is included in (46). This reveals that the attestation of the nonverbal communication verbs *nod* and *wave* in the ROC goes back to EModE and not to the LModE period as initially suggested by my historical data from the OED (Chapter 5).

(46) To penitent Magdalen.
Mary, but late the cage of Hell,
Thy heavenly change what Muse can tell?
Those twinkling eyes that did allure
To sordid lust, now droppe the pure
Pearle of Contrition; and that haire}
That wandering Cupids did ensnare,}
And **wav'd** its pride in every streete,}
Now humbly licks her Saviours feete,}
And from those blessed roots derives
Vertue, more worth than thousand lives.
To cleanse thy stain'd affections then,
Still weepe and wipe, kind Magdalen.

EEBO 1639, Thomas Bancroft (fl. 1633–1658); *Tvvo Bookes of Epigrammes, and Epitaphs Dedicated to Two Top-branches of Gentry: Sir Charles Shirley, Baronet, and William Davenport, Esquire*

Strikingly, the attestation of these ROCs with *nod* and *wave* in EModE coincides with the gradual development of instrumental NP objects such as *their hedde* and *their wings* in the early examples provided by Visser *noddes their hedde* (1553) and *waue their wings* (1584–1587) (Visser 1963–1973: § 425, I: 418–419).[55] Like ROCs, instrumental objects are also coreferential with the subject and characteristic of non-verbal communication verbs (for the features of instrumental objects see Ross 1970b, Levin 1993). What is relevant about this finding is that it supports the hypothesis outlined in Chapter 3 that the formal restriction of coreferentiality of ROCs could indeed date back to EModE, as

55 Further evidence of the development of instrumental objects in English in the transition from EModE to LModE is provided by Rohdenburg (2018). For instance, he shows that the instrumental object with the verb *stamp* (as in *She stamped her foot*) only starts to become frequent in the eighteenth century and gradually replaces its prepositional counterpart (*She stamped with her foot*) by the twentieth century.

happened to be originally the case of the *way*-construction, as described in Traugott and Trousdale (2013).

6.3.2 Diachronic distribution

As shown in Fig. 6.6, most LModE ROCs accumulate in the second subperiod of LModE (1780–1849), and more specifically in the thirties and forties of the nineteenth century. Interestingly, this diachronic distribution remains constant across the different verb classes: manner of speaking verbs (mos), nonverbal expression verbs (nve), and verbs that allow for both interpretations according to Levin's classification of verbs (see Fig. 6.7). Even if we take into account twelve of the fourteen examples discarded from Fig. 6.6 and Fig. 6.7 due to the fact that the date of publication of these works cannot be determined exactly, the graphic representations of the results keep the same camel shape, with the second subperiod being the most prolific (data not shown). This finding ties in well with our previous results based on the OED, which suggest that the ROC becomes grammatically stable around the nineteenth century.

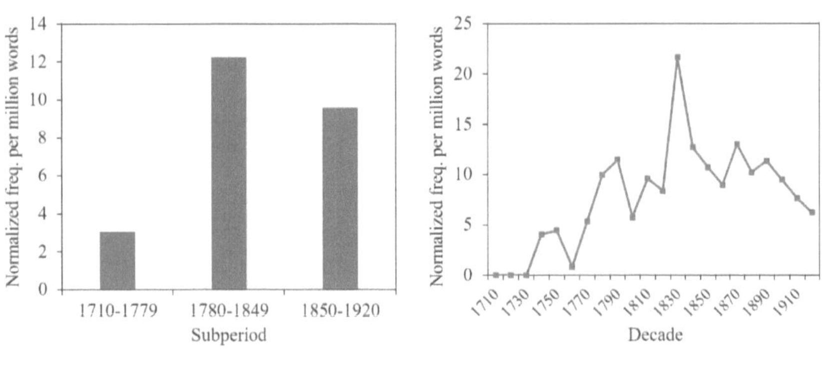

Fig. 6.6: Distribution of the LModE ROC per subperiod and decade

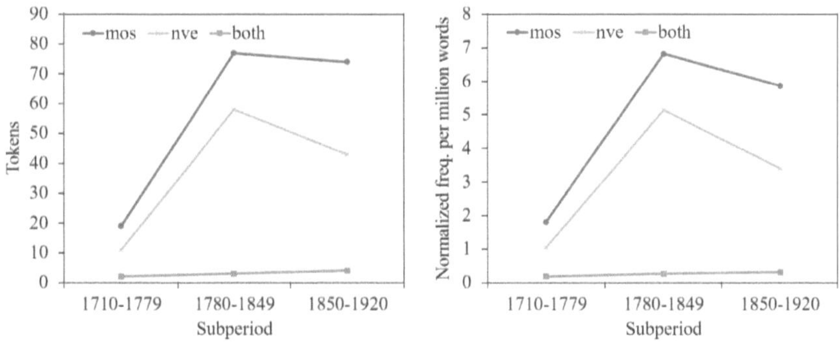

Fig. 6.7: Distribution of the LModE ROC across verb classes per subperiod. Note that I excluded from Fig. 6.6 and Fig. 6.7 fourteen ROCs due to their unknown date of publication. This leaves a total of 291 ROCs out of the 305 attested in CLMET3.0.

6.3.3 Textual distribution

One of the reasons why CLMET3.0 was selected to conduct historical research on the ROC stems from results obtained from previous studies, which suggest that the PDE ROC is primarily a written language phenomenon (Bouso 2012, Martínez-Vázquez 2015). As mentioned in § 6.1, CLMET3.0 has a strong emphasis on narrative texts (fictional and non-fictional), though this corpus also contains texts from other literary genres such as drama, letters and treatises. ROCs occur in all of them, but clearly drama and narrative fiction are the preferred ones for LModE ROCs.

6.3.3.1 Drama

Normalized frequencies show that drama is the preferred genre for ROCs, however, only twenty instances were attested in the whole corpus, which is less than 10 % of my overall data (cf. Fig. 6.8).

These instances are more or less evenly distributed across time with a slight decrease in use in the third subperiod of LModE. Interestingly, as shown in Fig. 6.9, ROCs in verse mainly accumulate in the first subperiod of LModE, whereas those ROCs in prose form mainly accumulate in the second and third subperiods. This could be related

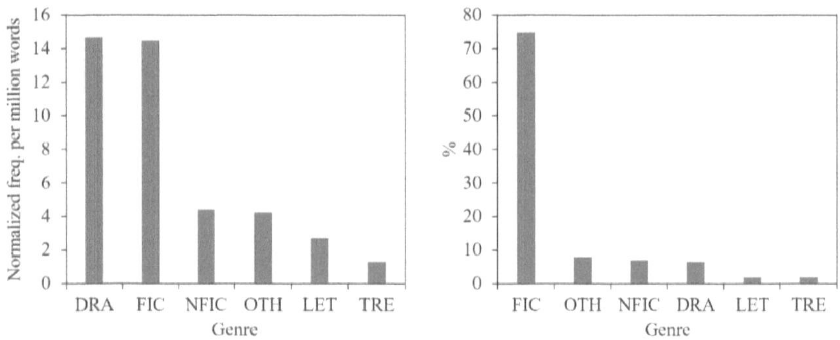

Fig. 6.8: Normalized frequencies and percentages of ROCs across genres in CLMET3.0. Based on 305 ROCs.

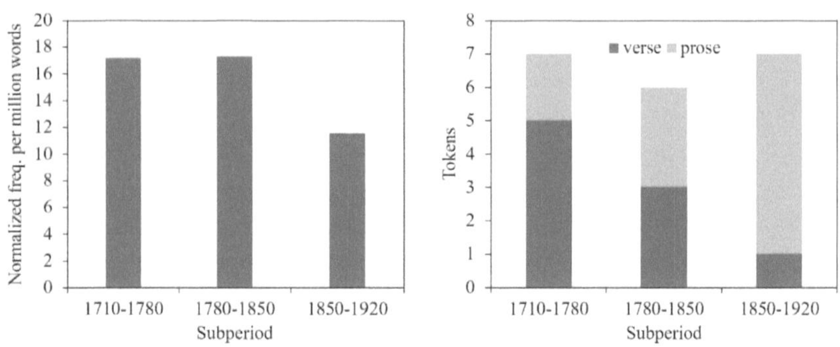

Fig. 6.9: Distribution of ROCs in drama across subperiods and writing style

to the progressive development of the use of prose in English drama (Alden 1909).

ROCs in verse form in LModE drama have been found in Johnson's *Irene* (1726–49), Garrick's *A Christmas Tale* (1774), Sheridan's *The Rivals* (1775), Shelley's *Prometheus Unbound* (1820), and Gilbert's *The Grand Duke* (1896) (cf. Tab. 6.30).

Johnson's *Irene* (1726–49) is fully written in blank verse, Shelley's *Prometheus Unbound* (1820) has been categorized in the literature as a lyrical drama, and the rest of the plays, though not entirely written in verse, have some verse excerpts throughout. More specifically, the ROCs in verse from Sheridan's *The Rivals*, Gilbert's *The Grand Duke*, and Garrick's *A Christmas Tale* have been identified in the *epilogue* and the *songs* chanted by one of the characters of the play (see example (47)). As noted in § 6.3.1.2.1 and § 6.3.1.2.4, the attestation of ROCs in verse form explains the idiosyncratic nature of some ROCs with the nonverbal communication verbs *smile* and *sigh*, which emerge to fit the rhyme of the stanzas they are embedded in.

(47) SONG
(. . .)
NOT. When off the loser's popped
(By pleasing legal fiction),
And friend and foe}
Have wept their woe}
In counterfeit affliction,
The winner must adopt
The loser's poor relations—
Discharge his debts,
Pay all his bets,
And take his obligations.

CLMET3.0 1896, Gilbert; *The Grand Duke*

Although not explicitly mentioned in Chapter 5, 28 of the earliest ROCs for the 51 verbs attested in the OED are in texts written in verse and some of them come from verse drama. It could well be the case that poetry (including verse drama) is the seeding ground of the construction since both the ROC and poetry in general tend to show condensed syntax and an expressive meaning. The ROC is a marked linguistic structure[56] which blends into a transitive construction what could be more easily expressed and processed in a longer sentence with a prepositional phrase, as in (49) and (50), where the argument structure of the verbs involved in the construction is not altered.

(48) Mr Chester waved his hand, and **smiled** a courteous welcome.

(49) Mr Chester waved his hand, and expressed a courteous welcome with a smile.

56 Note that Omuro (1997, 809–810) justifies the marked status of these constructions by claiming that they are not acquired by children at an early age.

(50) Mr Chester waved his hand, and expressed a courteous welcome by smiling.

ROCs in prose form in LModE drama are distributed across plays as shown in Tab. 6.31. These ROCs occur both in the dialogues of characters and in stage directions. Examples of the former are included in (51)-(54), whereas examples of the latter are given in (55) and (56). As shown in Fig. 6.10 further below, up to seven instances have been found in stage directions in the whole corpus. This is, in my view, a very high figure taking into account (i) the fact that the construction is very low in frequency, and (ii) that drama comprises a lower number of words with respect to other literary genres in CLMET3.0 (1,362,779 words; see Tab. 6.3 in § 6.1).

(51) HARMONY. Nay, 'tis truth: and I sincerely lament that human beings should be such strangers to one another as we are. We live in the same street, without knowing one another's necessities; and oftentimes meet and part from each other at church, at coffee-houses, play-houses, and all public places, without ever speaking a single word, or **nodding** "Good bye!" though 'tis a hundred chances to ten we never see one another again.

CLMET3.0 1793, Inchbald; *Everyone Has his Fault*

(52) Stu. Come hither, Dawson. My limbs are on the rack, and my soul shivers in me, till this night's business be complete. Tell me thy thoughts: is Bates determined? or does he waver?
Daw. At first he seemed irresolute; wished the employment had been mine; and **muttered** curses on his coward hand, that trembled at the deed.
CLMET3.0 1753, Moore; *The Gamester*

(53) SAFIE. I can only **weep** my thanks, of late I have been unused to kindness.

CLMET3.0 1823, Peake; *Presumption, or the Fate of Frankenstein*

(54) WOLF. Well done, my cat-o'-mountains, never spare 'em; out with your claws, and bristle up your backs; the rascals dare not look upon your eyes, they glare so terribly; tear 'em and eat 'em. What between Wolf and Cat they 've had a bargain; I 've set my fangs in some of them with a vengeance. (WOLF discovers GUNTRAM sculking.) What sculker have we here? Come out—Thou villain! thou cutpurse! who made thee a soldier, sirrah? Nature intended thee for an attorney—Come, brush your memory

up, **mumble** a prayer, and be quick! Thou ’rt hardly worth the time ’twill take to kill thee.

CLMET3.0 1800, Cumberlan; *Joanna of Montfaucon*

(55) (The men embark on the “Xebeque.” Marco and Giuseppe embracing Gianetta and Tessa. The girls **wave** a farewell to the men$_{REC}$ as the curtain falls.)

CLMET3.0 1889, Gilbert & Sullivan; *The Gondoliers*

(56) (Gloria **smiles** assent, and releases his hand after a final pressure. She then retires behind the garden seat, leaning over the back beside Mrs. Clandon.)

CLMET3.0 1897, Shaw; *You Never Can Tell*

Tab. 6.30: Plays that show ROCs in verse form in LModE

Work	**Date of publication**	**Period**	**Tokens**
Johnson’s *Irene*	1726–49	1	2
Garrick’s *A Christmas Tale*	1774	1	1
Sheridan’s *The Rivals*	1775	1	2
Shelley’s *Prometheus Unbound*	1820	2	3
Gilbert’s *The Grand Duke*	1896	3	1

Tab. 6.31: Plays that show ROCs in prose form in LModE

Work	**Date of publication**	**Period**	**Tokens**
Moore’s *The Gamester*	1753	1	1
Murphy’s *The Apprentice*	1756	1	1
Inchbald’s *Everyone Has His Fault*	1793	2	1
Cumberland’s *Joanna of Montfaucon*	1800	2	1
Peake’s *Presumption, or the Fate of Frankenstein*	1823	2	1
Gilbert & Sullivan’s *The Gondoliers*	1889	3	1
Shaw’s *The Devil’s Disciple*	1897	3	1
Shaw’s *You Never Can Tell*	1897	3	1
Pinero’s *The Gay Lord Quex*	1899	3	1
Barrie’s *What Every Woman Knows*	1918	3	2

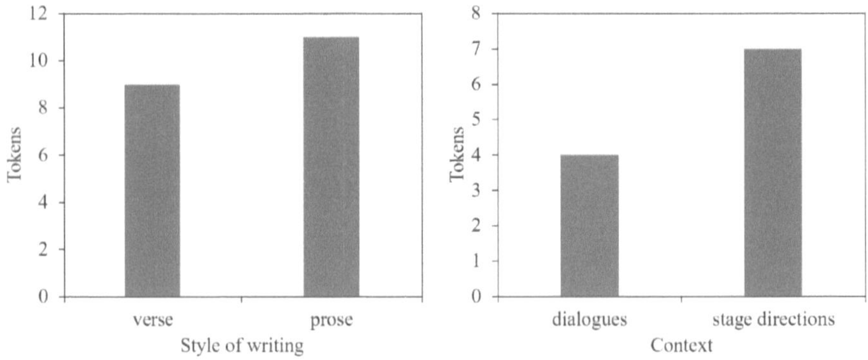

Fig. 6.10: Distribution of ROCs in drama across writing style and context

6.3.3.2 Narrative fiction

That the ROC is characteristic of narrative fiction is not a new notion. From previous historical and synchronic work on the ROC such as Jespersen (1909–1949), Visser (1963–1973), Bouso (2012) and Martínez-Vázquez (2015, 163) we know that this is the favoured genre for ROCs. Jespersen (1909–1949) mentions early instances primarily from nineteenth century novels such as Emily Brontë's *Wuthering Heighs* and Austen's *Mansfield Park* (cf. Tab. 5.1 from § 5.2.1.1), and Visser (1963–1973) hypothesizes that the origins of these nonprototypical transitive structures are to be found in LModE novels (cf. § 2.3.5). From a synchronic perspective, corpus research based on COCA (Bouso 2012; Martínez-Vázquez 2015, 163) shows that ROCs mostly accumulate in fiction over the other four major genres in which this corpus is subdivided: (i) magazines, (ii) academic journals, (iii) newspapers, and (iv) transcripts of unscripted conversation on different TV and radio programs. My historical findings from CLMET3.0 concur with this previous research on the ROC. As previously seen in Fig. 6.8 above, normalized frequencies per million words show that narrative fiction is the second most preferred genre for the construction, and most importantly the ROCs attested in this genre account for more than 70 % of my overall data.

As shown in Fig. 6.11, the vast majority of my examples from narrative fiction accumulate in the second subperiod of LModE, and with the exception of a couple of instances, all ROCs are in prose form.[57] These findings are probably a direct consequence of the continuous development of the English novel, which arose in the Augustan Age (1713–1789), grew largely during the Romantic Age (1789–1832), and became the most important literary form during the Victorian period (1832–1900) (Carter and McRae 1996, 78, 122–123). To be more specific, and to judge from a fine-grained qualitative analysis of the data (cf. § 6.3.1), we could say that the ROC develops alongside a subtype of novel known as sentimental novel which flourished precisely in the middle of the eighteenth century. At this point in time, the term 'sentimental' was no longer related to the term 'moral' but it came to mean "concerned with the emotions" (Ousby 1988, 888–889). Two early instances of the British sentimental novel are Richardson's *Pamela* (1740) and Brooke's *The Fool of Quality* (1765–70) (Ousby 1988, Head 2006). Richardson's *Pamela* is not included in CLMET3.0; it is, however, *Clarissa*, which is also written by Richardson and is another example of sentimental novel. *Clarissa* and *The Fool of Quality* accumulate a total of thirteen examples of ROCs in my database, which is, almost half of the examples attested for the first period of LModE (1710–1780) (cf. Fig. 6.6).

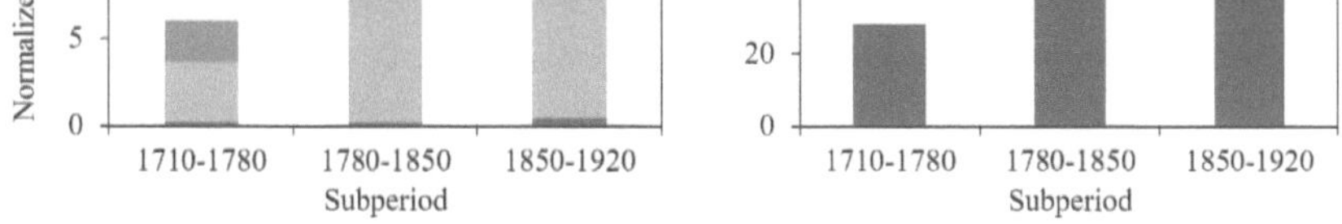

Fig. 6.11: Distribution of ROCs in narrative fiction across subperiods and writing style

57 The ROCs in verse come from an English translation by Edward Fairfax of a famous Italian poem entitled *La Gerusalemme liberata* (Torquato Tasso 1581) and from one of the poems read by a character of the novel.

In narrative fiction ROCs occur both in dialogue and in narrative. In both cases the narrator is typically a third person narrator who reports on expressive communicative scenes such as the ones illustrated in examples (57)-(59).

(57) Perhaps, the very notion of returning as a suspected criminal to that part of the country where a portion of his youth had been passed, was sufficient to disquiet and deject him. All this while his poor Madeline seemed actuated by a spirit beyond herself; she would not be separated from his side—she held his hand in hers—she **whispered** comfort and courage at the very moment when her own heart most sank. The magistrate wiped his eyes when he saw a creature so young, so beautiful, in circumstances so fearful, and bearing up with an energy so little to be expected from her years and delicate appearance. Aram said but little; he covered his face with his right hand for a few moments, as if to hide a passing emotion, a sudden weakness.

CLMET3.0 1832, Bulwer-Lytton; *Eugene Aram*

(58) His face was purple and his eyes dim, as he put her down and left her. He rode by his General's side, and smoked his cigar in silence as they hastened after the troops of the General's brigade, which preceded them; and it was not until they were some miles on their way that he left off twirling his moustache and broke silence. And Rebecca, as we have said, wisely determined not to give way to unavailing sentimentality on her husband's departure. She **waved** him an adieu from the window, and stood there for a moment looking out after he was gone. The cathedral towers and the full gables of the quaint old houses were just beginning to blush in the sunrise. There had been no rest for her that night. She was still in her pretty ball-dress, her fair hair hanging somewhat out of curl on her neck, and the circles round her eyes dark with watching.

CLMET3.0 1843, Thackeray; *Vanity Fair*

(59) "I thought we should outride him--he can't manage a pony any more than a child. But he will surely be here soon?" "Who will be here soon?" asked Olive, considerably surprised. "Are you speaking of Mr. Gwynne?" "Mr. Gwynne, no! Far better fun than that, isn't it, Charley? Shall we tell the secret or not? Or else shall we tell half of it, and let her puzzle it out till he comes?" The boy **nodded** assent. "Well, then, there is coming to see you to-day Charley's tutor, who was away for the holidays. He only arrived at Farnwood last night, and since then he has been talking of nothing else but his old friend, Miss Olive Rothesay. So I told him to meet me here, and, lo! he comes."

CLMET3.0 1850, Craik; *Olive*

These excerpts clearly show that the ROC can be considered a type of represented discourse.[58] However, the very low frequency of the ROC no doubt explains why it is never mentioned in the literature discussing represented discourse in detail such as Leech and Short (1981), Coulmas (1986), Fludernik (1993), Semino and Short (2004), and Busse (2020). In general terms, the three main types of represented discourse that are commonly mentioned in the literature are the following: (i) *direct discourse* as in *She said '<u>I will wait for you</u>'*, where the exact words spoken are repeated; (ii) *simple indirect discourse* which reports the content of what was said, as in *She said <u>she would wait for us</u>*; and (iii) *free indirect discourse*, which is halfway between direct and indirect discourse in that it reports the content of what was said without "being strictly subordinate to a "higher" verb of saying/thinking" (McHale 1978, 252; see also Poutsma 1929, 630).

As shown in (60) and (61), simple indirect discourse may be "derived" by applying a set of transformations to direct discourse. These are: (i) the suppression of quotation marks, and insertion of the conjunction *that* before the reported declarative; and (ii) the conversion of personal pronouns (e.g. from first to third person), verb tenses (e.g. present tense in direct discourse becomes past tense in indirect discourse), and deictics (e.g. the temporal adverbs *now* and *tomorrow* are replaced by *then* and *the next day*, respectively).

(60) **She said to herself**, "No, no, I can't just now, but tomorrow I'll drink in spite of the pledge I've signed with the N.E.R. and shoot the moon". → **direct discourse**[59]

(61) **She said to herself** that she couldn't just then, but that the next day she would drink in spite of the pledge she had signed with the N.E.R. and "shoot the moon". → **simple indirect discourse**

The ROC could be described as a subtype of simple indirect discourse. First, as in simple indirect discourse, ROCs report the content of what was felt: in examples (62) and (63), the feelings of *disbelief* and *gratitude*. Second, but for a few examples, ROCs show suppression of quotation marks, and conversion of personal/possessive pronouns. Since

58 Note that Martínez-Vázquez (2015) also mentions in passing this dimension of ROCs.

59 Examples taken from McHale (1978, 250 ff).

the content of what was felt in ROCs is expressed in the form of an NP, there is no conversion of verb tenses and deictic elements. In this last aspect ROCs differ from the prototypical simple indirect discourse where there is always a verb involved; as noted by Downing and Locke (2006, 299), simple indirect discourse may report the content of statements (64), questions (65) or directives (66).

(62) She **smiled** disbelief (vs. direct discourse → *She* ***smiled*** *'I don't believe you'*)

(63) He **grunted** his gratitude. (vs. direct discourse → *He* ***grunted*** *'I thank you'*)
(Visser 1963–1973: I, § 142: 133)

(64) 'I won't be long,' she said → She said she **wouldn't be** long.

(65) 'Can you leave this book here?' he said → He asked if I **could leave** that book there.

(66) 'Do it yourselves!' I said → I told them **to do** it themselves.

As mentioned earlier on in § 2.3.5, Visser (1963–1973: I, § 142: 133) suggested a possible historical connection between ROCs and the use of direct discourse involving verbs of sounds and gestures in novels, as in *She smiled 'I don't believe you'* and *He grunted 'I thank you'*. On a different level, Ruano San Segundo (2016, 2017, 2018a, 2018b) analysed direct discourse with verbs of this kind such as *growl*, *thunder*, *pout* and *whimper* in Dickens' narrative and showed that these constructions are quite common in nineteenth century novels, as is precisely the case of the ROC. As shown in Fig. 6.11 above, the ROC, in fact, in narrative fiction is used equally with both, manner of speaking verbs and verbs of nonverbal communication.

6.3.4 Concluding remarks

The aim of this chapter was to examine the development of the ROC over the LModE period by assessing its frequency, distribution across verb classes, time periods and text types, as well as its form and function in CLMET3.0. The results show that the ROC is a low-frequency phenomenon in LModE, but increased in frequency from the middle of the eighteenth century onwards. Collexeme analysis allowed me to identify five protypical verbs of the LModE ROC, namely the manner of speaking verbs *mutter* and *murmur* and the verbs of nonverbal communication *smile*, *nod* and *wave* which seem to have promoted the grammatical constructionalization of the ROC. The study of these verbs revealed different levels of specificity of the ROC: more abstract ROC subschemas are formed with the manner of speaking verbs *murmur* and *mutter*, whereas lower-level verb-specific subschemas are formed with the verbs *smile*, *nod* and *wave* when these verbs occur in semi-fixed ROCs such as *smile* + *assent/welcome/approval*, *nod assent* and *wave* (poss/a/Ø) *adieu(s)/farewell(s)*. On the whole, to judge from the low frequency of occurrence of ROCs and their restriction to specific text types (i.e. narrative fiction, drama and poetry), most likely ROCs are not part of the constructicon or linguistic knowledge of a large set of population.

As for its temporal and textual distribution, my results indicate that the heyday of the British ROC was the second subperiod of LModE (1780–1850), and that its consolidation was probably influenced by the emergence and subsequent development of the English novel as a literary genre, and most particularly by the fashionable use of verbs of sounds and gestures in direct discourse constructions in LModE sentimental novels (see Visser 1963–1973: I, § 142: 133; Ruano San Segundo 2016, 2017, 2018a, 2018b). Apart from these two *extralinguistic factors*, a couple of *intralinguistic factors* that have also contributed to the flourishment of the ROC during this period are:

i. The increase in verbs of sound emission in type and token frequency during ModE (Fanego 2017).
ii. The development during the LModE period of other transitivizing constructions such as (a) the *way*-construction (Israel 1996, Traugott and Trousdale 2013, Perek 2018, Fanego 2019, Perek 2020), (b) the cognate object construction which interestingly is also confined to "literary diction" (see Visser 1963–1973: I, § 424 (b): 415; Lavidas 2018), and (c) the dummy *it* object construction (see Visser 1963–1973: I, § 492 ff; Mondorf 2016). All these transitivizing constructions seem to have strengthened the representation of the ROC, and all of them seem to be working jointly together in a large scale transitivization process affecting the English language.

To bring this chapter to an end, we should refer here more explicitly to one of the research questions presented at the end of Chapter 4, namely the one concerning the constructional changes that can be identified in the development of the ROC. The results included in this chapter, alongside those in Chapter 5, lead us to conclude that some constructional changes are clearly observable in the historical development of the ROC. The construction has considerably increased its token frequency in the nineteenth century, and expanded its range of collocates throughout the course of the LModE period. The former is evinced by the relatively lower number of ROCs attested for the first subperiod of LModE (1710–1780) with respect to the other two subperiods, and the latter by the expansion of the ROC during the LModE period to include *modern* verbs of sound emission such as *purr* and *coo*. Finally, in § 6.3.1.2.5 a morphophonological change has been proposed for the PDE ROC subschema with *nod*: this subschema shows a tendency to leave out the indefinite determiner which was characteristic of its LModE subschema (LModE *nod <u>an</u> affirmative* > PDE *nod Ø yes/nod Ø agreement*). As I see it, in Traugott and Trousdale's theory of language change, this morphophonological change, as well as the increase in token frequency and expansion of collocates of the ROC during LModE would qualify as post-constructionalization constructional changes. These changes take place later than the process of constructionalization of the ROC in EModE, the period in which the ROC seems to develop its formal restriction of coreferentiality (cf. § 6.3.1.2.5).

Fig. 6.12 aims to summarize the historical development of the ROC presented so far. It shows the precursors of the ROC in LME, its subsequent process of constructionalization in EModE, and final grammatical constructionalization in LModE; the latter stemming from its considerable increase in token frequency during the nineteenth century and its expansion of collocates, mainly to modern verbs of sound emission. Chapter 7 will go forward in time with the development of the ROC, addressing further post-constructionalization constructional changes affecting the ROC in PDE, namely those concerning its productivity and schematicity.[60]

60 In Fig. 6.12 the underlined verbs with an asterisk (i.e. *nod* and *wave*) have been attested in the ROC in EEBO in the seventeenth century (1474–1700) (see § 6.3.1.2.5). This means that the availability of ROCs with these verbs in the English language goes back to EModE and not to the LModE period as suggested by the OED.

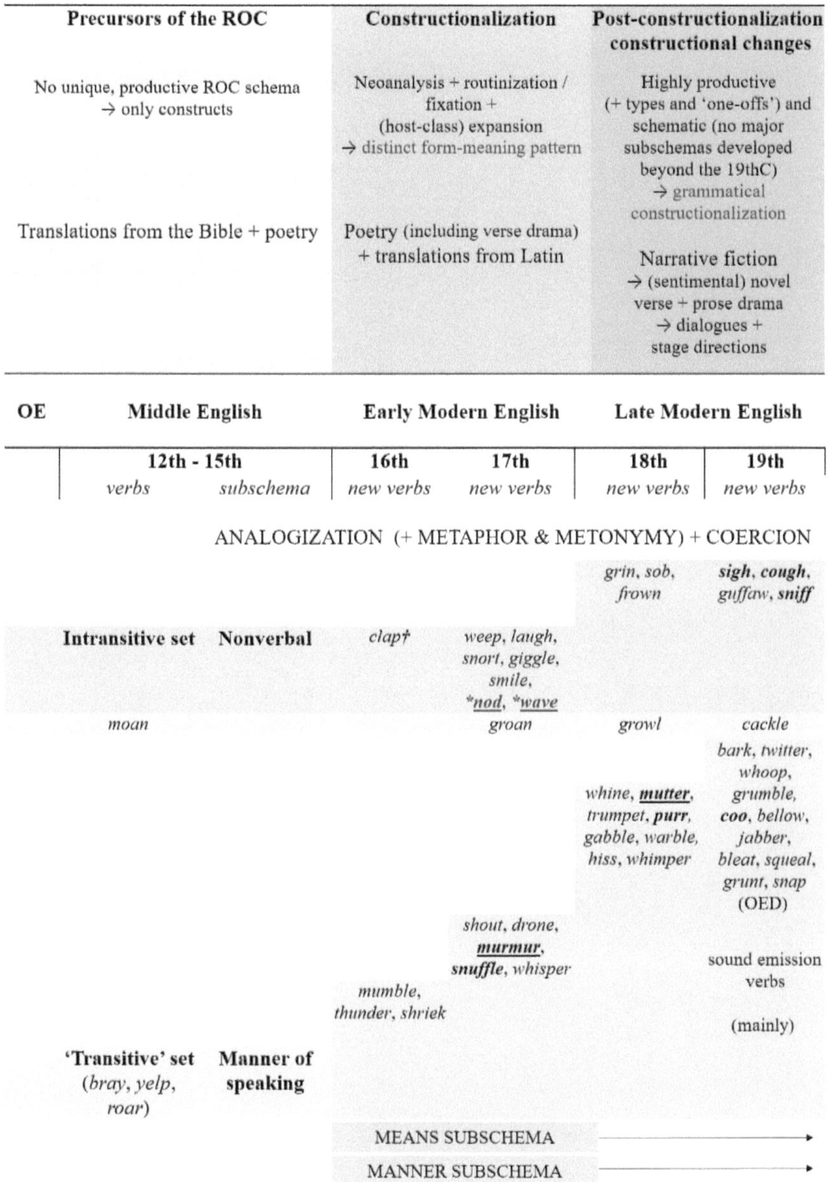

Fig. 6.12: Historical development of the ROC up to the 20th century. Precursors, constructionalization and post-constructionalization constructional changes. Based on Jespersen (1909–1949: III, §§ 12.1–12.8 and §§ 14.1–14.6), Visser (1963–1973: I, § 133: 100–127), the OED, EEBO (1474–1700) and CLMET3.0 (1710–1920).

7. Development of the ROC in American English

One of the major findings presented in Chapter 6 is the confirmation that the ROC proliferated quite recently in British English, more specifically in the early decades of the nineteenth century (§ 6.3.2). Moreover, since more than 70 % of my data on the ROC was found in narrative fiction (§ 6.3.3), I suggested there that there was a connection between the spread of the British ROC and the British novel, which arose essentially in the eighteenth century and developed precisely over the course of the nineteenth century (§ 6.3.3.2).

A second major finding was that the considerable increase in use of the ROC in the transition from the eighteenth to the nineteenth century appears to indicate that the overall development of the British ROC lines up historically with the development of the British *way*-construction, with both construction types becoming grammatically "stable" or "fairly productive" from the nineteenth century onwards (Israel 1996, 222; Perek 2018, 70). These two major findings lead us to address the following two research questions:

— First, is the ROC in fact a British innovation that later spread to American English?
— Second, given the parallel Late Modern English development between the ROC and the *way*-construction, one of the questions that arises at this point is whether we can also find parallelisms regarding their subsequent development in the twentieth century. More precisely, has the ROC, like the *way*-construction, increased its productivity after its consolidation over the LModE period?

The structure of this chapter will be as follows. I will first provide an account of the data sources and methodology used to address the two previous research questions. In § 7.2, I will discuss the frequency and distribution (diachronic and textual) of the ROC in American English. Finally, in § 7.3 I will examine the productivity of the ROC and the *way*-construction.

7.1 Data sources and methodology

In order to provide an answer to the research questions posed at the beginning of this chapter, I have used the online version of the *Corpus of Historical American English* (COHA). Apart from being the largest historical corpus of this variety available to date, COHA is also the corpus used by Perek (2018) in his study on the productivity and schematicity of the *way*-construction in its recent history. COHA contains more than 400 million words of texts retrieved from various digitized and online sources such as the *Project Gutenberg* (1810–1930), the *Making of America* (1810–1900), the *Internet Archive* (1810–1900) and the *Library of Congress*. Similarly to CLMET3.0, COHA includes descriptive meta-data: author, author's year of birth and death, full title of the work, genre, subgenre, source, year of publication, number of words of each text, and some publication information. Despite its very large size, COHA is a "well-constructed" corpus that has been "carefully lemmatised and tagged for part-of-speech" (Davies 2012, 122).

There are considerable differences in the total number of words included in the first decades of the nineteenth century with respect to the last decades of the twentieth century. However, on the whole, the number of words per decade becomes more uniform after the 1880s when it reaches 20,000,000 words for each subperiod. As shown in Tab. 7.1, the four genres that make up the corpus (fiction, popular magazines, newspapers and non-fiction books) are not completely balanced either. For instance, the newspaper genre is clearly underrepresented: it consists of only 40,124,656 words against the 207,633,395 words conforming fiction. Finally, it should be noted that the fiction genre accounts for 48–55 % of the total number of words for each decade (1810s-2000s), and that fiction in COHA is understood in a very broad sense, encompassing novels, drama, short stories, poetry and movie scripts; some of these subgenres, however, are rather poorly represented, as happens with the last three just mentioned.

Regarding the methodology employed, for the retrieval of the data, this time I opted for a top-down approach based on the search strings in (1) and (2) and the common delocutive nouns in (3).

Tab. 7.1: Composition of COHA by genre and decade. Adapted from Davies (2012, 123)

Decade	Fiction	Popular magazines	Newspapers	Non-fiction books	Total number of words	% of the total no. of words for fiction
1810s	641,164	88,316	0	451,542	1,181,022	0.54
1820s	3,751,204	1,714,789	0	1,461,012	6,927,005	0.54
1830s	7,590,350	3,145,575	0	3,038,062	13,773,987	0.55
1840s	8,850,886	3,554,534	0	3,641,434	16,046,854	0.55
1850s	9,094,346	4,220,558	0	3,178,922	16,493,826	0.55
1860s	9,450,562	4,437,941	262,198	2,974,401	17,125,102	0.55
1870s	10,291,968	4,452,192	1,030,560	2,835,440	18,610,160	0.55
1880s	11,215,065	4,481,568	1,355,456	3,820,766	20,872,855	0.54
1890s	11,212,219	4,679,486	1,383,948	3,907,730	21,183,383	0.53
1900s	12,029,439	5,062,650	1,433,576	4,015,567	22,541,232	0.53
1910s	11,935,701	5,694,710	1,489,942	3,534,899	22,655,252	0.53
1920s	12,539,681	5,841,678	3,552,699	3,698,353	25,632,411	0.49
1930s	11,876,996	5,910,095	3,545,527	3,080,629	24,413,247	0.49
1940s	11,946,743	5,644,216	3,497,509	3,056,010	24,144,478	0.49
1950s	11,986,437	5,796,823	3,522,545	3,092,375	24,398,180	0.49
1960s	11,578,880	5,803,276	3,404,244	3,141,582	23,927,982	0.48
1970s	11,626,911	5,755,537	3,383,924	3,002,933	23,769,305	0.49
1980s	12,152,603	5,804,320	4,113,254	3,108,775	25,178,952	0.48
1990s	13,272,162	7,440,305	4,060,570	3,104,303	27,877,340	0.48
2000s	14,590,078	7,678,830	4,088,704	3,121,839	29,479,451	0.49
TOTAL	207,633,395	97,207,399	40,124,656	61,266,574	**406,232,024**	0.51

(1) [v*] delocutive noun

(2) [v*] my|your|its|his|her|our|their|a|me|you|it|him|them|**delocutive noun**

(3) *hello(s), goodbye(s), good-bye, thanks, thank-you, thank you*

This top-down approach differs from the bottom-up approach adopted in the other corpus-based studies undertaken in Chapter 6. One of the aims of this chapter is indeed to assess the frequency and distribution of the ROC in American English, but my main concern now is not so much to identify the various formal variants of the construction in earlier stages of English, but rather to assess the productivity of the ROC and compare it to that of the *way*-construction. With these goals in mind, the top-down approach will suffice.

As argued in § 6.1 and § 6.2.1.1, the ROC is a highly schematic construction. It is thus not feasible to retrieve all instances of ROCs in large corpora such as COHA or COCA; but at the same time, in order to test the productivity of the ROC it is necessary to obtain a large and varied sample of ROCs which involves as many verb types as possible. For this reason, as shown in (1) to (3) above, the search strings employed consisted of: (i) any type of verb in any of its forms (i.e. [v*]), and (ii) any of the delocutive nouns *hello(s)*, *goodbye(s)*, *good-bye*, *thanks*, *thank-you* and *thank you.*

Taking into account the ROC schema proposed in Chapter 5 (§ 5.1.2), and repeated here in (4) for ease of exposition, the nouns can be bare (see search string in (1) above), or can be preceded by a possessive determiner, an indefinite article, or a personal pronoun functioning as recipient of the expressive message (see search string represented in (2) above).

(4) **Syntax:** $SUBJ_i$ [$V_{INTRmanner/means}$ (OBJ1) $OBJ2_i$]. Where OBJ2 = $(POSS)_i$ NP
Semantics: 'Sentient $agent_i$ cause Y_i become expressed while/$by_{manner/means}$ doing V'

With respect to the reasons to restrict my search to a particular set of delocutive nouns (i.e. the formulae *hello*, *goodbye*, *thank you* and their derivatives), one of them was the evident need to constrain the analysis to a sample that was controlled and manageable. In addition, delocutive nouns were selected instead of deverbal (e.g. *acquiescence* and *assent*), predicative expressive nouns (e.g. *discontent* and *delight*), or emotional abstract nouns (e.g. *sweetness* and *blessedness*) for the reasons specified below.

First, delocutive nouns constitute a rather closed set of reaction objects. As mentioned in § 5.1, delocutive nouns derive from conventional independent utterances and can be of two different types: interjections and formulae (Ameka 1992; see also Quirk et al. 1985, 852–853 for a few examples of the major types of formulae). The focus in this chapter is on formulae which differ from interjections in that they are not spontaneous immediate responses but are intentional and are socially expected reactions to situations (Ameka 1992, 109). For the purposes of this study, I have only selected three formulae, but the rest of the delocutive nouns mentioned by Quirk et al. (1985) and Ameka (1992) should not be neglected in future investigations.

Second, the reaction object type involving delocutive nouns frequently occurs in my British English data (delocutive nouns amount to 73 out of the 305 ROCs attested), therefore, my searches in COHA could be expected to yield a sufficient number of such nouns for analysis. Third, and most importantly for my purposes here, delocutive nouns are the most flexible reaction object type since they can freely occur with manner of speaking verbs and verbs of nonverbal communication (§ 6.3.1). By contrast, deverbal nouns such as *assent* tend to occur more frequently with verbs of manner of speaking (e.g. *The Dudgeons all murmur assent*), and predicative expressive nouns such as *delight* are more likely to occur with verbs of nonverbal communication (e.g. *Max chuckled his delight*). Because of their flexibility, delocutive nouns seemed the most appropriate for exploring the frequency and productivity of the ROC in the recent history of American English.

Before conducting the searches based on the strings in (1)-(2) above, I first designed the online interface of COHA as indicated in Tab. 7.2. The reasons for doing it in this way were the following:

(i) To sort out the queries according to their frequency, including hapaxes.
(ii) To display all hits from COHA adjusting to the search strings in (1)-(2).
(iii) To show the maximum number of keywords in context (KWIC) allowed (i.e. 1,000 words).
(iv) To group together my findings in the online interface by words (e.g. BOW THEIR THANKS; BOWED THEIR THANKS) instead of lemmas (e.g. [BOW] [THEIR] [THANKS]), or parts of speech (e.g. BOW (VVI) THEIR (APPGE) THANKS (NN2)).

The second step was to extract the relevant data. As for the tokens I discarded, they fall into the following six categories:

1. Duplicates to the extent that they could be detected.
2. Examples not relevant, such as *heard* a hello, *wish* a goodbye, *mean* good-bye.

Tab. 7.2: Options selected in the online interface of COHA

SORT/LIMIT	**OPTIONS**
Sorting: Frequency	Hits= 2000 (Maximum allowed by the the online interface. Neither of the two designed search strings went over 2,000 hits).
Minimum: Frequency = 1	Keywords in context = 1000 (maximum allowed by the system) Group by = words Raw frequency Save lists = no

3. Unclear metaphorical structures involving the verbs *work* (*their mouths worked goodbyes*), *wreathe* (*I should have wreathed my thanks*), and *leave* in example (5).

(5) The hall and staircase were quite deserted. He walked with her to the top of the first flight. "Do we **leave** good-bye here?" he asked. "Yes," she said smiling; "I think so." (COHA, 1905, FIC, WomansWill)

4. Idiomatic or fixed expressions such as *pay/vote/voice/owe/lavish thanks.*
5. Examples involving non-descriptive verbs of communication such as *tell* in example (6) and *say* in example (7).

(6) "Yes, he told me to **tell** you good-bye." (COHA, 1936, FIC, DrumsAlongMohawk)

(7) I'll **say** my goodbyes, got miles and miles to go before sunset. (COHA, 2004, FIC, Mov:ColdMountain)

The label 'descriptive' is taken from Snell-Hornby (1983, 15), who uses it to refer to verbs "that describe rather than state an action"; examples of descriptive verbs, in this sense, would be *stare* 'to look with a wide-eyed gaze' (as opposed to *look*), *strut* 'to walk in a stiff, self-satisfied way' (as opposed to *walk*), and also manner of speaking verbs such as *mutter* and *murmur* (as opposed to *say* and *tell*; see Snell-Hornby 1983, 27). More specifically, manner of speaking verbs describe "physical characteristics of the speech act" (Zwicky 1971, 223), whereas non-descriptive verbs of communication such as *tell* and *say* do "not include further specification, such as a manner or instrument component" (Levin 1993, 204). As explicitly indicated in § 5.1.2, this aspect is a fundamental characteristic of the ROC as it allows us to distinguish the ROC from ordinary communicative constructions such as *Jack announced his displeasure, Peter communicated his disapprobation*, etc.

6. I also discarded examples involving speech act verbs such as *acknowledge*, *claim*, *offer* and so on in examples (8)-(10). The main reasons for excluding these verb types are that their overall meaning differs from the constructional meaning of the ROC (cf. *?express thanks by acknowledging/claiming/offering*); and that speech act verbs do not involve a process of (de)transitivization (for details see Visser's and Liu's [Type 4] in Tab. 2.1 (§ 2.1) and comments therein).

(8) (. . .) in his mind one thing he could say to satisfy her, to **acknowledge** his thanks and the size of her care, to honor her fears but belittle them gently (COHA, 1975, FIC, LastValley)

(9) FERDINAND. Ferdinand Julio! thy prompt compliance **claims** our thanks. (COHA, 1839, FIC, Velasco)

(10) We **offer** our thanks to those readers who have followed us with patient attention to the close. (COHA, 1869, MAG, NewEngYaleRev)

After excluding all these tokens, only 961 examples complied with the syntax and semantics of the ROC (the schema included in (4) above). The number of verb types attested in my data reaches a total of 80. These 80 verb types are distributed across the following six verb classes: verbs of sound emission – and related verb classes – (*bang*, *bark* and *bawl*), verbs of gestures (*blink*, *bow* and *dimple*), verbs of bodily processes – verbs of inhalation and substance emission – (*snuffle*, *bleed* and *breathe*), verbs of instrument of communication – oral and written – (*call*, *phone* and *write*), verbs of activity (*dance*, *drink* and *flutter*), and verbs of light emission (*flare*, *glisten* and *reflect*). The full list of verb types included in each verb class is shown in Tab. 7.3. It is worth mentioning here that in this classification I have not distinguished between verbs of manner of speaking and verbs of sound emission. As seen in § 6.1 and § 6.3.1.1, verbs of manner of speaking have been regarded in the more specialized literature as essentially intransitive verbs of sound emission (Visser 1963–1973: I, § 132: 99–100; Levin and Song 1997; Martínez-Vázquez 2005).

Regarding the fuzzy boundary between verbs of manner of speaking and verbs of sound emission, Hilpert (p.c.) suggests that a distributional semantic analysis – like the ones conducted by Perek (2016a, 2016b, 2018) for the *way*-construction – could be useful in the future to provide a more fine-grained classification of these verbs, and, most particularly, when dealing with a greater number of ROCs and not just with those involving delocutive nouns. As explained by Perek (2016b), "in distributional semantics, the semantic similarity between two words is related to the number of their shared frequent collocates in a vast corpus of naturally occurring texts". Thus, distributional semantic analyses capture "the extent to which words can be substituted in context" (2016b, 159). For a reliable assessment of the semantic similarity between verbs, however, Perek (2018, 77) recommends keeping only those verbs with an overall frequency of 1,000. This requirement certainly poses a problem for its application to the ROC, as seen in previous chapters, ROC verbs, in general terms, are characterized by their low frequency. In fact, only a few of them, namely the verbs *laugh*, *shout*, *sigh*, *smile*, and *whisper* reach the minimum frequency of 1,000 in CLMET3.0 (cf. Tab. 6.8 in § 6.2.1.1).

In Chapter 6 I distinguished a manner subschema and a means subschema in allusion to the two major verb classes that collexeme analysis (§ 6.2.1.2) identifies as prototypes in the consolidation of the construction during the LModE period; these are the typical verbs of manner of speaking *mutter* and *murmur* (manner subschema), and the typical verbs of nonverbal communication *smile*, *nod* and *wave* (means subschema). In the results presented in § 7.2 and § 7.3, however, I finally decided not to make such a distinction.

This is mainly justified by two major problems I encountered after several failed attempts at manually coding my examples, and after discussing many of the ROCs with the help of a second linguist annotator. These two major problems are the already mentioned fuzzy boundary between verbs of manner of speaking and verbs of sound emission, and

Tab. 7.3: Classification into different verb classes of the 80 verb types identified in the sample[a]

1. Verbs of sound emission – and related verb classes – (38 types): *bang, bark, bawl, bellow, call* (= *to shout out*), *chirp, croak, crow, cry, echo, fumble, grumble, grunt, gurgle, holler, honk, hum, moan, mumble, murmur, mutter, quack, resound, shout, sing, snort, sputter, squeal, stammer, stutter, toot, tut-tut, warble, whinny, whisper, woof, yell* and *yelp*. Number of tokens: 174.

2. Verbs of gestures (21 types): *blink, bow, dimple, embrace, gesture, giggle, grin, hug, kiss, look, mouth, nod, pat, peck, rain* (= *weep*), *skim, smile, smooch, wag, wave* and *weep*. Number of tokens: 737.

3. Verbs of bodily processes – verbs of inhalation and substance emission – (5 types): *snuffle, bleed, breathe, gush* and *sigh*. Number of tokens: 12.

4. Verbs of instrument of communication (7 types): oral communication: *call* (= *to make a telephone call*) and *phone* (= *to telephone*); written communication: *write, scribble, type, wire* and *cable*. Number of tokens: 11.

5. Verbs of activity (6 types): *dance, drink, flutter, fuck, play* and *pray*[b]. Number of tokens: 11.

6. Verbs of light emission (3 types): *flare, glisten* and *reflect*. Number of tokens: 3.

a Based on 948 ROCs (excluding 13 coordinated ROCs).The graphs in § 7.3 on the productivity of the ROC are based on this count.

b In the three instances attested in COHA with *pray*, this verb is interpreted as a *verb of activity*: the agents express thanks/goodbye by the act of praying as shown in (1)-(3):

(1) He again dropped upon his knees and, crossing himself, **prayed** his thanks. Roddy fell into the bathrobe and into the steamer chair (COHA, 1909, FIC, WhiteMice).

(2) From the dining hall they heard the scrape of chairs on the bare wood floor as the Family rose to **pray** thanks for the meal. (COHA, 1979, FIC, CallDarknessLight)

(3) Father Martin **prays** his goodbye and Godspeed. (COHA, 1997, FIC, Isolation)

the lack of enough linguistic cues and extralinguistic context. Examples (11) and (12) with the verbs *grunt* and *gurgle* will serve us here to better illustrate these two controversial issues.

(11) "For the last time, I hope," Barone said. "We all hope," Downer said. "Yes, but I'm anxious to move," the twenty-nine-year-old officer said. He did not say where he wanted to move. A group of foreigners meeting in a rundown flat never knew who might be eavesdropping. Sazanka sat silently on the sofa and untied his Nikes. He massaged his thick feet. Barone tossed him a bottled water from the refrigerator in the kitchenette. **The Japanese grunted his thanks**. Sazanka's command of English was the weakest, and

he tended to say very little. Downer shared his uncle's view of the Japanese, and Sazanka's silence made him happy. (COHA, 1999, FIC, TomClancysOp-center)

(12) He stepped toward the door, his hand on the light switch. "You take the bed. I'll sleep on the couch. If you're sick, you clean it up." He shut the light off but hesitated in the doorway, silhouetted against the glow spilling down the hall from the living room, his outline fuzzy in the near-darkness. **I gurgled my thanks** and lay my head back, closing my eyes. "You're wrong, though," he said, and it seemed to come from some place far off and fast slipping away as I drifted toward sleep. "It's not destiny. It's damnation." He might have left then, but I was gone before he was. The next morning the couch and the apartment were empty. (COHA, 1997, FIC, FantasySciFi)

Regarding these two specific examples, Martínez-Vázquez (2014a) points out that "it is difficult to tell whether "thanks" stands for a speech act [verbal communication] or a guttural thanking signal [nonverbal communication]" (177). If this ambiguity could be solved, in the first option provided by Martínez-Vázquez, where "thanks" stands for a speech act, these verbs would be functioning as manner of speaking verbs and they would therefore adjust to the manner subschema of the ROC (i.e. 'Sentient $agent_i$ cause Y_i become expressed by_{manner} doing V'). On the other hand, in the second option, where "thanks" stands for a guttural thanking signal, these verbs would be functioning as verbs of sound emission and consequently they would adjust to the means subschema of the ROC (i.e. 'Sentient $agent_i$ cause Y_i become expressed by_{means} doing V'). Zwicky's definition of manner of speaking verbs previously given in § 6.3.1.1 confirms this crucial difference between verbs of manner of speaking and verbs of sound emission. This definition reads as follows, "[manner of speaking verbs are] verbs referring to intended acts of communication by speech" (1971, 223), where "by speech" refers to a verbal rather than a nonverbal type of communication.

The ambiguity represented in examples (11) and (12) above leads us to the second major problem in the coding of my data, i.e. the lack of enough linguistic cues and extralinguistic context. The presence of these two kinds of information would enable us to ascertain whether a manner subschema (verbal communication) or a means subschema (nonverbal communication) is at work in examples (11) and (12) above.

Far from being isolated cases, it should be highlighted here that ambiguous examples like these are quite recurrent in my findings. This is not just simply due to the fuzzy boundary between verbs of manner of speaking and verbs of sound emission – most particularly when these verbs have human subjects as in (11) and (12) –, but also because of the great complexity of my data. For instance, as happened with my examples from Chapter 6 (see § 6.3.1.1 and § 6.3.1.2.4), many of the ROCs attested in COHA involve some kind of metaphor and/or metonymy. For illustrative purposes, I include below some of these metaphorical/metonymic examples with the verbs of sound emission *bang* (13), *squeal* (14), *toot* (15) and *whisper* (16), the verbs of gestures *blink* (17), *kiss* (18), *rain* (= *weep*) (19), *smile* (20), and *wave* (21)-(22), the verb of light emission *flare* (23), and the verb of substance emission *bleed* (24).

(13) At a safe distance Mario$_{\text{SUBJECT}}$ hung his arm out the door$_{\text{SOUND EMITTER}}$ and **banged** a goodbye with his middle finger. (COHA, 1978, FIC, Road-Tamazunchale)

(14) The show finds its subject in Conrad Birdie, an Elvis Presleyish crooner, and in his shrieking teen-age worshipers. But happily the show's object is to uncover fun wherever it lurks, whether in fathers or fantasy, peashooters or TV shows. If so vagrant a method makes things slightly untidy, it also keeps them fresh. Where the method richly pays off is in its not giving Conrad (well played by Dick Gautier) too much houseroom, in its saying bye-bye to him oftener than it **squeals** hello. (COHA, 1960, MAG, Time)

(15) With that, the gangplank was raised, the Rotterdam$_{\text{SOUND EMITTER}}$ **tooted** goodbye, the pickets lowered their standards, and the U.S. State Department sighed with relief. (COHA, 1963, MAG, Time)

(16) No technique-detective or brushstroke spy, Author Eliot is instead one of the sun philosophers who value the lights that men and artists live by. Light is the sensuous hero of Sight and Insight: "Velásquez' light is like transparent golden bees swarming the honeyed shadow, while Rogier van der Weyden's is like water over marble... even when stealing into Vermeer's darkest interior by a narrow window, light is welcomed as a lover. The far corners **whisper** hello to light (...)". (COHA, 1959, MAG, Time)

(17) A reader from Staunton, Virginia, described "a bright red" disc in the night sky above his home. "In the middle were four round black circles," he reports. "When the object floated over the apartments, it seemed to stop and turn one of its sides up. Then it did something really wonderful -- it **blinked** a good-bye. Its speed seemed to go from 200 miles an hour to God-knows-what, and it was gone." (COHA, 1992, FIC, Omni)

(18) Harvard wants you to study odd, neglected corners of art that have long since **kissed** their ninth lives good-bye, such as the persistence of the Roman funerary-portrait formula into Byzantine decoration, or how Pontormo's

figures can be explained by inferring an extra joint in each limb and digit. (COHA, 1993, FIC, FlightDragonKyn)

(19) Kate said nothing in words but her dark longlashed eyes **rained [= weep]** thanks upon him. (COHA, 1936, FIC, CrookedTrailsStraight)

(20) The benevolent uncle prudently forbore any reference to guest or drawing-room for the evening, and leading the conversation into unlooked-for channels, only betrayed by unusual kindness of manner a remembrance of the unhappy incidents of the day. A practiced observer, however, might have detected the tenor of his thoughts, in the liberal amount of cream and sugar -- twice as much as she desired -- infused into the tea of the gentle niece, whose pained heart throbbed sensitively, while her lips **smiled** thanks. (COHA, 1853, FIC, ClovernookRecollections)

(21) Xylophones for chests and torsos, violin bows that had **waved** goodbye and hugged grandchildren and lifted in toasts to the passing of traditions, gourd whistles between eyes and mouths. (COHA, 1992, FIC,Omni)

(22) The prickly pears **waved** good-bye with puckered, grayish pads. (COHA, 2007, NF, AnimalVegetable)

(23) Away from the fire the stars fired up, and one, falling, **flared** its good-bye and left the congregation no poorer. (COHA, 1971, FIC, DreamMuseum)

(24) [Y]ou will find your heart **bleeding** thanks with every step you take. (COHA, 1940, FIC, HowGreenWasMyValley)

Contrary to the ROC, due to the now abundant research on the *way*-construction (§ 3.2.1.2), there has been some agreement on the identification of the subschemas of the *way*-construction (Israel 1996, Traugott and Trousdale 2013, Perek 2016a, 2018, 2020, Fanego 2019; supplementing the earliest accounts by Jackendoff 1990 and Goldberg 1995). Given that in § 7.2 and § 7.3 I will explicitly refer to the three main subschemas of the *way*-construction, for the sake of clarity, I will describe them in some level of detail here. These are: a) the *means subschema* – also referred to as causative path-creation subschema (Traugott and Trousdale 2013), or simply path-creation sense (Perek 2018), b) the *manner subschema* or intransitive motion subschema (Traugott and Trousdale 2013), and c) the *co-occurrence subschema* – also known as the non-causative accompanying activity subschema (Traugott and Trousdale 2013), or simply incidental-action sense (Perek 2018).

In the *means subschema*, "the verb refers to the means whereby the 'path' is created" (Perek 2018, 68 and 69; see also Israel 1996, 223). This is the case of the verbs *hack*, *talk* and *bribe* in the *way*-constructions represented in (25)-(27). In these examples the creation of the path may be: literal with the actual removal of physical obstacles (25), more abstract (26), or even metaphorical as in (27), "where an institution (*city government*) is construed as a container, and becoming a member of this institution as motion into this container" (Perek 2018, 69).

(25) [F]armers [. . .] were beginning to **hack** their way through primeval forests.

(26) [W]e **talked** our way into the VIP area.

(27) They [. . .] **bribed** their way into city government.

Examples from Perek (2018, 67–68)

The means subschema of the *way*-construction is considered by many as the primary or basic sense of the construction (Goldberg 1995, Traugott and Trousdale 2013; see also Fanego 2019). For instance, contrary to Israel (1996), Traugott and Trousdale point out that "[t]he productive subschema of the *way*-construction is a path-creation schema" (2013, 88); and Goldberg explains that "the most common interpretation of this construction involves motion through a crowd, mass, obstacle, or other difficulty – that is, there is some reason why a path needs to be created" (1995, 204).

This definition by Goldberg, which explicitly alludes to the notion of difficulty, reflects well the historical origins of the *way*-construction. As mentioned in § 3.2.1.2 and § 5.2.3.2, the constructionalization of the *way*-construction, as argued in Traugott and Trousdale (2013), goes back to EModE, among other reasons because this is the period in which it expands to verbs of obstruction such as *fight*, *battle*, *force*, *push*, *drag* and *dig* (Traugott and Trousdale 2013, 84–85). As we shall see towards the end of § 7.3, in PDE, however, though still common, this difficulty reading should be seen as a typical implicature but not necessarily as part of the semantics of the construction (Perek 2018).

As for the *manner subschema*, this is exemplified in (28) with the manner of motion verb *stumble*. This subschema indicates "the manner in which motion is performed" (Perek 2018, 69): rate (*inch*, *run*, *speed*), terrain (*swim*, *wade*), difficulty (*stagger*, *trudge*), path shape (*thread*, *wend*), among many others.

(28) He **stumbled** his way to the back of the room. (Perek 2018, 68)

Regarding the history of this subschema, there are notable differences in the accounts provided by Israel (1996), and Traugott and Trousdale

(2013). Contrary to Israel (1996, 221–223), Traugott and Trousdale (2013) claim that "there is little or no direct continuity between the use of *go* and manner verbs like *scramble*, *wing* and *worm*" (79). As explained in § 5.2.3.2 (Fig. 5.11), Traugott and Trousdale (2013, 80) certainly include some manner of motion verbs (e.g. *ride*) as part of what they call the intransitive motion subschema, nevertheless, in their account, the intransitive motion subschema is no longer productive in EModE as it is restricted to the deictic motion verbs *come* and *go*). In their study, manner of motion verbs such as *worm* only seem to enter the *way*-construction around the eighteenth century, and they do so as part of the means subschema, which was the most productive subschema at the time. To be more specific, Traugott and Trousdale's claim is that they enter the construction via analogy with verbs of obstruction such as *force* and *dig*, which also indicate *manner* to some degree.

Finally, the *co-occurrence subschema* of the *way*-construction is exemplified by instances such as the ones in (29) and (30).

(29) I got out of the car and **smoked** my way toward the restaurant.
(= *he went toward the restaurant smoking*) (Perek 2018, 68)

(30) He **whistled** his way across the room.
(= *he went across the room whistling*) (Perek 2016a)

In these examples "the action described by the verb [i.e. *smoking* and *whistling*] merely occurs concomitantly with motion" (Perek 2018, 69; see also Israel 1996, 225). Goldberg and Jackendoff (2004) had already made a similar point when dealing with the examples in (31) claiming that "the *way* construction allows the subevents to be simply simultaneous rather than causally related" (2004, 541).

(31) a. The car **honked** its way down the road.
b. The dog **barked** its way out of the room.
c. Bill **whistled** his way past the house.

The simultaneous action may be volitional or accidental. This is more explicitly shown by Traugott and Trousdale with examples in (32) and (33), where the first action (*shooting*) is volitional, and the second one (*plashing*) is accidental. In their own words, "*plash* (. . .) is not volitional and therefore intended, light splashing is an inevitable accompaniment of a steamer in motion" (2013, 87).

(32) and **shot** my way home the next day; having... equally divided the game between the three (1820–2 Hunt, *Memoirs of Henry Hunt* [CL 2]; Traugott and Trousdale 2013, 87)

(33) The steamer ... **plashed** its way forward. (1842 Borrow, *Bible in Spain* [CL 2]; Traugott and Trousdale 2013, 87)

Worth of note here is that Fanego (2019, 687) proposes to treat examples like the one in (33) separately as part of a fourth subschema she labels 'resultant sound subschema'. In (33), for instance, the splashing sound of water is not simply an accompanying accidental action but the sound also *results* from or is caused by the steamer's motion. This semantic nuance that distinguishes between the resultant sound subschema from the co-occurrence subschema of the *way*-construction is relevant in that it casts some more light on how the *way*-construction is networked with the intransitive motion construction (e.g. *The toddler walked to the door*): while the co-occurrence subschema is characteristic of the *way*-construction, the resultant sound subschema is mostly a feature of the intransitive motion construction (see Fanego 2019, 694).

Apart from Fanego's insights on the semantic complexities of the *way*-construction, there has also been some disagreement regarding the history of the co-occurrence subschema (Israel 1996, 223 and 225; Traugott and Trousdale 2013, 88; Perek 2018, 87; Fanego 2019, 697). Part of this controversy lies in how the manner subschema is conceived in the LModE period: (i) as a fully productive subschema in its own right; this is the account proposed by Israel (1996) and this seems to be also the view adopted by Perek (2018); or (ii) as a LModE extension of the means subschema which, as noted above, is the account proposed by Traugott and Trousdale (2013). In the first case, the origins of the co-occurrence subschema are uncertain: it could stem from either the manner or the means subschema (Israel 1996, 225; Perek 2018, 87). In the second case, however, the co-occurrence subschema is treated as a further development of this LModE extension of the means subschema:

> The productive subschema of the *way*-construction is a **path-creation schema** that is no longer restricted to transitive verbs. It has further subschemas: **a)** a causative path-creation subschema (itself with two sub-subnetworks, one involving obstruction (e.g. *force*), the other not (e.g. *make*)), and **b)** a **non-causative subschema**, designating **'iterative path-traversal with accompanying activity'** (e.g. *worm*, ***shoot***, *trash-talk*). (Traugott and Trousdale 2013, 88; emphasis mine)

On this particular matter, as seen in Chapter 5 (Fig. 5.11), though considering other proposals too, my discussion mostly follows Traugott and Trousdale's historical account of the *way*-construction because: (i) it improves on Israel (1996); (ii) it provides further historical data based on MED, HC and CLMET-EV – not just from the OED (as is the case of Israel 1996) – ; (iii) it is also a much more elaborated account that shows how the different subschemas of the *way*-construction emerged and interacted in earlier stages, ultimately leading to the *way*-construction as we know it in PDE: [[SUBJ$_i$ [V POSS$_i$ *way*] DIR] ↔ ['SEM$_i$ traverse the path PP while/by doing V']]; and (iv) finally, it crucially distinguishes between a causative (path-creation) subschema and a non-causative (accompanying activity) subschema, and, therefore their account provides evidence of the gradual process of transitivization undergone by the English language (Chapter 2).

7.2 Frequency and distribution

As already noted, the methodology described in § 7.1 allowed me to identify a total of 961 ROCs in COHA. This is a considerable amount of ROCs, especially since my searches are restricted to only a set of common delocutive nouns (i.e. *hello*, *goodbye*, *thank you* and their derivatives), and my previous historical study on British English only yielded 305 ROCs for the 40 verbs selected for analysis. These ROCs are distributed across decades as shown in Fig. 7.1. From this figure, it becomes clear that the ROC has been in use in American English since as early as the 1820s and it has increased in frequency up to PDE.

Now, if we compare the diachronic frequency of the American ROC to that of the American *way*-construction (see Fig. 7.2), we observe a strong parallel between the ROC, and the co-occurrence (incidental-action) subschema of the *way*-construction (e.g. *He whistled his way across the room = he went across the room whistling*). First, both can be described as "a novelty in the first half of the 19th century"; and second, both show a "steady increase in frequency starting in the early 20th century" (Perek 2018, 72).

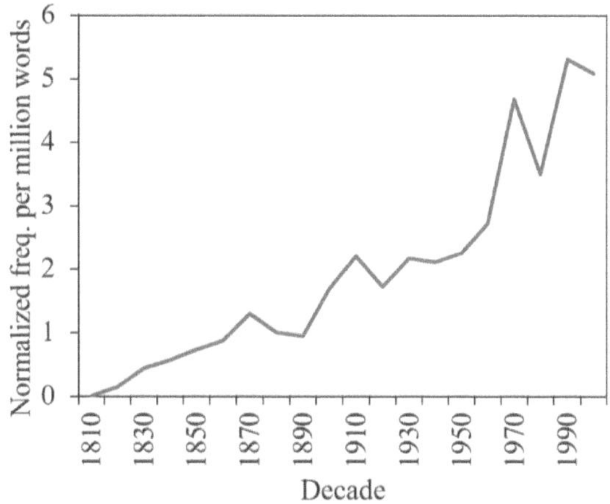

Fig. 7.1: Diachronic distribution of the American ROC

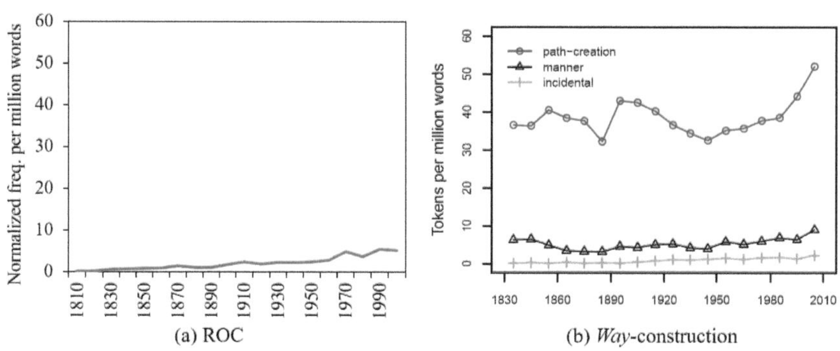

Fig. 7.2: Diachronic distribution of the American ROC and the *way*-construction. The figures corresponding to the *way*-construction have been adapted from Perek (2018, 73).

As I see it, these results support – or at least do not contradict – the hypothesis that the ROC is a British innovation that later spread to American English. More specifically, my data so far indicates that the period when the American ROC ranks lowest in token frequency (1810–1849) coincides with the heyday of the British ROC (1780–1849). This is more explicitly shown in Fig. 7.3. In addition to this, as with

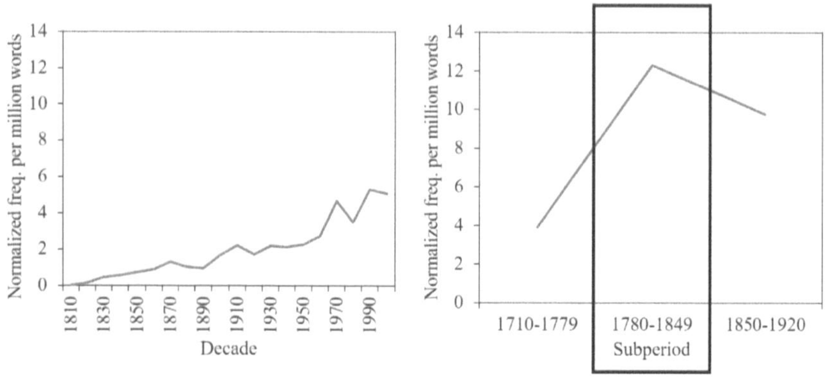

Fig. 7.3: Diachronic distribution of the American ROC and the British ROC. American ROC (1810–2009; based on 961 ROCs) and British ROC (1710–1920; based on 303 ROCs).

my British data (§ 6.3.3.1), most of the ROCs extracted from COHA come from fiction (see Fig. 7.4 where this genre preference remains constant across decades), and crucially, the American novel developed later in time than the British novel (see Carter and McRae 1996, 78 and 122–123). This also applies to the sentimental novel, which shows an unprecedented emphasis on "emotional response" (Rowland 2008, 193; see also Ousby 1988, 888–889), and, as previously seen in § 6.3.3.2, this genre accounts for almost half of the examples attested for the British ROC in the second half of the eighteenth century.[61]

Though quite promising, these results should not be taken as conclusive and a larger sample of ROCs should be analysed so as to confirm whether this trend (British > American) found with the set of delocutive nouns considered, also applies to deverbal nouns (e.g. *acqui-escence* and *assent*), predicative expressive nouns (e.g. *discontent* and *delight*), and emotional abstract nouns (e.g. *sweetness* and *blessedness*).

If this trend is confirmed, the ROC would show a difference with regard to the *way*-construction. Despite their parallel steady increase in

61 As demonstrated by Hart (2004), this emphasis on feeling is also a feature of the American sentimental novel. Regarding the later development of the American sentimental novel, see Samuels (1992, 2012).

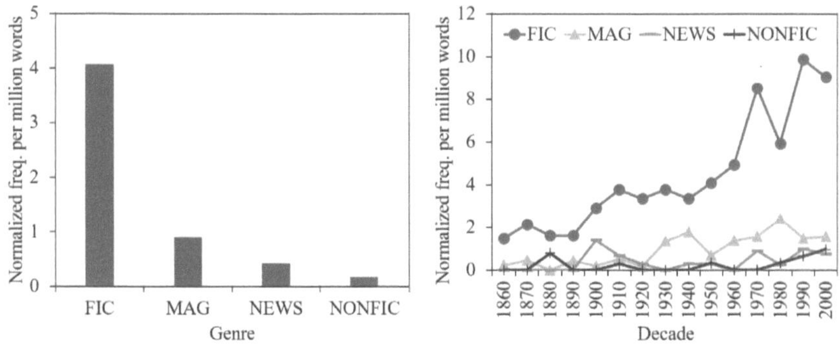

Fig. 7.4: Distribution of the American ROC across genres and decades. Note here that the genre of newspapers has no representation at all in COHA until the decade of the 1860s. This is the reason why I included the diachronic and textual distribution of the American ROC across genres *only* from the 1860s onwards. The results are thus calculated on the basis of a total of 933 ROCs.

frequency over the course of the twentieth century, the *way*-construction on the whole was already considerably frequent in American English during the first half of the nineteenth century (cf. Fig. 7.2). This aspect alongside the semantic diversity of Perek's data (2015b; see also Perek 2018, 86), are some of the reasons that led him to think of the American *way*-construction as being "ahead" of the British one – as opposed to Israel (1996), whose study is mostly based on British data.

7.3 Productivity of the ROC and the *way*-construction

The second research question to be discussed in this chapter has to do with the productivity of the ROC, and, in line with my results from Chapters 5 and 6, with whether we also keep on finding similarities between the ROC and the *way*-construction regarding their most recent history. More specifically, has the ROC, like the *way*-construction, increased its productivity after its grammatical constructionalization over the LModE period?

Though there is little consensus on how to define the terms 'productive' and 'productivity', Barðdal (2008, 9–54) manages to show that three subconcepts of productivity arise when one pays close attention to a considerable number of the uses of these two labels. These three subconcepts are:

(i) Productivity as *generality*, in the sense of being abstract (Kay and Fillmore 1999, 31):

> . . . a construction-based approach appears to provide promise of accounting for both for the relatively idiomatic and for the abstract and more fully productive aspects of language.

(ii) Productivity as *regularity*, in the sense of being rule-based (Pinker 1999, 17):

> The theory that regular forms are generated by rule and irregular forms are retrieved by rote is pleasing . . . because it explains the differences in productivity between the two patterns. . .

(iii) Productivity as *extensibility*, in the sense of occurring with new items (Haspelmath 2002, 98):

> . . . a morphological rule or pattern is said to be productive if (and to the extent that) it can be applied to new bases and new words can be formed with it.

One should bear in mind that these three subconcepts of productivity rather than being mutually exclusive are closely related to each other (Barðdal 2008, 22). For instance, general categories are always extendable but not all extendable categories are general; that is, the relation between generality and extensibility is one of *entailment*, whereas the relation between extensibility and generality is one of possible *co-occurrence*. Barðdal exemplifies this interrelationship between generality and extensibility with the category of weak or regular verbs as opposed to the category of strong or irregular verbs in English. The category of regular verbs that forms the past tense with the *–ed* dental suffix is general and extendable, whereas the category of irregular verbs that forms the past tense without suffixation in some cases (e.g. *beat*), and in others with changes of vowel/consonant in the stem (e.g. *stick/stuck*, *keep/kept*) is extendable but clearly not general; this last aspect is evinced by the fact that learners of English allocate verbs to the category of irregular verbs only when they fulfil "certain morphological and/or phonological requirements" (Barðdal 2008, 23 ff; see Bybee and Slobin 1982, 285).

The subconcept of productivity that is most relevant for my purposes here is that of extensibility, which is the one most commonly adopted in the literature (see Petré 2012, De Smet 2020, Ungerer and Hartmann 2020, Fanego 2020, among others) and quite crucially, this is also the one used by Perek (2016a, 2018) in his study on the recent change in the productivity of the *way*-construction. In addition to this, the subconcept of *generality*, as a feature of grammatical constructions, nowadays refers to *schematicity*. Although tightly connected with productivity (see § 4.3.1; Barðdal 2008), as also evinced further below by historical data for the ROC and the *way*-construction, the concept of schematicity should be kept apart from the concept of productivity (for this distinction see Traugott and Trousdale 2013, 113–120; see also Perek 2020).

Baayen and colleagues (Baayen and Lieber 1991, Baayen 1992, 1993, 2009) have proposed a number of corpus-based measures to gauge the productivity of constructions; among these are: realized productivity, expanding productivity, and potential productivity. Regarding these measures, Hilpert (2013) points out that they differ across different corpora due to corpus size and "thematic breadth of the texts that are included"; thus, "fruitful uses of productivity measures (. . .) include comparisons of different (. . .) categories within the same corpus or comparisons of multiple measures for the same category, again based on the same corpus" (128).

Baayen (2009) explains that realized productivity is estimated by type frequency in a corpus (905). On the other hand, expanding productivity, refers to the extent to which a particular construction contributes to "the growth rate of the vocabulary in a corpus" (905) and this is calculated by the sum of its hapaxes (i.e. one-token occurrences or, in this case, verbs that occur only once in the construction) divided by the sum total of hapaxes in the corpus. Finally, potential productivity measures "the extent to which the market for a category is saturated" (902); and this is estimated by the sum of its hapaxes divided by its token frequency. Tab. 7.4 summarizes the operationalizations for each of these three measures of productivity. Given that these three measures focus on different aspects of productivity they complement each other (Baayen 2009, 906; Hilpert 2013, 132). For instance, a construction may have a high realized productivity (i.e. type frequency) and still be judged less productive than other competing constructions in terms of potential productivity (i.e. hapax/token frequency ratio).

All these productivity measures are relevant, still potential productivity is particularly interesting as it is a good indication of the degree of cognitive ease with which speakers can produce and process new constructions (see van Marle 1985). For instance, the ADJ-*en* construction, instantiated by *weaken* and *widen*, is less productive nowadays than the V-*er* construction, instantiated by *baker*, *smoker* or *reporter*. As shown by Hilpert (2014b, 82), a search in the BNC (100 million words) only yields one hapax (*madden*) of the forty-four types attested for the ADJ-*en* construction. On the other hand, for the V-*er* construction, speakers are able to more freely create innovative combinations such as *applauder*, or even the non-existent word *zibber* to refer to a man whose invented job is to *zib* (Berko Gleason 1958).

As for expanding productivity, or the extent to which a particular construction contributes to the "the growth rate of the vocabulary in a corpus" (Baayen 2009, 905), this measure is more fruitfully applied to morphological constructions (i.e. the ADJ-*en* and V-*er* constructions just mentioned) rather than to argument structure constructions, such as the ROC and the *way*-construction. Yet, as demonstrated by Mondorf (2016), some *neologisms* or *nonce verbs* created by conversion have been brought to light by valency-increasing constructions such

Tab. 7.4: Measures of productivity. Adapted from Hilpert (2013, 132)

Measures	Operationalizations
Realized productivity	sum of all types of a construction (= type frequency)
Expanding productivity	sum of hapaxes of a construction divided by sum total of hapaxes in the corpus
Potential productivity	sum of hapaxes of a construction divided by token frequency

as the *way*-construction and the dummy *it* object construction. This is shown in examples (34) and (35).

(34) The story has Fred **yabba-dabba-dooing** his way into the vice presidency. . . [*The Guardian*, 1994; Mondorf 2016, 96]

(35) a1616 Shakespeare *Macbeth* (1623) ii. iii. 16 Ile **Deuill-Porter** it no further. (OED, s.v. *devil*, n. C1.a.; meaning "to act as a porter of hell"; Mondorf 2016, 94)

In the case of the ROC the only potential contribution in my data to the vocabulary of the English language could have been the reduplicated verb of sound emission *tut-tut* in example (36), which is not attested in the OED (cf. OED, *tut*, v. (1832)). This verb, however, does not count as a hapax in COHA as it occurs in two constructions in the corpus (see example (37)), although from the very same year.

(36) "Doctor, I have seen you on TV and I have great respect for the work you are doing." Seed **tut-tuts** his thanks. (COHA, 1998, NEWS, WashPost)

(37) If you don't talk, they will. Those are the facts. (Dalton doesn't respond. Chas **tut-tuts** at him.) (COHA, 1998, FIC, Play:TrestleAtPope)

Considering the observations above, the present study on the recent change in the productivity of the ROC excludes expanding productivity as it does not seem to be as relevant as the other two productivity measures. In what follows, attention will be paid therefore to realized (i.e. type frequency) and potential productivity (i.e. hapax/token frequency ratio), and to whether the results obtained for the *way*-construction (Perek 2016a, 2018) and the ROC are somewhat similar.

As shown in Fig. 7.5, the three subschemas of the *way*-construction described in detail in § 7.1, namely, the means (path-creation) subschema (e.g. *They **hacked** their way through the jungle*), the manner subschema (e.g. *They **trudged** their way through the snow*), and the co-occurrence (incidental-action) subschema (e.g. *He **whistled** his way across the room*), "have kept attracting more and more new verb types [i.e. verb stems]" (Perek 2018, 74), and exactly the same expanding tendency has been found for its three subschemas in terms of hapax legomena.

Out of the three subschemas of the *way*-construction, the one that stands out is the co-occurrence subschema: despite its novel and marginal status with respect to the more established means and manner

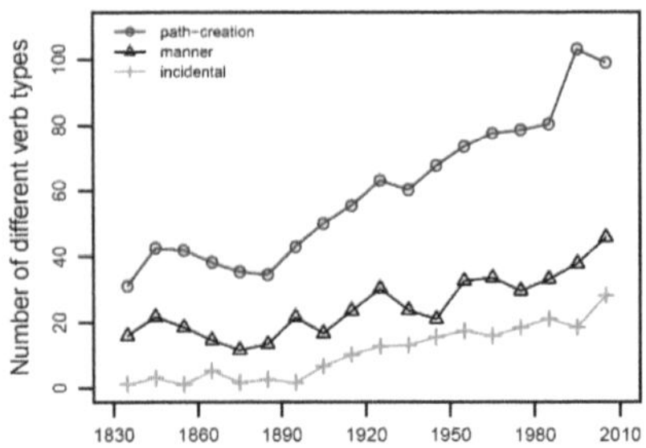

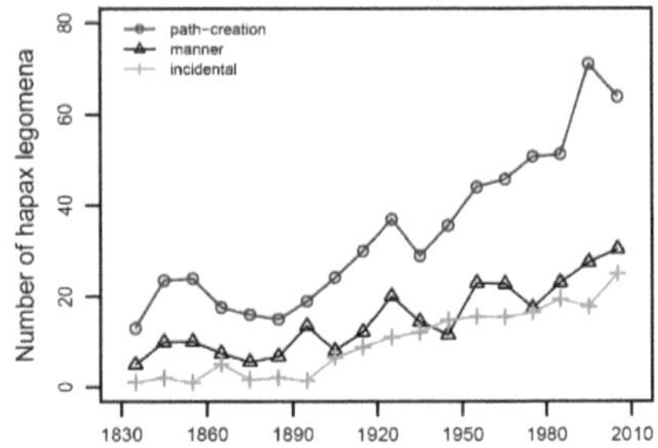

Fig. 7.5: Type frequency and hapax legomena of the *way*-construction

subschemas (Fig. 7.2), it shows the most drastic changes in both frequencies: verb types and hapax legomena. In addition to this, its high number of hapax legomena alongside its overall low token frequency results in high potential productivity. This is shown in Fig. 7.7 further below. Following Perek (2018), from this figure we can say that, first, the hapax/token frequency ratio of the co-occurrence subschema is very unstable at the start, but it reaches one and 0.8 in several decades when all or almost all tokens are hapaxes (this applies in particular to the 1860s). Second, the hapax/token frequency ratios of the co-occurrence subschema of the *way*-construction over the nineteenth and twentieth centuries are much higher than those calculated for the same period for the means and manner subschemas of the *way*-construction. The co-occurrence subschema can therefore be considered as the most productive subschema of the *way*-construction. Interestingly, although they do not apply these corpus-based measures to their historical study of the *way*-construction, Traugott and Trousdale (2013) also regard the co-occurrence subschema as the most productive.

Similarly to the *way*-construction, my data from COHA indicates that the ROC has also increased its productivity over the nineteenth and twentieth centuries. As shown in Fig. 7.6, the ROC has kept attracting more and more verb types, and also shows a considerable number of hapax legomena from different verb classes. A simple linear regression analysis confirms the positive correlation between time (independent variable), and verb types (dependent variable): the Pearson product-moment correlation coefficient indicates

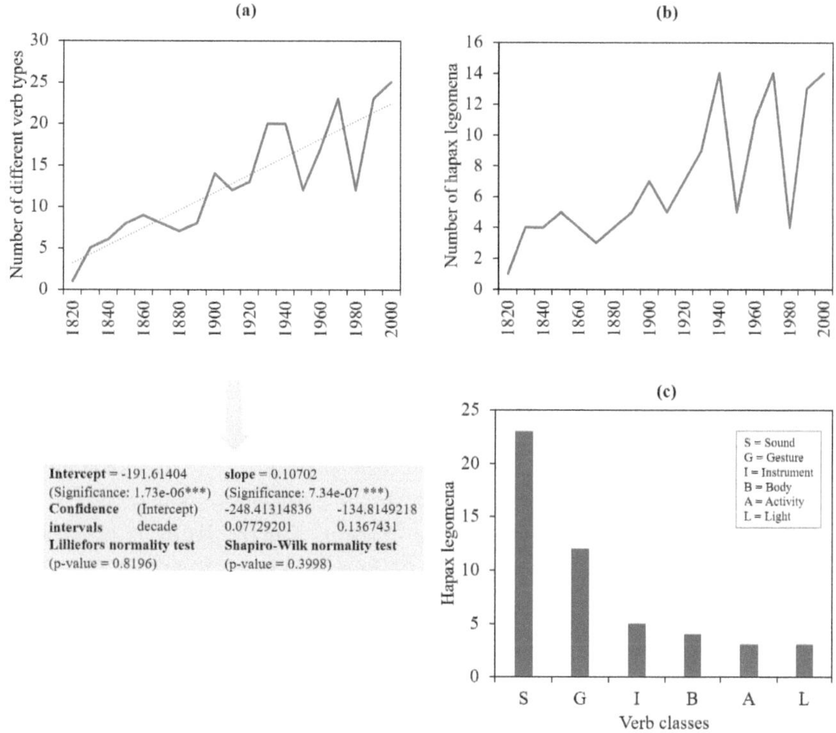

Intercept = -191.61404	**slope** = 0.10702
(Significance: 1.73e-06***)	(Significance: 7.34e-07 ***)
Confidence (Intercept)	-248.41314836 -134.8149218
intervals decade	0.07729201 0.1367431
Lilliefors normality test	**Shapiro-Wilk normality test**
(p-value = 0.8196)	(p-value = 0.3998)

Fig. 7.6: Type frequency, and hapax legomena of the ROC across time and verb classes. Fig. 7.6, Fig. 7.7, and Fig. 7.8 are based on 948 ROCs (excluding 13 coordinated ROCs). The verb types considered were specified in Tab. 7.3 (§ 7.1).

that the strength of the correlation is strong with a greater value than 0.7 (r = 0.8788677). Note that Fig. 7.6 also includes a table with the results from a couple of normality tests (the Lilliefors normality test and the Shapiro-Wilk normality test) that serve here to validate the linear regression model.

Although the ROC is a relatively low-frequency phenomenon (Fig. 7.2) and shows a considerable number of hapax legomena (Fig. 7.6), its hapax/token frequency ratios over the nineteenth and twentieth centuries are not as high as the ones calculated for the co-occurrence subschema of the *way*-construction. This is shown in 7.7 which compares the potential productivity of both constructions.

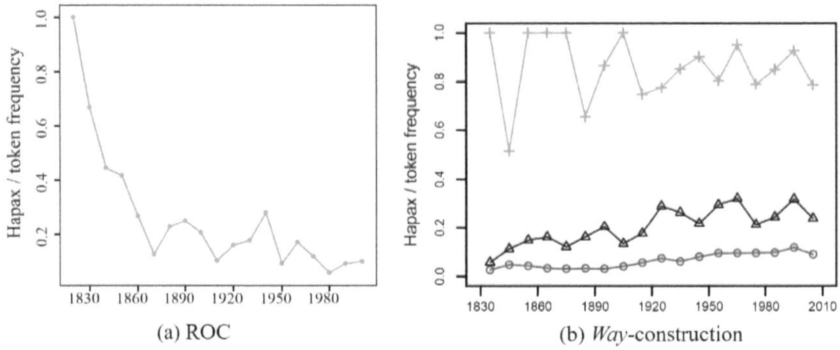

Fig. 7.7: Potential productivity of the ROC and the *way*-construction

Using Baayen's definition of potential productivity provided above (i.e. "the extent to which the market for a category is saturated"), we can say that Fig. 7.7 shows that "the market" for the ROC is more saturated than "the market" for the co-occurrence subschema of the *way*-construction, where, as previously noted, in some decades all or almost all tokens are hapaxes. This difference is partly explained by the fact that the co-occurrence subschema of the *way*-construction is "clearly dominated by different types of verbs describing sound emission" (Perek 2018, 86–87), and, as mentioned in previous chapters (see in particular Fig. 5.10 in Chapter 5), this is a verb class that only increases in type and token frequency in Modern English.

In the case of the ROC, it is relevant to point out here that the peaks of innovation represented in Fig. 7.7 also come in the form of verbs of sound emission. More explicitly, out of the 50 hapaxes attested in the whole sample (i.e. 948 ROCs excluding 13 coordinated ROCs), more than twenty qualify as verbs of sound emission – or related verb classes. Note, however, that this is not the only verb class that had an impact on the productivity of the ROC over the nineteenth and twentieth centuries, but other verb classes, though less significantly, had an impact on its productivity too. More concretely, I am referring to verbs of instrument of communication (I), verbs of bodily processes (B), verbs of activity (A), verbs of light emission (L), and finally, verbs of gestures (G), many of which entered the ROC by analogy with extremely high

Tab. 7.5: Hapaxes attested for each verb class

Verb classes	**Hapaxes**	
(S) Verbs of sound emission	(a)	**Verbs of sound emission proper** (x6): *bang, gurgle, hum, sputter, toot* and *tut-tut*;
	(b)	**Verbs of sounds made by animals** (x11): *bark, chirp, croak, crow, honk, quack, snort, squeal, warble, woof* and *yelp*;
	(c)	**Verbs of manner of speaking** (x3): *bawl, grumble*, and *moan*;
	(d)	**Others (verbs of sound existence, . . .)** (x3): *echo, fumble* and *resound*
(G) Verbs of gestures	—	*blink, dimple, embrace, gesture, giggle, pat, peck, rain* (= *weep*), *skim, smooch, wag* and *weep*
(I) Verbs of instrument of communication	—	*cable, phone, scribble, type* and *wire*
(B) Verbs of bodily processes – verbs of inhalation and substance emission	—	*snuffle, bleed, gush* and *sigh*
(A) Verbs of activity	—	*drink, flutter* and *fuck*
(L) Verbs of light emission	—	*flare, glisten* and *reflect*

token frequency verbs such as *wave* and *kiss* (cf. Fig. 7.9 at the end of the chapter). In Fig. 7.6 the exact number of hapaxes attested for each verb class has been included, and Tab. 7.5 lists the specific hapaxes found in my data.

To sum up, the results presented so far reveal that the parallelisms between the ROC and the *way*-construction should not be restricted to their constructionalization in EModE, and their grammatical constructionalization over the LModE period. Just like the *way*-construction, the ROC has further increased its productivity after all these gradual steps in its development. In both constructions, this increase in productivity has been shown to be continual and with some peaks of innovation. The former, that is, that the productivity of both constructions has been continual, is evinced by the fact that both constructions kept attracting more and more verb types over the nineteenth and twentieth centuries. The latter is justified by their hapax/token frequency ratios.

In the case of the co-occurrence subschema of the *way*-construction, the peaks of innovation mainly come in the form of verbs of sound emission, while in the ROC, these adopt the form of verbs of sound emission, and other verb classes such as verbs of instrument of communication, verbs of activity and verbs of light emission. This is particularly important as it reveals that the ROC not only has become more productive over the course of the nineteenth and twentieth centuries but also it has become more schematic (general) as the ROC now incorporates verb classes that were not available in its prior history (cf. § 5.2.3 for the verb classes attested in the historical record). Fig. 7.8 serves to better illustrate this point.

At the start of the nineteenth century, we only find in the ROC verbs of sound emission, verbs of gestures, and verbs of bodily processes and, as we move into the twentieth century, (modern) verbs of instrument of communication, verbs of activity and verbs of light emission start to come into play. Note here that this is just as predicted by my historical data from Chapter 5, where I also suggested that twentieth-century incorporations into the ROC may have escaped the eye of the readers and editors of the OED, most likely due to the overall low frequency of the construction.

Some of these recent incorporations enter the construction due to extralinguistic factors. This is the case of *modern* verbs of instrument of communication such as *type*, *wire*, *cable* and *phone* in examples

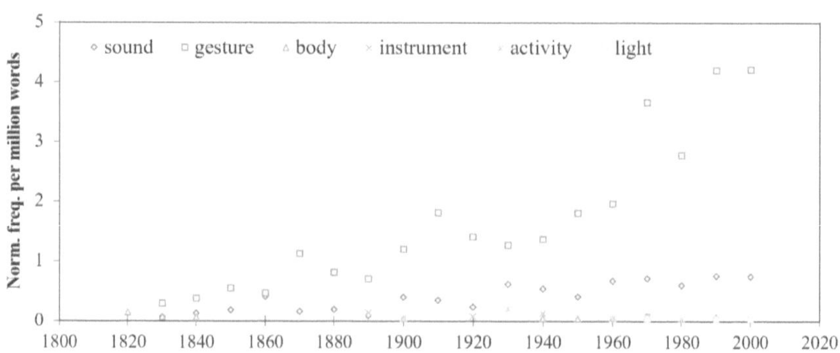

Fig. 7.8: Diachronic distribution of the verb classes attested in the American ROC

(1)-(4) from Tab. 7.6. The verb *type* is first used as a communication verb in 1736 (OED, s.v. *type*, v. 3. "To reproduce by means of type"), whereas the verbs *wire* and *cable* are used in such way only in the nineteenth century, namely in 1859 (OED, s.v. *wire*, v. 6. "To send (a message) electronically"), and 1871 (OED, s.v. *cable*, v. 3. "To transmit (a message, news, etc.), or communicate, by submarine telegraph."); finally, the verb *phone* is first recorded in the OED in 1885 (s.v. *phone*, v. 1. "To make a telephone call").[62] Other recent incorporations that entered the ROC via *coercion* are verbs of activity such as *drink*, and *flutter* in examples (5) and (6), and *play* and *dance* in the excerpt represented in (7) from Anderson's drama *Winterset* (1935).

Finally, verbs of light emission such as *flare*, *glisten* and *reflect* in examples (8)-(10) entered the ROC via *metaphor*, and low-frequency verbs such as *peck* and *smooch* (in examples (11) and (12)) via *analogization* with the verbs functioning as prototypes during this period (1810s-2000s). In particular, the verbs *peck* and *smooch* by analogy with *kiss*. Note in this regard that his verb amounts up to 217 ROCs in my data, despite the fact that this verb is also a quite recent incorporation, as seen in Tab. 5.10, the earliest example in the historical records I consulted only goes back to the nineteenth century.[63]

Finally, just like the ROC, the *way*-construction has also become more schematic over the course of the twentieth century. Apart from the *modern* verbs of sound emission characteristic of the newly formed co-occurrence subschema (cf. Fig. 7.2), the means and the manner subschemas of the *way*-construction went from describing more concrete to more neutral and abstract (even sometimes metaphorical) types of motion (Israel 1996, 224; see also Perek 2016a, 2018, 2020). For instance, the manner subschema at the start of the nineteenth century was dominated by verbs describing difficult motion such as *edge* and *plod* in examples (38) and (39), and over time motion verbs that do not

62 For similar results with these verbs involved in other argument structure constructions see Barðdal (2008), Colleman and De Clerck (2011), and De Clerck et al. (2011).

63 I also checked CLMET3.0 where only six examples of ROCs with *kiss* were attested, the earliest one from 1826.

Tab. 7.6: Recent examples with verbs of instrument of communication, activity, light emission and low-frequency verbs of gestures

(1) Belle snaps at my lifeless strands and I daydream of punting her across the room. "You'd look so good if you got some highlights. Please let me do a makeover on you, Milan? Please?" "Highlights would look beautiful," says my mother. "Shh," I say. "You should let your sister fix your hair," says our mother. "Shh," I tell them as I **type** my hellos to Las Ricky Chickies [i.e. an Internet forum in honor of sexy male pop star Ricky Biscayne].

COHA, **2006**, FIC, MakeHimLookGood

Instrument of communication

(2) She was directed to the man who owned the land on which the teams and men were now resting, and found that she could make a deal to lease the property at a reasonable figure. She made a freckle-faced boy happy with a bright new dime, and sent him back to her men with instructions for them to pitch the tents permanently and proceed to make the spot the Julia headquarters of the outfit. She **wired** her thanks to Demarest and assured him that the order would go forward next day, if the dealers had it ready.

COHA, **1922**, FIC, SheBoss AWestern

Instrument of communication

(3) From Addis Ababa, where he has been waiting the British Government's pleasure since last May, he **cabled** his thanks to Winston Churchill for helping to restore his country's independence.

COHA, **1942**, MAG, Time

Instrument of communication

(4) They went back to the house for a while. After he packed his kit and **phoned** good-bye to some neighbors -- landholders, friendly folk whose ancestors had dwelt here for generations beyond counting -- she flew him to Aerogare Bordeaux.

COHA, **1975**, FIC, BeyondBedroomWall

Instrument of communication

(5) All that occurred to her was to act in accordance with her manner of procedure on the bars: build a deliberate sequence leading to a strong but unhooked finish. She raised her glass and drank it all down, to make clear to Hector she entirely accepted his invitation to **drink** goodbye. She smiled to show that she considered all was well between them.

COHA, **1967**, FIC, Harpers

Activity

(6) "Howdy, Miss Emily," I said as I creaked open the screen door, my hand springing up, my fingers **fluttering** hello.

COHA, **2001**, FIC, IcySparksNovel

Activity

Tab. 7.6: *Continued*

(7)	LUCIA. (. . .) Maybe you don't know, folks! Tonight we **play** goodbye to the piano! Good-bye forever! No more piano on the streets! No more music! No more money for the music-man! Last time, folks! Good-bye to the piano -- good-bye forever! (. . .) LUCIA. Hoy! Hoy! Maybe it rains tonight, maybe it snows tomorrow! Tonight we **dance** good-bye. (*He sings the air lustily.* A POLICEMAN *comes in from the left and looks on.* TWO OR THREE PEDESTRIANS *follow him.*) POLICEMAN. Hey, you! (LUCIA *goes on singing.*) Hey, you! LUCIA. (Still playing.) What you want? POLICEMAN. Sign off! LUCIA. What you mean? I get off the street! POLICEMAN. Sign off! LUCIA. (Still playing.) What you mean? (The POLICEMAN *walks over to him.* LUCIA *stops playing and the* DANCERS *pause.*) (. . .) LUCIA. It's the last time. We **dance** good-bye to the piano. POLICEMAN. You'll **dance** good-bye to something else if I catch you cranking that thing again. COHA, **1935**, FIC, Play:Winterset
	Activity
(8)	Collingsworth got up, and, as if suddenly aware of his presence, they got up, too. "I must be going," he said. Blackman came to him and held out his hand. "Come again, any time, fish or no fish." "But have the warm mouth," Moreau said, taking his hand. Away from the fire the stars fired up, and one, falling, **flared** its good-bye and left the congregation no poorer. Simple stories, conceits, language, logic, history, formulas -- they were all fairy tales, images and symbols, acquisitions and wisdoms that the fanciful and exploring mind had conjuredand explicated. Not fairy tales, though. Wonders. Rich wonders. And hungry old men would listen. He saw again to his horse and sat on a downed log by his dead fire. He must learn more of the stars, that final wonder of all. COHA, **1971**, FIC, DreamMuseum
	Light emission

Continued on next page

Tab. 7.6: *Continued*

(9) I raised my arm and let # the paper poppy float down to the water. In the deep waves # hundreds of red poppies bobbed among the clouds. # My Mother's Eyes # My mother's eyes # watch day after night, # week into month # Her eyes see the man # shrivel to shroud of skin # and skeleton # Eyes that brim with tears # the color of the oceans # he once sailed # Those eyes yearn # for the dear morning sky # after the storm # Brown eyes # red and swollen # **glisten** good-bye # Chinook # The fish feels heavy in my grasp. Her dark body still # as my hands return her to the cold salty waters. I rub # clean the smooth scales of the Chinook, her eyes stare # with horror. The Black Robe had stared at me that way. # I told him we would let our children go to his school. # His mouth relaxed. His eyes danced. Spittle sprayed # from my labret as I went on.

COHA, **1999**, FIC, Frontiers

Light emission

(10) Jencie's face grew tense. Please help me, her eyes pleaded. Mamie's heart was pounding. She could feel everyone staring at her. "M-m-m. . . any a m-m. . . odern man has failed that test," she whispered, and she heard Jencie pick up the cue. Mamie's relief did not last long. Jencie was stuck again. Mamie was determined to say the next line without hesitating. She delivered the words slowly and clearly, "I question his motives." Jencie's eyes **reflected** her thanks. It was the last scene of the last act, and Mamie realized Chip was in trouble. If he fluffed his lines now, the whole effect of the surprise ending would be ruined. I wish I hadn't agreed to be prompter, Marnie said to herself for the hundredth time that evening. Her throat was tight, and her stomach ached. Chip stopped. He couldn't remember his next line.

COHA, **2003**, MAG, ChildDigest

Light emission

(11) The rig pulled up in front of the hotel. "I have to get back," Julie said. "Rex will see me home. Now you have it straight, Mort? Main Hall at two-thirty o'clock. I'll see you. right afterward." She **pecked** him good-bye. "Sure. Sure." He stepped down to the street. "Night, Julie."

COHA, **1971**, FIC, DreamMuseum

Gesture

(12) I barely noticed how boring it had all become-until one day I suddenly realized that our morning routine of **smooching** good-bye at the train station had somehow fallen by the wayside.

COHA, **2001**, MAG, Cosmopolitan

Gesture

involve difficulty such as *pace* (40), *fly* (41) and *ooze* (42) start to come into play.

<u>*Difficult motion*</u>

(38) She **edged** her way through the narrow space between her car and the next and climbed in behind the wheel.

(39) The horse was **plodding** its way through the snow-drifts and it was evident that the animal would soon become exhausted.

<u>*Neutral motion*</u>

(40) He slowly **paced** his way down the line of standing gangster.

(41) I must **fly** my way across the ocean.

(42) Between them a pale shaft of sun managed to **ooze** its way through the grime on the glass panes.

As for the means subschema, at the start of the nineteenth century this subschema was mainly dominated by verb classes of the type included in (43)-(48) which describe "forceful actions leading to the creation of an actual path through some concrete obstacle" (83). However, over the course of the twentieth century, verbs describing abstract (metaphorical motion) such as *mumble*, *grin* and *think* in examples (49)-(51) or *bribe* in example (27) from § 7.1, start to become more frequent. Perek justifies the inclusion of these examples as part of the means subschema as follows: "the path (. . .) does not exist before the action described by the verb is performed", more than describing the literal creation of a path through a physical obstacle, as in the prototypical examples of the means subschema in (43)-(48), they refer to "the abstract way that some goal is achieved" (2018, 71–72).

<u>*Difficult motion*</u>

(43) **Verbs of destruction** (*blast*, *break*, *crush*, *smash*)
The steamers were using dynamite in an attempt to **blast** their way <u>through the ice</u>.

(44) **Harm** (*beat*, *shoot*)
[T]hese men might [. . .] try to **shoot** their way <u>into Don Chafin's stronghold</u>.

(45) **Separation** (*cut, hack, hew, plow, saw, split, rip, tear, trim*)
[N]ow **cutting** their way through the tangled woods, they toiled courageously forward.

(46) **Hitting** (*claw, kick, paw, punch, slam, trash*)
He found that a bullet [. . .] had **punched** its way through the cloth.

(47) **Pushing and pulling** (*hitch, jostle, poke, pull, push, shove, shoulder, wedge*)
It occupied all Cap's faculties to **push** her way through the overhanging and interlacing branches of the trees.

(48) **General damage** (*batter, burn, hammer, pierce, strike, wear*)
He screamed in agony as the white metal **burned** its way through his flesh.

Abstract motion

(49) **Sound emission and manner of speaking** (*bellow, groan, mumble, snarl, stammer, wail, whisper*)
Macmillan [. . .] **mumbled** his way through a string of "Splendids," "Jolly goods," and "God bless you alls."

(50) **Social interaction** (*chat, chatter, grin, joke, kid, laugh, nod, quarrel, smile, talk*)
Duhamel **grinned** his way into the spotlight, chopping wood sans shirt and outshining his romantic foil, Topher Grace.

(51) **Cognitive verbs** (*brood, puzzle, think, worry*)
I was trying to **think** my way around the gun in his hand.

The interesting changes in the schematicity of the verb slot and, at a broader level, of the constructional meaning of the *way*-construction are analysed in detail in Perek (2020), to which I refer the reader interested in a description of the different types of conceptual metaphor underlying some of the abstract uses of the subschema just mentioned. To sum up, the striking parallelisms between the overall historical development of the *way*-construction and the ROC described so far are summarized in Fig. 7.10 and 7.11 at the end of this chapter.

These figures amplify those presented in Chapter 5 (Figs. 5.11 and 5.12) and Chapter 6 (Fig. 6.12), and add up the further post-constructionalization constructional changes proposed in § 6.3.1.2.5 and here in Chapter 7. These are: (i) the further increase in productivity and in schematicity of both constructions over the course of the twentieth century, (ii) and the post-constructionalization constructional change that affected the ROC subschema with *nod*, and which consisted in leaving out the indefinite article that was characteristic of its LModE subschema (**LModE** *nod an affirmative* > **PDE** *nod **Ø** yes/nod **Ø** agreement*).

Regarding this second type of post-constructionalization constructional change, a comment should be made here considering my historical data from American English. As shown in Fig. 7.9, the constructs attested for the ROC verb-specific subschemas with the most frequent verbs in my data, i.e. the nonverbal communication verbs *kiss*, *nod* and *wave*, show a clear preference for the bare and the possessive patterns. Also, as can be seen in Tab. 7.7 below, the vast majority of ROCs attested for *kiss* and *wave* occur in the bare pattern and in combination with the delocutive noun *goodbye*. This result seems to confirm the hypothesis put forward in § 6.3.1.2.5: the ROC subschema with *wave* may have also undergone some fixation and/or "morphological and phonological reduction" (LModE *wave an adieu* > PDE *wave **Ø** adieu*; LModE *wave a farewell* > PDE *wave **Ø** farewell*), as is clearly the case of the ROC subschemas with *nod* (LModE *nod an affirmative* > PDE *nod **Ø** yes/nod **Ø** agreement*) and *kiss* (see also Haïk 2011).

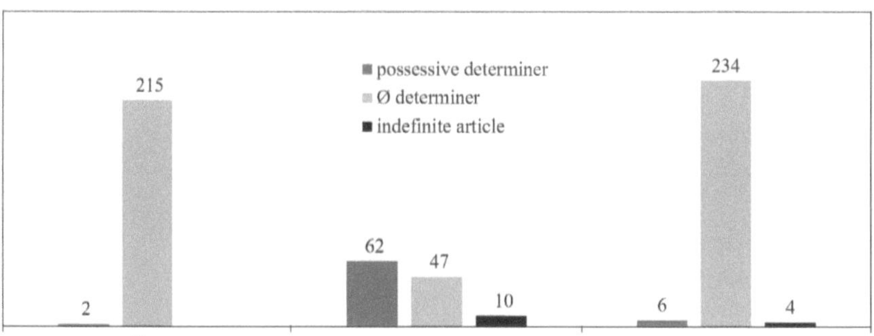

Fig. 7.9: Structural patterns for the ROC verb-specific subschemas with *kiss*, *nod* and *wave*. Based on the delocutive nouns *hello(s)*, *goodbye(s)*, *good-bye*, *thanks*, *thank-you* and *thank you*.

Tab. 7.7: Distribution of ROs in the bare pattern of the ROC verb-specific subschemas with *kiss* and *wave*

	Kiss	*Wave*
Ø goodbye(s), Ø good-bye	204	216
Ø hello	11	16
Ø thanks	0	2
Total	215	234[a]

a I excluded from the count the example below that may allow for two interpretations: the possessive and the bare pattern.

(4) Through the window she searched for Grace, hoping to **wave** her thanks, but she saw only unconscious people sitting on plastic stools at the red Formica counter, sipping coffee, huddled over newspapers, oblivious of the announced magic of this day, unaware of how quickly the past was slipping by, breaking old connections, one by one. (COHA, 1981, FIC, Stroll)

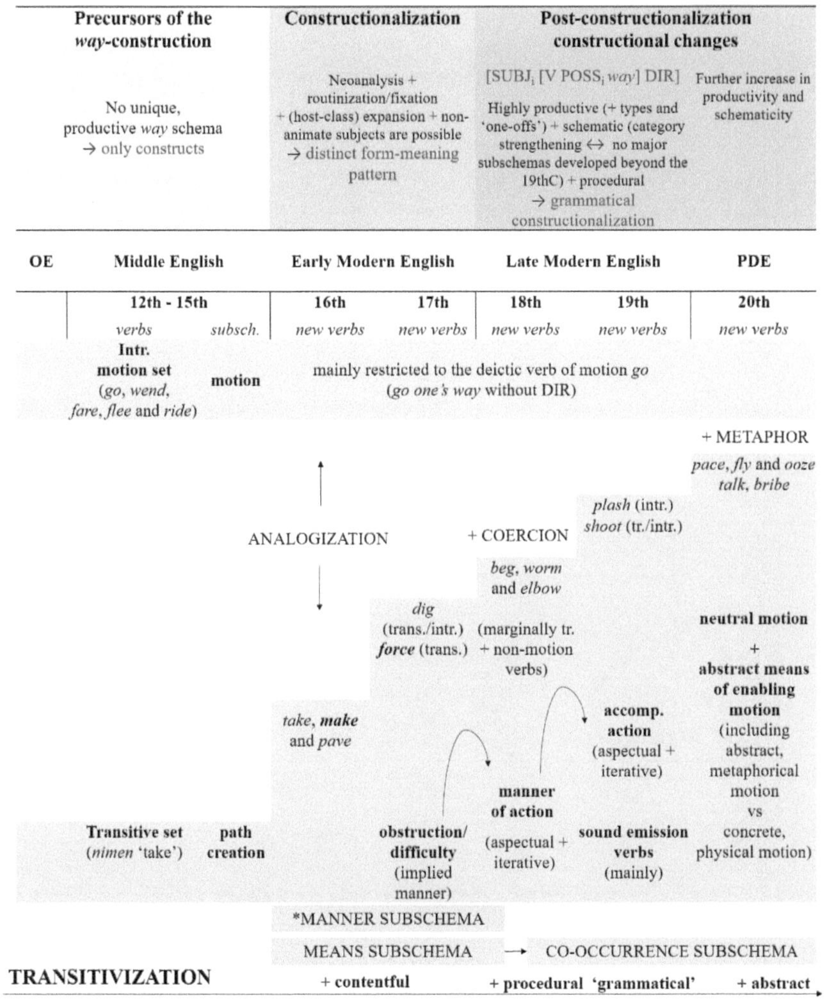

Fig. 7.10: Historical development of the *way*-construction up to the 21st century. Precursors, constructionalization and post-constructionalization constructional changes. Based on insights from Jackendoff (1990), Goldberg (1995), Israel (1996), Gisborne and Patten (2011), Mondorf (2011), Traugott and Trousdale (2013), Barðdal and Gildea (2015), Perek (2016a, 2018, 2020) and Fanego (2019).

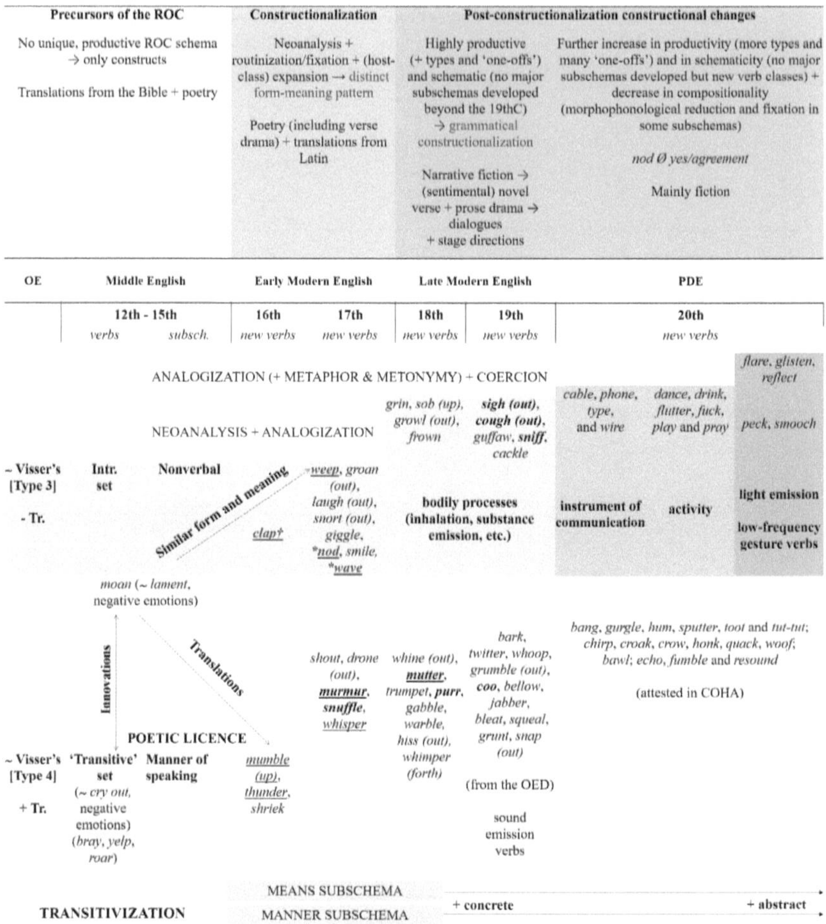

Fig. 7.11: Historical development of the ROC up to the 21st century. Precursors, constructionalization and post-constructionalization constructional changes. Based on historical data from Jespersen (1909–1949: III, §§ 12.1–12.8 and §§ 14.1–14.6), Visser (1963–1973: I, § 133: 100–127), the OED, EEBO (1474–1700), CLMET3.0 (1710–1920) and COHA (1810s-2000s).

8. Summary and conclusion

8.1 The reaction object construction

As repeatedly noted, reaction object constructions (ROCs) such as *She* ***mumbled*** *her adoration* and *Pauline* **smiled** *her thanks* consist of an intransitive verb (*mumble, smile*) followed by a reaction object that expresses an emotion or an attitude (*adoration, thanks*) such that the whole syntactic unit acquires the extended meaning [X_i express Y_i by V-ing] as in 'She expressed her adoration by mumbling' and 'Pauline expressed her thanks by smiling'. These expressive structures have eluded systematic investigation until the last quarter of the twentieth century when a number of linguists started to pay attention to the "strange restrictions" (Ross 1970a) that converted the ROC into a particularly suitable linguistic phenomenon to be addressed from the perspective of Construction Grammar (Goldberg 1995, 2006, 2019). One of the major proponents of this theory, Adele Goldberg, was in fact the first to describe the ROC as a form-meaning pairing when explaining that in structures such as *Pauline smiled her thanks* "the whole is not built up from the lexical items in a straightforward way (. . .) [but] is itself associated with meaning" (Goldberg 1995, 10).

Such characterization of the English ROC was later adopted by Martínez-Vázquez, who published a number of works where she outlined some of the properties of the construction, and studied its frequency and context of occurrence in PDE and Spanish (2010, 2014a, 2014b, 2015, 2016, 2017). Though from a synchronic perspective the English ROC has now received considerable attention (Felser and Wanner 2001, Mateu 2001, 2012, 2014, Mirto 2007, 2012, 2017, Kogusuri 2009b, 2011, Haïk 2011, Bouso 2012 among many others; cf. § 3.2), the situation changes when one examines this construction from a diachronic angle. Only monumental historical grammars such as Jespersen (1909–1949) and F. Th. Visser (1963–1973) mention this linguistic phenomenon, and this just in passing. The former deals with it in a section devoted to objects of result, that is, objects that express what results from the action denoted by the verb, among which he includes some historical instances of ROCs going back to the nineteenth century; while Visser provides some examples of the construction when dealing with the large-scale transitivization process that has affected English verbs since OE times. This monograph attempts to fill this gap in the diachronic study of the ROC by exploring issues such as *when* and *how* the ROC emerges, *how* it develops over time and *what mechanisms of change* (e.g. neoanalysis/reanalysis, analogization/analogy, coercion, metaphor, etc.) and *factors* (intralinguistic and/or extralinguistic) may have propelled its development.

8.2 Summary of the book

In order to accomplish these aims I structured this monograph in two blocks, a theoretical part and an empirical one. Part I, entitled *Transitivization, Reaction Objects and Construction Grammar* consists of three chapters (i.e. Chapters 2–4). In Chapter 2 I explain the process of transitivization of the English language and compare Old and Modern English verb valency (§ 2.1). I also summarize there the causes that led to the sharp difference between these two periods in the number of verbs with transitive and intransitive uses (§ 2.2 and § 2.3). Chapter 3 is devoted to the review of the literature on the reaction object where I first examine the general treatment of the object in historical and contemporary reference grammars (§ 3.1), and secondly the features of reaction objects in relation to other nonprototypical object types such as cognate objects and *way*-objects (§ 3.2). The chapter concludes by putting forward the hypotheses specified in (i) and (ii).

(i) *Hypothesis 1*: This is formulated as follows. In ME the *way*-object did not show its modern formal restrictions as it did not require the coreferential possessive determiner nor the directional that are compulsory in the PDE *way*-construction (e.g. *Bill$_i$ belched his$_i$ way* *out of the restaurant*$_{\text{DIRECTIONAL}}$). More precisely, the ME *way*-object could occur accompanied by a preposition (*ryde on your wey* 'ride on your way'), or an adverb (*she dryueth forth hir weye* 'she drives forth her way'), with a demonstrative (*þane wei he nam* 'that way he took') or article (*went the ways*) and in the plural (*went the ways*) (see Traugott and Trousdale 2013, 80–81), whereas the routinization or fixation of the coreferential possessive determiner and the directional starts to take place in EModE (1500–1700 approx.) (cf. § 3.2.1.2). In Traugott and Trousdale's (2013) words, in EModE there is an increasing preference for "POSS[essive] rather than definite article" (83) and "DIR[ectional] becomes distinctly preferred" (84). Just like *way*-objects, we may hypothesize that the PDE formal restriction of coreferentiality of ROCs, as shown in *She$_i$ mumbled her$_i$ adoration* and *Pauline$_i$ smiled her$_i$ thanks*, also goes back to EModE.

(ii) *Hypothesis 2*: Since the origins of the cognate object construction and the *way*-construction lie in the use of cognate objects and *way*-objects with transitive verbs (Visser 1963–1973: I, § 424: 414–415; Traugott and Trousdale 2013; Lavidas 2018; see § 3.2.1.1 and § 3.2.1.2), we may start from the assumption that reaction objects follow the same path of development as these other transitivizing/valency-increasing constructions, occurring first with more transitive-like verbs and then expanding to intransitives.

The nonprototypical features of reaction objects described in detail in § 3.2.1.3 confirm that they are best discussed within the framework of Construction Grammar. This claims that our *entire* linguistic knowledge consists of a large network of constructions (form-meaning pairings) "*and nothing else in addition*" (Hilpert 2014b, 2; emphasis in the original). Hence the last chapter in Part I (Chapter 4) aims to show how Construction Grammar (Goldberg 1995, 2006, Hilpert 2014b; cf. § 4.1–§ 4.3) – and Diachronic Construction Grammar in particular (Hilpert 2013, Traugott and Trousdale 2013; cf. § 4.4) –, can be used as a heuristic tool to arrive at a better understanding of the *idiosyncratic nature* and *historical development of the ROC*. Regarding the former,

Construction Grammar prompts us to reflect on how we can account for the *nonprototypical features* of reaction objects described in Chapter 3 and more specifically, on the basis of one of the major tenets of this theory (§ 4.3.3), if linguistic knowledge consists *only* of a large network of constructions how the ROC relates to other constructions within the English network of constructions such as, for instance, the highly frequent English ditransitive construction exemplified by *Joe gave Sally the Ball* (cf. § 4.3.3 and § 4.4.2 for a description of the types of relations among constructions). Regarding its historical pathway, I tackled the following research questions: (i) when and how does the ROC become a construction, that is, a *new* form-meaning pairing with its own morpho-syntactic and semantic constraints?, (ii) what constructional changes (i.e. changes in form and/or function, in frequency and distribution) can be identified in its development?, (iii) which of these changes qualify as pre- and post-constructionalization constructional changes?, and (iv) what mechanisms of change (e.g. neoanalysis/reanalysis, analogization, coercion, metaphor, etc.), and (v) factors (intralinguistic and/or extra-linguistic) have played a role in its development (cf. § 4.4)?

The hypotheses in (i) and (ii) outlined above and the research questions mentioned in the previous paragraph (i)-(v) are closely interrelated as they concern the *nature* and *evolution* of the ROC. These were approached empirically in Part II, *Hands-On with Data: A Usage-Based Approach to the History of the ROC* where, on the one hand, I describe the idiosyncratic nature of the modern ROC (§ 5.1.1) and explain how the ROC relates to other constructions within the English network of constructions (§ 5.1.2); and on the other hand, I examine its emergence (§ 5.2) and subsequent development in British and American English (Chapters 6 and 7 respectively). The material used to carry out these investigations were Jespersen and Visser's historical grammars, the *Oxford English Dictionary* (OED), the *Corpus of Late Modern English Texts, version 3.0* (CLMET3.0) and the *Corpus of Historical American English* (COHA). Additionally, I have made use of the *Early English Books Online* (EEBO), FrameNet and Google Books n-grams as secondary sources to confirm specific aspects of the ROC not revealed by the main sources and the methodology adopted. In line with previous investigations on argument structure constructions (see McMillion 2006, Mantlik 2011, Lavidas 2013, van Gelderen 2014, Siemund 2014, among many others), the OED this time again proved to be a valuable resource and a crucial starting point for the historical analysis of the ROC and has determined the path I followed in my subsequent investigation reported on in Chapter 6. In the following paragraphs I will outline the main contributions from these chapters.

In Chapter 5 I offer a detailed characterization of the idiosyncratic nature of the modern ROC (§ 5.1.1), and argue that it qualifies as a *multiple inheritance construction* (see De Smet, Ghesquière, and Van de Velde 2013, Trousdale 2013, and Hilpert 2019) that shares features with several well-established constructions in the English language, namely the experiencer construction (*Bob likes Sue*), the resultative construction (*She kissed him unconscious*), and the ditransitive and communicative constructions (*Joe gave Sally the Ball*; *She wired Jo a message*, respectively) (§ 5.1.2; see in particular Fig. 5.3). On the historical dimension, the data sources consulted as well as the methodology adopted (§ 5.2.1 and § 5.2.2) indicate that the origins of this hybrid construction go back to the LME period (§ 5.2.3). Most importantly, the OED data seems to confirm *Hypothesis 2* above that the ROC followed the same path of development as other transitivizing/valency-increasing constructions such as the cognate object construction and the *way*-construction, occurring first with more transitive-like verbs (e.g. the manner of speaking verbs *bray*, *yelp* and *roar*, and the nonverbal expression verbs *moan* and *weep*), and then, expanding to intransitives, namely verbs of nonverbal expression such as *grin* and *frown*, unergative verbs describing involuntary bodily processes such as *cough* and *sniff*, and modern verbs of sound emission such as *purr* (1620)[64] and *coo* (1672) (cf. § 5.2.3.2, Fig. 5.11 for a representation of the historical development of the *way*-construction and Fig. 5.12 for the historical development of the ROC).

Chapter 6 addresses the development of the ROC in British English during LModE (1710–1920) assessing constructional changes in form, function, frequency and distribution (across verbs, time and text types). The results show that the proliferation of the British ROC took place in the transition from the eighteenth to the nineteenth century

64 In parentheses the date of the first attestation of the verb in the English language according to the OED.

(§ 6.3.2) and is related to the literary language, and to specific text types (§ 6.3.3). In particular, its rise in frequency seems to be connected with the British (sentimental) novel, which arose and developed during this period (Ousby 1988, Head 2006), and with LModE drama to judge from the considerable high number of ROCs embedded in the lyrical verses, dialogues and the stage directions of several plays of the period which, quite importantly, developed "a widely shared theatrical vocabulary, especially from the 1590s on" (Dessen and Thomson 1999, x; Dessen 2009). As for the distribution of the ROC across verbs (§ 6.2 and § 6.3.1), *collexeme analysis* (Stefanowitsch and Gries 2003) reveals that a number of verbs functioned as prototypes promoting the consolidation of the ROC schema during this period (cf. § 6.2.1). At a deeper level of analysis (§ 6.3.1), my LModE data also shows different levels of specificity (or abstractness) of the ROC schema, more abstract ROC verb-specific subschemas formed by the prototypes *mutter* and *murmur*, and lower-level ROC verb-specific subschemas formed by the prototypes *nod* and *wave* which, due to their restricted semantics occurring with a limited number of reaction objects (routines or formulae and deverbal nouns indicating some type of agreement; see § 6.3.1.2.2 and § 6.3.1.2.3) have undergone some morphophonological reduction and fixation in PDE: from *nod/wave* + **a** + reaction object to *nod/wave* + **Ø** + reaction object; as in from *wave* ***a*** *goodbye* to *wave* ***Ø*** *goodbye*; for *nod* see Tab. 6.27 and Tab. 6.28 in § 6.3.1.2.5; and for *wave* see Tab. 6.29 in § 6.3.1.2.5 and Fig. 7.9 in § 7.3). From a methodological point of view, one relevant aspect of this diachronic corpus-based study is that it follows a *bottom-up approach*, among other reasons to provide an answer to *Hypothesis 1* above concerning the formal restriction of coreferentiality of the ROC described in detail in Chapter 3 (Tab. 3.8 in § 3.2.1.3). Since in my LModE data there is an overwhelming preference for coreferential ROCs – those where the reaction object is coreferential with the subject, whether covertly or overtly expressed, as in *She*$_i$ *mumbled her*$_i$ *adoration* and *Pauline*$_i$ *smiled her*$_i$ *thanks* vs *The soldiers chanted his victory* and *his Majesty nods my pardon* –, I assumed that the formal restriction of coreferentiality most likely starts to develop in EModE (1500–1700), as was also the case with the *way*-construction, in Traugott and Trousdale's (2013) account. In addition to this, during EModE intransitive verbs of gestures such as *weep* (= 'shed tears over'), *clap, nod* and *wave* that used to occur with a dative/instrumental object in Old English as in *he ongan wepan hluttrum tearum* 'he began to weep [with] pure tears' (c900), or a prepositional/instrumental object in later periods, as in *with hondes clap* (?c1350), *noddynge wyth the heed* (c1440) and *with her wynges she waveth* (1526), start to be *neoanalysed* as transitives as shown in the following early examples with *clap, nod* and *wave*: *clapping their hands* (1593), *noddes their hedde* (1553), and *waue their wings* (1584–1587).[65] Like the ROC, these transitive structures involving an NP instrumental object also show the coreferentiality constraint (Massam 1990, 180; Jackendoff 1990, 216; see also Ross 1970b), and what is even more interesting, the earliest ROCs attested with these transitivized gesture verbs in my data also go back to the EModE period (in order of appearance in my data): *He*$_i$ *... clap him good lucke*$_i$ (1591), *Ile*$_i$ *weepe my passion*$_i$ 'I'll weep my passion' (1602), *that haire*$_i$ *wav'd its pride*$_i$ (1639) and *a man*$_i$ *may nod a lie*$_i$ (1660). This finding could be interpreted as an additional hint in support of the assumption that EModE is the key period in the development of the formal restriction of coreferentiality both in the ROC and in the *way*-construction (for specific details on the *way*-construction see § 3.2.1.2 and § 5.2.3.2).

Chapter 7 moves on in time with the subsequent development of the ROC in American English from the 1810s to the 2000s, and examines further constructional changes regarding the frequency, distribution, form and function of the ROC. This chapter is structured around two research questions that are prompted by my findings in Chapters 5 and 6. The first of these questions asks whether the ROC is a British innovation that later spread to American English, where the ROC has been shown to be relatively high frequent and productive nowadays (Martínez-Vázquez 2010, 2014a, 2015) (cf. § 7.2). My results indicate that this is probably the case, since most of the ROCs extracted from COHA belong to the genre of fiction and the period when the American ROC ranks lowest in token frequency (1810–1849) coincides with the

65 The examples involving dative/prepositional and NP instrumental objects have been taken from Jespersen (1909–1949, III: 238; examples with *weep*) and Visser (1963–1973: § 425, I: 418–419; examples with *clap, nod* and *wave*). Date of attestation in parentheses.

heyday of the British ROC (1780–1849); to this, it should be added that the American sentimental novel developed later in time than the British sentimental novel (Samuels 1992, 2012). As for the second research question, this asks whether there are further parallelisms regarding the development of the ROC and the *way*-construction after their simultaneous consolidation over the LModE period (cf. § 7.3). Like the *way*-construction, the ROC not only increases its productivity over the course of the twentieth century but also its schematicity, as it attracted new verb classes such as novel verbs of instrument of communication (e.g. *wire*, *cable* and *phone*), verbs of activity (e.g. *dance*, *drink*, *flutter* and *play*), and verbs of light emission (e.g. *flare*, *glisten* and *reflect*) (Figs. 7.7 and 7.8). Another relevant finding presented in this chapter is the confirmation that modern intransitive verbs of sound emission such as *purr* (1620)[66] and *coo* (1672) constitute one explanatory factor for the simultaneous consolidation of the ROC and the *way*-construction during the LModE period. In my data from COHA (1810s-2000s) these verbs turn out to be one of the major sources of innovation of the ROC (cf. Fig. 7.6 and Tab. 7.5). Similarly, in Perek's data (2016a, 2018) for the *way*-construction this verb class is responsible for the subsequent increase in frequency of its co-occurrence subschema (e.g. *he **whistled** his way across the room = he went across the room whistling*) over the course of the twentieth century (see Figs. 7.5 and 7.7 and comments therein). In light of the results presented in this empirical part, the history of the ROC could be outlined as described in the following section.

8.3 Writing the history of the ROC: A proposal of when, how and why the ROC develops

The roots of the ROC lie in the LME period when originally intransitive verbs of manner of action such as *moan*, *bray*, *yelp* and *roar* start taking

66 In parentheses the date of the first attestation of the verb in the English language according to the OED.

reaction objects describing negative emotions: *monen his sinfulhed* 'moan his sinfulness' (= 'the state or character of being sinful'; OED, s.v. *sinfulness*, n.), *bray þy braþez breme* 'cry out/bray your terrible agony', *ȝelpe his sorwe* 'yelp his sorrow' and *rore his sikis* 'roar its [the heart] suffering'. The earliest recorded example of ROC involves the verb *moan*. This is a transitive verb formed by conversion (cf. OED, s.v. *moan*, v. 1. trans. a.) which used to occur with the transitivizing prefix *be-* (*bemoan*) when used transitively and without it when used intransitively (Visser 1963–1973: I, § 144: 134–135; see also Marchand 1969, 146–147; cf. § 2.3.1.1). The next gesture verbs attested in the ROC in my data are the verbs *clap* and *weep* in the ROCs *clap him good lucke* (1591) and *weepe my passion* 'weep my passion' (1602), respectively. The verb *weep*, apart from showing the same transitive/intransitive alternation as *moan* (e.g. *moan* and *bemoan*; *weep* and *beweep*), when used intransitively without the transitivizing prefix *be-*, like the gesture verb *clap*, could also occur with the so-called dative/instrumental object as in *he ongan wepan hluttrum tearum* 'he began to weep [with] pure tears' (cf. OED, s.v. *weep*, v. I. intr. 1. a.; see § 2.3.2 and § 3.1.1.1). This is in my view quite a relevant feature as it may have helped to pave the way to the next generation of gesture verbs attested in the ROC in EModE. These are the transitivized gesture verbs *wave* (*that haire*$_i$ *wav'd its pride*$_i$ (1639)) and *nod* (*a man*$_i$ *may nod a lie*$_i$ (1660)) which – like *clap* in *with hondes clap* (?c1350) and *weep* in *he ongan wepan hluttrum tearum* 'he began to weep [with] pure tears' (c900) – also used to hold an instrumental object as shown in *with her wynges she waveth* 'she waves with her wings' (1526) and *noddynge wyth the heed* 'nodding with the head' (c1440). As when the gesture verbs *wave* and *nod* were later neoanalysed as transitives these verbs were primarily restricted to coreferential object types (e.g. *waue their wings* 'wave their wings' (1584–1587) and *noddes their hedde* 'nod their heads' (1553)), EModE can be considered the period when the ROC develops its coreferentiality constraint. Finally, it should be mentioned here that during EModE a number of manner of speaking verbs such as *mumble*, *thunder* and *whisper* also entered the ROC via Latin translations from Erasmus and Virgil's works (see examples (4), (5) and (11) in Tab. 5.8).

To sum up these first stages in the historical development of the ROC, the EModE features of the ROC just described – these concerning the development of the coreferentiality constraint of the ROC and the incorporation of new manner of speaking verbs to the ROC schema via Latin translations – lead us to think of EModE as the period when the ROC becomes a construction or a *new* form-meaning pairing with its own morphosyntactic and semantic constraints as represented in (1). These constraints have been described in detail in § 5.1.2 (constraints (i)-(v)), and two of them are the ones just mentioned: (i) the coreferentiality constraint indicated in (1) in the subscript $_i$, and (ii) the means and manner interpretations of the ROC signalled in (1) in the subscript $_{manner/means}$. The means interpretation of the ROC is mainly accounted for by verbs of gestures such as *weep*, *clap*, *wave* and *nod* in the ROCs *weepe <u>my passion</u>* 'weep my passion' (1602), *clap him <u>good lucke</u>* (1591), *wav'd <u>its pride</u>* (1639) and *nod <u>a lie</u>* (1660), which carry the meaning 'Sentient agent$_i$ cause Y$_i$ become expressed by$_{means}$ *weeping/clapping/waving/nodding*'. On the other hand, the manner interpretation of the ROC (i.e. ['Sentient agent$_i$ cause Y$_i$ become expressed by$_{manner}$ doing V']) is represented, for instance, by manner of speaking verbs such as *mumble* and *thunder* in the ROCs *momblest vp <u>thy prayer</u>* 'mumble up your prayer' (1534) and *thunder <u>sore threatenings</u>* (1548).

(1) **Syntax:** SUBJ$_i$ [V$_{INTRmanner/means}$ (OBJ1) OBJ2$_i$]. Where OBJ2 = (POSS)$_i$ NP
Semantics: 'Sentient agent$_i$ cause Y$_i$ become expressed while/by$_{manner/means}$ doing V'

From the ideas presented above, it can be tentatively assumed that the process of constructionalization or coming into being of the ROC over the course of the EModE period was quite similar to that of the *way*-construction (Traugott and Trousdale 2013, 76–93), as the constructionalization of the *way*-construction was also accompanied by a number of 'pre-constructionalization constructional changes' such as (i) *neoanalysis*, (ii) *routinization* or *fixation*, and (iii) *host-class expansion*. To be more precise, in Traugott and Trousdale's theory of language change, 'pre-constructionalization constructional changes' like the ones just mentioned are changes that accompany constructionalization or the creation of a *new* form-meaning pairing. In their own words, these changes "precede and enable or 'feed' constructionalization", and typically involve "expansion of pragmatics [through host-class expansion], semanticization of that pragmatics [through conventionalization, routinization or fixation], mismatch between form and meaning [through neoanalysis/reanalysis], and some small distributional changes" (Traugott and Trousdale 2013, 27).

As mentioned in § 5.2.3.2, in the case of the *way*-construction the 'pre-constructionalization constructional changes' that enable its constructionalization during EModE are: **(i)** the ***neoanalysis*** of *way* as a complement of the motion verb *go* (i.e. the interpretation of *way* as a fake object in *go one's way* possibly by analogy with the transitive acquisition subschema verb + POSS + *way*, which involves transitive acquisition verbs such as *nimen* 'take' and *take* as in *þane wei he nam* 'that way he took'), **(ii)** the ***routinization or fixation*** of the coreferential possessive determiner and the directional which are compulsory in the PDE *way*-construction (e.g. *Bill*$_i$ *belched his*$_i$ *way out of the restaurant*-$_{\text{DIRECTIONAL}}$), and **(iii)** the ***host-class expansion*** of the *way*-construction to new verbs such as *make* and *pave*, and some other verbs denoting obstruction such as *force* in *a dozen of them*$_i$ *went into the Kitchin, forcing their way*$_i$ *against all the Bolts and Locks.*

As for the ROC, the 'pre-constructionalization constructional changes' that enable its constructionalization in EModE are: **(i)** the ***neoanalysis*** of the originally intransitive verbs of gestures *weep*, *clap*, *wave* and *nod* as transitives (e.g. from *he ongan wepan hluttrum tearum* 'he began to weep [with] pure tears' (c900) to *weep pure tears* and *weepe my passion* (1602); from *with hondes clap* (?c1350) to *clapping their hands* (1593) and *clap him good lucke* (1591); from *with her wynges she waveth* 'she waves with her wings' (1526) to *waue their wings* 'wave their wings' (1584–1587) and *that haire wav'd its pride* (1639); and from *noddynge wyth the heed* 'nodding with the head' (c1440) to *noddes their hedde* 'nod their heads' (1553) and *a man*$_i$ *may nod a lie* (1660)); **(ii)** the ***routinization*** **or** ***fixation*** of its formal restriction of coreferentiality, as mentioned above these verbs of gestures only seem to allow for coreferential object types (i.e. instrumental or reaction objects); and **(iii)** the ***host-class expansion*** of the ROC schema during this period (EModE) to other intransitive verbs such as the verbs of gestures *smile* in *smile a lie* (1660), and *giggle* in *giggle applause* (a1657), and the manner of speaking verbs *shout* in *shouting their emulation* (a1616) and *murmur* in *murmur'd soft applause* (1637), two of which (i.e. the verbs *smile* and *murmur*) will become part of the set of prototypes of the LModE ROC (see § 6.2.1.2).

After the constructionalization of the ROC schema in EModE, my historical data from CLMET3.0 indicates that the ROC considerably increases its frequency during the LModE period (1710–1920) mainly due to a number of intralinguistic and extralinguistic factors such as (i) the boom of intransitive verbs of sound emission in the Modern period (Fanego 2017; see Fig. 5.10), many of which came to be used metonymically as manner of speaking verbs as in *the audience roared* *__their approval__* (Martínez-Vázquez 2014a, 176), (ii) the proliferation of other transitivizing/valency-increasing constructions such as the cognate object construction (Lavidas 2013, 2014, 2018), the *way*-construction (Israel 1996, Traugott and Trousdale 2013), and the dummy *it* object construction (Mondorf 2016), and (iii) the rise in the mid-eighteenth century of the British novel (Carter and McRae 1996, 78). Crucially, the British sentimental novel aimed at describing the emotions and affective relations of characters and made extensive use of verbs of gestures and sounds to introduce the words of characters (Ousby 1988, 888–889; Ruano San Segundo 2016, 2017, 2018a, 2018b) (cf. § 2.3.5, § 6.3.3.2 and § 6.3.4).

Once the ROC propagated and consolidated in LModE (1710–1920), like the *way*-construction (Perek 2016a, 2018), over the course of the nineteenth and twentieth centuries, it kept on undergoing further constructional changes. More specifically, the ROC during this period (1810s-2000s) increased its productivity and schematicity and also fixed some of its constructs with Ø determiners (e.g. *nod Ø yes/agreement*, *kiss Ø goodbye*, *wave Ø goodbye*). Note that I treat this fixation with Ø determiners as cases of morphophonological reduction as, according to my data, the presence of the indefinite article used to be a common feature of ROCs in LModE which provided the reaction object its unambiguous nominal status (e.g. *nodded* ***an*** *affirmative*, *wave* ***a*** *farewell*). As for its increase in productivity and schematicity over the course of the nineteenth and twentieth centuries, the ROC expanded via *analogization* to very low-frequency or weakly established verbs of gestures such as *peck* and *smooch* (e.g. *She pecked him* *__good-bye__*), and via *coercion* to verbs of bodily processes (e.g. the verb of substance emission *cough* and the verb of inhalation *sniff*), to modern verbs of sound emission (e.g. the onomatopoeic verb *coo*), to newly formed verbs of instrument of communication (e.g. *wire*, *cable* and *phone*) and, more strikingly, to other verbs completely unrelated to the act of communication such as verbs of activity (e.g. *dance*, *drink*, *flutter* and *play*) and verbs of light emission (e.g. *flare*, *glisten* and *reflect*) which require a more *metaphorical* interpretation (e.g. *The stars fired up, and one, falling, flared* <u>*its good-bye*</u>).

As previously mentioned, the changes just described (i.e. increase in frequency during the LModE period, and over the course of the nineteenth and twentieth centuries increase in productivity and schematicity as well as morphophonological reduction and fixation of some constructs), affected the ROC after its constructionalization in EModE (1500–1700 approx.). These changes are known in Traugott and Trousdale's (2013) theory of constructionalization as 'post-constructionalization constructional changes'. In their own words, these are changes that follow or are fed by constructionalization and they "involve expansion of collocations [that is, increase in productivity, this understood as "extensibility" or "occurring with new items" (Barðdal 2008; Haspelmath 2002, 98); the expansion of collocations is sometimes accompanied by an increase in schematicity if these new items represent new verb classes], and may also involve morphological and phonological reduction" (Traugott and Trousdale 2013, 27; see § 4.4.1). Finally, it is worth mentioning that the ROC could also have acquired a more procedural ('grammatical') meaning over time. More specifically, like the *way*-construction in examples such as *he whistled his way across the room* (= *he went across the room whistling*) and *she giggled her way up the stairs* (= *she went up the stairs giggling*), when the ROC involves certain verbs of bodily processes (e.g. *pant*) and verbs of sound emission (e.g. *giggle*), it may also imply iteration. This is shown in the following correspondences with the verbs *pant* and *giggle*: *a reeking Post,..halfe breathles,* ***panting forth*** *. . . salutations* (= *half breathless the reeking post expressed his salutations* <u>*panting/with a pant*</u>) and *I* ***giggled*** *a hello* (= *I expressed a hello* <u>*giggling/with a giggle*</u>).

As a summary of the ideas presented in this section, I refer the reader to Fig. 7.11 (§ 7.3) from Chapter 7 that shows the proposed historical development of the ROC just outlined: (i) the **precursors** in LME with the originally intransitive verbs *moan*, *bray*, *yelp* and *roar*, (ii) the **constructionalization** of the ROC in EModE via the *neoanalysis* as transitives of originally intransitive verbs of gestures taking instrumental objects (i.e. *weep*, *clap*, *wave* and *nod*), the *routinization* or *fixation* of its formal restriction of coreferentiality, and the *host-class expansion* of the ROC through *analogization* to other semantically similar verbs to the ones already attested in LME (e.g. the verbs of gestures *smile* and *giggle*, and the manner of speaking verbs *shout* and *murmur*), and finally, (iii) the subsequent **'post-constructionalization constructional changes'** of the ROC up until the twenty-first century, these involving its increase in frequency during LModE, and over the course of the nineteenth and twentieth centuries, the increase in productivity and schematicity of the ROC expanding to new verb types and classes (unergative verbs describing involuntary bodily processes, modern verbs of sound emission, novel verbs of instrument of communication, verbs of activity and verbs of light emission), and the morphophonological reduction and fixation of some of its constructs (e.g. *nod Ø yes/agreement*, *kiss Ø goodbye* and *wave Ø goodbye*).

8.4 Theoretical implications and suggestions for further research

The history of the English reaction object construction outlined above on the basis of diachronic data used in this monograph by no means intends to be conclusive; surely more insights will be gained by complementing these corpus-based studies with further data and exploring aspects such as those described below.

First, the data presented for ME (1100–1500) and EModE (1500–1700) is based on Visser (1963–1973: I, § 133: 100–127), the OED, and on two comprehensive searches conducted in EEBO (1474–1700) for the gesture verbs *nod* (four ROCs in approx. 2,000 tokens) and *wave* (one ROC in approx. 9,000 tokens). Thus, a more comprehensive study that explores the frequency in the ROC of other verbs, as well as the distribution, form and function of the ROC during ME and EModE could serve to confirm empirically the claim made here that the precursors of the ROC lie indeed in LME, and that during EModE the

ROC becomes a distinct form-meaning pattern with its own morpho-syntactic and semantic constraints shown in (1) above, and repeated in (2) below for the sake of clarity. As repeatedly noted, the development of the formal restriction of coreferentiality, and the means and manner interpretations of the ROC seem to go back to EModE with the incorporation into the ROC of (i) some transitivized gesture verbs that only seem to allow for coreferential object types (i.e. *weep*, *clap*, *wave* and *nod*), and via Latin translations of (ii) manner of speaking verbs such as *mumble* and *thunder* that require a manner interpretation of the ROC (['Sentient agent$_i$ cause Y$_i$ become expressed by$_{manner}$ doing V']) rather than a means interpretation (['Sentient agent$_i$ cause Y$_i$ become expressed by$_{means}$ doing V']). See examples in (3) and (4) for early ROCs showing the means and the manner interpretations, respectively.

(2) **Syntax:** SUBJ$_i$ [V$_{INTRmanner/means}$ (OBJ1) OBJ2$_i$]. Where OBJ2 = (POSS)$_i$ NP
Semantics: 'Sentient agent$_i$ cause Y$_i$ become expressed while/by$_{manner/means}$ doing V'

(3) *Means interpretation*: ['Sentient agent$_i$ cause Y$_i$ become expressed by$_{means}$ doing V']
a. EModE *weepe my passion* 'weep [= shedding tears] my passion' (1602)

(4) *Manner interpretation*: ['Sentient agent$_i$ cause Y$_i$ become expressed by$_{manner}$ doing V']
a. EModE *momblest vp thy prayer* 'mumble up your prayer' (1534)
b. EModE *thunder sore threatenings* (1548)

Second, the bottom-up corpus-based study for the LModE (1710–1920) period using CLMET3.0, though quite comprehensive, does not take into account all the verbs mentioned by Levin (1993) for the reasons specified in § 6.1 (i.e. attestation in the OED and heterogeneity). Therefore, future investigations could complement this study by (a) analysing the remaining verbs, and semantically related verb classes mentioned by Levin (1993) such as the whole set of verbs of sounds made by animals, verbs of sound emission, and verbs of bodily processes; and (b) updating Levin's lists of verbs by retrieving new semantically similar verbs from the *Historical Thesaurus of the Oxford English Dictionary* (HTOED; cf. Fanego 2012, Miura 2015). Also, since the genre of drama is clearly underrepresented in CLMET3.0 (1,362,779 words for drama against the 15,784,689 words for narrative fiction; see Tab. 6.3

in § 6.1), and this seems to have played some role in the development of the ROC (cf. Fig. 6.8 in § 6.3.3.1 for details), it could also be useful to check other databases such as *Chadwyck-Healey Literature Collections Online*, in particular *English Drama 1280–1915* and *American Drama 1714–1915*. As mentioned above in § 8.2, in my LModE data there is a considerable high number of ROCs embedded in the lyrical verses, dialogues and the stage directions of several plays of the LModE period (cf. § 6.3.3.1 for details). Thus, one research question that seems to be worth pursuing in this field is how the change from verse to prose in English drama (1660–1800; see Alden 1909), as well as the development of "a widely shared theatrical vocabulary [in the stage directions of English drama (1580–1642)]" (Dessen and Thomson 1999, x; see also Dessen 2009) affected the overall historical development of the ROC, especially in the transition from Early to Late Modern English.

Finally, the corpus-based study conducted in Chapter 7, using COHA, focuses on the frequency and productivity of the ROC in American English from the 1810s to the 2000s but only takes into account a set of a subtype of delocutive reaction objects, i.e. the routines or formulae *hello(s)*, *goodbye(s)*, *good-bye*, *thanks*, *thank-you* and *thank you*, mainly because they show a greater degree of flexibility, freely occurring with verbs of manner of speaking and verbs of nonverbal communication (see § 6.3.1). This leaves for further research other types of delocutive nouns (e.g. interjections), and also deverbal illocutionary nouns (e.g. *acquiesce* in *the Chief Justice smiled <u>acquiescence</u>* and *assent* in *Tristram nodded <u>assent</u>*), predicative expressive nouns (e.g. *discontent* in *Dumouriez growls ominous <u>discontent</u>* and *disdain* in *the poor animals snort <u>disdain</u>*), and emotional abstract nouns (*sweetness* and *blessedness* in *She smiled ineffable <u>Sweetness</u> and <u>Blessedness</u>*). Last, the data from American English presented in this chapter suggests that the ROC has been a British innovation that subsequently spread to the American variety either due directly to British influence or just simply as a result of the later development of the American sentimental novel, by comparison with the British sentimental novel (Ousby 1988, Samuels 1992, 2012, Head 2006). Though it is quite plausible that the development of the ROC in American English takes place later than in British English, as mentioned above, and also more explicitly in § 7.2, (a) not enough data has been collected for this English variety, (b) nor it has been possible yet to conduct a detailed study of the American ROC considering its distribution across different novels and authors. In this regard, De Smet's *Corpus of English Novels* (26,227,428 words; 1881–1922; CEN) seems to be a suitable corpus to keep on exploring the most likely later development of the American ROC, and the several reasons for this being the case such as, for instance, the nineteenth century development of the American sentimental novel, changes in authors' particular styles, extravagance (Haspelmath 1999), and other interceding factors that still await to be discovered. Results that confirm this line of development of the ROC would provide support to the view that particular text types may evoke a specific linguistic phenomenon, leading us to consider, in this particular case, the sentimental novel as part of the meaning pole of the LModE ROC (Hilpert p.c. 2018). This would, in fact, fit in well within Goldberg's (2019, 7) new definition of constructions, in which context is key.

Overall, however, this monograph hopes to have made the best possible use of "bad" (Labov 1994, 11), "imperfect" data (Janda and Joseph 2003, 14) and to have attained some insights into the idiosyncratic nature and historical development of the reaction object construction from the perspective of Construction Grammar (Goldberg 1995, 2006, Hilpert 2013, 2019, Traugott and Trousdale 2013), used here as a tool for both theoretical description and historical analysis. Some comments have been made in Chapter 6 (§ 6.3.4) regarding the levels of specificity of the ROC in Late Modern British English. Following Barðdal (2008, 6), Traugott and Trousdale (2013, 14) and Hilpert (2018, 2019), I see these levels of specificity (i.e. schemas, subschemas and constructs) *primarily* as units of linguistic description rather than mental representations of particular individuals. In Traugott and Trousdale's words (2013), "[i]n our view schemas and subschemas [also constructs] are the *subparts of the linguistic system that the linguist picks out for discussion and analysis. They are not meant to be mental representations*, though nothing prevents there being an overlap between such representations and linguists' categories" (2013, 14; emphasis mine). I take Traugott and Trousdale's sensitive standpoint mainly because – contrary to other linguistic phenomena such as the LModE ditransitive construction (Wolk et al. 2013) – the ROC during this period was a low-frequency structure restricted to specific text types such as novels, drama and poetry. The *marginal* status the ROC had in LModE has changed in PDE, since in the present day the ROC is no doubt more productive and schematic allowing a greater degree of variability. This new status of the PDE ROC becomes a much more promising scenario for experimental type of research (see Barðdal 2008, Perek 2015a, Perek and Hilpert 2016, Ungerer 2019), and make more solid claims regarding (i) the cognitive reality of the ROC (i.e. its mental representation) and its levels of specificity or abstraction (i.e. schemas, subschemas and constructs) (Barðdal 2008, 101–136), (ii) its interconnections with other constructions and its interpretations – *subpart links* and *polysemy links* using the terminology of Construction Grammar –, and (iii) also its degree of acceptability or "tolerance" (Perek and Hilpert 2016) among speakers of English, and other Germanic (and non-Germanic) languages where this construction – except for Spanish and French – remains, to the best of my knowledge, unexplored (cf. § 3.2).

Leaving aside the *cognitive nature* of the ROC, and focusing now more on its *historical dimension* and how it fits within the English language system, this monograph has shown that the reaction object construction is clearly part of the large-scale process of transitivization of English verbs that Visser originally unearthed, and that has recently caught the attention of Mondorf (2011, 2016), Eitelmann and Mondorf (2018), and Lavidas (2009, 2013, 2014, 2018), who mainly focused on the competition between the *way*-construction and reflexive structures (e.g. *She worked her way to the top* vs. *She worked herself to the top*; Mondorf 2011), on the dummy *it* object construction (e.g. *Snake legs it to freedom*; Mondorf 2016), and the aspectual cognate object construction (e.g. *She smiled an enigmatic smile*; Lavidas 2018). More specifically, this monograph has shown striking parallelisms between the ROC and these three transitivizing/valency-increasing constructions; all of them (i) occur with low-frequency, or weakly established verbs, such as verbs of gestures (e.g. *peck* and *smooch*), unergative verbs describing involuntary bodily processes (e.g. *cough* and *sniff*), modern verbs of sound emission (e.g. *purr* and *coo*), or adjective/noun to verb conversions (e.g. the deadjectival verb *rough* in *rough it* and the denominal verb *king* in *king it*), and (ii) all of them acquire more prominence in ModE (Israel 1996, Traugott and Trousdale 2013, Mondorf 2016, Lavidas 2018). These investigations concerning transitivization and, on a broader level, the ongoing state of flux in verbs' argument structure throughout the history of English should not be neglected by advocates of Construction Grammar who could complement them by revisiting Visser's list of transitivized verbs, and analysing, for instance, the history of *other unexplored transitivizing structures* such as the superlative object construction (e.g. *She worked* <u>*her hardest*</u>; cf. Tab. 3.1 in § 3.1.1.1). Similar findings to the ones presented here for these neglected phenomena would contribute to the characterization of ModE as the enlightening era of resultative constructions.

List of Figures

List of Tables

Summary

This monograph deals with the characterization and diachronic development of the so-called English reaction object construction (ROC; Levin 1993, 98), as in *She mumbled her adoration* and *The door jingled a welcome*. The ROC consists of an originally intransitive verb – particularly manner of speaking verbs such as *mumble*, but also verbs of gestures and sounds such as *smile* and *jingle* – followed by a nonprototypical object that expresses a reaction or an attitude of some kind (*adoration*, *welcome*). The result of this syntactic amalgam is a valency-increasing construction whose overall extended meaning is "express, communicate, signal X by V-ing", as in 'She expressed/communicated her adoration by mumbling' and 'The door expressed/signalled a welcome by jingling'. The theoretical framework adopted to account for the idiosyncratic nature of these expressive structures as well as their historical development is that of Construction Grammar and its application to language change (Goldberg 1995, 2006, Hilpert 2013, Traugott and Trousdale 2013). From a methodological perspective, this first historical study on the ROC relies on a number of complementary historical sources that address the different stages in the evolution of the construction. The hypothesis is put forward that ROCs are part and result of the large-scale process of transitivization that has affected English since OE times (Visser, 1963–1973: I, §§ 132–144). Thus ROCs follow a similar historical pathway as other transitivizing constructions such as the cognate object construction (*The hart lept a great leap*) and the *way*-construction (*She giggled her way up the stairs*), which occurred first with transitive verbs and then expanded to intransitives (cf. Visser, 1963–1973: I, § 424 (b); Traugott and Trousdale 2013; Lavidas 2018). The results confirm this idea, and they also reveal striking parallels in the development of the ROC and the *way*-construction.

List of References

Dictionaries

B&T = Bosworth, Joseph, and T. Northcote Toller, eds. 1882–1898. With supplements by Toller 1908–1921 and Alistair Campbell 1972. *An Anglo-Saxon Dictionary*. Oxford: Oxford University Press. http://bosworth.ff.cuni.cz/.

HTOED = Kay, Christian, Jane Roberts, Michael Samuels, and Irené Wotherspoon, eds. 2009. *Historical Thesaurus of the Oxford English Dictionary*. Oxford: Oxford University Press. http://public.oed.com/historical-thesaurus-of-the-oed/.

MED = Kurath, Hans, Sherman M. Kuhn, and Robert E. Lewis, eds. 1952–2001. *Middle English Dictionary*. Ann Arbor: University of Michigan Press. http://quod.lib.umich.edu/m/med/.

OED = Simpson, John A., ed. 2000-. *Oxford English Dictionary Online*. Oxford: Oxford University Press. http://www.oed.com/.

Corpora

BNC = *The British National Corpus*, version 3 (BNC XML Edition). 2007. Distributed by Oxford University Computing Services on behalf of the BNC Consortium. http://www.natcorp.ox.ac.uk/.

CEN = De Smet, Hendrik. 2008. *Corpus of English Novels (CEN)*. Katholieke Universiteit Leuven: https://perswww.kuleuven.be/~u0044428/.

CLMET = De Smet, Hendrik. 2005. *Corpus of Late Modern English Texts (CLMET)*. Katholieke Universiteit Leuven: https://perswww.kuleuven.be/~u0044428/.

CLMET-EV = De Smet, Hendrik. 2006. *Corpus of Late Modern English Texts (extended version) (CLMET-EV)*. Katholieke Universiteit Leuven: https://perswww.kuleuven.be/~u0044428/.

CLMET3.0 = De Smet, Hendrik, Hans-Jürgenand Diller, and Jukka Tyrkkö. 2011. *Corpus of Late Modern English Texts, version 3.0 (CLMET3.0)*. Katholieke Universiteit Leuven: https://perswww.kuleuven.be/~u0044428/.

COCA = Davies, Mark. 2008-. *The Corpus of Contemporary American English (COCA): 520 million words, 1990-present*. http://corpus.byu.edu/coca/.

COHA = Davies, Mark. 2010-. *The Corpus of Historical American English (COHA): 400 million words, 1810–2009*. https://www.english-corpora.org/coha/.

DOE Web Corpus = Healey, Antonette diPaolo, John Price Wilkin, and Xin Xiang. 2009. *Dictionary of Old English Web Corpus*. Toronto: Dictionary of Old English Project. http://tapor.library.utoronto.ca/doecorpus/.

EEBO = Petré, Peter. 2013. *EEBOCorp 1.0*. Katholieke Universiteit Leuven: https://lirias.kuleuven.be/handle/123456789/416330.

HC = Rissanen, Matti, Merja Kytö, Leena Kahlas-Tarkka, Matti Kilpiö, Saara Nevanlinna, Irma Taavitsainen, Terttu Nevalainen, and Helena Raumolin-Brunberg. 1991. *The Helsinki Corpus of English Texts*. University of Helsinki: http://www.helsinki.fi/varieng/CoRD/corpora/HelsinkiCorpus/.

PPCEME = Kroch, Anthony, Beatrice Santorini, and Lauren Delfs. 2004. *The Penn-Helsinki Parsed Corpus of Early Modern English* (PPCEME). Philadelphia: University of Pennsylvania. CD-ROM, 1st ed: http://www.ling.upenn.edu/hist-corpora/.

PPCMBE = Kroch, Anthony, Beatrice Santorini, and Ariel Diertani. 2010. *The Penn-Helsinki Parsed Corpus of Modern British English* (PPCMBE). Philadelphia: University of Pennsylvania. CD-ROM, 1st ed: http://www.ling.upenn.edu/hist-corpora/.

PPCME2 = Kroch, Anthony, and Ann Taylor. 2000. *The Penn-Helsinki Parsed Corpus of Middle English* (PPCME2). Philadelphia: University of Pennsylvania. CD-ROM, 2nd ed: http://www.ling.upenn.edu/hist-corpora/.

YCOE = Taylor, Ann, Anthony Warner, Susan Pintzuk, and Frank Beths. 2003. *The York-Toronto-Helsinki Parsed Corpus of Old English Prose* (YCOE). University of York. Oxford Text Archive, 1st ed: http://www-users.york.ac.uk/~lang22/YcoeHome1.htm.

Online sources

Byram-Wigfield, Ben. 2006. William's vision of *Piers Plowman*. Accessed August 20, 2020. http://www.ancientgroove.co.uk/books/Piers_Plowman.pdf.

Chadwyck-Healey Literature Collections Online. *American Drama 1714–1915*. (1, 500 dramatic works). Accessed August 20, 2020. http://collections.chadwyck.co.uk/.

Chadwyck-Healey Literature Collections Online. *Eighteenth-Century Fiction 1700–1780*. (96 complete works of English prose by writers from the British Isles). Accessed August 20, 2020. http://collections.chadwyck.co.uk/.

Chadwyck-Healey Literature Collections Online. *English Drama 1280–1915*. (3, 900 plays in verse and prose). Accessed August 20, 2020. http://collections.chadwyck.co.uk/.

Chadwyck-Healey Literature Collections Online. *Nineteenth-Century Fiction 1782–1903*. (250 British and Irish novels). Accessed August 20, 2020. http://collections.chadwyck.co.uk/.

Collins, William. 1746. "The Passions. An Ode for Music". Odes on several descriptive and allegorical subjects. Accessed August 20, 2020. http://spenserians.cath.vt.edu/TextRecord.php?textsid=34216.

Erasmus, Desiderius. 1544 [1467–1536]. *Evangelium Matthaei D. Erasmi Rot. Paraphrasis, Lvgdvni apud seb. gryphivm.*

Accessed August 20, 2020. http://www.galiciana.bibliotecadegalicia.xunta.es/museos_gal/es/consulta/registro.cmd?id=9549.
FanFiction. 2013. *A smoked glass crow.* Accessed August 20, 2020. https://www.fanfiction.net/s/8972962/.../A-Smoked-Glass-Cr...FanFiction.Net.
FrameNet. Accessed August 20, 2020. https://framenet.icsi.berkeley.edu/fndrupal/.
Google Books Ngram Viewer. Accessed August 20, 2020. https://books.google.com/ngrams.
Stanton, Bill. 1995. *Pearl.* This being a translation in verse of the Middle English poem *Pearl* by un unknown poet. Accessed August 20, 2020. http://www.billstanton.co.uk/pearl/menu.php.
The Challoner revision of the Douay-Rheims Bible. 1899. Accessed August 20, 2020. http://www.intratext.com/IXT/ENG0011/_INDEX.HTM.

Software

Gries, Stefan Th. 2014. Coll.analysis 3.5. A script for R to compute perform collostructional analyses. Accessed August 20, 2020. http://www.linguistics.ucsb.edu/faculty/stgries/teaching/groningen/.
Petré, Peter. 2016. *EEBOCorp Concordancer 1.7.* Accessed August 20, 2020. https://lirias.kuleuven.be/handle/123456789/436853.
R Core Team. 2019. R: A language and environment for statistical computing. R Foundation for Statistical Computing. Accessed August 20, 2020. https://www.R-project.org/.
Scott, Mike. 2012. *WordSmith Tools version 6.* Liverpool: Lexical Analysis Software. Accessed August 20, 2020. http://www.lexically.net/wordsmith/version6/.

Secondary sources

Alden, Raymond MacDonald. 1909. The development of the use of prose in the English drama: 1660–1800. *Modern Philology* 7 (1):1–22.

Aldezabal, Izaskun, Maxux Aranzabe, Aitziber Atutxa, and Mikel Lersundi. 2002. *Levin-ek English verb classes and alternations (1993) liburuan proposatzen dituen ingeleserako alternantziak euskararekin parekatuz*. University of the Basque Country, LSI Department: Internal report TR 13–2002. Accessed August 20, 2020. http://ixa.si.ehu.es/node/4099.

Algeo, John. 1998. Vocabulary. In *The Cambridge history of the English language. Volume I: 1776–1997*, edited by Suzanne Romaine, 57–92. Cambridge: Cambridge University Press.

Allen, Cynthia L. 1986. Reconsidering the history of *like*. *Journal of Linguistics* 22 (2):375–409.

Allen, Cynthia L. 1995. *Case marking and reanalysis: Grammatical relations from Old to Early Modern English*. Oxford: Clarendon Press.

Amberber, Mengistu. 1996. The transitivity of verbs of saying revisited. In *WCCFL 14: The Proceedings of the Fourteenth West Coast Conference on Formal Linguistics*, edited by José Camacho, Lina Choueiri, and Maki Watanabe, 1–15. Stanford: CSLI Publications.

Ameka, Felix. 1992. Interjections: The universal yet neglected part of speech. *Journal of Pragmatics* 18 (2):101–118.

Atkins, Beryl T., and Beth Levin. 1991. Admitting impediments. In *Lexical acquisition: Exploiting on-line resources to build a lexicon*, edited by Uri Zernik, 233–262. Hillsdale, New Jersey: Lawrence Erlbaum Associates.

Aue-Apaikul, Panida. 2006. *Transitivized instransives in English: Syntactic, semantic and constructional Issues*. PhD diss. University of Wisconsin, Madison.

Baayen, Harald. 1992. Quantitative aspects of morphological productivity. In *Yearbook of Morphology 1991*, edited by Geert E. Booij, and Jaap van Marle, 109–149. Dordrecht: Kluwer Academic Publishers.

Baayen, Harald. 1993. On frequency, transparency and productivity. In *Yearbook of Morphology 1992*, edited by Geert E. Booij, and Jaap van Marle, 181–208. Dordrecht: Kluwer Academic Publishers.

Baayen, Harald. 2009. Corpus linguistics in morphology: Morphological productivity. In *Corpus linguistics. An international handbook. Volume 2*, edited by Anke Lüdeling, and Merja Kytö, 899–919. Berlin: De Gruyter Mouton

Baayen, Harald, and Rochelle Lieber. 1991. Productivity and English derivation: A corpus-based study. *Linguistics* 29 (5):801–844.

Barðdal, Jóhanna. 2008. *Productivity: Evidence from case and argument structure in Icelandic.* Amsterdam: John Benjamins.

Barðdal, Jóhanna, Elena Smirnova, Lotte Sommerer, and Spike Gildea. 2015. *Diachronic construction grammar.* Amsterdam: John Benjamins.

Barðdal, Jóhanna, and Spike Gildea. 2015. Diachronic construction grammar: Epistemological context, basic assumptions and historical implications. In *Diachronic construction grammar*, edited by Jóhanna Barðdal, Elena Smirnova, Lotte Sommerer, and Spike Gildea, 1–49. Amsterdam: John Benjamins.

Baugh, Albert C., and Thomas Cable. 2002. *A history of the English language.* 5th ed. London: Routledge.

Benveniste, Émile. 1966 [1958]. *Problèmes de linguistique générale.* Paris: Gallimard.

Bergs, Alexander, and Gabriele Diewald, eds. 2008. *Constructions and language change.* Berlin: De Gruyter Mouton

Bergs, Alexander, and Gabriele Diewald, eds. 2009. *Contexts and constructions.* Amsterdam: John Benjamins.

Berko Gleason, Jean. 1958. The child's learning of English morphology. *Word* 14 (2–3):150–177.

Boas, Hans C. 2003. *A constructional approach to resultatives.* Stanford: CSLI Publications.

Boas, Hans C. 2010. The syntax–lexicon continuum in construction grammar: A case study of English communication verbs. *Belgian Journal of Linguistics* 24 (1):54–82.

Boas, Hans C., and Ivan A. Sag, eds. 2012. *Sign-based construction grammar.* Stanford: CSLI Publications.

Börjars, Kersti, Nigel Vincent, and George Walkden. 2015. On constructing a theory of grammatical change. *Transactions of the Philological Society* 113 (3):363–382.

Bouso, Tamara. 2012. *Reaction object constructions in Contemporary American English: A preliminary corpus-based study.* MA diss. Universidade de Santiago de Compostela.

Bouso, Tamara. 2014a. On the nonprototypical status of reaction objects and other nonsubcategorized objects. In *Building interdisciplinary knowledge. Approaches to English and American studies in Spain*, edited by Esther Álvarez López, Emilia María Durán Almarza, and Alicia Menéndez Tarrazo, 307–314. Oviedo: AEDEAN & KRK Ediciones.

Bouso, Tamara. 2014b. "They threw their caps. . ., shouting their emulation": Reaction object constructions in Early and Late Modern English. 8th International Conference on Construction Grammar (ICCG 8), University of Osnabrück, Germany, September 3–6.

Bouso, Tamara. 2014c. *Whispering adieus* and *smiling a welcome*: Changes in argument structure in the history of English. International Symposium on Verbs, Clauses and Constructions. Theory, Variation and Change (VCC Symposium 2014), University of La Rioja, Spain, October 22–24.

Bouso, Tamara. 2017. *Muttering contempt* and *smiling appreciation*: Disentangling the history of the Reaction Object Construction in English. *English Studies 98* (2):194–215

Brems, Lieselotte. 2003. Measure noun constructions: An instance of semantically-driven grammaticalization. *International Journal of Corpus Linguistics* 8 (2):283–312.

Brinton, Laurel J. 1988. *The development of English aspectual systems: Aspectualizers and post-verbal particles.* Cambridge: Cambridge University Press.

Brinton, Laurel J., and Elizabeth Closs Traugott. 2005. *Lexicalization and language change.* Cambridge: Cambridge University Press.

Broccias, Cristiano. 2008. Towards a history of English resultative constructions: The case of adjectival resultative constructions. *English Language and Linguistics* 12 (1):27–54.

Brugmann, Karl. 1904. *Die Demonstrativpronomina der indogermanischen Sprachen: Eine bedeutungsgeschichtliche Untersuchung.* Leipzig: BG Teubner.

Brunner, Thomas, and Thomas Hoffmann. 2020. The *way*-construction in World Englishes. *English World-Wide* 41 (1):1–32.

Busse, Beatrix. 2020. *Speech, writing, and thought presentation in 19th-century narrative fiction: A corpus-assisted approach.* Oxford: Oxford University Pres.

Bybee, Joan L., and Dan I. Slobin. 1982. Rules and schemas in the development and use of the English past tense. *Language* 58 (2):265–289.

Caballero, Rosario. 2015. Reconstructing speech events: Comparing English and Spanish. *Linguistics* 53 (6):1391–1431.

Caballero, Rosario. 2016. Showing versus telling: Representing speech events in English and Spanish. *Review of Cognitive Linguistics* 14 (1):209–233.

Cantos-Gómez, Pascual. 2013. *Statistical methods in language and linguistic research.* Sheffield, UK: Equinox Publishing.

Cappelle, Bert, Edwige Dugas, and Vera Tobin. 2015. An afterthought on *let alone. Journal of Pragmatics* 80:70–85.

Carter, Ronald, and John McRae. 1996. *The Penguin guide to English literature: Britain and Ireland.* London: Penguin Books.

Chomsky, Noam. 1965. *Aspects of the theory of syntax.* Cambridge, MA: MIT Press.

Claridge, Claudia, and Leslie Arnovick. 2010. Pragmaticalisation and discursisation. In *Historical Pragmatics*, edited by Andreas H. Jucker, and Irma Taavitsainen, 165–192. Berlin: De Gruyter Mouton.

Colleman, Timothy, and Bernard De Clerck. 2008. Accounting for ditransitive constructions with *envy* and *forgive. Functions of Language* 15 (2):187–215.

Colleman, Timothy, and Bernard De Clerck. 2011. Constructional semantics on the move: On semantic specialization in the English double object construction. *Cognitive Linguistics* 22 (1):183–209.

Collins, Daniel E. 2001. *Reanimated voices: Speech reporting in a historical-pragmatic perspective.* Amsterdam: John Benjamins.

Cortés-Rodríguez, Francisco J., and Marta González-Orta. 2006. Anglo-saxon verbs of sound: Semantic architecture, lexical representation and constructions. *Studia Anglica Posnaniensia* 42:249–284.

Coulmas, Florian, ed. 1986. *Direct and indirect speech.* Berlin: De Gruyter Mouton.

Coussé, Evie, Peter Andersson, and Joel Olofsson, eds. 2018. *Grammaticalization meets construction grammar.* Amsterdam: John Benjamins.

Croft, William. 2001. *Radical construction grammar: Syntactic theory in typological perspective.* Oxford: Oxford University Press.

Croft, William, and D. Alan Cruse. 2004. *Cognitive linguistics.* Cambridge: Cambridge University Press.

Davies, Mark. 2012. Expanding horizons in historical linguistics with the 400-million word *Corpus of Historical American English. Corpora* 7 (2):121–157.

De Clerck, Bernard, Filip Verroens, Dominique Willems, and Timothy Colleman. 2011. The syntactic flexibility of (new) verbs of instrument of communication: A corpus-based study. *Functions of Language* 18 (1):57–86.

De Dios, Tania. 2014. *He was eating* vs. **He was devouring*: Throwing some light on the workings of object deletion. In *New alleys to significance: Interdisciplinary approaches to English studies*, edited by Alejandra Moreno Álvarez, and Irene Fernández Pérez, 279–290. Palma de Mallorca: Edicions UIB.

De Dios, Tania. 2015. *After 15 years of sobriety I found out he was drinking and using again*: Taboo avoidance as a trigger for object drop? 13th International Cognitive Linguistics Conference (ICLC-13), Northumbria University, UK, July 20–25.

De Smet, Hendrik, Lobke Ghesquière, and Freek Van de Velde, eds. 2013. *On multiple source constructions in language change.* Amsterdam: John Benjamins.

De Smet, Hendrik. 2005. A corpus of Late Modern English texts. *International Computer Archive of Modern and Medieval English* 29:69–82.

De Smet, Hendrik. 2020. What predicts productivity? Theory meets individuals. *Cognitive Linguistics* 31(2):251–278.

Dehé, Nicole, Ray Jackendoff, Andrew McIntyre, and Silke Urban, eds. 2002. *Verb-particle explorations*. Berlin: De Gruyter Mouton.

Denison, David. 1993. *English historical syntax: Verbal constructions*. London: Longman.

Dessen, Alan C. 2009. Stage directions and the theater historian. In *The Oxford handbook of Early Modern theatre*, edited by Richard Dutton, 513–527. Oxford: Oxford University Press.

Dessen, Alan C., and Leslie Thomson. 1999. *A dictionary of stage directions in English drama, 1580–1642*. Cambridge: Cambridge University Press.

Deutschbein, Max. 1931. *System der neuenglischen syntax*. 4th ed. Leipzig: Queller & Meyer.

Devereux, Edward James. 1968. *A checklist of English translations of Erasmus to 1700*. Oxford: Oxford Bibliographical Society.

Diessel, Holger. 2019. *The grammar network: How linguistic structure is shaped by language use*. Cambridge: Cambridge University Press.

Diessel, Holger, and Martin Hilpert. 2016. Frequency effects in grammar. In *Oxford Research Encyclopedia of Linguistics*. Accessed August 20, 2020. https://doi.org/10.1093/acrefore/9780199384655.013.120.

Diller, Hans-Jürgen, Hendrik De Smet, and Jukka Tyrkkö. 2010. A European database of descriptors of English electronic texts. *The European English Messenger* 19(2):29–35.

Dirven, René, Louis Goossens, Yvan Putseys, and Emma Vorlat. 1982. *The scene of linguistic action and its perspectivization by speak, talk, say and tell*. Amsterdam: John Benjamins.

Dixon, Robert M. W., and Alexandra Y. Aikhenvald, eds. 2000. *Changing valency: Case studies in transitivity*. Cambridge: Cambridge University Press.

Dorfeld, Karl. 1885. *Über die Function des Präfixes ge- (got. ga-) in der Composition mit Verben. Teil I.: Das Präfix bei Ulfilas und Tatian*. PhD diss. Ludewigs-Universität Giessen.

Downing, Angela, and Philip Locke. 2006. *English grammar: A university course*. 2nd ed. London: Routledge.

Dyka, Susanne, Iva Novakova, and Dirk Siepmann. 2017. A web of analogies: Depictive and reaction object constructions in Modern English and French fiction. In *Computational and corpus-based phraseology*, edited by Ruslan Mitkov, 87–101. Switzerland: Springer International Publishing AG.

Eitelmann, Matthias, and Britta Mondorf. 2018. The role of cognate objects in language variation and change. In *Exact repetition in grammar and discourse*, edited by Rita Finkbeiner, and Ulrike Freywald. Berlin: Mouton de Gruyter.

Faber, Pamela B., and Jesús Sánchez Martínez. 1990. Semántica de prototipos: El campo semántico de los verbos que expresan la manera de hablar frente al de los verbos de sonido en inglés y español. *Revista Española de Lingüística Aplicada (RESLA)* 6:19–29.

Faber, Pamela B., and Ricardo Mairal Usón. 1999. *Constructing a lexicon of English verbs*. Berlin: De Gruyter Mouton.

Fanego, Teresa. 2012. Motion events in English: The emergence and diachrony of manner salience from Old English to Late Modern English. *Folia Linguistica Historica* 33 (1):29–86.

Fanego, Teresa. 2017. *The trolley rumbled through the tunnel*: On the history of the English intransitive motion construction. *Folia Linguistica Historica* 51 (38):29–73.

Fanego, Teresa. 2019. A construction of independent means: The history of the *Way* construction revisited. *English Language and Linguistics* 23 (3):671–699.

Fanego, Teresa. 2020. On the history of the English progressive construction *Jane came whistling down the street*. *Journal of English Linguistics* 48 (4):1–36.

Fauconnier, Gilles, and Mark Turner. 1998. Conceptual integration networks. *Cognitive Science* 22 (2):133–187.

Fellbaum, Christiane. 1986. *On the middle construction in English*. Bloomington: Indiana University Linguistics Club.

Felser, Claudia, and Anja Wanner. 2001. The syntax of cognate and other unselected objects. In *Structural aspects of semantically complex verbs*, edited by Nicole Dehé, and Anja Wanner, 105–130. Bern: Peter Lang.

Fillmore, Charles J. 1968. The case for case. In *Universals in linguistic theory*, edited by Emmon Bach, and Robert T. Harms, 1–89. New York: Holt, Rinehart and Winston.

Fillmore, Charles J. 1986. Pragmatically controlled zero anaphora. In *Proceedings of the Twelfth Annual Meeting of the Berkeley Linguistics Society*, 95–107. Berkeley: Berkeley Linguistics Society.

Fillmore, Charles J., Paul Kay, and Mary Catherine O'Connor. 1988. Regularity and idiomaticity in grammatical constructions: The case of *let alone*. *Language* 64 (3):501–538.

Fischer, Olga. 1992. Syntax. In *The Cambridge history of the English language. Volume II: 1066–1476*, edited by Norman Blake, 207–408. Cambridge: Cambridge University Press.

Fischer, Olga, and Frederike van Der Leek. 1983. The demise of the Old English impersonal construction. *Journal of Linguistics* 19 (2):337–368.

Flach, Susanne. 2020. Constructionalization and the sorites paradox: The emergence of the *into*-causative. In *Nodes and networks in diachronic construction grammar*, edited by Lotte Sommerer, and Elena Smirnova, 46–67. Amsterdam: John Benjamins.

Fludernik, Monika. 1993. *The fictions of language and the languages of fiction: The linguistic representation of speech and consciousness*. London: Routledge.

García García, Luisa. 2012. Morphological causatives in Old English: The quest for a vanishing formation. *Transactions of the Philological Society* 110 (1):122–148.

Gisborne, Nikolas, and Amanda Patten. 2011. Construction grammar and grammaticalization. In *The Oxford handbook of grammaticalization*, edited by Bernd Heine, and Heiko Narrog. Oxford: Oxford University Press.

Givón, Talmy. 1984. *Syntax: A functional-typological introduction. Volume I*. Amsterdam: John Benjamins.

Goldberg, Adele E. 1995. *Constructions: A construction grammar approach to argument structure*. Chicago: University of Chicago Press.

Goldberg, Adele E. 2006. *Constructions at work: The nature of generalization in language*. Oxford: Oxford University Press.

Goldberg, Adele E. 2013. Constructionist approaches. In *The Oxford handbook of construction grammar*, edited by Thomas Hoffmann, and Graeme Trousdale, 15–31. Oxford: Oxford University Press.

Goldberg, Adele E. 2019. *Explain me this: Creativity, competition, and the partial productivity of constructions*. Princeton: Princeton University Press.

Goldberg, Adele E., and Ray Jackendoff. 2004. The English resultative as a family of constructions. *Language* 80 (3):532–568.

Görlach, Manfred. 1999. *English in nineteenth-century England. An introduction*. Cambridge: Cambridge University Press.

Grady, Joe. 1998. The "conduit metaphor" revisited: A reassessment of metaphors for communication. In *Discourse and cognition: Bridging the gap*, edited by Jean-Pierre Koenig, 205–218. Stanford: CSLI Publications.

Gries, Stefan Th. 2012. Frequencies, probabilities, and association measures in usage-/exemplar-based linguistics: Some necessary clarifications. *Studies in Language* 36 (3):477–510.

Gries, Stefan Th., and Anatol Stefanowitsch. 2004a. Covarying collexemes in the *into*-causative. In *Language, Culture, and Mind*, edited by Michel Achard, and Suzanne Kemmer, 225–236. Stanford: CSLI Publications.

Gries, Stefan Th., and Anatol Stefanowitsch. 2004b. Extending collostructional analysis: A corpus-based perspective on alternations. *International Journal of Corpus Linguistics* 9 (1):97–129.

Gross, Maurice. 1981. Les bases empiriques de la notion de prédicat sémantique. *Langages* (63):7–52.

Guerra-García, Fátima, and Elena Sacramento-Lechado. 2011. *Tutorial de FunGramKB Suite para los Lexicones*. Accessed August 20, 2020. http://www.fungramkb.com/resources/papers/tutorial2.pdf.

Haïk, Isabelle. 2011. Kissing goodbye. *Corela. Cognition, Représentation, Langage* 9 (2):1–26.

Hale, Kenneth, and Samuel Jay Keyser. 1993. On argument structure and the lexical expression of syntactic relations. In *The view from Building 20: Essays in linguistics in honor of Sylvain Bromberger*, edited by Ken Hale, and Samuel Jay Keyser, 53–109. Cambridge, MA: MIT Press.

Harley, Heidi. 2005. How do verbs get their names? Denominal verbs, Manner Incorporation, and the ontology of verb roots in English. In *The syntax of aspect: Deriving thematic and aspectual interpretation*, edited by Nomi Erteschik-Shir, and Tova Rapoport, 42–64. Oxford: Oxford University Press.

Hart, Hilary. 2004. *Sentimental spectacles: The sentimental novel, natural language, and early film performance*. PhD diss. University of Oregon.

Hartmann, Stefan. 2016. *Wortbildungswandel: Eine diachrone Studie zu deutschen Nominalisierungsmustern*. Berlin: De Gruyter Mouton.

Haspelmath, Martin. 1993. More on the typology of inchoative/causative verb alternations. In *Causatives and transitivity*, edited by Bernard Comrie, and Maria Polinsky, 87–120. Amsterdam: John Benjamins.

Haspelmath, Martin. 1999. Why is grammaticalization irreversible? *Linguistics* 37 (6):1043–1068.

Haspelmath, Martin. 2002. *Understanding morphology*. London: Arnold.

Head, Dominic, ed. 2006. *The Cambridge guide to literature in English*. 3rd ed. Cambridge: Cambridge University Press.

Hermodsson, Lars. 1952. *Reflexive und intransitive Verba im älteren Westgermanischen*. Uppsala: Almqvist & Wiksell.

Hilpert, Martin. 2013. *Constructional change in English: Developments in allomorphy, word formation, and syntax*. Cambridge: Cambridge University Press.

Hilpert, Martin. 2014a. Collostructional analysis: Measuring associations between constructions and lexical elements. In *Corpus methods for semantics: Quantitative studies in polysemy and synonymy*, edited by Dylan Glynn, and Justyna A. Robinson, 391–404. Amsterdam: John Benjamins.

Hilpert, Martin. 2014b. *Construction grammar and its application to English*. 1st ed. Edinburgh: Edinburgh University Press.

Hilpert, Martin. 2018. Three open questions in diachronic construction grammar. In *Grammaticalization meets construction Grammar*, edited by Evie Coussé, Peter Andersson, and Joel Olofsson, 21–39. Amstedam: John Benjamins.

Hilpert, Martin. 2019. *Construction grammar and its application to English*. 2nd ed. Edinburgh: Edinburgh University Press.

Hiltunen, Risto. 1983. *The decline of the prefixes and the beginnings of the English phrasal verb*. Turku: Turun Yliopisto.

Himmelmann, Nikolaus P. 2004. Lexicalization and grammaticization: Opposite or orthogonal. In *What makes grammaticalization? A look from its fringes and its components*, edited by Walter Bisang, Nikolaus P. Himmelmann, and Björn Wiemer, 21–44. Berlin: De Gruyter Mouton.

Höche, Silke. 2009. *Cognate object constructions in English. A cognitive-linguistic account*. Tübingen: Gunter Narr Verlag.

Hoffmann, Sebastian. 2004. Using the OED quotations database as a corpus – a linguistic appraisal. *ICAME Journal* 28:17–30.

Hoffmann, Thomas, and Graeme Trousdale, eds. 2013. *The Oxford handbook of construction grammar*. Oxford: Oxford University Press.

Hollmann, Willem B. 2003. *Synchrony and diachrony of English periphrastic causatives: A cognitive perspective*. PhD diss. University of Manchester.

Hopper, Paul J., and Sandra A. Thompson. 1980. Transitivity in grammar and discourse. *Language* 56 (2):251–299.

Hopper, Paul J., and Elizabeth Closs Traugott. 2003. *Grammaticalization*. 2nd ed. Cambridge: Cambridge University Press.

Horrocks, Geoffrey, and Melita Stavrou. 2010. Morphological aspect and the function and distribution of cognate objects across languages. In *Lexical semantics, syntax, and event structure*, edited by Malka Rappaport Hovav, Edit Doron, and Ivy Sichel, 284–308. Oxford: Oxford University Press.

Huddleston, Rodney, Geoffrey K. Pullum, Laurie Bauer, Betty Birner, Ted Briscoe, Peter Collins, David Denison, David Lee, Anita Mittwoch, Geoffrey Nunberg, Frank Palmer, John Payne, Peter Peterson, Lesley Stirling, and Gregory Ward. 2002. *The Cambridge grammar of the English language*. Cambridge: Cambridge University Press.

Isherwood, Christopher. 1935. *Mr Norris changes trains*. London: Leonard and Virginia Woolf at the Hogarth press.

Israel, Michael. 1996. The *way* constructions grow. In *Conceptual structure, discourse and language*, edited by Adele E. Goldberg, 217–230. Stanford: CSLI Publications.

Jackendoff, Ray. 1990. *Semantic structures*. Cambridge, MA: MIT Press.

Jackendoff, Ray. 1997. Twistin' the night away. *Language* 73 (3):534–559.

Janda, Richard D., and Joseph D. Brian. 2003. On language, change, and language change; or, of history, linguistics, and historical linguistics. In *The handbook of historical linguistics*, edited by Richard D. Janda, and Joseph D. Brian, 3–180. Oxford: Blackwell Publishing.

Jespersen, Otto. 1909–1949. *A Modern English grammar on historical principles*. 7 Volumes. Copenhagen: Munksgaard. Reprint, London: George Allen & Unwin, 1961.

Jones, Michael Allan. 1988. Cognate objects and the case-filter. *Journal of Linguistics* 24 (1):89–110.

Kastovsky, Dieter. 1992. Semantics and vocabulary. In *The Cambridge history of the English language. Volume I: The beginnings to 1066*, edited by Richard M. Hogg, 290–408. Cambridge: Cambridge University Press.

Kay, Paul, and Charles J. Fillmore. 1999. Grammatical constructions and linguistic generalizations: The *What's X doing Y?* construction. *Language* 75 (1):1–33.

Khan, Zeeshan. 1994. Bangla verb classes and alternations. In *Verb classes and alternations in Bangla, German, English, and Korean*, edited by Douglas A. Jones, Robert C. Berwick, Franklin Cho, Zeeshan Khan, Karen T. Kohl, Naoyuki Nomura, Anand Radhakrishnan, Ulrich Sauerland, and Brian Ulicny, 36–50. Cambridge, MA: Massachussetts Institute of Technology. Center for Biological and Computational Learning and the Artificial Intelligence Laboratory. Accessed August 20, 2020. https://dspace.mit.edu/handle/1721.1/7197.

Kirchner, Gustav. 1951. A special case of the object of result. *English Studies* 32:153–159.

Klages, Monika E. 1996. Act-effecting 'Affectedness': A semantic parameter for argument selection and semantic function assignment. 7th International Conference on Functional Grammar, University of Córdoba, Spain, September 23–27.

Kogusuri, Tetsuya. 2009a. Manner of speaking verbs and their clausal complements in English. *Tsukuba English Studies* 27:187–203.

Kogusuri, Tetsuya. 2009b. The syntax and semantics of reaction object constructions in English. *Tsukuba English Studies* 28:33–53.

Kogusuri, Tetsuya. 2011. On the passivization of the gesture expression construction. *Tsukuba English Studies* 29:149–168.

Kogusuri, Tetsuya. 2012. The passive of the gesture expression construction: Event structure and discourse function. Debrecen Workshop on Argument Structure (WAS), University of Debrecen, Hungary, May 25–27.

König, Ekkehard, and Peter Siemund. 2000. The development of complex reflexives and intensifiers in English. *Diachronica* 17 (1):39–84.

Labov, William. 1994. *Principles of linguistic change. Volume I. Internal factors.* Oxford: Blackwell.

Lakoff, George. 1987. *Women, fire, and dangerous things: What categories reveal about the mind.* Chicago: University of Chicago Press.

Lakoff, George, and Mark Johnson. 1980. *Metaphors we live by.* Chicago: University of Chicago Press.

Langacker, Ronald W. 1987. *Foundations of cognitive grammar. Volume I: Theoretical prerequisites.* Stanford: Stanford University Press.

Langacker, Ronald W. 2000. *Grammar and conceptualization.* Berlin: Mouton de Gruyter.

Langacker, Ronald W. 2009. Constructions and constructional meaning. In *New directions in cognitive linguistics*, edited by Vyvyan Evans, and Stéphanie Pourcel, 225–267. Amsterdam: John Benjamins.

Lass, Roger. 1992. Phonology and morphology. In *The Cambridge history of the English language. Volume II: 1066–1476*, edited by Norman Blake, 23–155. Cambridge: Cambridge University Press.

Lavidas, Nikolaos. 2009. *Transitivity alternations in diachrony: Changes in argument structure and voice morphology.* Newcastle upon Tyne: Cambridge Scholars Publishing.

Lavidas, Nikolaos. 2013. Null and cognate objects and changes in (in) transitivity: Evidence from the history of English. *Acta Linguistica Hungarica* 60 (1):69–106.

Lavidas, Nikolaos. 2014. Cognate arguments and the transitivity requirement in the history of English. *Lingua Posnaniensis* 56 (2):41–59.

Lavidas, Nikolaos. 2018. Cognate noun constructions in Early Modern English: The case of Tyndale's *New Testament*. In *Explorations in English historical syntax*, edited by Hubert Cuyckens, Hendrik De Smet, Liesbet Heyvaert, and Charlotte Maekelberghe, 51–76. Amsterdam: John Benjamins.

Leech, Geoffrey, and Mick Short. 1981. *Style in fiction*. London: Longman.

Lehmann, Christian. 1995. *Thoughts on grammaticalization*. 2nd ed. Munich: Lincom.

Lehrer, Adrienne. 1988. Checklist for verbs of speaking. *Acta Linguistica Hungarica* 38 (1–4):143–161.

Levin, Beth. 1991. Building a lexicon: The contribution of linguistics. *International Journal of Lexicography* 4 (3):205–226.

Levin, Beth. 1993. *English verb classes and alternations. A preliminary investigation*. Chicago: University of Chicago Press.

Levin, Beth, and Tova R. Rapoport. 1988. Lexical subordination. In *CLS 24*, edited by Lynn MacLeod, Gary Larson, and Diane Brentari, 275–289. Chicago: CLS Publications.

Levin, Beth, and Grace Song. 1997. Making sense of corpus data: A case study of verbs of sound. *International Journal of Corpus Linguistics* 2 (1):23–64.

Lindemann, John William Richard. 1970. *Old English preverbal ge-: Its meaning*. Charlottesville: University Press of Virginia.

Liu, Dilin. 2008. Intransitive or object deleting? Classifying English verbs used without an object. *Journal of English Linguistics* 36 (4):289–313.

Los, Bettelou. 2004. From resultative predicate to event-modifier: The case of *forth* and *on*. In *New perspectives on English historical linguistics: Selected papers from 12 ICEHL, Glasgow, 21–26 August 2002. Volume I: Syntax and morphology*, edited by Christian Kay, Simon Horobin, and Jeremy J. Smith, 83–102. Amsterdam: John Benjamins.

Los, Bettelou, Corrien Blom, Geert Booij, Marion Elenbaas, and Ans van Kemenade, ed. 2012. *Morphosyntactic change: A comparative study of particles and prefixes*. Cambridge: Cambridge University Press.

Macfarland, Talke. 1995. *Cognate objects and the argument/adjunct distinction in English*. PhD diss. Northwestern University, Illinois.

Mair, Christian. 2004. Corpus linguistics and grammaticalisation theory: Statistics, frequencies, and beyond. In *Corpus approaches to grammaticalization in English*, edited by Hans Lindquist, and Christian Mair, 121–150. Amsterdam: John Benjamins.

Mantlik, Annette. 2011. *The historical development of shell nouns: A diachronic study of abstract noun constructions in English*. PhD diss. Ludwig-Maximilians-Universität München.

Marchand, Hans. 1969. *The categories and types of present-day English word-formation: A synchronic-diachronic approach*. 2nd ed. München: C.H.Beck Verlag.

Martínez-Vázquez, Montserrat. 1998. Effected objects in English and Spanish. *Languages in Contrast* 1 (2):245–264.

Martínez-Vázquez, Montserrat. 2005. Communicative constructions in English and Spanish. In *The dynamics of language use: Functional and contrastive perspectives*, edited by Christopher S. Butler, María de los Ángeles Gómez González, and Susana M. Doval-Suárez, 79–109. Amsterdam: John Benjamins.

Martínez-Vázquez, Montserrat. 2010. Reaction object constructions in English. A corpus-based study. In *Language windowing through corpora/Visualización del lenguaje a través de corpus*, edited by Isabel Moskowich, Begoña Crespo, Inés Lareo, and Paula Lojo, 551–561. A Coruña: Universidade da Coruña.

Martínez-Vázquez, Montserrat. 2014a. Expressive object constructions in English. A corpus based analysis. *Revista Canaria de Estudios Ingleses* 69:171–186.

Martínez-Vázquez, Montserrat. 2014b. Reaction object constructions in English and Spanish. *ES. Revista de Filología Inglesa* 35:193–217.

Martínez-Vázquez, Montserrat. 2015. Nominalized expressive acts in English. *Verbum* (Special issue *Nominalisations et corpus*, edited by Evelyne Jacquey, and Marie Laurence Knittel) 37 (1):147–170.

Martínez-Vázquez, Montserrat. 2016. La construcción *llorar las penas*: Un nuevo caso de tipología germánica en una lengua romance. *Verba. Anuario Galego de Filoloxía* 43:107–128.

Martínez-Vázquez, Montserrat. 2017. Cultural influence on the expression of cathartic conceptualization in English and Spanish: A corpus-based analysis. *International Journal of Society, Culture & Language* 5 (2):1–14.

Massam, Diane. 1990. Cognate objects as thematic objects. *Canadian Journal of Linguistics* 35:161–190.

Mastrofini, Roberta. 2014. English manner of speaking verbs and their Italian translations: A cross-linguistic comparison. *Athens Journal of Philology* 1 (2):83–98.

Mateu, Jaume. 2001. Unselected objects. In *Structural aspects of semantically complex verbs*, edited by Nicole Dehé, and Anja Wanner, 83–104. Bern: Peter Lang.

Mateu, Jaume. 2012. Conflation and incorporation processes in resultative constructions. In *Telicity, change, and state: A cross-categorical view of event structure*, edited by Violeta Demonte, and Louise McNally, 252–278. Oxford: Oxford University Press.

Mateu, Jaume. 2014. Change of state and the co-event conflation pattern: The case of unselected object constructions. SFB Kolloquium, Heinrich-Heine-Universität Düsseldorf, Germany, April 17.

Matsumoto, Masumi. 1996. The syntax and semantics of the cognate object construction. *English Linguistics (by the English Linguistic Society of Japan)* 13:199–220.

McColm, Daniel. 2015. *A comparison of the way-construction and the fake reflexive resultative construction: A diachronic construction grammar account*. MA diss. University of Edinburgh.

McColm, Daniel. 2019. *The way-construction in English, Dutch and German*. PhD diss. University of Edinburgh.

McHale, Brian. 1978. Free indirect discourse: A survey of recent accounts. *PTL: A Journal for Descriptive Poetics and Theory of Literature* 3 (2):249–287.

McMillion, Allan. 2006. *Labile verbs in English: Their meaning, behavior and structure*. PhD diss. Stockholm University.

Méndez-Naya, Belén, and María José López-Couso. 1997. What is really meant by *impersonal*? On impersonal and related terms. *Atlantis. Journal of the Spanish Association for Anglo-American Studies* 19:185–192.

Michaelis, Laura A. 2004. Type shifting in construction grammar: An integrated approach to aspectual coercion. *Cognitive Linguistics* 15 (1):1–67.

Michaelis, Laura A., and Knud Lambrecht. 1996. Toward a construction-based theory of language function: The case of nominal extraposition. *Language* 72 (2):215–247.

Mirto, Ignazio Mauro. 2007. *Dream a little dream of me*: Cognate predicates in English. 26th International Conference on Lexis and Grammar, Bonifacio, France, October 2–6. Accessed August 20, 2020. http://infolingu.univ-mlv.fr/Colloques/Bonifacio/proceedings/mirto.pdf.

Mirto, Ignazio Mauro. 2012. Alternanze argomentali: Oggetti interni e reaction objects come nomi predicativi di costrutti a verbo supporto. In *SLE 53 Linguaggio e cervello – Semantica/Language and the brain – Semantics*, edited by Valentina Bambini, Irene Ricci, and Pier Marco Bertinetto, 589–612. Roma: Bulzoni.

Mirto, Ignazio Mauro. 2017. The so-called *reaction object construction*: Reaction or co-predication? In *Lucrările celui de al șaselea simpozion internațional de lingvistică*, edited by Maria Stanciu Istrate, and Daniela Răuțu, 540–549. Bucharest: Univers Enciclopedic Gold Publishing House.

Miura, Ayumi. 2015. *Middle English verbs of emotion and impersonal constructions: Verb meaning and syntax in diachrony*. Oxford: Oxford University Press.

Möhlig, Ruth, and Monika E. Klages. 2002. Detransitivization in the history of English from a semantic perspective. In *Selected papers from 11 ICEHL, Santiago de Compostela, 7–11 September 2000. Volume I: English historical syntax and morphology*, edited by Teresa Fanego, Javier Pérez-Guerra, and María José López-Couso, 231–254. Amsterdam: John Benjamins.

Moltmann, Friederike. 1989. Nominal and clausal event predicates. In *CLS 25*, 300–314. Chicago: CLS Publications.

Mondorf, Britta. 2010. Genre effects in the replacement of reflexives by particles. In *Syntactic variation and genre*, edited by Heidrun Dorgeloh, and Anja Wanner, 219–246. Berlin: De Gruyter Mouton.

Mondorf, Britta. 2011. Variation and change in English resultative constructions. *Language Variation and Change* 22 (3):397–421.

Mondorf, Britta. 2016. "Snake legs it to freedom": Dummy *it* as pseudo-object. *Corpus Linguistics and Linguistic Theory* 12 (1):73–102.

Mondorf, Britta, and Ulrike Schneider. 2016. Detransitivisation as a support strategy for causative *bring*. *English Language and Linguistics* 20 (3):439–462.

Mufwene, Salikoko S. 1978. English manner-of-speaking verbs revisited. In *CLS 14*, edited by Donka Farkas, Wesley M. Jacobsen, and Karol W. Todrys, 278–288. Chicago: CLS Publications.

Neels, Jakob. 2015. Adding a diachronic dimension to the case of *let alone*. 22nd International Conference on Historical Linguistics (ICHL 22), University of Naples Federico II, Italy, July 27–31

Noël, Dirk. 2007. Diachronic construction grammar and grammaticalization theory. *Functions of Language* 14 (2):177–202.

Omuro, Takeshi. 1995. On the similarities and differences between nonverbal communication verbs and manner-of-speaking verbs in English (1). *Gengobunka Ronshu (Studies in Language and Culture)* 17 (1):107–127.

Omuro, Takeshi. 1996. On the similarities and differences between nonverbal communication verbs and manner-of-speaking verbs in English (2). *Gengobunka Ronshu (Studies in Language and Culture)* 17 (2):125–154.

Omuro, Takeshi. 1997. Semantic extension: The case of nonverbal communication verbs in English. In *Studies in English linguistics: A festschrift for Akira Ota on the occasion of his eightieth birthday*, edited by Masatomo Ukaji, Toshio Nakao, Masaru Kajita, and Shuji Chiba, 806–825. Tokyo: Taishukan.

Omuro, Takeshi. 2000. Gainen imiron-kihontekina mekanizumu to zirei kenkyu (Conceptual semantics-The basic mechanism and a case study). In *Seisei Gengo Riron: Nyumon (Generative linguistic theory: An introduction)*, edited by Shinichi Tanaka, Jun Abe, and Takeshi Omuro, 123–191. Tokyo: Hitsuji Shobou.

Ousby, Ian, ed. 1988. *The Cambridge guide to literature in English.* Cambridge: Cambridge University Press.

Patten, Amanda. 2012. *The English it-cleft: A constructional account and a diachronic investigation.* Berlin: De Gruyter Mouton.

Peitsara, Kirsti. 1997. The development of reflexive strategies in English. In *Grammaticalization at work. Studies of long-term developments in English*, edited by Matti Rissanen, Merja Kytö, and Kirsi Heikkonen, 277–370. Berlin: De Gruyter Mouton.

Perek, Florent. 2015a. *Argument structure in usage-based construction grammar: Experimental and corpus-based perspectives.* Amsterdam: John Benjamins.

Perek, Florent. 2015b. Plotting our way through the data: The *way*-construction revisited. 6th International Conference of the French Association for Cognitive Linguistics (AFLiCo 6), Université Grenoble Alpes, France, May 27–29. Accessed August 20, 2020. http://www.fperek.net/pdfs/abstract_aflico6.pdf.

Perek, Florent. 2016a. Productivity and schematicity of the *way*-construction in Late Modern English. Workshop "Historische Konstruktionsgrammatik: Konvergenzen und Divergenzen im Sprach- und Konstruktionswande" (Diachronic construction grammar: Convergence and divergence in language and constructional change), Heinrich-Heine-Universität Düsseldorf, Germany, February 17–18. Accessed August 20, 2020. http://www.fperek.net/pdfs/slides-dusseldorf.pdf.

Perek, Florent. 2016b. Using distributional semantics to study syntactic productivity in diachrony: A case study. *Linguistics* 54 (1):149–188.

Perek, Florent. 2018. Recent change in the productivity and schematicity of the *way*-construction: A distributional semantic analysis. *Corpus Linguistics and Linguistic Theory* 14 (1):65–97.

Perek, Florent. 2020. Productivity and schematicity in constructional change. In *Nodes and networks in diachronic construction grammar*, edited by Lotte Sommerer, and Elena Smirnova, 142–166. Amsterdam: John Benjamins.

Perek, Florent, and Martin Hilpert. 2016. Constructional tolerance: Cross-linguistic differences in the acceptability of non-conventional uses of constructions. In *Constructions across grammars*, edited by Martin Hilpert, and Jan-Ola Östman, 131–168. Amsterdam: John Benjamins.

Perek, Florent, and Martin Hilpert. 2017. A distributional semantic approach to the periodization of change in the productivity of constructions. *International Journal of Corpus Linguistics* 22 (4): 490–520.

Petré, Peter. 2012. General productivity: How *become* waxed and *wax* became a copula. *Cognitive Linguistics* 23 (1): 27–65.

Perlmutter, David M., and Scott Soames. 1979. *Syntactic argumentation and the structure of English.* Berkeley: University of California Press.

Pinker, Steven. 1989. *Learnability and cognition: The acquisition of argument structure.* Cambridge, MA: MIT Press.

Pinker, Steven. 1999. *Words and rules. The ingredients of language.* New York: Basic Books.

Poppe, Erich. 2009. Standard average European and the Celticity of English intensifiers and reflexives: Some considerations and implications. *English Language and Linguistics* 13 (2):251–266.

Postal, Paul M., and Geoffrey K. Pullum. 1988. Expletive noun phrases in subcategorized positions. *Linguistic Inquiry* 19 (4):635–670.

Poutsma, Hendrik. 1926. *A grammar of Late Modern English: For the use of continental, especially Dutch, students. Part II: The parts of speech. Section II: The verb and the particles.* Groningen: P. Noordhoff.

Poutsma, Hendrik. 1929. *A grammar of Late Modern English: For the use of continental, especially Dutch, students. Part I: The sentence. Section II: The composite sentence.* 2nd ed. Groningen: P. Noordhoff.

Quirk, Randolph, Sidney Greenbaum, Geoffrey Leech, and Jan Svartvik. 1985. *A comprehensive grammar of the English language.* London: Longman.

Real Puigdollers, Cristina. 2009. The nature of cognate objects. A syntactic approach. In *Proceedings of ConSOLE XVI*, edited by Sylvia Blaho, Camelia Constantinescu, and Bert Le Bruyn, 157–178.

Reddy, Michael. 1979. The conduit metaphor: A case of frame conflict in our language about language. In *Metaphor and thought*, edited by Andrew Ortony, 284–324. Cambridge: Cambridge University Press.

Rohdenburg, Günter. 1995. Betrachtungen zum Auf- und Abstief einiger präpositionaler Konstruktionen im Englischen. *NOWELE* 26:67–124.

Rohdenburg, Günter. 2007. Functional constraints in syntactic change: The rise and fall of prepositional constructions in Early and Late Modern English. *English Studies* 88 (2):217–233.

Rohdenburg, Günter. 2009. Reflexive structures. In *One language, two grammars? Differences between British and American English*, edited by Günter Rohdenburg, and Julia Schlüter, 166–181. Cambridge: Cambridge University Press.

Rohdenburg, Günter. 2018. On the differential evolution of simple and complex object constructions in English. In *Explorations in English historical syntax*, edited by Hubert Cuyckens, Hendrik De Smet, Liesbet Heyvaert, and Charlotte Maekelberghe, 77–104. Amsterdam: John Benjamins.

Rojo, Ana, and Javier Valenzuela. 2005. Verbs of sensory perception. An English-Spanish comparison. *Languages in Contrast* 5 (2):219–243.

Ron Vaz, Pilar. 2003. Los verbos de posesión en inglés y en español. In *Gramática de construcciones: Contrastes entre el inglés y el español*, edited by Montserrat Martínez-Vázquez, 59–90. Huelva: Grupo de Investigación Gramática Contrastiva.

Rosca, Andreea. 2011. *A lexical-constructional approach to light emission and sound emission verbs*. MA diss. Universidad de la Rioja. Accessed August 20, 2020. http://biblioteca.unirioja.es/tfe_e/TFE000105.pdf.

Ross, John Robert. 1970a. On declarative sentences. In *Readings in English transformational grammar*, edited by Roderick A. Jacobs, and Peter S. Rosenbaum, 222–277. Waltham, MA: Ginn and Company.

Ross, John Robert. 1970b. Two types of idioms. *Linguistic Inquiry* 1 (1):144.

Rowland, Ann. 2008. Sentimental fiction. In *The Cambridge companion to fiction in the Romantic period*, edited by Richard Maxwell, and Katie Trumpener, 191–206. Cambridge: Cambridge University Press.

Ruano San Segundo, Pablo. 2016. A corpus-stylistic approach to Dickens' use of speech verbs: Beyond mere reporting. *Language and Literature* 25 (2):113–129.

Ruano San Segundo, Pablo. 2017. Reporting verbs as a stylistic device in the creation of fictional personalities in literary texts. *Atlantis. Journal of the Spanish Association for Anglo-American Studies* 39 (2):105–124.

Ruano San Segundo, Pablo. 2018a. An analysis of Charles Dickens's gender-based use of speech verbs. *Gender and Language* 12 (2):192–217.

Ruano San Segundo, Pablo. 2018b. Dickens's hyperbolic style revisited: Verbs that describe sounds made by animals used to report the words of male villains. *Style* 52 (4):475–493.

Rudzka-Ostyn, Brygida. 1988. Semantic extensions into the domain of verbal communication. In *Topics in cognitive linguistics*, edited by Brygida Rudzka-Ostyn, 507–554. Amsterdam: John Benjamins.

Ruiz Narbona, Esaúl. 2020. *Transitivising mechanisms in Old English: Preverbs versus the deverbal causative formation.* Munich: Utzverlag.

Ruppenhofer, Josef, and Laura A. Michaelis. 2010. A constructional account of genre-based argument omissions. *Constructions and Frames* 2 (2):158–184.

Salkoff, Morris. 1988. Analysis by fusion. *Lingvisticae Investigationes* 12 (1):49–84.

Sams, Jessica. 2008. *A syntactic analysis of written English quotatives.* PhD diss. University of Colorado at Boulder.

Samuels, Shirley. 1992. *The culture of sentiment: Race, gender, and sentimentality in nineteenth-century America.* Oxford: Oxford University Press.

Samuels, Shirley. 2012. *Sentimentalism and domestic fiction.* Oxford: Oxford Bibliographies.

Sandford, Jodi L. 2016. Agreement on *croak* and *groan*: Theory and verification of manner of speaking verbs in English. *Cognitive Semantics* 2 (1):80–101.

Schmid, Hans-Jörg. 2000. *English abstract nouns as conceptual shells: From corpus to cognition*. Berlin: De Gruyter Mouton.

Schmid, Hans-Jörg, and Annette Mantlik. 2015. Entrenchment in historical corpora? Reconstructing dead authors' minds from their usage profiles. *Anglia* 133 (4):583–623.

Semino, Elena, and Mick Short. 2004. *Corpus stylistics: Speech, writing and thought presentation in a corpus of English writing*. London: Routledge.

Shakespeare, William. 1997a. The history of Troilus and Cressida. In *The Riverside Shakespeare*, edited by G. Blakemore Evans, and J. J. M. Tobin, 482–532. 2nd ed. Boston: Houghton Mifflin.

Shakespeare, William. 1997b. The tragedy of Coriolanus. In *The Riverside Shakespeare*, edited by G. Blakemore Evans, and J. J. M. Tobin, 1444–1488. 2nd. Boston: Houghton Mifflin.

Shakespeare, William. 1997c. The tragedy of King Lear. In *The Riverside Shakespeare*, edited by G. Blakemore Evans, and J. J. M. Tobin, 1303–1354. 2nd ed. Boston: Houghton Mifflin.

Shakespeare, William. 1997d. The winter's tale. In *The Riverside Shakespeare*, edited by G. Blakemore Evans, and J. J. M. Tobin, 1616–1654. 2nd ed. Boston: Houghton Mifflin.

Siemund, Peter. 2014. The emergence of English reflexive verbs: An analysis based on the *Oxford English Dictionary*. *English Language and Linguistics* 18 (1):49–73.

Simpson, Jane. 1983. Resultatives. In *Papers in lexical-functional grammar*, edited by Lori Levin, Malka Rappaport, and Annie Zaenen, 143–157. Bloomington: Indiana University Linguistics Club.

Slobin, Dan I. 2006. What makes manner of motion salient? Explorations in linguistic typology, dicourse, and cognition. In *Space in languages: Linguistic systems and cognitive categories*, edited by Maya Hickmann, and Stéphane Robert, 59–81. Amsterdam: Benjamins.

Snell-Hornby, Mary. 1983. *Verb descriptivity in German and English: A contrastive study in semantic fields*. Carl Winter: Heidelberg.

Sommerer, Lotte, and Elena Smirnova, eds. 2020. *Nodes and networks in diachronic construction grammar*. Amsterdam: John Benjamins.

Stefanowitsch, Anatol. 2006. Negative evidence and the raw frequency fallacy. *Corpus Linguistics and Linguistic Theory* 2 (1):61–77.

Stefanowitsch, Anatol. 2013. Collostructional analysis. In *The Oxford handbook of construction grammar*, edited by Thomas Hoffmann, and Graeme Trousdale, 290–307. Oxford: Oxford University Press.

Stefanowitsch, Anatol, and Stefan Th. Gries. 2003. Collostructions: Investigating the interaction of words and constructions. *International Journal of Corpus Linguistics* 8 (2):209–243.

Stefanowitsch, Anatol, and Stefan Th. Gries. 2005. Covarying collexemes. *Corpus Linguistics and Linguistic Theory* 1 (1):1–43.

Stefanowitsch, Anatol, and Susanne Flach. 2020. *Too big to fail* but *big enough to pay for their mistakes*: A collostructional analysis of the patterns [*too* ADJ *to* V] and [ADJ *enough to* V]. In *Current trends in Computational Phraseology*, edited by Gloria Corpas, and Ulrich Heid, 247–272. Amsterdam: John Benjamins.

Talmy, Leonard. 1985. Lexicalization patterns: Semantic structure in lexical forms. In *Language typology and syntactic description. Volume 3: Grammatical categories and the lexicon*, edited by Timothy Shopen, 57–149. Cambridge: Cambridge University Press.

Talmy, Leonard. 1988. Force dynamics in language and cognition. *Cognitive Science* 12 (1):49–100.

Talmy, Leonard. 2000. *Toward a cognitive semantics. Volume 1: Concept structuring systems. Volume 2: Typology and process in concept structuring.* Cambridge, MA: MIT Press.

Tanaka, Shoichi. 1990. On the transitive constructions of intransitive verbs. *Bulletin of the Faculty of Liberal Arts, Nagasaki University, Humanities* 30–2, 37–58.

Tanaka, Shoichi. 1991. On the argumenthood of *that*-clauses which "communication verbs" take. *Tsukuba English Studies* 10:69–82.

Taylor, John R. 2002. *Cognitive grammar.* Oxford: Oxford University Press.

Toda, Tatsuhiko. 2006. *I hugged him good-bye* ni tsuite: Higengoteki dentatsudoushi to nijuumokutekigo koubun (On *I hugged him good-bye*: Non-verbal communication verbs and the double object construction). In *Bonds of language: A festschrift for Dr. Yasuaki Fujiwara on the occasion of his sixtieth birthday*, edited by Yuji

Ushiro, Satoshi Ota, Shinichi Tanaka, Eiji Yamada, Kazuaki Ota, Naohiro Takizawa, and Koichi Nishida, 175–188. Tokyo: Kaitakusha.

Traugott, Elizabeth Closs. 1992. Syntax. In *The Cambridge history of the English language. Volume I: The beginnings to 1066*, edited by Richard M. Hogg, 168–289. Cambridge: Cambridge University Press.

Traugott, Elizabeth Closs, and Graeme Trousdale. 2013. *Constructionalization and constructional changes.* Oxford: Oxford University Press.

Trousdale, Graeme. 2008a. Constructions in grammaticalization and lexicalization: Evidence from the history of a composite predicate construction in English. In *Constructional approaches to English grammar*, edited by Graeme Trousdale, and Nikolas Gisborne, 33–67. Berlin: De Gruyter Mouton.

Trousdale, Graeme. 2008b. Words and constructions in grammaticalization: The end of the English impersonal construction. In *Studies in the history of the English language IV: Empirical and analytical advances in the study of English language change*, edited by Susan M. Fitzmaurice, and Donka Minkova, 301–326. Berlin: De Gruyter Mouton.

Trousdale, Graeme. 2013. Multiple inheritance and constructional change. *Studies in Language* 37 (3):491–514.

Ungerer, Tobias. 2019. Priming as evidence of links between constructions: A study of aspects of the English resultative network. International Cognitive Linguistics Conference (ICLC-15), Kwansei Gakui University, Japan, August 6–11.

Ungerer, Tobias, and Stefan Hartmann. 2020. Attack of the snowclones: A corpus-based analysis of extravagant formulaic patterns. UK Cognitive Linguistics Conference 2020 (Virtual UK-CLC 2020), University of Birmingham, United Kingdom, July 27–29.

Urban, Margaret, and Josef Ruppenhofer. 2001. Shouting and screaming: Manner and noise verbs in communication. *Literary and Linguistic Computing* 16 (1):77–97.

van Gelderen, Elly. 2011. Valency changes in the history of English. *Journal of Historical Linguistics* 1 (1):106–143.

van Gelderen, Elly. 2014. Change in *psych*-verbs: A reanalysis of little v. *Catalan Journal of Linguistics* 13:99–122.

van Gelderen, Elly. 2015. Changing argument structure in the history of English: Filling up the vP. 22nd International Conference on Historical Linguistics (ICHL 22), University of Naples Federico II, Italy, July 27–31.

van Gelderen, Elly. 2018. *The diachrony of verb meaning: Aspect and argument structure*. London: Routledge.

van Marle, Jaap. 1985. *On the paradigmatic dimension of morphological creativity*. Dordrecht: Foris Publications.

Vanderveken, Daniel. 1990. *Meaning and speech acts. Volume 1: Principles of language use*. Cambridge: Cambridge University Press.

Vergaro, Carla, Jodi L. Sandford, Roberta Mastrofini, and Yhara M. Formisano. 2014. 'Hollering from across the yard': Fictive path in manner of speaking events. *Language and Cognition* 6 (3):408–426.

Verschueren, Jef. 1985. *What people say they do with words: Prolegomena to an empirical-conceptual approach to linguistic action*. Norwood: Ablex.

Visser, Frederikus Theodorus. 1963–1973. *An historical syntax of the English language. Volume I: Syntactical units with one verb*. Leiden: E. J. Brill.

Wierzbicka, Anna. 1987. *English speech act verbs: A semantic dictionary*. Sydney: Academic Press.

Wolk, Christoph, Joan Bresnan, Anette Rosenbach, and Benedikt Szmrecsanyi. 2013. Dative and genitive variability in Late Modern English: Exploring cross-constructional variation and change. *Diachronica* 30 (3):382–419.

Wustmann, Rudolf. 1894. *Verba perfectiva, namentlich im Heliand: Ein Beitrag zum Verständnis der germanischen Verbalkomposition*. Leipzig: F.W. Grunow.

Zehentner, Eva. 2019. *Competition in language change: The rise of the English dative alternation*. Berlin: De Gruyter Mouton.

Zipf, George K. 1935. *The psycho-biology of language: An introduction to dynamic philology*. Cambridge, MA: MIT Press.

Zubizarreta, Maria Luisa. 1985. The relation between morphophonology and morphosyntax: The case of romance causatives. *Linguistic Inquiry* 16 (2):247–289.
Zubizarreta, Maria Luisa. 1987. *Levels of representation in the lexicon and in the syntax*. Dordrecht: Foris Publications.
Zwicky, Arnold M. 1971. In a manner of speaking. *Linguistic Inquiry* 2 (2):223–233.

Author's Bio

Tamara Bouso holds a PhD in English Linguistics from the University of Santiago de Compostela (Spain). Her research interests include language variation and change, Diachronic Construction Grammar, and transitivization processes in the history of English.

Linguistic Insights

Studies in Language and Communication

This series aims to promote specialist language studies in the fields of linguistic theory and applied linguistics, by publishing volumes that focus on specific aspects of language use in one or several languages and provide valuable insights into language and communication research. A cross-disciplinary approach is favoured and most European languages are accepted.

The series includes two types of books:

- Monographs – featuring in-depth studies on special aspects of language theory, language analysis or language teaching.
- Collected papers – assembling papers from workshops, conferences or symposia.

Each volume of the series is subjected to a double peer-reviewing process.

Vol. 1 Maurizio Gotti & Marina Dossena (eds)
Modality in Specialized Texts. Selected Papers of the 1st CERLIS Conference.
421 pages. 2001. ISBN 3-906767-10-8 · US-ISBN 0-8204-5340-4

Vol. 2 Giuseppina Cortese & Philip Riley (eds)
Domain-specific English. Textual Practices across Communities and Classrooms.
420 pages. 2002. ISBN 3-906768-98-8 · US-ISBN 0-8204-5884-8

Vol. 3 Maurizio Gotti, Dorothee Heller & Marina Dossena (eds)
Conflict and Negotiation in Specialized Texts. Selected Papers of the 2nd CERLIS Conference.
470 pages. 2002. ISBN 3-906769-12-7 · US-ISBN 0-8204-5887-2

Vol. 4 Maurizio Gotti, Marina Dossena, Richard Dury, Roberta Facchinetti & Maria Lima
Variation in Central Modals. A Repertoire of Forms and Types of Usage in Middle English and Early Modern English.
364 pages. 2002. ISBN 3-906769-84-4 · US-ISBN 0-8204-5898-8

Editorial address:

Prof. Maurizio Gotti Università di Bergamo, Dipartimento di Lingue, Letterature e Culture Straniere Piazza Rosate 2, 24129 Bergamo, Italy
Fax: +39 035 2052789, E-Mail: m.gotti@unibg.it

Vol. 5 Stefania Nuccorini (ed.)
Phrases and Phraseology. Data and Descriptions.
187 pages. 2002. ISBN 3-906770-08-7 · US-ISBN 0-8204-5933-X

Vol. 6 Vijay Bhatia, Christopher N. Candlin & Maurizio Gotti (eds)
Legal Discourse in Multilingual and Multicultural Contexts.
Arbitration Texts in Europe.
385 pages. 2003. ISBN 3-906770-85-0 · US-ISBN 0-8204-6254-3

Vol. 7 Marina Dossena & Charles Jones (eds)
Insights into Late Modern English. 2nd edition.
378 pages. 2003, 2007.
ISBN 978-3-03911-257-9 · US-ISBN 978-0-8204-8927-8

Vol. 8 Maurizio Gotti
Specialized Discourse. Linguistic Features and Changing Conventions.
351 pages. 2003, 2005.
ISBN 3-03910-606-6 · US-ISBN 0-8204-7000-7

Vol. 9 Alan Partington, John Morley & Louann Haarman (eds)
Corpora and Discourse.
420 pages. 2004. ISBN 3-03910-026-2 · US-ISBN 0-8204-6262-4

Vol. 10 Martina Möllering
The Acquisition of German Modal Particles. A Corpus-Based Approach.
290 pages. 2004. ISBN 3-03910-043-2 · US-ISBN 0-8204-6273-X

Vol. 11 David Hart (ed.)
English Modality in Context. Diachronic Perspectives.
261 pages. 2003. ISBN 3-03910-046-7 · US-ISBN 0-8204-6852-5

Vol. 12 Wendy Swanson
Modes of Co-reference as an Indicator of Genre.
430 pages. 2003. ISBN 3-03910-052-1 · US-ISBN 0-8204-6855-X

Vol. 13 Gina Poncini
Discursive Strategies in Multicultural Business Meetings.
2nd edition. 338 pages. 2004, 2007.
ISBN 978-3-03911-296-8 · US-ISBN 978-0-8204-8937-7

Vol. 14 Christopher N. Candlin & Maurizio Gotti (eds)
Intercultural Aspects of Specialized Communication.
2nd edition. 369 pages. 2004, 2007.
ISBN 978-3-03911-258-6 · US-ISBN 978-0-8204-8926-1

Vol. 15 Gabriella Del Lungo Camiciotti & Elena Tognini Bonelli (eds)
Academic Discourse. New Insights into Evaluation.
234 pages. 2004. ISBN 3-03910-353-9 · US-ISBN 0-8204-7016-3

Vol. 16 Marina Dossena & Roger Lass (eds)
Methods and Data in English Historical Dialectology.
405 pages. 2004. ISBN 3-03910-362-8 · US-ISBN 0-8204-7018-X

Vol. 17 Judy Noguchi
The Science Review Article. An Opportune Genre in
the Construction of Science.
274 pages. 2006. ISBN 3-03910-426-8 · US-ISBN 0-8204-7034-1

Vol. 18 Giuseppina Cortese & Anna Duszak (eds)
Identity, Community, Discourse. English in Intercultural Settings.
495 pages. 2005. ISBN 3-03910-632-5 · US-ISBN 0-8204-7163-1

Vol. 19 Anna Trosborg & Poul Erik Flyvholm Jørgensen (eds)
Business Discourse. Texts and Contexts.
250 pages. 2005. ISBN 3-03910-606-6 · US-ISBN 0-8204-7000-7

Vol. 20 Christopher Williams
Tradition and Change in Legal English. Verbal Constructions in Prescriptive Texts.
2nd revised edition. 216 pages. 2005, 2007. ISBN 978-3-03911-444-3.

Vol. 21 Katarzyna Dziubalska-Kolaczyk & Joanna Przedlacka (eds)
English Pronunciation Models: A Changing Scene.
2nd edition. 476 pages. 2005, 2008. ISBN 978-3-03911-682-9.

Vol. 22 Christián Abello-Contesse, Rubén Chacón-Beltrán, M. Dolores López-Jiménez & M. Mar Torreblanca-López (eds)
Age in L2 Acquisition and Teaching.
214 pages. 2006. ISBN 3-03910-668-6 · US-ISBN 0-8204-7174-7

Vol. 23 Vijay K. Bhatia, Maurizio Gotti, Jan Engberg & Dorothee Heller (eds)
Vagueness in Normative Texts.
474 pages. 2005. ISBN 3-03910-653-8 · US-ISBN 0-8204-7169-0

Vol. 24 Paul Gillaerts & Maurizio Gotti (eds)
Genre Variation in Business Letters. 2nd printing.
407 pages. 2008. ISBN 978-3-03911-681-2.

Vol. 25 Ana María Hornero, María José Luzón & Silvia Murillo (eds)
Corpus Linguistics. Applications for the Study of English.
2nd printing. 526 pages. 2006, 2008. ISBN 978-3-03911-726-0

Vol. 26 J. Lachlan Mackenzie & María de los Ángeles Gómez-González (eds)
Studies in Functional Discourse Grammar.
259 pages. 2005. ISBN 3-03910-696-1 · US-ISBN 0-8204-7558-0

Vol. 27 Debbie G. E. Ho
Classroom Talk. Exploring the Sociocultural Structure of Formal ESL Learning.
2nd edition. 254 pages. 2006, 2007. ISBN 978-3-03911-434-4

Vol. 28 Javier Pérez-Guerra, Dolores González-Álvarez, Jorge L. Bueno-Alonso & Esperanza Rama-Martínez (eds)
'Of Varying Language and Opposing Creed'. New Insights into Late Modern English.
455 pages. 2007. ISBN 978-3-03910-788-9

Vol. 29 Francesca Bargiela-Chiappini & Maurizio Gotti (eds)
Asian Business Discourse(s).
350 pages. 2005. ISBN 3-03910-804-2 · US-ISBN 0-8204-7574-2

Vol. 30 Nicholas Brownlees (ed.)
News Discourse in Early Modern Britain. Selected Papers of CHINED 2004.
300 pages. 2006. ISBN 3-03910-805-0 · US-ISBN 0-8204-8025-8

Vol. 31 Roberta Facchinetti & Matti Rissanen (eds)
Corpus-based Studies of Diachronic English.
300 pages. 2006. ISBN 3-03910-851-4 · US-ISBN 0-8204-8040-1

Vol. 32 Marina Dossena & Susan M. Fitzmaurice (eds)
Business and Official Correspondence. Historical Investigations.
209 pages. 2006. ISBN 3-03910-880-8 · US-ISBN 0-8204-8352-4

Vol. 33 Giuliana Garzone & Srikant Sarangi (eds)
Discourse, Ideology and Specialized Communication.
494 pages. 2007. ISBN 978-3-03910-888-6

Vol. 34 Giuliana Garzone & Cornelia Ilie (eds)
The Use of English in Institutional and Business Settings.
An Intercultural Perspective.
372 pages. 2007. ISBN 978-3-03910-889-3

Vol. 35 Vijay K. Bhatia & Maurizio Gotti (eds)
Explorations in Specialized Genres.
316 pages. 2006. ISBN 3-03910-995-2 · US-ISBN 0-8204-8372-9

Vol. 36 Heribert Picht (ed.)
Modern Approaches to Terminological Theories and Applications.
432 pages. 2006. ISBN 3-03911-156-6 · US-ISBN 0-8204-8380-X

Vol. 37 Anne Wagner & Sophie Cacciaguidi-Fahy (eds)
Legal Language and the Search for Clarity / Le langage juridique et la quête de clarté. Practice and Tools / Pratiques et instruments.
487 pages. 2006. ISBN 3-03911-169-8 · US-ISBN 0-8204-8388-5

Vol. 38 Juan Carlos Palmer-Silveira, Miguel F. Ruiz-Garrido & Inmaculada Fortanet-Gómez (eds)
Intercultural and International Business Communication.
Theory, Research and Teaching.
2nd edition. 343 pages. 2006, 2008. ISBN 978-3-03911-680-5

Vol. 39 Christiane Dalton-Puffer, Dieter Kastovsky, Nikolaus Ritt & Herbert Schendl (eds)
Syntax, Style and Grammatical Norms. English from 1500–2000.
250 pages. 2006. ISBN 3-03911-181-7 · US-ISBN 0-8204-8394-X

Vol. 40 Marina Dossena & Irma Taavitsainen (eds)
Diachronic Perspectives on Domain-Specific English.
280 pages. 2006. ISBN 3-03910-176-0 · US-ISBN 0-8204-8391-5

Vol. 41 John Flowerdew & Maurizio Gotti (eds)
Studies in Specialized Discourse.
293 pages. 2006. ISBN 3-03911-178-7

Vol. 42 Ken Hyland & Marina Bondi (eds)
Academic Discourse Across Disciplines.
320 pages. 2006. ISBN 3-03911-183-3 · US-ISBN 0-8204-8396-6

Vol. 43 Paul Gillaerts & Philip Shaw (eds)
The Map and the Landscape. Norms and Practices in Genre.
256 pages. 2006. ISBN 3-03911-182-5 · US-ISBN 0-8204-8395-4

Vol. 44 Maurizio Gotti & Davide Giannoni (eds)
New Trends in Specialized Discourse Analysis.
301 pages. 2006. ISBN 3-03911-184-1 · US-ISBN 0-8204-8381-8

Vol. 45 Maurizio Gotti & Françoise Salager-Meyer (eds)
Advances in Medical Discourse Analysis. Oral and Written Contexts.
492 pages. 2006. ISBN 3-03911-185-X · US-ISBN 0-8204-8382-6

Vol. 46 Maurizio Gotti & Susan Šarcević (eds)
Insights into Specialized Translation.
396 pages. 2006. ISBN 3-03911-186-8 · US-ISBN 0-8204-8383-4

Vol. 47 Khurshid Ahmad & Margaret Rogers (eds)
Evidence-based LSP. Translation, Text and Terminology.
584 pages. 2007. ISBN 978-3-03911-187-9

Vol. 48 Hao Sun & Dániel Z. Kádár (eds)
It's the Dragon's Turn. Chinese Institutional Discourses.
262 pages. 2008. ISBN 978-3-03911-175-6

Vol. 49 Cristina Suárez-Gómez
Relativization in Early English (950-1250). the Position of Relative Clauses.
149 pages. 2006. ISBN 3-03911-203-1 · US-ISBN 0-8204-8904-2

Vol. 50 Maria Vittoria Calvi & Luisa Chierichetti (eds)
Nuevas tendencias en el discurso de especialidad.
319 pages. 2006. ISBN 978-3-03911-261-6

Vol. 51 Mari Carmen Campoy & María José Luzón (eds)
Spoken Corpora in Applied Linguistics.
274 pages. 2008. ISBN 978-3-03911-275-3

Vol. 52 Konrad Ehlich & Dorothee Heller (Hrsg.)
Die Wissenschaft und ihre Sprachen.
323 pages. 2006. ISBN 978-3-03911-272-2

Vol. 53 Jingyu Zhang
The Semantic Salience Hierarchy Model. The L2 Acquisition of Psych Predicates
273 pages. 2007. ISBN 978-3-03911-300-2

Vol. 54 Norman Fairclough, Giuseppina Cortese & Patrizia Ardizzone (eds)
Discourse and Contemporary Social Change.
555 pages. 2007. ISBN 978-3-03911-276-0

Vol. 55 Jan Engberg, Marianne Grove Ditlevsen, Peter Kastberg & Martin Stegu (eds)
New Directions in LSP Teaching.
331 pages. 2007. ISBN 978-3-03911-433-7

Vol. 56 Dorothee Heller & Konrad Ehlich (Hrsg.)
Studien zur Rechtskommunikation.
322 pages. 2007. ISBN 978-3-03911-436-8

Vol. 57 Teruhiro Ishiguro & Kang-kwong Luke (eds)
Grammar in Cross-Linguistic Perspective.
The Syntax, Semantics, and Pragmatics of Japanese and Chinese.
304 pages. 2012. ISBN 978-3-03911-445-0

Vol. 58 Carmen Frehner
Email – SMS – MMS
294 pages. 2008. ISBN 978-3-03911-451-1

Vol. 59 Isabel Balteiro
The Directionality of Conversion in English. A Dia-Synchronic Study.
276 pages. 2007. ISBN 978-3-03911-241-8

Vol. 60 Maria Milagros Del Saz Rubio
English Discourse Markers of Reformulation.
237 pages. 2007. ISBN 978-3-03911-196-1

Vol. 61 Sally Burgess & Pedro Martín-Martín (eds)
English as an Additional Language in Research Publication and Communication.
259 pages. 2008. ISBN 978-3-03911-462-7

Vol. 62 Sandrine Onillon
Pratiques et représentations de l'écrit.
458 pages. 2008. ISBN 978-3-03911-464-1

Vol. 63 Hugo Bowles & Paul Seedhouse (eds)
Conversation Analysis and Language for Specific Purposes.
2nd edition. 337 pages. 2007, 2009. ISBN 978-3-0343-0045-2

Vol. 64 Vijay K. Bhatia, Christopher N. Candlin & Paola Evangelisti Allori (eds)
Language, Culture and the Law.
The Formulation of Legal Concepts across Systems and Cultures.
342 pages. 2008. ISBN 978-3-03911-470-2

Vol. 65 Jonathan Culpeper & Dániel Z. Kádár (eds)
Historical (Im)politeness.
300 pages. 2010. ISBN 978-3-03911-496-2

Vol. 66 Linda Lombardo (ed.)
Using Corpora to Learn about Language and Discourse.
237 pages. 2009. ISBN 978-3-03911-522-8

Vol. 67 Natsumi Wakamoto
Extroversion/Introversion in Foreign Language Learning.
Interactions with Learner Strategy Use.
159 pages. 2009. ISBN 978-3-03911-596-9

Vol. 68 Eva Alcón-Soler (ed.)
Learning How to Request in an Instructed Language Learning Context.
260 pages. 2008. ISBN 978-3-03911-601-0

Vol. 69 Domenico Pezzini
The Translation of Religious Texts in the Middle Ages.
428 pages. 2008. ISBN 978-3-03911-600-3

Vol. 70 Tomoko Tode
Effects of Frequency in Classroom Second Language Learning.
Quasi-experiment and stimulated-recall analysis.
195 pages. 2008. ISBN 978-3-03911-602-7

Vol. 71 Egor Tsedryk
Fusion symétrique et alternances ditransitives.
211 pages. 2009. ISBN 978-3-03911-609-6

Vol. 72 Cynthia J. Kellett Bidoli & Elana Ochse (eds)
English in International Deaf Communication.
444 pages. 2008. ISBN 978-3-03911-610-2

Vol. 73 Joan C. Beal, Carmela Nocera & Massimo Sturiale (eds)
Perspectives on Prescriptivism.
269 pages. 2008. ISBN 978-3-03911-632-4

Vol. 74 Carol Taylor Torsello, Katherine Ackerley & Erik Castello (eds)
Corpora for University Language Teachers.
308 pages. 2008. ISBN 978-3-03911-639-3

Vol. 75 María Luisa Pérez Cañado (ed.)
English Language Teaching in the European Credit Transfer System. Facing the Challenge.
251 pages. 2009. ISBN 978-3-03911-654-6

Vol. 76 Marina Dossena & Ingrid Tieken-Boon van Ostade (eds)
Studies in Late Modern English Correspondence. Methodology and Data.
291 pages. 2008. ISBN 978-3-03911-658-4

Vol. 77 Ingrid Tieken-Boon van Ostade & Wim van der Wurff (eds)
Current Issues in Late Modern English.
436 pages. 2009. ISBN 978-3-03911-660-7

Vol. 78 Marta Navarro Coy (ed.)
Practical Approaches to Foreign Language Teaching and Learning.
297 pages. 2009. ISBN 978-3-03911-661-4

Vol. 79 Qing Ma
Second Language Vocabulary Acquisition.
333 pages. 2009. ISBN 978-3-03911-666-9

Vol. 80 Martin Solly, Michelangelo Conoscenti & Sandra Campagna (eds)
Verbal/Visual Narrative Texts in Higher Education.
384 pages. 2008. ISBN 978-3-03911-672-0

Vol. 81 Meiko Matsumoto
From Simple Verbs to Periphrastic Expressions: The Historical Development of Composite Predicates, Phrasal Verbs, and Related Constructions in English.
235 pages. 2008. ISBN 978-3-03911-675-1

Vol. 82 Melinda Dooly
Doing Diversity. Teachers' Construction of Their Classroom Reality.
180 pages. 2009. ISBN 978-3-03911-687-4

Vol. 83 Victoria Guillén-Nieto, Carmen Marimón-Llorca & Chelo Vargas-Sierra (eds)
Intercultural Business Communication and Simulation and Gaming Methodology.
392 pages. 2009. ISBN 978-3-03911-688-1

Vol. 84 Maria Grazia Guido
English as a Lingua Franca in Cross-cultural Immigration Domains.
285 pages. 2008. ISBN 978-3-03911-689-8

Vol. 85 Erik Castello
Text Complexity and Reading Comprehension Tests.
352 pages. 2008. ISBN 978-3-03911-717-8

Vol. 86 Maria-Lluisa Gea-Valor, Isabel García-Izquierdo & Maria-José Esteve (eds)
Linguistic and Translation Studies in Scientific Communication.
317 pages. 2010. ISBN 978-3-0343-0069-8

Vol. 87 Carmen Navarro, Rosa Mª Rodríguez Abella, Francesca Dalle Pezze & Renzo Miotti (eds)
La comunicación especializada.
355 pages. 2008. ISBN 978-3-03911-733-8

Vol. 88 Kiriko Sato
The Development from Case-Forms to Prepositional Constructions in Old English Prose.
231 pages. 2009. ISBN 978-3-03911-763-5

Vol. 89 Dorothee Heller (Hrsg.)
Formulierungsmuster in deutscher und italienischer Fachkommunikation. Intra- und interlinguale Perspektiven.
315 pages. 2008. ISBN 978-3-03911-778-9

Vol. 90 Henning Bergenholtz, Sandro Nielsen & Sven Tarp (eds)
Lexicography at a Crossroads. Dictionaries and Encyclopedias Today, Lexicographical Tools Tomorrow.
372 pages. 2009. ISBN 978-3-03911-799-4

Vol. 91 Manouchehr Moshtagh Khorasani
The Development of Controversies. From the Early Modern Period to Online Discussion Forums.
317 pages. 2009. ISBN 978-3-3911-711-6

Vol. 92 María Luisa Carrió-Pastor (ed.)
Content and Language Integrated Learning. Cultural Diversity.
178 pages. 2009. ISBN 978-3-3911-818-2

Vol. 93 Roger Berry
Terminology in English Language Teaching. Nature and Use.
262 pages. 2010. ISBN 978-3-0343-0013-1

Vol. 94 Roberto Cagliero & Jennifer Jenkins (eds)
Discourses, Communities, and Global Englishes
240 pages. 2010. ISBN 978-3-0343-0012-4

Vol. 95 Facchinetti Roberta, Crystal David, Seidlhofer Barbara (eds)
From International to Local English – And Back Again.
268 pages. 2010. ISBN 978-3-0343-0011-7

Vol. 96 Cesare Gagliardi & Alan Maley (eds)
EIL, ELF, Global English. Teaching and Learning Issues
376 pages. 2010. ISBN 978-3-0343-0010-0

Vol. 97 Sylvie Hancil (ed.)
The Role of Prosody in Affective Speech.
403 pages. 2009. ISBN 978-3-03911-696-6

Vol. 98 Marina Dossena & Roger Lass (eds)
Studies in English and European Historical Dialectology.
257 pages. 2009. ISBN 978-3-0343-0024-7

Vol. 99 Christine Béal
Les interactions quotidiennes en français et en anglais. De l'approche comparative à l'analyse des situations interculturelles.
424 pages. 2010. ISBN 978-3-0343-0027-8

Vol. 100 Maurizio Gotti (ed.)
Commonality and Individuality in Academic Discourse.
398 pages. 2009. ISBN 978-3-0343-0023-0

Vol. 101 Javier E. Díaz Vera & Rosario Caballero (eds)
Textual Healing. Studies in Medieval English Medical, Scientific and Technical Texts.
213 pages. 2009. ISBN 978-3-03911-822-9

Vol. 102 Nuria Edo Marzá
The Specialised Lexicographical Approach. A Step further in Dictionary-making.
316 pages. 2009. ISBN 978-3-0343-0043-8

Vol. 103 Carlos Prado-Alonso, Lidia Gómez-García, Iria Pastor-Gómez & David Tizón-Couto (eds)
New Trends and Methodologies in Applied English Language Research. Diachronic, Diatopic and Contrastive Studies.
348 pages. 2009. ISBN 978-3-0343-0046-9

Vol. 104 Françoise Salager-Meyer & Beverly A. Lewin
Crossed Words. Criticism in Scholarly Writing?
371 pages. 2011. ISBN 978-3-0343-0049-0.

Vol. 105 Javier Ruano-García
Early Modern Northern English Lexis. A Literary Corpus-Based Study.
611 pages. 2010. ISBN 978-3-0343-0058-2

Vol. 106 Rafael Monroy-Casas
Systems for the Phonetic Transcription of English. Theory and Texts.
280 pages. 2011. ISBN 978-3-0343-0059-9

Vol. 107 Nicola T. Owtram
The Pragmatics of Academic Writing.
A Relevance Approach to the Analysis of Research Article Introductions.
311 pages. 2009. ISBN 978-3-0343-0060-5

Vol. 108 Yolanda Ruiz de Zarobe, Juan Manuel Sierra & Francisco Gallardo del Puerto (eds)
Content and Foreign Language Integrated Learning.
Contributions to Multilingualism in European Contexts
343 pages. 2011. ISBN 978-3-0343-0074-2

Vol. 109 Ángeles Linde López & Rosalía Crespo Jiménez (eds)
Professional English in the European context. The EHEA challenge.
374 pages. 2010. ISBN 978-3-0343-0088-9

Vol. 110 Rosalía Rodríguez-Vázquez
The Rhythm of Speech, Verse and Vocal Music. A New Theory.
394 pages. 2010. ISBN 978-3-0343-0309-5

Vol. 111 Anastasios Tsangalidis & Roberta Facchinetti (eds)
Studies on English Modality. In Honour of Frank Palmer.
392 pages. 2009. ISBN 978-3-0343-0310-1

Vol. 112 Jing Huang
Autonomy, Agency and Identity in Foreign Language Learning and Teaching.
400 pages. 2013. ISBN 978-3-0343-0370-5

Vol. 113 Mihhail Lotman & Maria-Kristiina Lotman (eds)
Frontiers in Comparative Prosody. In memoriam: Mikhail Gasparov.
426 pages. 2011. ISBN 978-3-0343-0373-6

Vol. 114 Merja Kytö, John Scahill & Harumi Tanabe (eds)
Language Change and Variation from Old English to Late Modern English.
A Festschrift for Minoji Akimoto
422 pages. 2010. ISBN 978-3-0343-0372-9

Vol. 115 Giuliana Garzone & Paola Catenaccio (eds)
Identities across Media and Modes. Discursive Perspectives.
379 pages. 2009. ISBN 978-3-0343-0386-6

Vol. 116 Elena Landone
Los marcadores del discurso y cortesía verbal en español.
390 pages. 2010. ISBN 978-3-0343-0413-9

Vol. 117 Maurizio Gotti & Christopher Williams (eds)
Legal Discourse across Languages and Cultures.
339 pages. 2010. ISBN 978-3-0343-0425-2

Vol. 118 David Hirsh
Academic Vocabulary in Context.
217 pages. 2010. ISBN 978-3-0343-0426-9

Vol. 119 Yvonne Dröschel
Lingua Franca English. The Role of Simplification and Transfer.
358 pages. 2011. ISBN 978-3-0343-0432-0

Vol. 120 Tengku Sepora Tengku Mahadi, Helia Vaezian & Mahmoud Akbari
Corpora in Translation. A Practical Guide.
135 pages. 2010. ISBN 978-3-0343-0434-4

Vol. 121 Davide Simone Giannoni & Celina Frade (eds)
Researching Language and the Law. Textual Features and Translation Issues.
278 pages. 2010. ISBN 978-3-0343-0443-6

Vol. 122 Daniel Madrid & Stephen Hughes (eds)
Studies in Bilingual Education.
472 pages. 2011. ISBN 978-3-0343-0474-0

Vol. 123 Vijay K. Bhatia, Christopher N. Candlin & Maurizio Gotti (eds)
The Discourses of Dispute Resolution.
290 pages. 2010. ISBN 978-3-0343-0476-4

Vol. 124 Davide Simone Giannoni
Mapping Academic Values in the Disciplines. A Corpus-Based Approach.
288 pages. 2010. ISBN 978-3-0343-0488-7

Vol. 125 Giuliana Garzone & James Archibald (eds)
Discourse, Identities and Roles in Specialized Communication.
419 pages. 2010. ISBN 978-3-0343-0494-8

Vol. 126 Iria Pastor-Gómez
The Status and Development of N+N Sequences in
Contemporary English Noun Phrases.
216 pages. 2011. ISBN 978-3-0343-0534-1

Vol. 127 Carlos Prado-Alonso
Full-verb Inversion in Written and Spoken English.
261 pages. 2011. ISBN 978-3-0343-0535-8

Vol. 128 Tony Harris & María Moreno Jaén (eds)
Corpus Linguistics in Language Teaching.
214 pages. 2010. ISBN 978-3-0343-0524-2

Vol. 129 Tetsuji Oda & Hiroyuki Eto (eds)
Multiple Perspectives on English Philology and History of Linguistics.
A Festschrift for Shoichi Watanabe on his 80th Birthday.
378 pages. 2010. ISBN 978-3-0343-0480-1

Vol. 130 Luisa Chierichetti & Giovanni Garofalo (eds)
Lengua y Derecho. líneas de investigación interdisciplinaria.
283 pages. 2010. 978-3-0343-0463-4

Vol. 131 Paola Evangelisti Allori & Giuliana Garzone (eds)
Discourse, Identities and Genres in Corporate Communication.
Sponsorship, Advertising and Organizational Communication.
324 pages. 2011. 978-3-0343-0591-4

Vol. 132 Leyre Ruiz de Zarobe & Yolanda Ruiz de Zarobe (eds)
Speech Acts and Politeness across Languages and Cultures.
402 pages. 2012. 978-3-0343-0611-9

Vol. 133 Thomas Christiansen
Cohesion. A Discourse Perspective.
387 pages. 2011. 978-3-0343-0619-5

Vol. 134 Giuliana Garzone & Maurizio Gotti
Discourse, Communication and the Enterprise. Genres and Trends.
451 pages. 2011. ISBN 978-3-0343-0620-1

Vol. 135 Zsuzsa Hoffmann
Ways of the World's Words.
Language Contact in the Age of Globalization.
334 pages 2011. ISBN 978-3-0343-0673-7

Vol. 136 Cecilia Varcasia (ed.)
Becoming Multilingual.
Language Learning and Language Policy between Attitudes and Identities.
213 pages. 2011. ISBN 978-3-0343-0687-5

Vol. 137 Susy Macqueen
The Emergence of Patterns in Second Language Writing.
A Sociocognitive Exploration of Lexical Trails.
325 pages. 2012. ISBN 978-3-0343-1010-9

Vol. 138 Maria Vittoria Calvi & Giovanna Mapelli (eds)
La lengua del turismo. Géneros discursivos y terminología.
365 pages. 2011. ISBN 978-3-0343-1011-6

Vol. 139 Ken Lau
Learning to Become a Professional in a Textually-Mediated World.
A Text-Oriented Study of Placement Practices.
261 pages. 2012. ISBN 978-3-0343-1016-1

Vol. 140 Sandra Campagna, Giuliana Garzone, Cornelia Ilie & Elizabeth Rowley-Jolivet (eds)
Evolving Genres in Web-mediated Communication.
337 pages. 2012. ISBN 978-3-0343-1013-0

Vol. 141 Edith Esch & Martin Solly (eds)
The Sociolinguistics of Language Education in International Contexts.
263 pages. 2012. ISBN 978-3-0343-1009-3

Vol. 142 Forthcoming.

Vol. 143 David Tizón-Couto
Left Dislocation in English. A Functional-Discoursal Approach.
416 pages. 2012. ISBN 978-3-0343-1037-6

Vol. 144 Margrethe Petersen & Jan Engberg (eds)
Current Trends in LSP Research. Aims and Methods.
323 pages. 2011. ISBN 978-3-0343-1054-3

Vol. 145 David Tizón-Couto, Beatriz Tizón-Couto, Iria Pastor-Gómez & Paula Rodríguez-Puente (eds)
New Trends and Methodologies in Applied English Language Research II.
Studies in Language Variation, Meaning and Learning.
283 pages. 2012. ISBN 978-3-0343-1061-1

Vol. 146 Rita Salvi & Hiromasa Tanaka (eds)
Intercultural Interactions in Business and Management.
306 pages. 2011. ISBN 978-3-0343-1039-0

Vol. 147 Francesco Straniero Sergio & Caterina Falbo (eds)
Breaking Ground in Corpus-based Interpreting Studies.
254 pages. 2012. ISBN 978-3-0343-1071-0

Vol. 148 Forthcoming.

Vol. 149 Vijay K. Bhatia & Paola Evangelisti Allori (eds)
Discourse and Identity in the Professions. Legal, Corporate and Institutional Citizenship.
352 pages. 2011. ISBN 978-3-0343-1079-6

Vol. 150 Maurizio Gotti (ed.)
Academic Identity Traits. A Corpus-Based Investigation.
363 pages. 2012. ISBN 978-3-0343-1141-0

Vol. 151 Priscilla Heynderickx, Sylvain Dieltjens, Geert Jacobs, Paul Gillaerts & Elizabeth de Groot (eds)
The Language Factor in International Business.
New Perspectives on Research, Teaching and Practice.
320 pages. 2012. ISBN 978-3-0343-1090-1

Vol. 152 Paul Gillaerts, Elizabeth de Groot, Sylvain Dieltjens, Priscilla Heynderickx & Geert Jacobs (eds)
Researching Discourse in Business Genres. Cases and Corpora.
215 pages. 2012. ISBN 978-3-0343-1092-5

Vol. 153 Yongyan Zheng
Dynamic Vocabulary Development in a Foreign Language.
262 pages. 2012. ISBN 978-3-0343-1106-9

Vol. 154 Carmen Argondizzo (ed.)
Creativity and Innovation in Language Education.
357 pages. 2012. ISBN 978-3-0343-1080-2

Vol. 155 David Hirsh (ed.)
Current Perspectives in Second Language Vocabulary Research.
180 pages. 2012. ISBN 978-3-0343-1108-3

Vol. 156 Seiji Shinkawa
Unhistorical Gender Assignment in Lahamon's *Brut*. A Case Study of a Late Stage in the Development of Grammatical Gender toward its Ultimate Loss.
186 pages. 2012. ISBN 978-3-0343-1124-3

Vol. 157 Yeonkwon Jung
Basics of Organizational Writing: A Critical Reading Approach.
151 pages. 2014. ISBN 978-3-0343-1137-3.

Vol. 158 Bárbara Eizaga Rebollar (ed.)
Studies in Linguistics and Cognition.
301 pages. 2012. ISBN 978-3-0343-1138-0

Vol. 159 Giuliana Garzone, Paola Catenaccio, Chiara Degano (eds)
Genre Change in the Contemporary World. Short-term Diachronic Perspectives.
329 pages. 2012. ISBN 978-3-0343-1214-1

Vol. 160 Carol Berkenkotter, Vijay K. Bhatia & Maurizio Gotti (eds)
Insights into Academic Genres.
468 pages. 2012. ISBN 978-3-0343-1211-0

Vol. 161 Beatriz Tizón-Couto
Clausal Complements in Native and Learner Spoken English. A corpus-based study with Lindsei and Vicolse. 357 pages. 2013. ISBN 978-3-0343-1184-7

Vol. 162 Patrizia Anesa
Jury Trials and the Popularization of Legal Language. A Discourse Analytical Approach.
247 pages. 2012. ISBN 978-3-0343-1231-8

Vol. 163 David Hirsh
Endangered Languages, Knowledge Systems and Belief Systems.
153 pages. 2013. ISBN 978-3-0343-1232-5

Vol. 164 Eugenia Sainz (ed.)
De la estructura de la frase al tejido del discurso. Estudios contrastivos español/italiano.
305 pages. 2014. ISBN 978-3-0343-1253-0

Vol. 165 Julia Bamford, Franca Poppi & Davide Mazzi (eds)
Space, Place and the Discursive Construction of Identity.
367 pages. 2014. ISBN 978-3-0343-1249-3

Vol. 166 Rita Salvi & Janet Bowker (eds)
Space, Time and the Construction of Identity.
Discursive Indexicality in Cultural, Institutional and Professional Fields.
324 pages. 2013. ISBN 978-3-0343-1254-7

Vol. 167 Shunji Yamazaki & Robert Sigley (eds)
Approaching Language Variation through Corpora. A Festschrift in Honour of Toshio Saito.
421 pages. 2013. ISBN 978-3-0343-1264-6

Vol. 168 Franca Poppi
Global Interactions in English as a Lingua Franca. How written communication is changing under the influence of electronic media and new contexts of use.
249 pages. 2012. ISBN 978-3-0343-1276-9

Vol. 169 Miguel A. Aijón Oliva & María José Serrano
Style in syntax. Investigating variation in Spanish pronoun subjects.
239 pages. 2013. ISBN 978-3-0343-1244-8

Vol. 170 Inés Olza, Óscar Loureda & Manuel Casado-Velarde (eds)
Language Use in the Public Sphere. Methodological Perspectives and Empirical Applications
564 pages. 2014. ISBN 978-3-0343-1286-8

Vol. 171 Aleksandra Matulewska
Legilinguistic Translatology. A Parametric Approach to Legal Translation.
279 pages. 2013. ISBN 978-3-0343-1287-5

Vol. 172 Maurizio Gotti & Carmen Sancho Guinda (eds)
Narratives in Academic and Professional Genres.
513 pages. 2013. ISBN 978-3-0343-1371-1

Vol. 173 Madalina Chitez
Learner corpus profiles. The case of Romanian Learner English.
244 pages. 2014. ISBN 978-3-0343-1410-7

Vol. 174 Chihiro Inoue
Task Equivalence in Speaking Tests.
251 pages. 2013. ISBN 978-3-0343-1417-6

Vol. 175 Gabriel Quiroz & Pedro Patiño (eds.)
LSP in Colombia: advances and challenges.
339 pages. 2014. ISBN 978-3-0343-1434-3

Vol. 176 Catherine Resche
Economic Terms and Beyond: Capitalising on the Wealth of Notions.
How Researchers in Specialised Varieties of English Can Benefit from Focusing on Terms.
332 pages. 2013. ISBN 978-3-0343-1435-0

Vol. 177 Wei Wang
Media representation of migrant workers in China. Identities and stances
198 pages. 2018. 978-3-0343-1436-7

Vol. 178 Cécile Desoutter & Caroline Mellet (dir.)
Le discours rapporté: approches linguistiques et perspectives didactiques.
270 pages. 2013. ISBN 978-3-0343-1292-9

Vol. 179 Ana Díaz-Negrillo & Francisco Javier Díaz-Pérez (eds)
Specialisation and Variation in Language Corpora.
341 pages. 2014. ISBN 978-3-0343-1316-2

Vol. 180 Pilar Alonso
A Multi-dimensional Approach to Discourse Coherence. From Standardness to Creativity.
247 pages. 2014. ISBN 978-3-0343-1325-4

Vol. 181 Alejandro Alcaraz-Sintes & Salvador Valera-Hernández (eds)
Diachrony and Synchrony in English Corpus Linguistics.
393 pages. 2014. ISBN 978-3-0343-1326-1

Vol. 182 Runhan Zhang
Investigating Linguistic Knowledge of a Second Language.
207 pages. 2015. ISBN 978-3-0343-1330-8

Vol. 183 Hajar Abdul Rahim & Shakila Abdul Manan (eds.)
English in Malaysia. Postcolonial and Beyond.
267 pages. 2014. ISBN 978-3-0343-1341-4

Vol. 184 Virginie Fasel Lauzon
Comprendre et apprendre dans l'interaction. Les séquences d'explication en classe de français langue seconde.
292 pages. 2014. ISBN 978-3-0343-1451-0

Vol. 185 Forthcoming.

Vol. 186 Wei Ren
L2 Pragmatic Development in Study Abroad Contexts
256 pages. 2015. ISBN 978-3-0343-1358-2

Vol. 187 Marina Bondi & Rosa Lorés Sanz (eds)
Abstracts in Academic Discourse. Variation and Change.
361 pages. 2014. ISBN 978-3-0343-1483-1

Vol. 188 Giuditta Caliendo
Rethinking Community. Discourse, Identity and Citizenship in the European Union.
240 pages. 2017. ISBN 978-3-0343-1561-6

Vol. 189 Paola Evangelisti Allori (ed.)
Identities in and across Cultures.
315 pages. 2014. ISBN 978-3-0343-1458-9

Vol. 190 Erik Castello, Katherine Ackerley & Francesca Coccetta (eds).
Studies in Learner Corpus Linguistics. Research and Applications for Foreign Language Teaching and Assessment.
358 pages. 2015. ISBN 978-3-0343-1506-7

Vol. 191 Ruth Breeze, Maurizio Gotti & Carmen Sancho Guinda (eds)
Interpersonality in Legal Genres.
389 pages. 2014. ISBN 978-3-0343-1524-1

Vol. 192 Paola Evangelisti Allori, John Bateman & Vijay K. Bhatia (eds)
Evolution in Genre. Emergence, Variation, Multimodality.
364 pages. 2014. ISBN 978-3-0343-1533-3

Vol. 193 Jiyeon Kook
Agency in Arzt-Patient-Gesprächen. Zur interaktionistischen Konzeptualisierung von Agency
271 pages. 2015. ISBN 978-3-0343-1666-8

Vol. 194 Susana Nicolás Román & Juan José Torres Núñez (eds)
Drama and CLIL. A new challenge for the teaching approaches in bilingual education.
170 pages. 2015. ISBN 978-3-0343-1629-3

Vol. 195 Alessandra Molino & Serenella Zanotti (eds)
Observing Norm, Observing Usage. Lexis in Dictionaries and in the Media.
430 pages. 2015. ISBN 978-3-0343-1584-5

Vol. 196 Begoña Soneira
A Lexical Description of English for Architecture. A Corpus-based Approach.
267 pages. 2015. ISBN 978-3-0343-1602-6

Vol. 197 M Luisa Roca-Varela
False Friends in Learner Corpora. A corpus-based study of English false friends in the written and spoken production of Spanish learners.
348 pages. 2015. ISBN 978-3-0343-1620-0

Vol. 198 Rahma Al-Mahrooqi & Christopher Denman
Bridging the Gap between Education and Employment. English Language Instruction in EFL Contexts.
416 pages. 2015. ISBN 978-3-0343-1681-1

Vol. 199 Rita Salvi & Janet Bowker (eds)
The Dissemination of Contemporary Knowledge in English. Genres, discourse strategies and professional practices.
171 pages. 2015. ISBN 978-3-0343-1679-8

Vol. 200 Maurizio Gotti & Davide S. Giannoni (eds)
Corpus Analysis for Descriptive and Pedagogical Purposes. ESP Perspectives.
432 pages. 2014. ISBN 978-3-0343-1516-6

Vol. 201 Ida Ruffolo
The Perception of Nature in Travel Promotion Texts. A Corpus-based Discourse Analysis.
148 pages. 2015. ISBN 978-3-0343-1521-0

Vol. 202 Ives Trevian
English suffixes. Stress-assignment properties, productivity, selection and combinatorial processes.
471 pages. 2015. ISBN 978-3-0343-1576-0

Vol. 203 Maurizio Gotti, Stefania Maci & Michele Sala (eds)
Insights into Medical Communication.
422 pages. 2015. ISBN 978-3-0343-1694-1

Vol. 204 Carmen Argondizzo (ed.)
European Projects in University Language Centres. Creativity, Dynamics, Best Practice.
371 pages. 2015. ISBN 978-3-0343-1696-5

Vol. 205 Aura Luz Duffé Montalván (ed.)
Estudios sobre el léxico. Puntos y contrapuntos.
502 pages. 2016. ISBN 978-3-0343-2011-5

Vol. 206 Maria Pavesi, Maicol Formentelli & Elisa Ghia (eds)
The Languages of Dubbing. Mainstream Audiovisual Translation in Italy.
275 pages. 2014. ISBN 978-3-0343-1646-0

Vol. 207 Ruth Breeze & Inés Olza (eds)
Evaluation in media discourse. European perspectives.
268 pages. 2017. ISBN 978-3-0343-2014-6

Vol. 208 Vijay K. Bhatia & Maurizio Gotti (eds)
Arbitration Discourse in Asia.
331 pages. 2015. ISBN 978-3-0343-2032-0

Vol. 209 Sofía Bemposta-Rivas, Carla Bouzada-Jabois, Yolanda Fernández-Pena, Tamara Bouso, Yolanda J. Calvo-Benzies, Iván Tamaredo (eds)
New trends and methodologies in applied English language research III.
Synchronic and diachronic studies on discourse, lexis and grammar processing.
280 pages. 2017. ISBN 978-3-0343-2039-9

Vol. 210 Francisco Alonso Almeida, Laura Cruz García & Víctor González Ruiz (eds)
Corpus-based studies on language varieties.
285 pages. 2016. ISBN 978-3-0343-2044-3

Vol. 211 Juan Pedro Rica Peromingo
Aspectos lingüísticos y técnicos de la traducción audiovisual (TAV).
177 pages. 2016. ISBN 978-3-0343-2055-9

Vol. 212 Maria Vender
Disentangling Dyslexia. VenderPhonological and Processing Deficit in Developmental Dyslexia.
338 pages. 2017. ISBN 978-3-0343-2064-1

Vol. 213 Zhilong Xie
Bilingual Advantages. Contributions of Different Bilingual Experiences to Cognitive Control Differences Among Young-adult Bilinguals.
221 pages. 2016. ISBN 978-3-0343-2081-8

Vol. 214 Larissa D'Angelo
Academic posters. A textual and visual metadiscourse analysis.
367 pages. 2016. ISBN 978-3-0343-2083-2

Vol. 215 Evelyne Berger
Prendre la parole en L2. Regard sur la compétence d'interaction en classe de langue.
246 pages. 2016. ISBN 978-3-0343-2084-9

Vol. 216 David Lasagabaster and Aintzane Doiz (eds)
CLIL experiences in secondary and tertiary education: In search of good practices.
262 pages. 2016. ISBN 978-3-0343-2104-4

Vol. 217 Elena Kkese
Identifying Plosives in L2 English: The Case of L1 Cypriot Greek Speakers.
317 pages. 2016. ISBN 978-3-0343-2060-3

Vol. 218 Sandra Campagna, Elana Ochse, Virginia Pulcini & Martin Solly (eds)
Languaging in and across Communities: New Voices, New Identities. Studies in Honour of Giuseppina Cortese.
507 pages. 2016. ISBN 978-3-0343-2073-3

Vol. 219 Adriana Orlandi & Laura Giacomini (ed.)
Defining collocation for lexicographic purposes. From linguistic theory to lexicographic practice.
328 pages. 2016. ISBN 978-3-0343-2054-2

Vol. 220 Pietro Luigi Iaia
Analysing English as a Lingua Franca in Video Games. Linguistic Features, Experiential and Functional Dimensions of Online and Scripted Interactions.
139 pages. 2016. ISBN 978-3-0343-2138-9

Vol. 221 Dimitrinka G. Níkleva (ed.)
La formación de los docentes de español para inmigrantes en distintos contextos educativos.
390 pages. 2017. ISBN 978-3-0343-2135-8

Vol. 222 Katherine Ackerley, Marta Guarda & Francesca Helm (eds)
Sharing Perspectives on English-Medium Instruction.
308 pages. 2017. ISBN 978-3-0343-2537-0

Vol. 223 Juana I. Marín-Arrese, Julia Lavid-López, Marta Carretero, Elena Domínguez Romero, Mª Victoria Martín de la Rosa & María Pérez Blanco (eds)
Evidentiality and Modality in European Languages. Discourse-pragmatic perspectives.
427 pages. 2017. ISBN 978-3-0343-2437-3

Vol. 224 Gilles Col
Construction du sens : un modèle instructionnel pour la sémantique.
292 pages. 2017. ISBN 978-3-0343-2572-1

Vol. 225 Ana Chiquito & Gabriel Quiroz (eds)
Pobreza, Lenguaje y Medios en América Latina.
362 pages. 2017. ISBN 978-3-0343-2142-6

Vol. 226 Xu Zhang
English Quasi-Numeral Classifiers. A Corpus-Based Cognitive-Typological Study.
360 pages. 2017. ISBN 978-3-0343-2818-0

Vol. 227 María Ángeles Orts, Ruth Breeze & Maurizio Gotti (eds)
Power, Persuasion and Manipulation in Specialised Genres. Providing Keys to the Rhetoric of Professional Communities.
368 pages. 2017. ISBN 978-3-0343-3010-7

Vol. 228 Maurizio Gotti, Stefania Maci & Michele Sala (eds)
Ways of Seeing, Ways of Being: Representing the Voices of Tourism.
453 pages. 2017. ISBN 978-3-0343-3031-2

Vol. 229 Dino Selvaggi
Plurilingual Code-Switching between Standard and Local Varieties.
A Socio-Psycholinguistic Approach
371 pages. 2018. ISBN 978-3-0343-2663-6

Vol. 230 Anca-Cristina Sterie
Interprofessional interactions at the hospital. Nurses' requests and reports of problems in calls with physicians.
371 pages. 2017. ISBN 978-3-0343-2734-3

Vol. 231 Xiaodong Zhang
Understanding Chinese EFL Teachers' Beliefs and Practices in the Textbook-Based Classroom.
189 pages. 2017. ISBN 978-3-0343-3053-4

Vol. 232 Manuela Caterina Moroni & Federica Ricci Garotti (Hrsg.)
Brücken schlagen zwischen Sprachwissenschaft und DaF-Didaktik.
345 pages. 2017. ISBN 978-3-0343-2667-4

Vol. 233 Dimitrinka Georgieva Níkleva
Necesidades y tendencias en la formación del profesorado de español como lengua extranjera
401 pages. 2017. ISBN 978-3-0343-2946-0

Vol. 234 Juan Santana-Lario & Salvador Valera (Hrsg.)
Competing patterns in English affixation.
272 pages. 2017. ISBN 978-3-0343-2701-5

Vol. 235 Francisco Salgado-Robles
Desarrollo de la competencia sociolingüística por aprendices de español en un contexto de inmersión en el extranjero
241 pages. 2018. ISBN 978-3-0343-2323-9

Vol. 236 Maria Chiara Janner
Sguardi linguistici sulla marca. Analisi morfosintattica dei nomi commerciali in italiano
345 pages. 2017. ISBN 978-3-0343-2667-4

Vol. 237 Bárbara Herrero Muñoz-Cobo & Otman El Azami Zalachi
La primavera del árabe marroquí.
192 pages. 2017. ISBN 978-3-0343-3104-3

Vol. 238 Consuelo Pascual Escagedo
El papel del oyente en la construcción de la conversación espontánea de estudiantes italianos en su interlengua y en su lengua materna
295 pages. 2017. ISBN 978-3-0343-3186-9

Vol. 239 Stefania M. Maci
The MS Digby 133 *Mary Magdalene*. Beyond scribal practices: language, discourse, values and attitudes.
336 pages. 2017. ISBN 978-3-0343-3256-9

Vol. 240 Eliecer Crespo-Fernández
Taboo in Discourse. Studies on Attenuation and Offence in Communication.
326 pages. 2018. ISBN 978-3-0343-3018-3

Vol. 241 Jana Altmanova, Maria Centrella, Katherine E. Russo (eds)
Terminology & Discourse / Terminologie et discours.
424 pages. 2018. ISBN 978-3-0343-2417-5

Vol. 242 Xavier Blanco et Inès Sfar (dir.)
Lexicologie(s) : approches croisées en sémantique lexicale.
442 pages. 2018. ISBN 978-3-0343-3056-5

Vol. 243 Yunfeng Ge
Resolution of Conflict of Interest in Chinese Civil Court Hearings. A Perspective of Discourse Information Theory.
302 pages. 2018. ISBN 978-3-0343-3313-9

Vol. 244 Carla Vergaro
Illocutionary Shell Nouns in English
322 pages. 2018. ISBN 978-3-0343-3069-5

Vol. 245 Paolo Frassi
L'adjectif en français et sa définition lexicographique.
270 pages. 2018. ISBN 978-3-0343-3394-8

Vol. 246 Suwilai Premsrirat and David Hirsh (eds)
Language Revitalization. Insights from Thailand
328 pages. 2018. ISBN 978-3-0343-3497-6

Vol. 247 Wei Wang
Researching Learning and Learners in Genre-based Academic Writing Instruction
282 pages. 2018. ISBN 978-3-0343-3297-2

Vol. 248 Isusi Alabarte, Alberto & Lahuerta Martínez, Ana Cristina (eds)
La comprensión lectora de lengua extranjera
Estudio de los factores de familiaridad, interés, género y métodos de evaluación
336 pages. 2018. ISBN 978-3-0343-3493-8

Vol. 249 Mercedes Eurrutia Cavero
Approche didactique du langage techno-scientifique
Terminologie et discours
374 pages. 2018. ISBN 978-3-0343-3512-6

Vol. 250 Aurora Ruiz Mezcua (ed.)
Approaches to Telephone Interpretation
Research, Innovation, Teaching and Transference
268 pages. 2018. ISBN 978-3-0343-3330-6

Vol. 251 Morini Massimiliano
A Day in the News
A Stylistic Analysis of Newsspeak
188 pages. 2018. ISBN 978-3-0343-3507-2

Vol. 252 Ignacio Guillén-Galve & Ignacio Vázquez-Orta (eds.)
English as a Lingua Franca and Intercultural Communication
Implications and Applications in the Field of English Language Teaching
414 pages. 2018. ISBN 978-3-0343-2763-3

Vol. 253 Bianca Del Villano
Using the Devil with Courtesy
Shakespeare and the Language of (Im)Politeness
216 pages. 2018. ISBN 978-3-0343-2315-4

Vol. 254 David Hirsh (ed.)
Explorations in Second Language Vocabulary Research
252 pages. 2018. ISBN 978-3-0343-2940-8

Vol. 255 Tania Baumann (ed.)
Reiseführer - Sprach- und Kulturmittlung im Tourismus / Le guide turistiche - mediazione linguistica e culturale in ambito turistico
270 pages. 2018. ISBN 978-3-0343-3402-0

Vol. 256 Ariadna Sánchez-Hernández & Ana Herraiz-Martínez (eds)
Learning second language pragmatics beyond traditional contexts
376 pages. 2018. ISBN 978-3-0343-3437-2

Vol. 257 Albert Bastardas-Boada, Emili Boix-Fuster, Rosa Maria Torrens (eds)
Family Multilingualism in Medium-Sized Linguistic Communities
336 pages. 2019. ISBN 978-3-0343-2536-3

Vol. 258 Yuyang Cai
Examining the Interaction among Components of English for Specific Purposes Ability in Reading. The Triple-Decker Model
296 pages. 2020. 978-3-0343-2913-2

Vol. 259 Catia Nannoni
Participe présent et gérondif dans la presse française contemporaine
176 pages. 2019. ISBN 978-3-0343-3631-4

Vol. 260 Nieves Rodríguez Pérez & Bárbara Heinsch (eds.)
Contextos multilingües. Mediadores interculturales, formación del profesorado de lenguas extranjeras
289 pages. 2019. ISBN 978-3-0343-3768-7

Vol. 261 Giuliana Elena Garzone, Mara Logaldo, Francesca Santulli (eds.)
Investigating Conflict Discourses in the Periodical Press
244 pages. 2020. ISBN 978-3-0343-3668-0

Vol. 262 Laura Nadal
Lingüística experimental y contraargumentación
233 pages. 2019. ISBN 978-3-0343-3791-5

Vol. 263 Claudia Claridge & Merja Kytö (eds.)
Punctuation in Context – Past and Present Perspectives
288 pages. 2019. ISBN 978-3-0343-3790-8

Vol. 264 Maurizio Gotti, Stefania Maci, Michele Sala (eds.)
Scholarly Pathways
530 pages. 2020. ISBN 978-3-0343-3860-8

Vol. 265 Ruth Breeze, Ana M. Fernández Vallejo (eds.)
Politics and populism across modes and media
350 pages. 2020. ISBN 978-3-0343-3707-6

Vol. 266 Jean Marguerite Jimenez
Understanding the Effects of Immediate Electronic Corrective Feedback on Second Language Development
252 pages. 2020. ISBN 978-3-0343-3815-8

Vol. 267 Sergio Rodríguez-Tapia, Adela González-Fernández (eds)
Lenguas y turismo: estudios en torno al discurso, la didáctica y la divulgación
380 pages. 2020. ISBN 978-3-0343-3881-3

Vol. 268 Ana Bocanegra-Valle (ed.)
Applied Linguistics and Knowledge Transfer. Employability, Internationalisation and Social Challenges
344 pages. 2020. ISBN 978-3-0343-3714-4

Vol. 269 Beatrice Garzelli
La traducción audiovisual español-italiano.Películas y cortos entre humor y habla soez
202 pages. 2020. ISBN 978-3-0343-4013-7

Vol. 270 Iván Tamaredo
Complexity, Efficiency, and Language Contact. Pronoun Omission in World Englishes
292 pages. 2020. ISBN 978-3-0343-3902-5

Vol. 271 Silvia Domenica Zollo,
Origine et histoire du vocabulaire des arts de la table. Analyse lexicale et exploitation de corpus textuels
239 pages. 2020. ISBN 978-3-0343-3890-5

Vol. 272 Paola Paissa, Michelangelo Conoscenti, Ruggero Druetta, Martin Solly (eds.)
Metaphor and Conflict / Métaphore et conflit
385 pages. 2021. 978-3-0343-4068-7

Vol. 273 María Martínez-Atienza de Dios,
Entre el léxico y la sintaxis: las fases de los eventos
178 pages. 2021. 978-3-0343-4173-8

Vol. 274 Noelia Castro-Chao,
Argument Structure in Flux. The Development of Impersonal Constructions in Middle and Early Modern English, with Special Reference to Verbs of Desire.
300 pages. 2021. 978-3-0343-4189-9

Vol. 275 Gabriella Carobbio, Cécile Desoutter, Aurora Fragonara (eds.)
Macht, Ratio und Emotion: Diskurse im digitalen Zeitalter / Pouvoir, raison et émotion: les discours à l'ère du numérique
246 pages. 2020. 978-3-0343-4184-4

Vol. 276 Miguel Fuster-Márquez, José Santaemilia, Carmen Gregori-Signes, Paula Rodríguez-Abruñeiras (eds.)
Exploring discourse and ideology through corpora
293 pages. 2021. 978-3-0343-3969-8

Vol. 277 Tamara Bouso
Changes in Argument Structure
The Transitivizing Reaction Object Construction
392. 2021. 978-3-0343-4095-3

Vol. 278 Forthcoming

Vol. 279 Luisa Chierichetti
Diálogos de serie. Una aproximación a la construcción discursiva de personajes basada en corpus
246 pages. 2021. 978-3-0343-4274-2

www.ingramcontent.com/pod-product-compliance
Ingram Content Group UK Ltd.
Pitfield, Milton Keynes, MK11 3LW, UK
UKHW041448071026
15587UKWH00010B/686

9 783034 340953